MW01625483

THE END OF EXPRESSIONISM

THE END OF EXPRESSIONISM

ART AND THE NOVEMBER REVOLUTION IN GERMANY, 1918–19

JOAN WEINSTEIN

THE UNIVERSITY OF CHICAGO PRESS
CHICAGO AND LONDON

JOAN WEINSTEIN is assistant professor of fine arts at the University of Pittsburgh.

The University of Chicago Press, Chicago 60637
The University of Chicago Press, Ltd., London

Printed in the United States of America

99 98 97 96 95 94 93 92 91 90 5 4 3 2 1

Library of Congress Cataloging-in-Publication Data

Weinstein, Joan.
 The end of expressionism: Art and the November Revolution in Germany / Joan Weinstein.
  p. cm.
 Bibliography: p. 307
 Includes index.
 ISBN 0-226-89059-7

 1. Expressionism (Art)—Germany. 2. Avant-garde (Aesthetics)—Germany—History—20th century. 3. Art and society—Germany—History—20th century. 4. Politics in art—Germany—History—20th century. 5. Germany—History—Revolution, 1918—Art and the revolution. I. Title.
N6868.5.E9W45 1989 88-23206
701′.03—dc19 CIP
This book is printed on acid-free paper.

To Martin Rips

Contents

Illustrations

Acknowledgments

Many people have contributed to the completion of this book. Above all I want to thank Karl Werckmeister, who over the years has demonstrated that it is possible to rewrite the history of modern German art based on the historical record. Beyond that, I thank him for his patience, his criticism and skepticism, and finally for his friendship.

I am also indebted to a number of people who have read and criticized my work. Chief among them is Beth Irwin Lewis, whose thoughtful criticism has, I hope, kept me on the right side of the polemical line. My thanks to Sanda Agalidi, who unfailingly shared her broader perspective on German art and history with me, and to Françoise Forster-Hahn, Barbara Buenger, Kenneth Barkin, and David Kunzle for criticizing parts of the manuscript.

The existing literature on art and revolution in Germany, whatever my disagreements with it, constituted a significant starting point for this study. In particular I want to acknowledge Barbara Miller Lane's *Architecture and Politics in Germany 1918–1945* (Boston 1968); William Bischoff's unpublished doctoral dissertation "Artists, Intellectuals, and Revolution: Munich 1918–19," (Harvard 1970); Marcel Franciscono's *Walter Gropius and the Creation of the Bauhaus in Weimar* (Urbana 1971); Wolfgant Pehnt's *Expressionist Architecture* (London 1973); Justin Hoffmann's essays in *München 1919: Bildende Kunst/Fotografie der Revolutions- und Rätezeit* (Munich 1979); Iain Boyd Whyte's *Bruno Taut and the Architecture of Activism* (Cambridge 1982); and Ida Rigby's *An alle Künstler* (San Diego 1983).

Financial aid from the German Academic Exchange Service and an Edward Dickson Travel Fellowship made research for this book possible. I thank the Robert Gore Rifkind Collection at the Los Angeles County Museum of Art for providing me access to their collection of expressionist periodicals.

I am grateful to a number of friends from UCLA who provided not only a high level of theoretical discourse but unstinting emotional support: Deborah Weiner, Steven Weiner, Tom Cummins, Kyle Huffman, Cecelia Klein, Kathleen Corrigan, Jane Williams, and Stacie Widdifield. I also want to thank the faculty of the art history department at the University of Pittsburgh for their generous support. Katherine Smith, Ernestine Kahn, Christian Kozoil, and Matthew Roper provided editorial and photographic assistance. Finally, I should like to express my thanks to Martin Rips, who has helped me keep my life in some skewed perspective. I value his contributions more than he knows.

INTRODUCTION 1

In late 1918 Germany experienced military defeat, economic collapse, revolution, and the inception of a parliamentary democracy, all within the space of a few months. This cataclysm propelled into the spotlight a number of artists who called themselves revolutionaries and who became, at least for a short time, active in politics. Among their ranks were names now familiar in the history of modern German art: the *Brücke* painters Max Pechstein and Karl Schmidt-Rottluff, Paul Klee from the *Blaue Reiter*, the architects Bruno Taut and Walter Gropius, and the young Otto Dix. Ignited by the events around them, these artists and others formed their own organizations modeled directly on those of revolutionary workers and soldiers. The names they gave them were meant to proclaim their revolutionary aspirations: the November Group, the Working Council for Art, the Action Committee of Revolutionary Artists. They imagined a revolution in which the arts would play a leading role, a revolution that would render a notion like "expressionism" as a valid criterion of political life. With confidence in their mission they issued excited manifestos that called for, among other things, complete artistic freedom, an end to the capitalist art market, and the creation of a new proletarian audience for their art. It is the formation of these artists' groups in Berlin, Dresden, and Munich, and their efforts to reinvent the art world with the November Revolution in Germany, that constitute the subject of this book.

The far-reaching behavior of these artists was the logical culmination of a German art world in which art and politics were explosively linked. The signs of this politicization were clearly visible, frequently discussed, and therefore hard to miss. William II set the stage with his famous 1901 speech on the Siegesallee:

> Art should contribute to the education of the people. Even the lower classes, after their toil and hard work, should be lifted up and inspired by ideal forces.

We Germans have permanently acquired these great ideals, while other peoples have more or less lost them. Only the Germans remain and are above all others called upon to guard these great ideals, to nurture and perpetuate them, and it is part of these ideals to enable the working and toiling classes, too, to become inspired by the beautiful and to help them liberate themselves from the constraints of their ordinary thoughts and attitudes.

But when art, as often happens today, shows us only misery, and shows it to us even uglier than misery is anyway, then art commits a sin against the German people. The supreme task of our cultural effort is to foster our ideals. If we are and want to remain a model for other nations, our entire people must share in this effort, and if culture is to fulfill its task completely it must reach down to the lowest levels of the population. That can be done only if art holds out its hand to raise the people up, instead of descending into the gutter.[1]

These words were not just the usual platitudes dredged up for another ceremonial function. They went directly to the heart of a struggle in imperial Germany over who was to define what was art. William II rigidly identified his rule with academic art and, as a result, rejected any art that did not conform to its standards. His grip on the art world, though, was slipping, as was evident in his words: he urgently sought cultural cohesion in the face of its opposite. Between the lines lay the specter of enemies both within and without, those who would challenge his authority, those who would stir up the working classes, and those who would threaten to import a foreign culture. This debate was carried out in a political language, whose hallmarks were xenophobia and fear of the working classes. Socialist became both an epithet and a rallying cry used to describe disparate forms of art—from the realism of Käthe Kollwitz's etchings, to Max Liebermann's impressionist paintings, to the expressionist art of Franz Marc. The revolutionary artists of 1918 were part and parcel of this politicized art world.

The fissures in the art world cracked wide open in November 1918, and the revolution seemed to open a window of opportunity for a handful of artists to put an end to the old order. It was one of those brief moments when the avant-garde fervently believed it could make a difference, not only remaking the art world in its own image, but actively taking part in revolutionary politics. This book has the broader purpose of analyzing a specific convergence of avant-garde art and political revolution. Already in 1918–19 artists and critics debated the revolutionary character of avant-garde art in terms with which we are familiar today: avant-garde art as anticipating political revolution; avant-garde art as separate and distinct from politics; avant-garde art as the refuge of revolution, safeguarding it until more propitious times; avant-garde art as mere bourgeois soul-searching. My intention here is to restore to this ideological debate a sense of a particularized history.[2]

At the center of discussion about art and revolution in 1918 was not the protest art of Dada, which existed still only at the margins of the German art world, but expressionism, which had been around for more than a decade. Although the flamboyant Dada movement—and the aggressive challenge it eventually posed to the status quo in art as in politics—figures in the final chapter of this book, it was the energetic art of the expressionists whose revolutionary credentials were so hotly debated in the months following the outbreak of revolution in Germany. Expressionism was a loosely defined term that encompassed the art of the Brücke and the Blaue Reiter, as well as cubism, futurism, and abstraction. What supposedly tied them together was a concern with the expression of inner feelings rather than with any verisimilitude to nature. The joining together of these seemingly different styles, however, had even more to do with the strictures of the German art world. They had all shared a common fate in pre-war Wilhelmine Germany; they were rejected by the state and its official institutions and scorned by most of the art-buying public. In a sense, it was the Wilhelmine state that had made such an all-purpose term as expressionism serviceable. This rejection by the state, and by the bourgeoisie, now bolstered many expressionist artists' belief that their art had anticipated the revolution. In their eyes the revolution had no need to usher in a new art, only to confirm an already existing one, "revolutionary" expressionism. Left unspoken, for the time being, were the dilemmas of how an art previously predicated on opposition to society could now be reclaimed as a catalyst to social integration and of whether expressionism as a style was marked by a destructive or constructive relationship to society.

The story that follows chronicles the difficulties faced by these artists in radically transforming the art world—the day-by-day organization and planning, the aggressive pronouncements and resigned retrenchments, the successes and failures as they met with official recalcitrance or grudging concessions. These events were played out differently in each city, dependent to a high degree upon the extent of revolutionary activity there, the compliance or resistance of art institutions, the local cultural traditions, and the fluctuations of the art market. Ultimately, this book centers on the difficult project of keeping alive the politically progressive claims of expressionist art during the revolution and on the underlying contradictions inherent in this attempt, which led critics to proclaim the end of expressionism, the "death" of the movement, by 1920. By this they did not mean that expressionism disappeared, that its practitioners suddenly abandoned it or that its patrons deserted it, but that its fateful history during the revolution had destroyed confidence in its ability to serve the avant-garde notion of art in the forefront of revolutionary politics. The claim to revolutionary status became problematical.

The struggle that emerged in Germany for control and containment of the revolution put into doubt the indiscriminate use of a term such as revolutionary. Revolution was a word everyone wanted to own, from the competing socialist parties to representatives of industry—all in an attempt to further their own political and economic interests. Each assumed for themselves and redefined the fundamental elements of socialist strategy: socialism as revolutionary change, evolutionary change, or even accelerated accumulation, industrial reconstruction, and state intervention in the economic cycle. Accrued power was often defended through revolutionary rhetoric and retained by counterrevolutionary action. What could it mean, then, to call expressionism revolutionary?

The point, however, is not to damn the expressionists for failing to achieve revolution, something not within their power. Why should one expect it of artists, when the politicians failed so miserably? Rather, the goal is a more concrete one—to understand the process whereby artists' responses to the rapidly changing, seemingly chaotic developments of the revolution were shaped by a socially structured environment of culture. In Germany, this culture was organized around institutions still governed directly or indirectly by the state, institutions which often continued unchanged or with only cosmetic alterations. Defined in the broadest terms, these included not only government art agencies and the academy, but also artists' groups organized in opposition to these institutions, the art press, and the art market. The economic and political conditions under which these institutions functioned, and their effects on the production and reception of art are essential to this discussion.

There are a number of obstacles to writing an institutional history of the art world during the November Revolution. First, the history and significance of the revolution are still very much disputed.[3] In this study I distinguish between three of its phases. The earliest, the "people's revolution" of November and December 1918, was characterized by optimistic proclamations of socialist equality and the brotherhood of mankind. On the morning of 9 November enthusiastic processions of factory workers and soldiers streamed from the suburbs into the city of Berlin. Meeting no resistance, they quickly took possession of public buildings, planting the red flag of the revolution on the rooftops and in the doorways. The capital fell into the hands of the workers and soldiers, who spontaneously set up councils modeled after Russian soviets in the factories and barracks. No one defended the old regime; power lay with the left. Among the most vivid images of this first phase of the revolution were ragged soldiers with red flags riding past the baroque monuments of past rulers, sailors looting the royal palace and drinking the royal family's champagne, crowds singing "The Internationale" as they listened expectantly to the speeches of their leaders.

The optimistic, often indiscriminate affiliations of November and December 1918 soon gave way to the political struggle for control of the revolution. At issue was the choice between proletarian dictatorship and parliamentary democracy. The competing socialist parties fought each other at almost every turn.[4] The largest socialist party, the Social Democratic Party (SPD), clearly favored parliamentary democracy.[5] Its political leaders assured the Supreme Command that they would fight bolshevism (which soon caused them to call out the troops against fellow socialists),[6] while its union leaders entered into a pact with industry preventing any wholesale nationalization. The Independent Social Democratic Party (USPD), which formed to the left of the SPD in 1917, first participated in the provisional socialist government empowered by the councils and then withdrew. With one wing supporting the government and the other working for its downfall, the party became irreparably split. Still further to the left were the Spartacists, who on 30 December 1918 formally constituted the German Communist Party (KPD) and supported proletarian dictatorship after the Russian model. Lacking mass support, the KPD represented a further split of the forces on the left. By January the revolution was in trouble: the tenuous socialist government had collapsed, the councils were largely neutralized, and elections to a National Constituent Assembly were imminent, which the communists promised to boycott.

The revolution had entered its second phase, a period of radicalization, violence, and internal controversy. In an atmosphere of approaching civil war in January, armed Spartacists occupied a number of buildings in Berlin, declaring the government deposed. The government, in response, called out the *Freikorps,* a temporary armed force composed mainly of antirepublican adventurers. The communist party leaders Karl Liebknecht and Rosa Luxemburg were captured and summarily murdered. The months from January until May saw the emergence of communist and anarchist positions, of short-lived revolutionary council governments in Munich, Brunswick, and Bremen, of continuous strikes and unrest, and their suppression by military intervention. The images of this phase of the revolution were quite different: bullet-riddled barricades, the machine-gun fire of the Freikorps troops, and the bodies piled up at the morgue for identification. And yet, even this phase of the revolution, with its street fighting, food shortages, and violent efforts to revive the council movement, did not affect the ability of some institutions to operate seemingly unchanged: bloody street battles one week, gallery openings the next.

The violent suppression of the "class revolution" ultimately yielded to a period of growing if uneasy political and economic stabilization.[7] The Versailles Treaty was finally signed on 28 June 1919, and a new constitution was approved by the National Assembly less than five weeks later. Although the new political order claimed the mantle of the revolution, it appeared to many suspiciously like a reconstitution of the coalition that had been in power in October 1918. Industrialists increasingly recovered control of the economy from the wartime state control, and inflation, favored by the industrialists and essentially unchecked by the government, led to an illusory recovery.[8] Political stability was created on the basis of an unstable economy; if this was not to be a lasting political stability, it was at least one able to withstand the revolutionary threat.

These three phases of the revolution indelibly marked the expressionist artists' groups. The initial euphoria of the council movement dominated their earliest manifestos. With little consideration for practicalities, they ecstatically proclaimed that "art and the people must form a unity."[9] The assumption was that the revolution would mean an end to the isolation of modern art as a luxury commodity and a new integration of art and the social life of the people. Their repeated use of the word "people" (*Volk*), with its lack of class distinction, was typical. The revolution further seemed to promise artists a kind of workers' control, freedom to regulate their own affairs, to choose their own juries and officials, to take a decisive voice in all public art matters. The chaotic, and violent, political struggles of January and March, however, forced expressionist artists to reexamine their vague confidence in the revolution to transform the art world. What was the political base for their art? How was the old public for art to be discounted and a new, economically viable, but still proletarian audience to be created? What changes were necessary in the economy? And in their art? Confronted with this political minefield, expressionist artists had to consider which political course might further their ambitious plans. Finally, with the political and economic stabilization of late 1919, expressionist artists were confronted with the contradiction not only between their political aspirations and the need to sell their work, but with the fundamental contradiction between enterprise and security in a capitalist economy.

While the account that follows is chronologically limited to one year in the history of German art, its repercussions extend much further. As an analysis of what happens when a revolution fails, and when art is implicated in its failure, it is a striking example of how art can resist change under the pressure of historical events. The story of expressionism during the November Revolution is not so much one of how art changed, but instead of how fast and of how radically the claims advanced for it did. The history of art during the November Revolution is also of importance for understanding the institutional framework for the arts that emerged in the Weimar Republic: the events of the revolution conditioned the degree and extent to which avant-garde artists integrated themselves into the culture of the new republic. Moreover, a history of art and the revolution reveals the ways in which the art world participated in—and legitimized—the continuity and rigidity of institutions that plagued the republic. Finally, this history frames the political debates about art that followed, including the rightist attacks on "Weimar culture." When the National Socialists attacked expressionism as "bolshevik," it was not a characterization of their own invention. Rather, it stemmed from these artists' fateful involvement in the November Revolution. No matter how much they accommodated themselves to the Weimar democracy, or, in the case of a few, tried to ingratiate themselves with the National Socialist government after 1933, the expressionists could not escape the rhetoric of political revolution that surrounded their art.

Narrated in the following chapters is the story of how expressionist artists' councils responded to the conflicting forces that shaped art in Germany during the November Revolution. The question has seldom been posed, though, as to why so many expressionist artists eagerly embraced the revolution in November 1918. That decision was conditioned in large part by the artists' previous histories, both collective and individual. The collective history had, first of all, to do with their unqualified hostility toward official art and the art politics of the state. "That old, fat, perverted institution," one of their sympathetic critics called the academy, adding the opinion that academic art—"the mummy realm of Anton von Werner, Franz von Stuck, and the craftsmen of the Siegesallee"—was only an "accumulation of trash."[10] In his history of the Berlin Secession, Peter Paret has suggested the reasons for this hostility. The emperor, and institutions connected with the Prussian royal household, still exercised extensive control over German cultural and intellectual affairs and thereby effectively excluded expressionist artists from official patronage. In Prussia, at least, state-supervised artists' groups, the academy, as well as most commissions presiding over purchases and awards, were all subject to the emperor's personal supervision. Since William II identified his rule so closely with academic art, he rejected any art that did not conform to its standards. This rejection, however, went beyond mere economic exclusion and turned into an aggressive attack on all other forms of art, an attack often expressed in political terms.

The political conflict between modern art and the autocratic structure of the Prussian state became institutionalized with the founding of the Berlin Secession in 1898. Although the Berlin Secession is usually described as the rallying point of impressionism in Germany, its significance lies less in any stylistic unity than in its successful challenge to state control of exhibitions and funding for artists. The conflict pitted a private association of artists, led by the impressionist painter Max Liebermann, against the authority of the Prussian Academy of Arts, headed by the emperor's friend and adviser, Anton von Werner. Through skillful leadership and management, the Berlin Secession was able to establish itself with a new purchasing clientele drawn from the wealthy educated bourgeoisie, which, in resistance to official art, sought a more internationally minded art ostensibly free of political design. No art, though, could remain outside the political debate for long. These rival artistic ideologies, representing distinct segments of German society, clashed repeatedly in the first decade of the century. An inescapable factor in these conflicts was the sheer number of artists in Berlin. The proletarianization (the word was common at the time) of the many in the face of the great financial success of the few contributed to the deep tensions within the art world and the tendency of artists and their supporters to turn to nonaesthetic criteria, often xenophobic or anti-Semitic, for judging works of art.[11]

The political debate about art intensified with expressionism, the first avant-garde challenge to both imperial and bourgeois culture in Germany. Although expressionism remained a marginal movement until about 1912, it was roundly condemned by those mainstream critics who did not totally ignore it. Part of the reason for this hostility toward the expressionists was their apparent attack on the values and institutions of imperial and bourgeois artistic culture. They rejected the realistic complication and patriotic pomposity of academic art, and, while they shared the internationalist outlook of the Berlin Secession, they scorned the group's exclusionary practices, its juries, and its satisfied patrons. The targets of their art and their elaborate theoretical writings were the philistinism of the bourgeoisie and the affirmative, materialist culture of Wilhelmine Germany. The Brücke artists indicted the hypocrisy of bourgeois sexual morality when they painted themselves and their models frolicking openly in the nude at the Moritzburg lakes.

Their slashing brushstrokes and non-naturalistic forms and colors were meant to proclaim their spontaneity and passion and to free art from its descriptive role. When the Brücke artists incorporated motifs and forms from African and South Seas sculpture in their work, they challenged the right of those in authority in the art world to determine aesthetic criteria. In Munich, artists associated with the Blaue Reiter also questioned contemporary definitions of culture when they promoted the art of children, primitives, and the insane (although all these artists still conformed to prevailing notions of primitive sexuality and the ahistoricity of tribal cultures, children, and the insane.)

By 1912, though, the expressionists could count on a rapidly developing network of support. These included Franz Pfemfert's journal *Die Aktion* and Herwarth Walden's *Der Sturm,* the name given to both his journal and his gallery. Their art was now featured in a number of major exhibitions, including the 1912 Sonderbund exhibition and Walden's First German Autumn Salon the following year. Expressionist artists could still feel secure, however, in their intention "to demolish insidiously [the bourgeoisie's] comfortable, solemnly elevated view of the world"[12]—as a writer in *Der Sturm* put it in the first (and most political) issue of the journal. Despite a few conspicuous success stories, such as Max Pechstein, their outsider status seemed assured when their work generally found little support in a slumping German art market before the war.

The expressionists' seeming hostility toward imperial and bourgeois culture was a starting point for their enthusiastic response to the November Revolution. But what about their actual relationship to the political left before the war? Since for so long now it has been accepted as axiomatic that expressionism was revolutionary, the question has seldom been posed as to what relationship the expressionists had to the political left before the revolution. Despite the fact that expressionist artists and their critics often used the rhetoric of politics and political revolution before the war, there has been no systematic discussion in the literature of socialism and avant-garde art in imperial Germany.[13] Without such a history, it is more difficult to discern continuities or breaks with the past, including revisions of legitimating ideologies with the revolution.

From the sketchy evidence available, it seems that although expressionists may have been antibourgeois, and even anticapitalist, they did not, for the most part, engage in organized political activity before the war. There were only a few who joined the SPD, most prominently Ludwig Meidner and Georg Tappert. Some may have rejected the reformist tactics and culture of the SPD. Others may have been disillu-

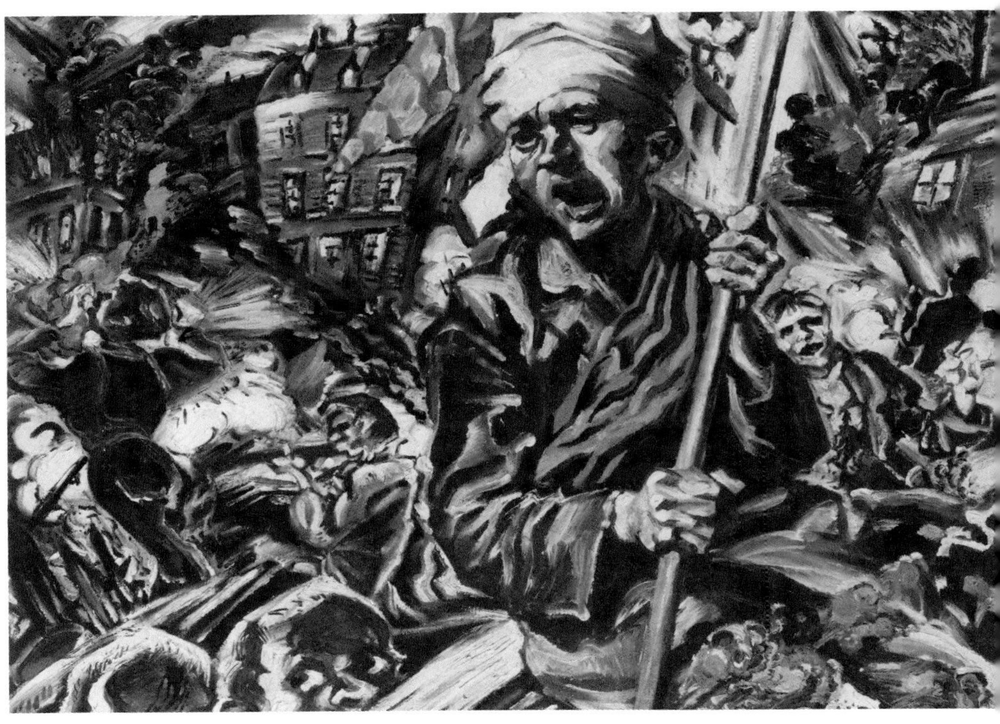

1.1 Ludwig Meidner, *Revolution (Barrikadenkampf)* [*Revolution (Fighting on the Barricade)*], 1912–13. Oil on canvas, 80 x 196 cm. Staatliche Museen Preussischer Kulturbesitz, Nationalgalerie, Berlin (West). Photo by Jörg P. Anders. Reproduced by courtesy of David Meidner, Kibbutz Schluchot, Israel.

sioned with the party's apparent lack of sympathy with their art. A few expressionists in Munich flirted with the anarchism of Erich Mühsam's *Gruppe Tat,* but almost none in Berlin participated in the anarcho-socialist groups in that city, from the *Neue Gemeinschaft* to the *Neue Freie Volksbühne*. For the most part, the expressionists sought to undermine bourgeois artistic and social values while preserving their art from political interference. Only occasionally did revolution become an explicit issue—as in the 1913 painting by Ludwig Meidner, *Revolution (Fighting on the Barricade)* (fig. 1.1), loosely modeled after Delacroix's *Liberty Leading the People*. In this painting, the central figure, head bandaged, holds aloft the red flag on the barricade; behind him fighting rages in the streets (shells explode, rifle-carrying figures shoot from behind barricades, bodies fall, houses burn). Meidner painted *Revolution* on the reverse side of one of his 1913 apocalyptic landscapes (fig. 1.2). Here, destruction prevails in the background (the seas rise, a comet strikes, dark clouds threateningly cover the sun, buildings stand

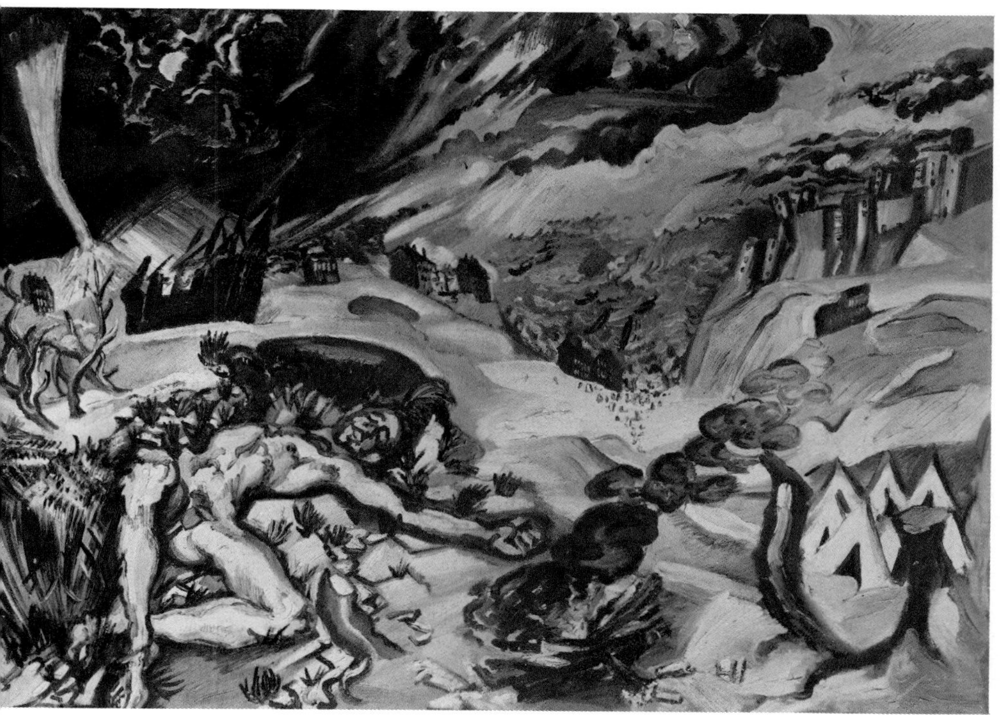

1.2 Ludwig Meidner, *Apokalyptische Landschaft (Apocalyptic Landscape),* 1913. Oil on canvas, 80 x 196 cm. Staatliche Museen Preussischer Kulturbesitz, Nationalgalerie, Berlin (West). Photo by Jörg P. Anders. Reproduced by courtesy of David Meidner, Kibbutz Schluchot, Israel.

poised to topple over the cliffs), while in the foreground a lone nude figure lies supine by a failing fire in a desolate landscape, his raised knee the only indication he is alive. Like most of Meidner's apocalyptic landscapes, fear dominates over hope. By placing these two images on opposite sides of the same canvas, Meidner seemed to imply that revolution was the alternative to apocalyptic destruction, the image of which offered little expectation of renewal after destruction. Meidner's seeming *parti pris* for revolution, however, had no specific reference point in 1913; the SPD, to which he belonged, promoted evolutionary reform, not revolution.

Revolution also appeared at times as a form of radical chic in the expressionist camp. This is most apparent in the "revolutionary balls" sponsored in 1913 and 1914 by *Die Aktion,* the most political of the expressionist journals. Guests at the carnival balls were instructed to appear in "costumes of revolutions from 1789 to 1989" or be forced to sport Jacobin caps and pay a fine.[14] So successful that they were repeated twice each year, they were also satirized in the pages of *Die Aktion* by the poet Franz Luft. He described a room dominated by a blood-red guillotine, where elegantly attired bandits, Jacobins, and lady liberties flirted, drank, and danced the evening away.[15]

Whatever the political commitments of the expressionists, their art was conspicuously debated in left-wing political terms. Karl Scheffler, the influential editor of *Kunst und Künstler* and a vocal partisan of impressionism, was among those to attack expressionism for its allegiance to the left. In his review of the Sturm gallery's influential First German Autumn Salon in 1913, Scheffler repeatedly referred to the expressionists as revolutionaries and condemned their art for its "proletarian outlook."[16] More importantly, a number of their supporters also sought to associate them with the left. The prominent Hamburg museum director Gustav Pauli considered the proletarian orientation of expressionism as one of its strengths. Unlike the "connoisseurs" and "sensitive epicures" to whom impressionism appealed, Pauli wrote, "the new expressionist art seems to me rather an art of the aspiring, struggling popular classes. The works of these artists would go better in a sober laborer's home than in a salon with silken wallpaper. This is proletarian art, and I mean this without any unfriendly second thoughts and in no way with a belittling intention."[17] Pauli did not go so far as to claim that the proletariat had already embraced expressionism, but nevertheless conjured up a potential alliance between the two.

Pauli's assessment followed closely the pronouncements of at least a few influential—and politically progressive—critics before the war, who had conspicuously advertised expressionism as the art of a future socialist, collectivist society. Among the most prominent was the art historian Wilhelm Hausenstein, a member of the SPD and an occasional instructor at the party's night school for workers. In his early writings, Hausenstein attempted to develop a sociological approach to art based on the writings of Karl Marx. In a 1913 book he described expressionism as the art of a future socialist society, based on its supposed antipathy to individualism. Hausenstein cited Franz Marc in particular as an example of an artist striving toward an anonymous, communal notion of beauty, a presupposition, he believed, for the art of a future collective society.[18] The characterization by Hausenstein and a few other SPD art critics of the socialist potential of expressionism may have hit home in 1918 and encouraged these artists to hope for the triumph of their art in a new socialist state.

The cultural and political traditions sketched above are meant to provide some context, however minimal, for expressionist artists' enthusiastic responses to the revolution. Still, these remarks have been directed primarily at the arts in Prussia, the most dominant of the German states. But Germany was not culturally or politically homogeneous, and local political and artistic traditions influenced how artists responded to the revolution. Dresden and Munich presented very different artistic and political profiles than Berlin did before the war. While Berlin was on the ascendancy as an art center, Munich was in a decline—a result of the social and political makeup of the city. Dresden, the center of baroque art in Germany, had never regained its artistic splendor, but managed to avoid many of the tensions that characterized the Berlin and Munich art worlds. Although expressionist artists in all three cities shared a common fate before the war, it is the subtle differences in their local reception that are so telling for their subsequent actions during the revolution.

As in Berlin, the main problem facing the Munich art community in the years before the First World War was the overabundance of artists and their vast annual output of paintings, which far outstripped the resources of the local art-buying public. Yet the political climate in Munich, and therefore the political context in which art developed there, differed in several important ways from Berlin, differences that were to have significant repercussions for the arts in the Bavarian capital during the revolution.

In the federal structure of the German empire, Bavaria, more than any other German state, retained a high degree of political autonomy. Consequently, the struggle between liberals and Catholics that had begun in the 1860s continued well into the twentieth century. Resurgent Catholicism finally secured a firm hold over Bavarian political culture in 1912, and with it came increasing polarization in the Munich art world.

In the 1880s, Munich was the most important art center in Germany, famed for its academy and its liberal tradition in the arts.[19] With the increasing proletarianization of artists, however, and with institutional resistance to international trends in the arts, Munich was also the site of the first successful challenge to the authority of imperial culture and its annual salon. Struggling against the vast numbers of works in the bazaarlike salon and official resistance to naturalism and impressionism, in 1892 a number of prominent Munich artists launched the Munich Secession to promote quality "international" art in "elite" exhibitions.[20] Unlike their subsequent Berlin counterpart, however, the Munich Secession very quickly achieved parity with the official Art Association (*Kunstgenossenschaft*), receiving state and royal patronage, honors, and influence. Because of this success, the vituperative political attacks by the crown and state on naturalist and impressionist art that characterized the Berlin art world did not emerge with the same vehemence in Munich.[21] By 1898 Munich was also the capital of the *Jugendstil* movement, a cosmopolitan art of design that appealed to the educated middle class.

These successes, however, were short-lived, and Munich declined as an art center after the turn of the century. The Bavarian capital rapidly lost status to Berlin, not only because of its smaller population (some five hundred thousand compared to two million and growing in Berlin), but with far fewer wealthy bourgeois, it had a distinctly smaller pool of art buyers. Already in 1901 a heated public debate emerged regarding Munich's decline as an art center;[22] two of the city's leading impressionist painters, Max Slevogt and Lovis Corinth, had already moved to Berlin, and by 1903 many of the best-known *Jugendstil* artists had abandoned the city as well.

As in Berlin, a vigorous avant-garde developed in Munich in the years before the war, one which also challenged the values and institutions of bourgeois culture—not only its resurgent Catholicism, with its imposition of censorship, but its moribund liberalism as well, which often acquiesced to Centrist parliamentary pressure. In his history of Munich avant-garde theater, Peter Jelavich has described a thriving bohemian subculture featuring a number of artist-run cabarets in the Schwabing district. With their provocative ridicule of religious institutions and middle-class sexual hypocrisy, they were easy targets for the censors. These cabarets were frequented by a number of painters, who also sought to develop cooperative ventures with the aim of eliminating middlemen in the sale of their art. Phalanx, led by the Russian-born Wassily Kandinsky, was Munich's first association of modern artists to bypass private galleries by establishing its own exhibition spaces. Kandinsky also became the key figure in the New Artists' Union (*Neue Künstlervereinigung*), which featured at its exhibitions expressionist painting along with recent French art. When the NKV refused to exhibit one of Kandinsky's abstract paintings at its 1911 exhibition, he resigned from the group and proceeded to organize the Blaue Reiter exhibitions and almanac. In 1913, a New Secession broke off from the Munich Secession, promoting a broad range of modern art, including expressionism. As in Berlin, a support network soon developed to promote the new art, including the Brakl, Thannhauser, and Goltz galleries. But here as well expressionist art found limited patronage. Kandinsky survived through independent financial means, while others relied on a few important buyers.

As in Berlin, few Munich expressionists seem to have been involved with the SPD—which in any case was weak in the Bavarian capital.

They did receive support, though, from the socialist art historian and critic Wilhelm Hausenstein, who resided in Munich, but even his art-political activities at the time appear more liberal than radical (he was a founding member of the Munich New Secession). One small segment of the bohemian art scene, however, became radicalized, and vociferously argued its politics to the rest of the Munich art world. Their radicalization followed the political crisis of 1912 in Bavaria, in which the Centre Party emerged for the first time in control of crown, cabinet, and parliament, ending years of liberalism. In October 1913 these artists and writers published the first issue of a new journal titled *Revolution,* which promoted political anarchism, sexual liberation, and expressionism.

The first issue of *Revolution* featured a programmatic statement by the anarchist Erich Mühsam, a writer and cabaret performer who had settled in bohemian Schwabing in 1908. In 1909 he had organized an offshoot of Gustav Landauer's anarchistic Socialist League, which Mühsam called the Gruppe Tat and which was a small cell of social outcasts, including unemployed youths, draft-evaders, vagabonds, prostitutes, and a few artists.[23] He now defined revolution as follows:

> Revolution is the movement between two conditions. One should not imagine it as a slowly turning roller, but as a bursting volcano, an exploding bomb, or a nun stripping herself.
>
> All revolution is active, singular, sudden, and uproots its own origins. . . .
>
> Destruction and construction are identical during a revolution. Every destructive desire is a creative desire (Bakunin). A few forms of revolution: tyrannicide, deposing a sovereign power, establishment of a religion, breaking old tablets (of convention and art), creating an art work, the sex act.[24]

Mühsam's provocative language implicitly dismissed SPD gradualism (a "slowly turning roller") and obliquely invoked in its place anarchist violence and the breaking of sexual taboos.[25] He further reinforced the notion of the avant-garde artist as a revolutionary, shattering the conventions of bourgeois art. In the same issue the expressionist writer Johannes Becher appealed to the identical down-and-outers of Mühsam's now-defunct Gruppe Tat in his "Song of Freedom":

> You mongrels, you boozers! Clowns! Fops! Onanists! Pederasts! Fetishists! Merchants, burghers, aviators, soldiers! Pimps, whores! You great harlots! Syphilitics! Brothers, all children of mankind! Wake up! Wake up! I summon you to a violent rebellion, to fiery anarchy. I inspire you, I provoke you to malevolent battle! Revolution! Revolutionaries! Anarchists![26]

Featured on the cover of the first issue was a woodcut titled *Revolution* (fig. 1.3) by the expressionist Richard Seewald. It shows troops firing

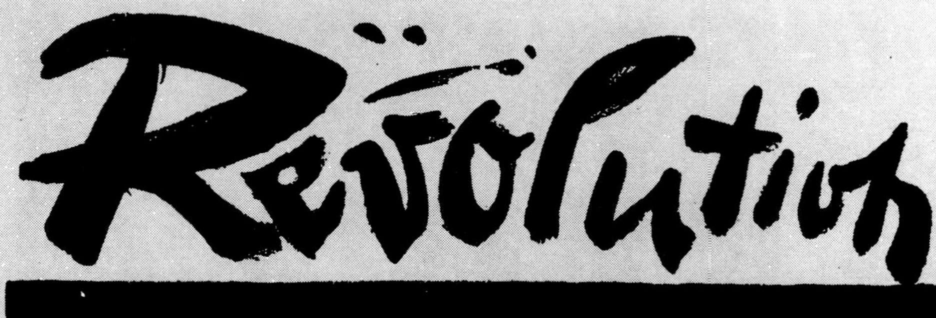

Auflage 3000 — Zweiwochenschrift — Preis 10 Pfg.

Jahrgang 1913 — Verlag: Heinrich F. S. Bachmair

Nummer 1 — München — 15. Oktober

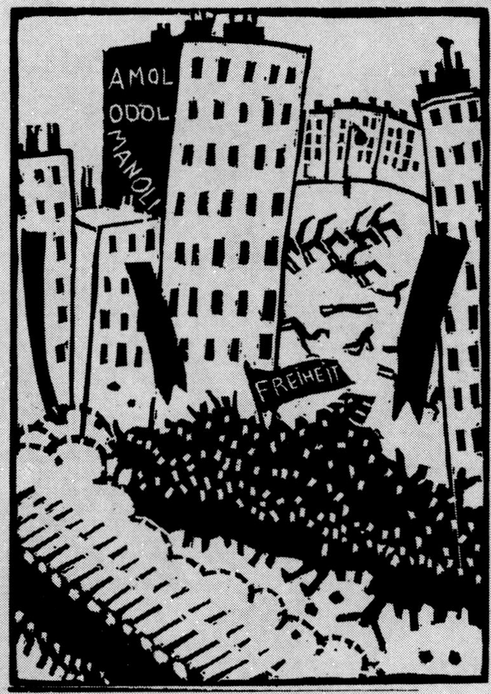

Richard Seewald: Revolution

(Original-Holzschnitt)

Inhalt:

Richard Seewald: Revolution — Johannes R. Becher: Freiheitlied — Erich Mühsam: Revolution — Hugo Ball: Der Henker — Leonhard Frank: Der Erotomane und diese Jungfrau — Klabund: Drei Gedichte — Fritz Lenz: Das endlose Sein — emmy hennings: Ich bin zu gleicher Zeit — Hans Harbeck: Georg Büchner — Franz Blei: über Maurice Barrès — Kurt Hiller: Alfred Kerr — Adam: Die katholischen Gegenfüßler — Leybold: Der Vortragsreisende Roda Roda — Klabund: Das Herz der Lasker — Bachmair: Die Aufregung in Wien — Notizen.

Mitarbeiter:

Adam, Hugo Ball, Johannes R. Becher, Gottfried Benn, Franz Blei, Max Brod, Friedrich Eisenlohr, Engert, Leonhard Frank, John R. v. Gorsleben, emmy hennings, Kurt Hiller, Friedrich Markus Hübner, Philipp Keller, Klabund, Else Lasker-Schüler, Iwan Lazang, Erich Mühsam, Heinrich Nowak, Karl Otten, Sebastian Scharnagl, Richard Seewald und andere.

1.3 Richard Seewald, *Revolution,* 1913. Woodcut, *Revolution* 1, no. 1 (15 October 1913).

on a crowd holding a banner labeled "freedom." Buildings in the background threaten to topple into a square where there is fighting between some isolated figures and a cavalry unit. The woodcut stood in a curious relationship to the texts by Mühsam and Becher: rather than a call to rebellion, it seemed to show its bloody suppression.

Seewald's woodcut belied the bravado of *Revolution*'s editorial line, which was challenged in the second issue of the journal. There the editors felt it necessary to defend themselves against the criticism that *Revolution* was not "revolutionary enough," that there were "too few daggers, swords, flags" in evidence and too much that was "lyrical."[27] Explaining why they "had not built any barricades" or "distributed bombs gratis," they implicitly conceded the futility of such acts at the present time and leveled the same charge at others: "Where does *Der Sturm* 'storm'? At best in the Autumn Salon."[28] Here already was the difficulty that would plague artists during the revolution in Munich: the relationship between expressionist art and revolutionary act. Although *Revolution* lasted only a few issues and involved only a small number of expressionists, its curious synthesis of anarchism and expressionism was to have a major impact on the promotion of expressionist art during the revolutionary Munich council republics in 1919. Although it was a quixotic and marginal movement in pre-war Munich, anarchism was to gain center stage there during the revolution. Several of the contributors to *Revolution,* and even a few artist-members of Mühsam's Gruppe Tat, went on to become key figures in the revolutionary artists' council in Munich.

It is much more difficult to make any conclusive statements about the pre-war art world in Dresden, the capital of Saxony. The firebombing of the city during the Second World War destroyed much of the archival material upon which an institutional history of the art world could be based. Moreover, the nature of scholarship in the German Democratic Republic has essentially limited the discussion of the Dresden art scene to issues central to orthodox communist definitions of art—and thereby directed attention away from the development of expressionism in that city.

By the turn of the century, Dresden's reputation as an art center rested mainly on its past laurels, despite the strength of its venerable art academy, founded in 1764. The liberal political tradition of the city, though, seems to have fostered a democratic forum for the arts. Impressionism was granted official recognition in Dresden earlier than elsewhere; already by the turn of the century the impressionist-influenced painter Gotthard Kühl was appointed to the academy, followed shortly thereafter by Robert Sterl.[29] When the liberal Artists'

Union (*Künstlervereinigung*) challenged the authority of the official Art Association (*Kunstgenossenschaft*) in 1910, it quickly achieved parity.

Such liberalism, though, did not immediately extend to expressionist art. When the Brücke was founded in 1905, it received some encouragement from the Emil Richter gallery, but its early exhibitions met with scathing reviews and few sales. By 1910–11 most of the Brücke members had left for Berlin where they had reason to expect better prospects. Only in 1913 did the expressionists find any critical support in Dresden when they exhibited at the more established Arnold gallery.[30] The following four years brought a modicum of success and a comparatively high degree of integration into the existing art establishment: the expressionists showed side by side with the academicians in special war exhibitions and at the Artists' Union.[31] This aura of conciliation allowed the artists' groups founded during the revolution in Dresden to look for common ground with the Artists' Union and even the academy—and concomitantly weakened their resolve to radically alter the status quo.

The pre-war history of expressionism in Berlin, Dresden, and Munich reveals few direct links with radical politics, only a generalized, and often unfocused, contempt for Wilhelmine culture and politics. From this history it would have been difficult to predict the active participation of so many expressionist artists in the November Revolution and their radical demands for the remaking of the German art world. There were some warning signs, particularly the way in which a few very prominent critics promoted expressionism in the same breath with socialism. It seems possible to conjure up a latent political radicalism in expressionism that was unleashed with the revolution. But the story is a much more complex one, complicated by these artists' fateful involvement in the First World War.

With the war, the political debate about expressionism seems to have ceased, at least temporarily. Expressionism now took its place in a fragile balance of forces given some encouragement by the imperial art administration in order to maintain broad support for the war effort.[32] Artists from the academy, the Secessions, and even the avant-garde initially supported the war in their statements and in their art, if not always on the same terms. Members of the Secession patriotically supported the German position in the journal *Kriegszeit*, published by the Berlin art dealer Paul Cassirer. Numerous artists of the younger generation immediately volunteered for active duty or for duty as medics. Members of the avant-garde, most notably Franz Marc, welcomed the war—if not as nationalist imperative, then as an apocalyptic solution for cultural crisis. More than a few saw extended action at the front, and several were killed in action, including the best-known expressionist of his day, Marc. Even the critical writing about expressionism quickly adjusted to the new political situation. The critic Adolf Behne, a member of the SPD and an early supporter of the new art, now advocated expressionism as the new national art, defending it against charges that it was international and therefore unpatriotic.[33]

When the German offensive collapsed after 1916, however, the initial war enthusiasm waned and artists increasingly agonized over their inability to reconcile the war and their art. The expressionist painter Karl Schmidt-Rottluff wrote despairingly in early 1917: "Either you are a painter and you shit on the whole caboodle or you join in and kiss painting goodbye."[34] Patriotic commitment gave way to detachment, disillusionment, defeatist cynicism, and in a few rare cases outright political opposition.[35] Franz Pfemfert's journal *Die Aktion* now devoted whole issues to Karl Marx and Rosa Luxemburg. (Because of the strict censorship, his opposition to the war had previously been expressed primarily by reproducing works of modern art from enemy countries.) The Munich journal *Zeit-Echo* went into exile in Switzerland, where its editor, Ludwig Rubiner, devoted its pages to anti-war activism and expressionism, couched in the anarchist rhetoric of freedom, communal ties, and the supremacy of the spirit. In Dresden, a number of expressionist artists and writers also linked their expressionism to anti-war activism. The painters Conrad Felixmüller and Raoul Hausmann (a cofounder of Berlin Dada in 1917), along with the writers Walter Rheiner and Felix Stiemer, formed the Expressionist Working Group (*Expressionistische Arbeitsgemeinschaft Dresden*), simultaneously promoting expressionism and radical politics. With the twenty-year-old Felixmüller as its guiding force, the Expressionist Working Group sponsored fifteen soirées featuring expressionist poetry and circulated radical political pamphlets among their members, including Spartacist letters and the resolutions of the Grunewald Conference.[36] These meetings led to the establishment of the Felix Stiemer publishing house and of the journal *Menschen*. A typical contribution to this journal was the anti-war verse by Richard Fischer, "Field of Honor," which blamed the continuation of the war not only on the politicians, but on capitalist war profiteers as well. It read in part:

> "On the field of honor"
> This Golgotha of murderous demise
> Ploughed and tended by hands
> that stink of money and lies![37]

The political protests by Pfemfert, Felixmüller, and others, no matter how vague, were still more the exception than the rule. What generally prevailed instead in the German art world was the promotion of art as a spiritual compensation for the miseries of war. One could lament the destruction of war without necessarily pointing to its causes. Taking into account the new disillusionment with the war—on the part of both artists and clients—the art dealer Paul Cassirer folded *Kriegszeit* and published in its place the pacifist *Der Bildermann*. The introduction to the first issue declared:

> Despite the horror of the times, our spirit has remained faithful to the old gods; in the midst of war we want to use our eyes as we used them before the war, even take pleasure as we once did. The strain of war has taught us to look horror calmly in the face, but it has also reawakened our longing for higher and purer things . . . [38]

With the awareness of possible defeat, art was increasingly projected as an alternative to the war, as spiritual escape. Expressionism, too, participated in this general trend.[39] Its promoters could point to interpretations from before the war that had conspicuously advertised it as a turning inward from historical reality and as a regeneration in the midst of catastrophe.[40] The spiritual element in expressionism, its speculative nature, had been there from the start, but it was only now that a public dissatisfied with the war seemed to suddenly discover it.

Under these circumstances, expressionist art began to achieve its first real success with a buying public. The founding of the journal *Das Kunstblatt* in 1917, recognized as an expressionist rival to the more conservative *Kunst und Künstler,* and its almost immediate success testify to the burgeoning new public for modern art.[41] This was the result not only of an ideological convergence between expressionist art and a war-weary bourgeois public, but also its conjuncture with economic conditions. High profits in the armaments industry and few available consumer goods led to a boom in the art market. As prices for older art became prohibitive, it opened a market for modern art, which also benefited from tax laws favoring living artists.[42] Many of expressionism's patrons now came from the newer industrial and financial sectors and often held reformist political and social views. Among the most prominent of these supporters were Walter Rathenau and Robert Bosch, vocal advocates of the de facto parliamentary democracy that emerged at the end of the war while Germany was still under imperial government.[43]

The success of expressionism, however, called into question its revolutionary status. At least a few expressionists felt the need to distance themselves from the "spiritualization" of the movement. The Dresden journal *Menschen*, for instance, repudiated any spiritual comfort for the miseries of the war, for which it held apolitical expressionist journals such as *Der Sturm* responsible.[44] Ludwig Rubiner in *Zeit-Echo* now attacked "art hedonism, pretenses of beauty, atelier-parasitism," and picture painters in general as "art servants . . . of a capitalist age."[45] From outside the expressionist camp the Berlin Dadaists also assailed the incipient success of the movement. Best known is Richard Huelsenbeck's reading of the first German Dada manifesto at an 18 April 1918 Dada evening held, ironically enough, in the New Secession building. It read in part:

> Under the pretense of internalization, the expressionists in literature and in painting have joined together to form a generation which already today longingly awaits its literary and art historical appreciation and is a candidate for honourable recognition by the bourgeoisie. Under the pretense of propagating the soul, they have . . . found their way back to those abstract-pathetic gestures which presuppose an empty, comfortable and inflexible life.[46]

Huelsenbeck attacked the success of expressionism as part of an escapist bourgeois culture culpable for the war.

This success was dealt a serious setback when the art market staggered in mid-1918 under the impact of a ten-percent war-profits tax. With the revolution the economic outlook for expressionist artists was even more precarious.[47] They were confronted once more with the uncertainty of their dependence on an art market catering to the wealthy. The painter and writer Ludwig Meidner melodramatically summed up expressionist sentiment when he lamented: "Is our position in society much better and safer than the proletarian's?! Aren't we, like beggars, dependent on the whims of the art-collecting bourgeoisie!"[48] Many expressionist artists now placed their hopes in the revolution to radically alter the economics of the art world and to bring their art to the "people" as a new clientele. The question with the revolution became: How could an art that had found financial success with a war-weary bourgeoisie after 1917, with its emphasis on the individual and his retreat from the world, now reenter that world and appeal to a different, proletarian public?

The dilemma may have seemed less daunting because of an important precedent. Expressionist artists could feel confirmed in their expectations by news of the prominence of modern art in Soviet Russia. Although the news was sketchy, impeded by the blockade, reports of the advancement of artists such as Wassily Kandinsky, Vladimir Tatlin, and Marc Chagall in the new Russian arts administration fired their imaginations. Just how vague and exaggerated was the news, and how enthusiastically it was received, is seen in a January 1919 letter written by the Stuttgart painter Oskar Schlemmer to a friend: "News from Russia has finally arrived. Moscow is said to be flooded with expressionism. They say Kandinsky and the moderns are splashing whole quarters with color, using blank walls and the sides of houses as the surfaces on which to paint modern pictures."[49] Developments in Russia could serve only to bolster the conviction that a socialist state could provide artists not only with artistic freedom, but with a living independent of the vagaries of a capitalist art market.

It is with this checkered history that expressionist artists confronted the political developments of November 1918. As they were swept up in the maelstrom of events, it seemed easy to ignore the acceptance of their art by a bourgeois public and to focus instead on the apparent victory of their colleagues and friends in Russia. They could confidently point to their contempt for Wilhelmine culture and the support they had received from influential socialist critics. Apparently distrustful of political parties, they could also look to the council movement as a viable alternative for achieving their goals. They now began their assault on the art world in the most logical place—Berlin.

BERLIN 2

November–January: The "People's Revolution" and Democratization of the Arts

Berlin, the capital of Prussia and the German Empire, was quite logically the nerve center of the revolution. It was here that Philipp Scheidemann of the SPD and Karl Liebknecht of the Spartacist group issued their competing proclamations announcing the revolution, here that the Provisional Council of People's Commissioners met, here that the Congress of Councils convened, here that the Freikorps troops were first called in to violently suppress revolutionary activity. It was also in Berlin in November that the first challenges to the imperial arts administration were issued and the first of the expressionist "artists' councils" founded. These were the Working Council for Art (*Arbeitsrat für Kunst*) and the November Group (*Novembergruppe*), whose names were meant to proclaim their revolutionary aspirations. Both, as we shall see, resembled the workers' and soldiers' councils in the earliest months of the revolution, uniting seemingly disparate leftist political perspectives in optimistic expectation of the benefits to be won from the revolution. Unlike the workers and soldiers, though, their authority was self-proclaimed, not mandated by factory or garrison, or even by a general assembly of their profession.

The Working Council for Art first came before the public in early December 1918 when it published its "guiding principles" as "A New Artistic Program" in major German art and architecture journals, as well as in Berlin's two leading socialist papers, the SPD *Vorwärts* and the USPD *Die Freiheit*.[1] In tone and phrase the manifesto resembled any number of declamatory texts published in the daily press that month by groups ranging from teachers to actors, who also included the key word "council" in their titles. Calling for a "rebuilding of our artistic life," the program nowhere mentioned the word revolution, referring only to "political upheaval." It read in part:

Art and the people must form a unity. Art should no longer be the pleasure of a few, but the happiness and life of the masses. The aim is the union of the arts under the wings of a great architecture. Henceforth, the artist alone, as the one who gives form to the perceptions of the people, is responsible for the visible raiment of the new state. He must determine the moulding of the general character of the city, up to coins and stamps.[2]

"A New Artistic Program" further enumerated six demands. The first four polemicized against Wilhelmine art institutions. Unequivocally rejecting anything to do with the old arts management, they demanded either the outright abolition or radical reform of the city planning administration, the royal academies, the Prussian Provincial Arts Commission, state-sponsored exhibitions, and state museums. The fifth demand adopted, quite literally, an iconoclastic and pacifist note: "the elimination of artistically worthless monuments" and the "prevention of precipitously planned war memorials."[3] To help achieve these ends, the WCA included as its sixth demand the formation of a federal position to assure the promotion of the arts in future legislation.

With the revolution, the overriding question in the art world became the fate of the old arts administration. Could artistic freedom be realized within the existing institutional framework, or was it necessary to dismantle the whole apparatus and begin anew? For the WCA the answer seemed clear: the target of the manifesto was the old imperial arts administration, which did not just disappear with the revolution, but for the time being continued convening courses, electing members to the academy, organizing exhibitions, and advising on state purchases. In opposition to these institutions, the WCA offered its "guiding principles," which were in themselves not completely new. They derived in large part from nineteenth-century theories of art such as those of Saint-Simon, Charles Fourier and William Morris, all of whom sought to reverse the privileged exclusivity of art ("no longer the pleasure of the few") and expand it instead into everyday life ("the happiness and life of the masses"). A key facet in these nineteenth-century theories had also been the linking of art and handicrafts, giving artistic shape to everyday objects (everything from coins to stamps), which the WCA also took up.[4]

Some eighty people representing many different segments of the German art world rallied to "A New Artistic Program." Among the painters signing were not only the expressionists Max Pechstein and Cesar Klein, or artists known for their social activism, such as Käthe

Kollwitz, but also Leo von König of the Berlin Secession and Theo von Brockhusen of the Free Secession. Signing were the young architects Walter Gropius and Bruno Taut, but also the older Paul Mebes and Paul Schmitthenner. Writers lending their support included the socialist critics John Schikowski and Wilhelm Hausenstein, ardent supporters of expressionism, as well as Julius Meier-Graefe, the leading promoter of impressionism in Germany. Just as the signatories represented no one artistic ideal, neither did they represent only one political position. Nowhere in the manifesto was any party-political position mentioned, only the intent to work with "like-minded" government officials. Probably because the manifesto was politically vague and because it basically demanded only a democratization of the arts could it garner such widespread support.

The initial leadership of the WCA mirrored the broad base of the members.[5] There was the 38-year-old architect Bruno Taut, an ardent social reformer with anarchist views who had been active in the garden city movement and had worked for the cooperative building societies. He was best known for his quixotic Glass Pavilion at the 1914 Werkbund exhibition, which had inscribed over its entrance the aphorism "Colored glass destroys hatred." His faith in art was not rewarded, though, as the war broke out shortly after the opening of the pavilion. Opposed to the war, Taut went to extreme lengths to avoid conscription, even contemplating suicide.[6] His pacifism became the basis for the futurist utopias he described in his wartime writings, including *Alpine Architecture* and *The City Crown.* Taut was also associated with the expressionist camp, which he had praised in a 1914 essay in *Der Sturm.*[7] Joining Taut in guiding the WCA was Wilhelm Valentiner, who in the final days of the war had enrolled in the SPD.[8] A former assistant to Wilhelm von Bode (director general of the royal museums), Valentiner had spent the years immediately before the war as a curator in the United States. Initially supportive of the war effort, he returned to Germany and quickly volunteered for active duty.[9] It was during his military training that he was exposed for the first time to expressionist art. His appreciation for the new art developed not through scholarly essays or other second-hand sources, but under the direct tutelage of Franz Marc, his instructor in officer training.[10] By October 1916 friends arranged his transfer to a desk job in Berlin, where he edited foreign press news. Quickly, Valentiner became one of the most enterprising promoters of expressionism in Berlin. He developed friendships with the collectors Princess Lichnowsky and Walter Rathenau and even delivered lectures on art to the German Crown Princess in an attempt to influence her opinions in favor of modern art.[11] The divergent backgrounds of the two initial leaders of the WCA—Taut the architect with anarchist views who had worked for the cooperative building societies, Valentiner the lecturer on art to the crown princess—indicate the width of the social spectrum that these men could think of reaching.

With the publication of Bruno Taut's "Architecture Program" at Christmas under the auspices of the WCA, however, the group moved decisively to the left. A polemical, rhetorically exaggerated assessment of the architectural profession, Taut's program had broader implications for all the arts. In it he proposed a comprehensive plan for the restructuring of the architectural profession. Essential here is his conception of the social role of art in revolutionary Germany. Taut stressed five points: the leading role of architecture as the embodiment of all the arts, the Gothic cathedral as a model for the unification of the arts and handicrafts in an organic society, the importance of a council system to control all building activities, decentralization, and the necessity of beginning work on a utopian building project uniting all the arts. Many of these tenets, including decentralization, council rule, and the Gothic precedent, could be found in the reformist anarchist writings of Gustav Landauer and Peter Kropotkin. Landauer's 1911 *Call to Socialism*, for example, presented similar plans for decentralized settlements which were to prefigure a future socialist society characterized not simply by political and economic liberation, but a prerequisite spiritual renewal as well.[12] Taut's further insistence on upholding an essentially nonutilitarian idea of art (a utopian building project) undoubtedly was meant as a repudiation of the German Werkbund in which he had been so active. An association of artists, manufacturers, and patrons founded in 1907, the Werkbund had as its original premise cooperation between artists and industrialists on the basis of equality. Already before the war, though, manufacturers had gained the upper hand, thereby coopting for Taut the issue of the aesthetic shape of everyday objects. With the publication of Taut's text, the WCA headed on a collision course with some of its more conservative members and began a process of radicalization that would accelerate in the coming months.

The other Berlin artists' group founded during the revolution was the November Group. Although membership in the two groups overlapped to a certain extent, there were nonetheless significant differences between them, both artistically and politically. The WCA was broader-based, including from the outset not only painters, but also sculptors, architects, critics, government officials, and patrons. It also attempted, at least initially, to unite artists practicing in a variety of styles. The NG was from the beginning more narrowly defined, composed almost exclusively of "expressionist, cubist, and futurist" artists (as they described themselves in the group's first public statement), and was essentially limited to painters and sculptors. Its organizers were among the most prominent expressionists in Berlin, who were the founders of the Berlin New Secession: Max Pechstein, Cesar Klein, Georg Tappert, and Heinrich Richter-Berlin, along with Moriz Melzer. Much as the New Secession in 1910 had attempted to dislodge the Berlin Secession as the corporate rallying center for modern artists, so the November Group now positioned itself not only to supplant the secession movement, but also to become the dominant artists' association in Germany.

In a retrospective account, Richter-Berlin recorded the events that led to the group's founding. His words are revealing not only of the mood at the time, but also of the artists' relationship to the drama unfolding in the streets around them. He wrote:

> When the revolution was a few days old many people always gathered at noon in the Potsdamer Platz to hear the latest. While crossing the Platz I met Max Pechstein. He had a plan. He believed one should start anew. I should rally my people (Tappert, Klein, Melzer) and he would bring the Brücke. He even had a name already: November Group! At this moment a lorry drove by loaded with masses of weapons, and the sailors sitting on top resounded: 'Citizens, comrades! The Potsdam garrison is advancing to wipe out the revolution. Arm yourselves! Resist!' Ten meters away from us the sculptor Leschnitzer and the graphic artist Leni had been standing. As I looked around, they disappeared in the subway. Max Pechstein considered it best to do the same thing. I was totally of the same opinion.[13]

If one can believe Richter-Berlin, the NG was hatched moments before a street battle, but by those who were only passive observers.

When some twenty artists came together for the first meeting of the NG on 3 December 1918, there was little consensus about what they wanted to achieve, other than to form a new organization.[14] They agreed only that the group was to be composed of pictorial artists, that it would be national in scope,[15] and that they would not accept an offer to merge with the WCA.[16] This last decision indicates that the NG insisted still on the preeminence of the fine arts, rather than unity with the handicrafts or with architecture. The group's first public statement, dated 13 December 1918, was not an elaboration of its aims, but a call to membership: "The future of art and the seriousness of the present hour force us revolutionaries of the spirit (expressionists, cubists, futurists) to unification and close alliance. We therefore direct to all artists, who shattered the old forms in art, the urgent request to announce their joining in the November Group."[17] The letter based potential membership almost solely on formal terms, defining "expressionists, cubists, and futurists" by their "shattering of old forms in art." The only potential link to the revolution came in the term "revolutionaries of the spirit," which reiterated a commonly held view that this art, by its very nature, had presaged the revolution. As compared with the first WCA manifesto, the NG statement was less concerned with specific demands for the democratization of the art world and mentioned only the hope for developing a program that would bring about a closer relationship between art and the people.[18] Unlike the WCA, the November Group did not send its announcements to the socialist daily press, but only to expressionist art journals.

The November Group was slow to formulate a specific program. A preliminary draft for a manifesto had no specific demands; instead it was a general plea for legitimacy.[19] Carrying no specific political reference points, it claimed only that the group "stood on the most fruitful ground of revolution," was ready to fight reaction, and had as its motto "liberty, equality, fraternity," the words of another revolution.[20] When a manifesto and guiding principles finally appeared in broadsheet form in January, however, they echoed the demands of the WCA, including reform of art education, reorganization of museums, destruction of artistically worthless monuments, and reform of exhibition policies.[21] The NG manifesto, though, still differed in a few significant regards. Nowhere did it mention the uniting of art and the masses, nor of reversing the privileged exclusivity of art. Its brief references to the economics of the art market seemed primarily concerned with protecting the interests of artists: it called for an end to capitalist influences on art exhibitions, protection of artistic property, and elimination of taxes on artworks, including free import and export.[22] Appended to these statements were the statutes of the group, already legally formulated in mid-December and registered with the proper authorities, spelling out membership and voting requirements, the length of the business year, and the relationship of regional groups to the central organization.[23]

While the political position of the November Group may have been deliberately vague in its manifesto, its leadership was more explicit as to where it stood. A rare letter by Georg Tappert provides a remarkably frank glimpse of the struggle of the artist to come to terms with the meaning of the revolution for art. Tappert was, by 1919, a fairly well-established figure in the art world, an expressionist painter known for his portraits and flower paintings. A cofounder of the New Secession, he had recently been appointed as a teacher at the State College for Art Education in Berlin. He was also a highly visible contributor to expressionist journals, including *Die schöne Rarität* in Kiel, which he helped edit. On 20 November 1918, after attending a political debate, he wrote a lengthy letter to his friend Franz Pfemfert, editor of the radical journal *Die Aktion*, which is worth quoting at length:

I wish you had been there [at the meeting], because the whole atmosphere of the gathering would have shown you how correct my expressions of opinion in this direction previously were. Whether Spartacus or U.S.(P.D.),—the people don't want anything to do with you, with us, and even a proletarian collar will not help us to hope for trust or understanding. What we are doing is foreign to them. They also don't want to understand; they are indifferent and will still be in ten or fifteen years! The proletarian youth of 1900 would have been a much more suitable object for *Die Aktion* and its efforts. In them there was an eagerness for literature, for art, for education! This youth waited for two hours before entrance into the theater in order to obtain spiritual and intellectual conception in the standing-room-only galleries. Today's young proletarian doesn't do this anymore. Class consciousness, political enlightenment hinders him in this; if he can't sit in the orchestra stalls, he renounces it entirely. . . .

You won't want to find me right, will think I judge the circumstances as an artist, as an owner of spiritual values. To that I would like to oppose that as the son of a convinced socialist I grew up with the teachings of socialism, got to know party life in all its forms, just as the proletariat in all its highs and lows. From the moment when I decided to become a painter I was seen as disloyal, as bourgeois. . . .

Your political work in *Die Aktion* will not be recognized by comrades, by manual laborers. You do not speak their language . . . In the best case you will be tolerated, but not understood. It will be the same with the Spartacus group; today you—we—are welcome as fellow-travelers; in the coming revolution they will break into your shops and inasmuch as they attain power they will decree what you may publish. If you give 10,000 workers the last *Rote Hahn* issue of Rottluff-Brust [Pfemfert's press had recently published a play by the expressionist Alfred Brust, with illustrations by Karl Schmidt-Rottluff] they won't know what to make of it. Not today, not in five years, for they stand on the ground of naturalism, on the ground of the real (material) mode of viewing. The proletarian is of the erroneous view that all of the new art is a product of bourgeois society and now demands that he as dictator lay down for artists in which paths the new (now naturally socialist) art should move.[24]

Tappert's political dilemma was inscribed in almost every line, his ambivalence about his socialist commitment neatly indicated in his repeated reference to Pfemfert as "you," quickly amended to "we." Although they had collaborated during the war (Tappert had contributed to *Die Aktion*), they were now moving apart politically. Tappert was suspicious of the USPD and the Spartacists because (at least as he perceived it) they favored naturalism and spurned the new art. A Spartacist victory, in his view, would mean subsuming art to politics and, therefore, the end of all artistic freedom. He concluded his letter by outlining the only two avenues he saw available to progressive intellectuals: either succumb to the political propaganda of the masses, thereby hastening the inevitable, if dreaded, "socialist dictatorship" or organize an international community of intellectuals—"who stand on the ground of socialism"—to oppose the "masses, the mass psychosis."[25] The November Group may have been his preferred alternative.

The vague revolutionary claims of the WCA and the November Group found almost immediate support in the expressionist art journals. Expressionism, according to the editor of *Das Kunstblatt,* had not only anticipated, but, with the help of journals such as his, had paved the way for the revolution. *Das Kunstblatt* therefore had no need to publish "a new program or new affirmations" because "a revolution was already long ago put into action in art."[26] Pfemfert, too, predicted the eventual success of expressionist art with the revolution, but saw a more difficult road ahead. Although *Die Aktion* turned increasingly away from writing on art in favor of promoting leftist politics, on 14 December 1918, Pfemfert published an excerpt from the little-known artist Peter Bender's manifesto "The Artist and the Revolution." Bender wrote that the proletarian revolution would mean the end of the old public for art, the "oppressors" and "exploiters," the "rich church, the powerful nobility, and the possessing burgher." They would be replaced by a new public, the victorious proletariat, which as yet, however, had no money to support the arts nor an understanding of them. Rather than calling for an end to art as it was previously known, Bender envisioned the crisis resolved in a utopian perspective: "As to the understanding (of art), the crisis is temporary, since the socialized humanity will raise the standard of living of all members of the human condition to the standard of living of the present bourgeoisie, and beyond that to the present court."[27] Revolution, then, meant a temporary crisis for all artists, to be resolved in a socialist future. In the meantime, there was no necessity, by implication, for artists to change their art. Only Herwarth Walden's *Der Sturm,* among the major expressionist journals, preferred for the time being to remain silent on the issue of art and revolution.

Even more instrumental in promoting the expressionist artists' groups and putting forward their demands were the SPD and USPD newspapers in Berlin, *Vorwärts* and *Die Freiheit* respectively. *Die Freiheit* published the WCA manifesto as well as a series of articles on the economic reorganization of the arts, which, without mentioning the artists's councils by name, were clearly in sympathy with them. First was "Socialism and the Artist" by Lu Märten, the author of the 1914 book *Art and the Proletariat* that had detailed the proletarianization of artists in Wilhelmine Germany. She now condemned the disastrous effects of capitalism on the arts, which restricted artistic freedom and relegated artworks to commodity items. Märten believed that a socialist state would remedy these disasters, but did not, however, provide any specifics.[28] *Die Freiheit* also published a three-part series called "The Intellectual Worker in the Socialist State" that focused on the possible socialization of intellectual work, including art. The author envisaged a society in which the state would someday be wealthy enough to support all artists.[29] The SPD newspaper *Vorwärts* also published the WCA manifesto, and its resident critic John Schikowski joined the group. His "The Revolution and Art," published in November, was a critique of Wilhelmine art policies and a plea for a universally conceived aesthetic environment in line with the WCA's "New Artistic Program." He promoted expressionist art, without having to name it:

> Is it a purely fortunate accident that simultaneous with the social and political revolution an upheaval in the artistic sphere takes place? A new spirit moves through art, an impulse toward intensification and absorption, which wants to elevate, transport and edify the souls, and wants to mean to those who have become free what religion once meant to those who were enslaved.[30]

Schikowski here held to the spirit claims made for expressionism during the war. *Vorwärts*, however, did not one-sidedly support expressionism. With the Christmas issue the newspaper documented the range of opinions about the future of art, posing to a broad cross section of the art world the question: "What do you expect for art from the new people's state?" The impressionist painter Max Liebermann, now a prominent member of the academy, demanded only artistic freedom, and therefore autonomy. A young member of the WCA decried the capitalist art market and proposed state support for artists. Another artist pleaded for artistic freedom and for the importance of the "new" art finding its way to public places rather than restricted exhibitions and museums. The architect and designer Peter Behrens, who was active in the Werkbund, repeated two of the catchphrases of the younger artists: antagonism to imperial art policies and the claim that art had presaged the revolution. But rather than hailing expressionist art "in opposition to courtly representation," he named instead the "technical and tectonic" in art, the "products of industry," which would bring artistic form to the broadest numbers of people. The art of the new "people's state," for Behrens, was the product of capitalist industry. Evident in these varied responses was the composite nature of the bourgeois aspirations that rallied to the SPD newspaper, from hopes for state support for the new art to calls for an art of industrial capitalism.

In this the responses mirrored quite accurately the support given the SPD, not only by workers and their trade-union representatives, but by many leaders of industry as well, who, for the time being, did not want to harm the cause of the Majority Socialists and the chances for the speedy summoning of a National Assembly. For its part, the Spartacist (later KPD) newspaper *Rote Fahne* carried no essays on art at all. Nor is it clear where its leaders stood on the issue of expressionist art. Rosa Luxemburg, for one, was conservative in her aesthetic tastes and expressed no interest in avant-garde art forms. At least one communist leader (Paul Levi), however, had already demonstrated an interest in expressionism.[31] For the time being, though, the party had more pressing concerns than art.

Support from the SPD and USPD newspapers lent political credibility to the vague revolutionary claims of the artists' councils. By December, however, it became more evident where the leadership of the November Group stood politically. Max Pechstein, Cesar Klein, and Heinrich Richter-Berlin now placed their art at the service of anti-Spartacist politics. Although all members of the November Group did not necessarily concur (one member warned in a letter against those in the group who "as 'spiritual' try to preserve the pseudo-cultural values of capitalism in the new freedom"[32]), the leadership, at least, seems to have been in accord.

Beginning in December 1918, Pechstein, Richter-Berlin, and Klein produced posters and pamphlet illustrations for an outfit called the Publicity Office (*Werbedienst*). Created in late October 1918 as a division of the Military Department of the Foreign Office, the Publicity Office was now under the control of the Council of People's Representatives. Running the office was the expressionist writer Paul Zech, a member of the SPD.[33] The first expressionist posters for the Publicity Office, identifiable by their torch insignia, were predominantly calls for a return to work, order, and the speedy summoning of a National Assembly in order to "protect" the revolution. In this sense, they were partisan propaganda, directed against the Spartacists.[34] Typical was Cesar Klein's poster in support of the National Assembly (fig. 2.1). His call for class reconciliation and national unity reprised the most common theme in poster production of the late war years, when political tensions on the homefront had threatened the war effort. His friezelike mass of people, arms raised in victory, recalled Ferdinand Hodler's famous frieze *Unanimity* at the Hannover town hall. Another Klein poster warned against strikes: "He Who Does Not Work is the Grave-Digger of His Children" (fig. 2.2). A similar emotional appeal to law and order was Max Pechstein's large-scale poster "Do Not Strangle the

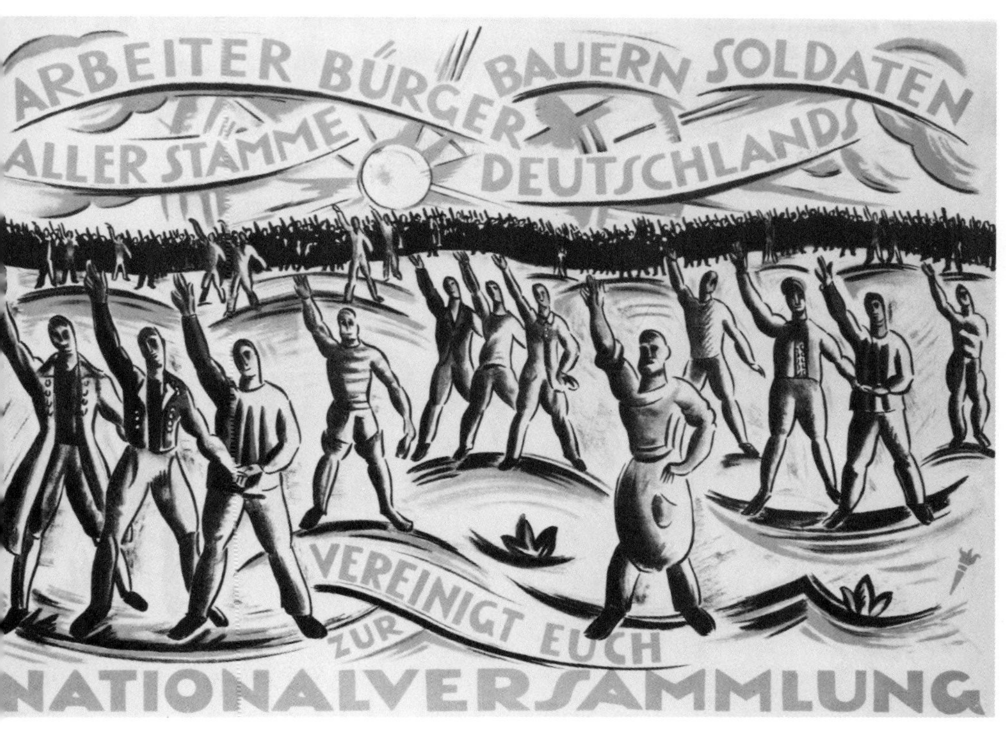

2.1 Cesar Klein, *Nationalversammlung* (*National Assembly*), poster for the Publicity Office, 1918–19. Color lithograph, 65 x 94 cm. The Robert Gore Rifkind Collection, Beverly Hills, California.

Young Freedom through Disorder and Fratricide, Otherwise Your Children Will Starve" (fig. 2.3).

The poster most often mentioned in connection with the Publicity Office campaign was Pechstein's "The National Assembly, the Corner-Stone of the German Socialist Republic" (fig. 2.4), which appeared in the last days before the disputed elections to the National Assembly boycotted by the KPD. It showed a worker, shirt sleeves rolled up, trowel in hand, literally atop a building cornerstone, left arm raised as he issues the call for the National Assembly. Pechstein's concentration on a single figure in an action pose recalled war-bond posters, where the figure held not a trowel, but a weapon.[35] He also provided covers for the Publicity Office brochures "Call to Socialism" and "Bestir Yourselves." The first was a collection of manifestos and poems by expressionist writers, all of which echoed a vague commitment to socialism. Pechstein's cover drawing captured the earliest revolutionary fervor with its ineluctable forward surge (fig. 2.5). "Bestir Yourselves" in-

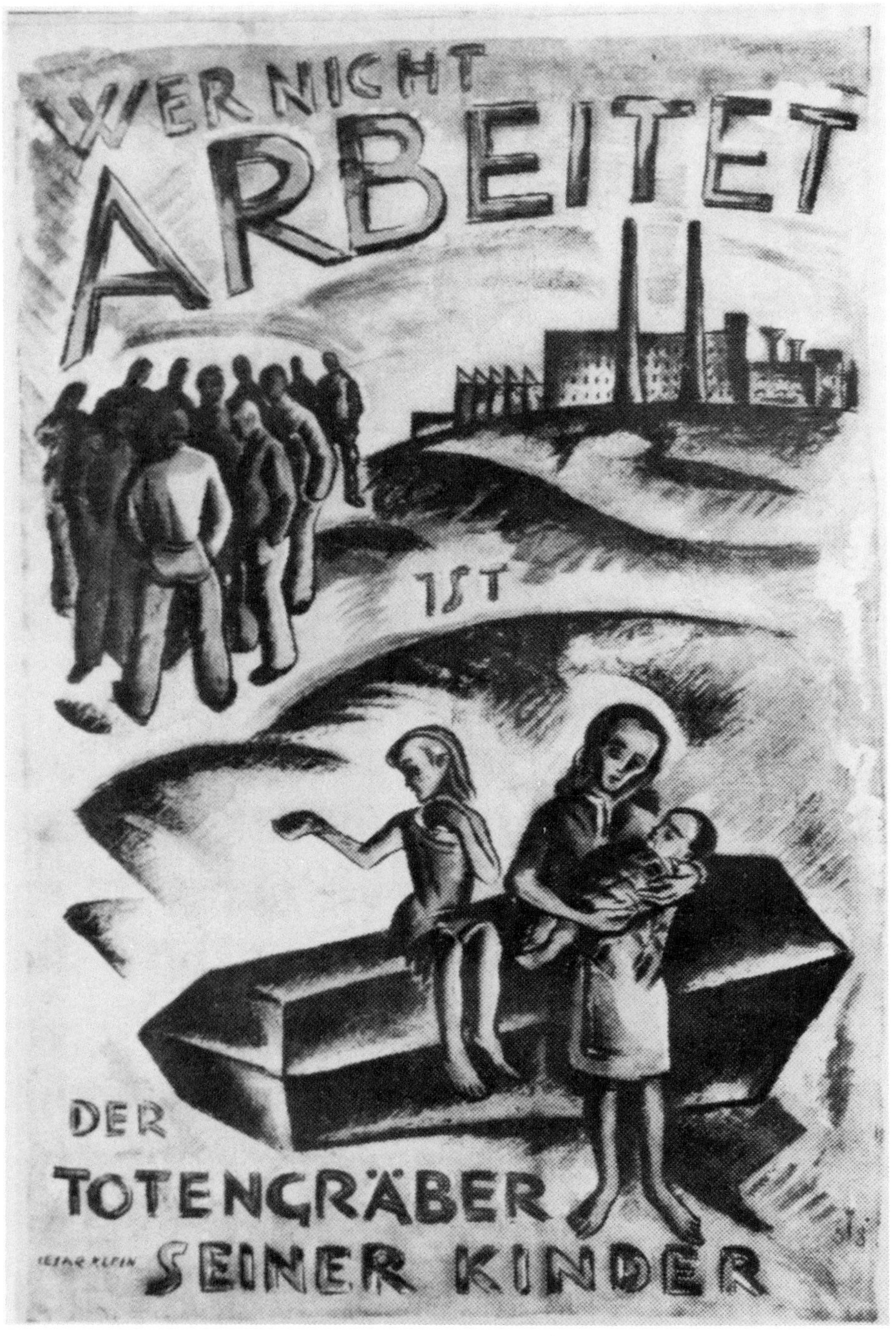

2.2 Cesar Klein, *Wer nicht arbeitet* (*He Who Does Not Work*), poster for the Publicity Office, 1918–19. Color lithograph, dimensions unknown. From the Imperial War Museum.

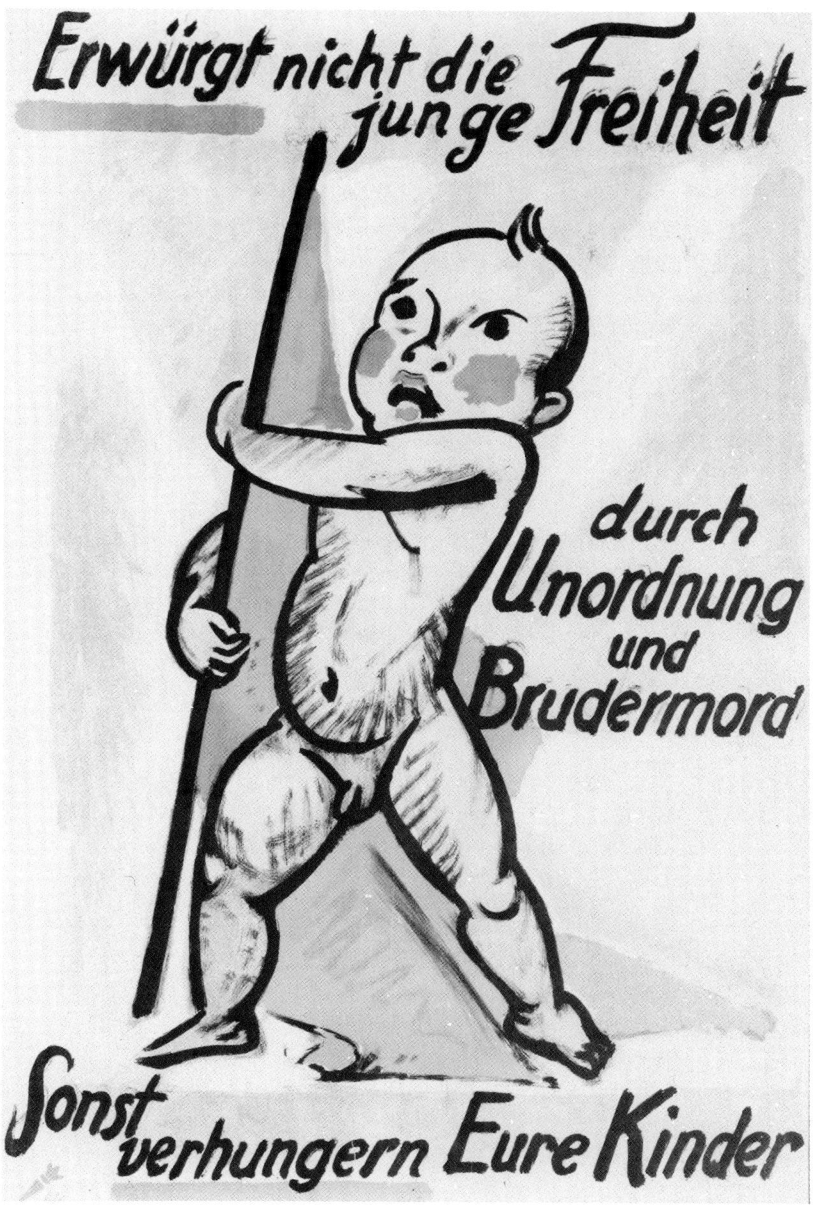

2.3 Max Pechstein, *Erwürgt nicht die junge Freiheit* (*Do Not Strangle the Young Freedom*), poster for the Publicity Office, 1918–19. Color lithograph, 99.1 x 65 cm. The Robert Gore Rifkind Collection, Beverly Hills, California.

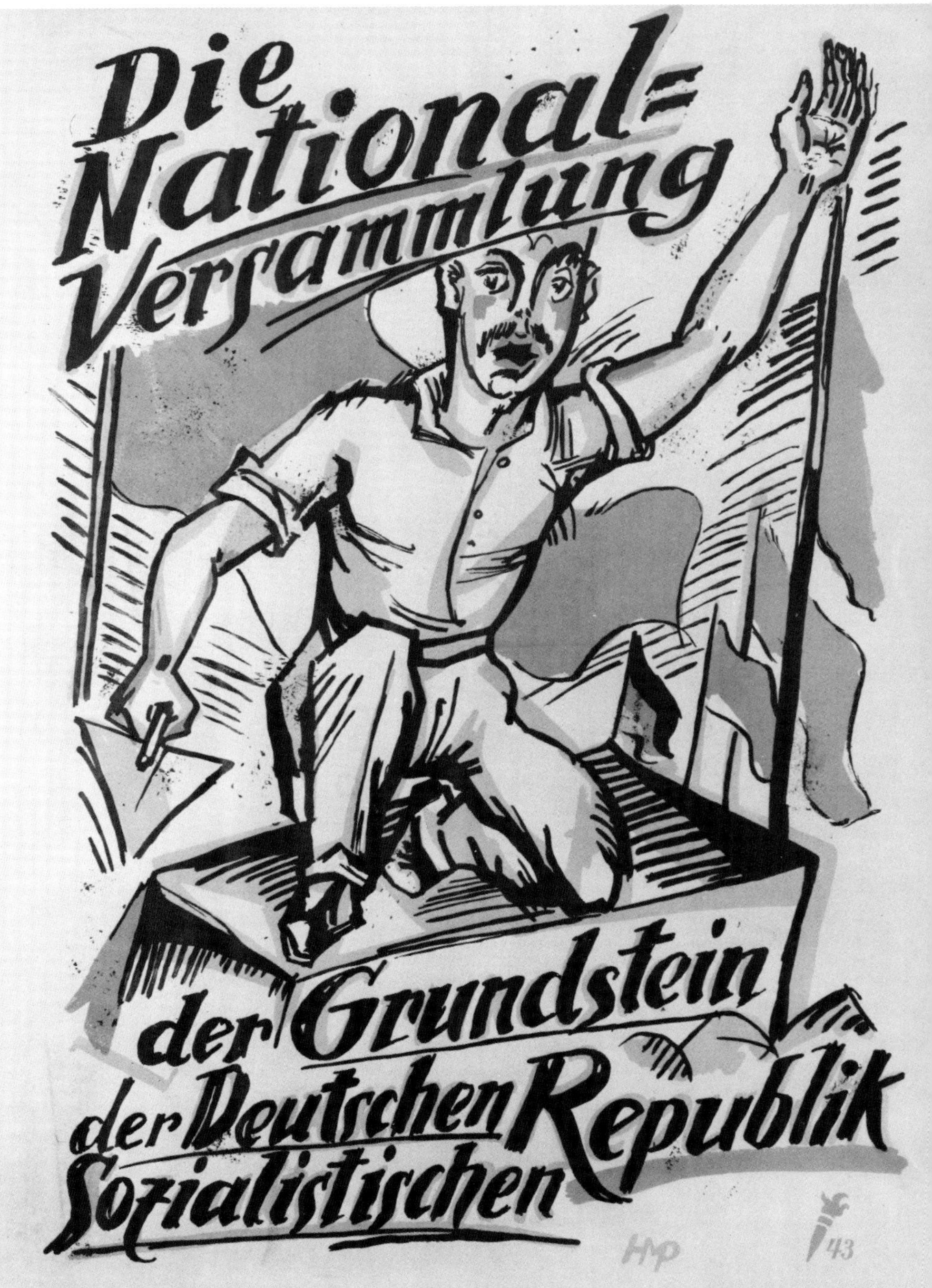

2.4 Max Pechstein, *Die Nationalversammlung* (*The National Assembly*), poster for the Publicity Office, 1918–19. Color lithograph, 67.8 x 50.2 cm. The Robert Gore Rifkind Collection, Beverly Hills, California.

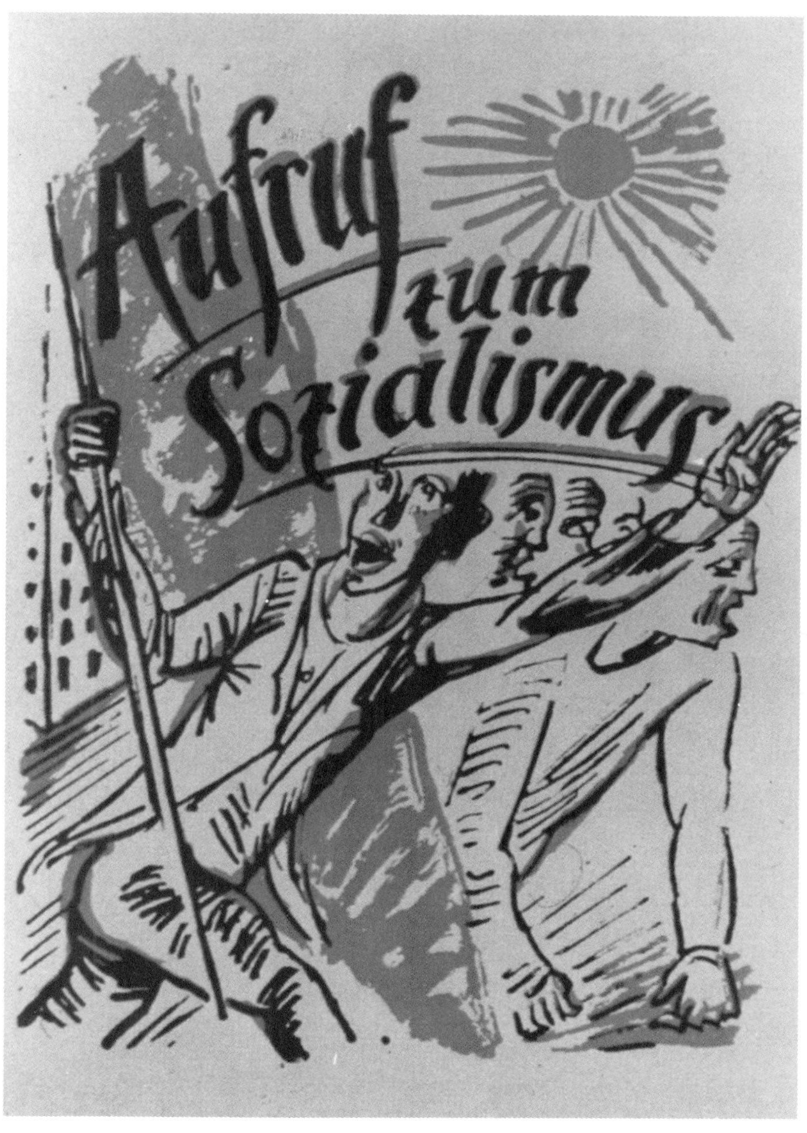

2.5 Max Pechstein, *Aufruf zum Sozialismus* (*Call to Socialism*), pamphlet cover, 1919. Color lithograph.

cluded specific instructions concerning polling places and voting procedures for the 19 January elections. Although produced under the auspices of an ostensibly politically independent agency, the pamphlet was decidedly anti-Spartacist. Among its pages, for example, were excerpts from the Munich satirical journal *Simplicissimus* deriding adherents of the council movement as buffoonish and ignorant.

The participation of expressionist artists in an officially sponsored propaganda campaign was a landmark event: the first time they had received state patronage, the first time they had placed their art at the service of party politics, the first time they had truly tried to reach a mass audience. But the grand experiment soon came to a crashing halt. When the political parties were due to produce their first postwar election posters in January, none of the socialist parties turned to expressionist artists. Even though these artists had eliminated the most gross expressionist distortions in their posters in an apparent attempt to appeal to a mass audience, in the serious matter of turning out the electorate, the parties relied on more readable artistic traditions.[36]

While the leaders of the November Group were producing their propaganda posters, the leaders of the WCA took their own more cautious first steps toward dealing with the provisional government. Optimistic about support for their efforts, they approached the governmental agency in Prussia still responsible for cultural matters, the *Kultusministerium* (Ministry of Ecclesiastical Affairs, Education, and Art). Like all other Prussian ministries in November 1918, one SPD and one USPD representative presided over the *Kultusministerium*. The SPD member was Konrad Hänisch, a member of the right wing of his party, who was appointed already during the war. The USPD member was Adolf Hoffmann, a former engraver and editor who belonged to the left wing of his party.[37] There is one telling account of a meeting between representatives of the WCA and the *Kultusministerium*. Arriving a few minutes late for their scheduled appointment, Bruno Taut, Wilhelm Valentiner, and the architect Walter Gropius were forced to wait behind a folded screen while Adolf Hoffman conferred with Wilhelm von Bode, the director general of the royal museums. Bode was under heavy criticism at the time from the modern camp for his accusations that those who supported modernist art abroad during the war had consorted with the enemy.[38] Taut, Valentiner, and Gropius listened helplessly as Hoffman authorized Bode to continue at his post. In their own subsequent meeting with the minister, the WCA representatives came away only with an assurance that their program would be put in the files.[39] Taut also tried in December to meet with the SPD minister

Hänisch to discuss the persistence of "reactionary circles" in matters of housing policy, but was apparently never granted a meeting.[40]

Nor were such experiences limited to the WCA. The editor of *Der Sturm*, Herwarth Walden, requested a meeting with Hänisch just days after the outbreak of the revolution. In his letter he argued for the superiority of expressionism, while assuring Hänisch that "we don't want to set up a dictatorship of expressionism, but we want to receive for our artistic efforts the same rights—also state support and help—as all other directions in art."[41] Hänisch's reply was that of a bureaucrat, polite but noncommital.[42] The minister wrote to yet another expressionist petitioner: "Artistic questions, as much as I recognize their importance, must in any case still in these first weeks take a back seat to more pressing issues."[43] By January Hänisch presided over the *Kultusministerium* alone, as the USPD withdrew *en bloc* from the government.

In these early days of the revolution the WCA had two high priorities for institutional reform, which represented to them the antidemocratic art practices of the imperial administration: museums and the academy. Expressionist art was barely represented in public museums throughout Germany, and the National Gallery in Berlin did not own a single painting by an expressionist artist—only a few graphic works. The *Gemäldegalerie* in Dresden, the city where the Brücke was founded, owned only one work by Pechstein. Even the state museum with the largest expressionist collection, the *Kunstmuseum* in Essen, boasted only six works.[44] Of the few expressionist paintings owned by public museums in Germany, almost all had been given to the museums as gifts. It was no wonder, then, that both the November Group and the Working Council for Art targeted museums for reform in their manifestos, advocating reorganization to make them "places of education for the people," with frequently changing exhibitions of contemporary art made accessible through lecture series and guided tours. Museums were to become, in the words of the November Group, "places for people's art."

Already on 22 November 1918, Ludwig Justi, director of the Berlin National Gallery, felt compelled to address the exclusion of expressionism from public collections in a published memorandum to the Prussian *Kultusministerium*. *The National Gallery and Modern Art* was a defensive plea in which Justi tried to convince not just his new superiors in the ministry, but the general public as well, that his tenure as director had been a period of bold democratic attempts in the face of conservative opposition from the Kaiser.[45] As evidence he offered the effective dismantling of the control of the Prussian Provincial Art Commission (the body that made recommendations on state purchases), the permission to exhibit works purchased during the war without the Kaiser's approval, and the new space for exhibiting works by living artists.[46] He now proposed further reform: doing away with paying days at the museum, expanding the existing "small commission" deciding on purchases into an impartial "commission of experts,"[47] and creating a separate Gallery of Living Artists. He concluded rather uncharacteristically: "State promotion of art should not limit itself to buying and exhibiting works that properly belong in a middle-class home, but commissions must be given for large-scale decoration of public buildings."[48]

Justi was attacked almost immediately as an opportunist by a prominent member of the expressionist camp. Paul Westheim, editor of *Das Kunstblatt* and a frequent columnist for the liberal *Frankfurter Zeitung*, publicly questioned Justi's sudden conversion to modern art. He pointed out that as late as 15 July 1918, when Justi had proposed new purchases by living artists, not a single one was by an expressionist.[49] Westheim also argued that the maintenance of any type of art commission was a conservative relic. For these reasons he found Justi unacceptable to direct any new Gallery of Living Artists.[50]

Despite Justi's apparent attempt to placate the artists' councils, the WCA soon offered its own alternative in the form of a detailed memorandum by Wilhelm Valentiner, titled *Reorganization of the Museums in Step with the New Times*.[51] As an experienced museum professional, Valentiner seemed the appropriate WCA member for the job. His was a rather dramatic plan, calling for a complete reorganization of German museums, with separate museums for international art, national art, and the works of living artists. The particulars were set out in great detail. The museum for international art, for instance, would be located in the provinces, either Coburg or Marburg, with twenty-three nonconnecting rooms beginning with primitive art and ending with contemporary art. The museums for national art were to be "educational places for the people" (a phrase repeated from the WCA manifesto), replete with sports fields, music halls, and libraries. In both the national and international museums a principle Valentiner called mixture was to be in effect: placing artworks in their historical settings by surrounding them with craft objects of the same period.

The more unconventional suggestions made Valentiner's proposals suspect in the eyes of much of the art establishment, as did his disregard for nineteenth-century German art, which he did not plan to include in the international museum. Despite these peculiarities, Valentiner's plans did not differ all that fundamentally from earlier proposals by reformers such as Alfred Lichtwark, the former director of the Hamburg Kunsthalle, and Fritz Wichert, director of the Mannheim Kunsthalle, which were also concerned with a comprehensive program of public education in the arts—that is, with bringing art to the general populace. (His section on national museums even quoted, uncredited, a Lichtwark speech of 1905 almost word for word).[52] Even his museum for the works of living artists sounded like Justi's Gallery of Living Artists. What all these programs had in common was that change in the art world was not dependent on change in society; quite the opposite, art—rather than revolution—was empowered with bringing about social reform. The main difference in Valentiner's plan was his favoring of expressionist art.

Despite its similarity to long-standing reform proposals, the press vehemently attacked Valentiner's plan as too radical. One conservative critic compared it to the plan of the Commissar for People's Enlightenment in revolutionary Russia, calling it "neither liberal nor democratic."[53] Another museum director pointed out the contradiction between expressionist artists demanding public collections of expressionist art and at the same time implying in their manifestos that they "preferred for their works the most modest wall of a worker's apartment to the death chamber" of any gallery.[54] Justi jumped into the fray with a long attack on "these dusty thoughts and platitudes," claiming that the majority of Valentiner's concerns had already been adequately addressed. He even went so far as to claim that the museums had achieved a degree of "socialization" of artworks when the royal family had turned over its art treasures to found the first public museums.[55]

By early December Justi recommended for purchase by the National Gallery two paintings by Erich Heckel, one by Oskar Kokoschka, and one sculpture by Ernst Barlach. Disagreement over the purchases caused the advisory commission to dissolve in acrimony. In the end, Justi prevailed, and the works were purchased, but they were bound to be seen as only a minor concession to the expressionist artists' councils. Little else was done by the museum, the academy, or the *Kultusministerium* to implement any reforms in the earliest months of the revolution. The ministry had to contend as well with more conservative members of the art community who staunchly resisted even cosmetic changes. Typical of their recalcitrance was a critic writing in *Wachtfeuer,* the journal of the conservative Berlin League of Pictorial Artists (*Verband bildender Künstler*): "And art becomes new and beautiful. Formerly Justi could not buy a single picture for the National Gallery if the Kaiser did not want it. Now he may buy, but now Westheim tells him that he has no character. He must be crucified. Rosa Luxemburg then certainly knows a good successor."[56] Westheim's criticism of Justi was sarcastically dismissed as the dictatorial views of the extreme left.

Next to the museum, the other institution to raise the ire of the artists' councils was the academy, which had long been a bastion of royal control of the arts. Under pressure from the Prussian *Kultusministerium*, on 3 December the Berlin academy instituted a reform commission, whose most prominent members were the impressionist painter Max Liebermann, the architect and designer Bruno Paul (who had cofounded the Workshops for Art in Crafts in Munich and was an active proponent of educational reform), and the sculptor and academy professor Louis Tuaillon.[57] At stake was whether the academy should expand its membership to include younger, expressionist artists. A preliminary vote of the commission showed only one member for the expansion (Bruno Paul), eleven against (led by Liebermann).[58] The academy also threatened to reject a plan developed by the *Kultusministerium* to alter the format of the annual Berlin Art Exhibition. The state-financed annual salon had for years been the prerogative of the academy and the conservative Association of Berlin Artists (*Verein Berliner Künstler*) and was an important showplace for artists seeking to attract a public. To no small degree the Secessions had formed against the mass market of the salon. On 22 November Max Schlichting, a prominent academician, vocal opponent of nonacademic art,[59] and chairman of the exhibition, requested a meeting with Konrad Hänisch to discuss a reorganization of the show.[60] What finally emerged from their meeting was a plan to divide the exhibition space on a separate but equal basis, with one-half given over to the direction of the Association of Berlin Artists, and the other to the combined leadership of the Berlin Secession, the Free Secession (which formed in 1913 after a split in the Berlin Secession and included both impressionists and expressionists), and the November Group.

The academy threatened to reject the new plan, since as a corporate body it was deprived of its longstanding control of the exhibition.[61] In the end, though, it acquiesced, perhaps because Schlichting was to remain titular head. Paul Westheim soon inveighed against the plan. Much as he had attacked Justi's "commission of experts," he derided the "first act of official art promotion of the new republic in Berlin" as similarly based on outmoded premises. Westheim argued that a democratic state would find it hard to support such an exhibition: if it were truly neutral, it would have to allow all seventeen thousand artists in Germany to exhibit, leading to an unmanageable "orgy of bad taste."

If, on the other hand, it limited those who could exhibit, this would be nothing more than resurrecting a privileged state art.[62] In spite of these warnings, the November Group planned to join the exhibition. The Prussian *Kultusministerium* could claim for the first time to have unified the entire Berlin art world under one roof, even if the "left" and "right" wings of the building would have nothing to do with one another.

For the time being this remained the only significant contribution of the Prussian *Kultusministerium* to a reorganization of the arts. Political uncertainty, and the open conflicts in the ministry, hampered any further attempts to democratize the art world. Museum officials retained their posts, where their main concern seemed to be the safeguarding of collections after reports of vandalism by soldiers occupying the royal palace.[63] The academy continued much as it always had. If in the early days of the revolution expressionist artists had been euphoric, assuming their art would triumph with the revolution and the hated institutions of the imperial art world would fade away, they soon became disillusioned as they met with resistance. This disillusionment soon accelerated dramatically, as events in the streets overtook the Working Council for Art and the November Group, and not just the political, but the cultural life of Berlin became radicalized.

January–June: Political and Artistic Radicalization

On 5 January the newly formed Communist Party organized mass demonstrations to protest what they considered the SPD's suppression of the revolution. Spartacist troops occupied several press offices and refused to leave. On 11 January Friedrich Ebert (SPD head of the rump Council of People's Representatives) called in the Freikorps, the temporary armed force composed of a small number of workers loyal to the republic and many more former soldiers who were antirepublican adventurers. On 13 January the fugitive Communist Party leaders Rosa Luxemburg and Karl Liebknecht were captured by the Freikorps and subsequently murdered.

Only four days after the double murder, elections to the disputed National Assembly took place as scheduled. The SPD gained the largest share of the vote (37.9 percent), while the USPD garnered only 7.6 percent. The KPD, as promised, boycotted the election. Between them, the socialists' parties did not have a majority. On 11 February Ebert was elected president and a coalition government was formed consisting of the SPD, the Centre Party, and the Democratic Party. The USPD refused to join, and thus the first socialist government of Germany ended after only a few short months.

Political tensions continued in the wake of the murders of Liebknecht and Luxemburg. In March the remnants of the Berlin councils called for a general strike to protest the murders; thousands took to the streets and the government declared martial law, calling out the Freikorps troops. In the ensuing clash, over one thousand workers were killed. In several cities, including Bremen and Brunswick, left-wing council governments were briefly established, only to be ousted by military intervention.

These events could not fail to cast a pall over the exuberant expectations for the triumph of expressionist art with the revolution. After remaining relatively silent in the early months, the conservative art press now entered the fray. Among them was Karl Scheffler, editor of *Kunst und Künstler* and one of the most vocal supporters of impressionism in Germany. In the lead article of the 1 February issue of *Kunst und Künstler* he wrote: "The war did not change anything in the essence of art; neither will the revolution."[64] Although Scheffler had never been a champion of imperial art and its bureaucracy, he was decidedly hostile toward the expressionists. His article was an attack on the WCA as well as a vigorous defense of capitalism and its benefit for the arts. Promoting a free-market economy for art as an alternative to the imperial arts administration, he criticized the "revolutionary" programs put forward by the WCA, particularly their demand that the masses should now become the public for art.[65] Scheffler confidently repudiated this demand, arguing instead for the "aristocratic principle" in art and for the "right of the minority."[66]

On the left, the USPD daily *Die Freiheit* came more and more to defend the artists' councils and their demands. Just days after the murders of Liebknecht and Luxemburg, the Berlin newspaper featured an appeal by WCA member Artur Degner, a 30-year-old painter who was also on the executive committee of the Berlin Secession. Without naming the WCA, Degner repeated the main tenets of the group. Offering hopes for full employment in a socialist economy, he argued that with the socialization of industry the number of public buildings requiring artistic decoration would increase. With such public projects, the easel painting, "the prototype of the bourgeois-capitalist art epoch," would recede. The necessary first step was to give control of the art world, and state funds, to radically inclined, "left-leaning" artists.[67] The day after the government suppression of street fighting in March, *Die Freiheit* came out unequivocally once more in support of the WCA. An article entitled "Revolutionary Art Politics" lamented the complete lack of change in the arts administration—change that had been so keenly anticipated in the first days of the revolution. The blame was laid squarely at the feet of the SPD:

> Earlier, to be sure, there was no Social Democrat who did not already protest in the name of good taste against the Wilhelmine art abomination. But today a government, which calls itself socialist, which so quickly causes machine guns and heavy artillery to be brought up against workers, does not dare to touch the monuments of a stained past epoch! Yet how much less bloody would that be. We have a Working Council for Art created in the revolution, but one disregards its proposals and protests.[68]

With the pronoun "we," *Die Freiheit* linked itself with the goals of the WCA and made explicit that the radical demands of the group were opposed not only to Wilhelmine art policies, but now to those of the SPD as well.

For its part, the Prussian *Kultusministerium* walked a cautious line between maintenance of the status quo and concessions to the left, with Hänisch ever mindful that his party could not govern without the support of the bourgeois parties. Hänisch had even contemplated offering each of the government coalition partners a ministry in his department, parceling out education, religious affairs, and art. Although it never came to pass, the specter was raised, however briefly, of the Centre or DDP administering art policy.[69] In mid-March the ministry announced the dissolution of the Prussian Provincial Arts Commission, a 21-member board that controlled state art purchases and commissions. Although the press credited the dissolution to WCA pressure,[70] the commission in reality had already lost most of its power, and more importantly, there was no word as yet as to how state purchases were henceforth to be decided.[71] The *Kultusministerium* also acted cautiously in the matter of reform of the academy. When on 3 February the reform commission decided that "as little as possible should be reformed," given the unstable political situation,[72] the *Kultusministerium* pressed it to make some concessions, particularly when it came to membership for younger artists.[73] An assistant to Hänisch urged the commission to make these modest reforms in order to "take the wind out of the sails of the young people who represent themselves as oppressed."[74] Yet the commission staunchly resisted, threatening to disband the academy rather than give in to political pressure.[75]

A publication put out soon after the suppression of the Berlin strikes by a government agency summed up the conciliatory middle-road the *Kultusministerium* hoped to pursue in cultural matters. *The Spirit of the New National Community* presented a compendium of essays outlining a new cultural, political, and economic program for the "people's state."[76] It was published by the *Reichszentrale für Heimatdienst*, an obscure propaganda/publicity agency responsible to the press division in the chancellor's office.[77] The title of the book implied the cooperation of all segments of society, a proposition already challenged by the violent street fighting just before its publication. The introduction made explicit its political sympathies:

> The revolutionary movement of society . . . gives [us] the right to say: that the life of man leads to a new order, that all future things, regardless of whether they are of a religious, cultural or economic nature, will be placed in the depth of a new European way of thinking. Nothing is more essential than to free us from the mistake that, in the case of the revolution, it is the naked appearance of a generation afflicted with catastrophic misfortune, unnerved by hunger, which wants collapse and only this.[78]

Revolution was not linked to defeat, destruction, or impoverishment, but instead to an all-embracing order reconciling religion, culture, and economics. Moreover, the new national community was oriented to a "European way of thinking"—and not to the bolshevik east.

The main thrust of the essays on culture in *The Spirit of the New National Community* centered on enlarging the public for art. This was a cause championed in many quarters, even before the war. One essay advocated the creation of art leagues in each German city (a kind of "academy for everyman") that would stage extensive lecture series, didactic exhibitions, and promote the sale of original art works.[79] These proposals, however, envisioned no fundamental change in the art market, nor with those who controlled it (a change radical artists hoped would emerge with the revolution). For the editors of *The Spirit of the New National Community*, aesthetic reform preempted political or social change. Art was meant to be a well-ordered response to what one author called the "agonizing confusion" and destructive "chaos" of revolution.

The revolution had intially appeared to offer artists an opportunity to radically reorganize the art world, to alter its institutional and economic structure, and to redress the complaints of past decades. It had even promised a modicum of security and social integration for a generation of artists who had considered themselves socially marginalized. With the increasing polarization of German politics, however, artists were increasingly confronted with political choices whereby they might realize these goals. As they saw their ambitions frustrated, opposition to imperial art policies turned into opposition to those of the SPD. For many a move to the left was also exacerbated by economic uncertainty.

When the expressionist painter Ludwig Meidner asked whether the artist was any better off than the proletarian and described the artist as "dependent on the whims of the art-collecting bourgeoisie," he pointed beyond political ideologies to the economic realities of art production.

The sudden upturn for expressionist artists in the heated 1917 war economy had faltered dramatically by July 1918. Artists were rudely confronted with the extent of their dependence on the vagaries of the art market.[80] Commentators in the art press lamented the current economic impoverishment of artists (even if the conservative press described it as a consequence of the revolution rather than of the war and the policies of the imperial government). The journal *Der Kunsthandel*, which commented frequently on the market, wrote in January:

> In no other area . . . have the consequences of the upheaval made themselves so strongly and decisively noticeable as in that of art. While in the weeks before the outbreak of the revolution the old war-boom prices were no longer to be maintained, since November 9th any interest on the part of the moneyed public for any kind of artwork has been completely suspended. Just as in the antiquities shops, there are no more buyers in the shops selling modern art.[81]

Der deutsche Künstler, the journal of the Economic Association of German Artists, worried: "What shall [the artist] live on if no one is inclined to give him a commission in these uncertain times in which everything is in question?"[82] Artists who had achieved a degree of financial success during the war now found themselves in serious economic straits. A case in point was the 47-year-old painter Lyonel Feininger, a member of both the WCA and the November Group. The former caricaturist had become quite successful during the war with his cubist-influenced land- and seascapes. But in March 1919 he wrote to a friend: "If the times were halfway normal I could sell a great deal and we all could live magnificently. But as it is, I do not know what the future will bring . . . In any case we must leave the expensive metropolis and consider going somewhere where life is modest and unpretentious. The war has devoured almost our entire fortune."[83] Germany's economy was a disaster. Raw materials and food were in short supply because of the Allied blockade, transportation was severely hampered, production was at a virtual standstill during the demobilization crisis, soldiers returning from the front fueled the already high unemployment rates, and the certainty of reparations assured no quick relief. These calamities reverberated in the art world. There was continually talk of yet another increase in the luxury tax, and persistent rumors of an impending tax on art estates led to wholesale selling off of existing collections, driving prices down.[84] The situation seemed even more desperate for architects: a serious lack of building materials had already led, by 1918, to a complete standstill in housing starts in Berlin—despite the huge number of homeless—and the impending reparations payments threatened to divert all materials outside Germany.

For many artists, then, socialism appeared as a solution not only to their social alienation, but to their economic plight as well. As seen in their manifestos, they envisioned a socialist state that would simultaneously insure artistic freedom, give modern artists control over the institutional art world, and guarantee a degree of financial assistance, whether by providing exhibition space to all artists, through state purchases, or with health and welfare benefits.[85] These convictions collided with political reality first in January and again in March, as the "people's revolution" gave way to class conflict. It was not only that the state had little money to support the arts, but that the government moved reluctantly or not at all to make institutional changes. Many artists began in these months to envision an alternative to government support: direct support from the proletariat. Peter Bender in his December essay for *Die Aktion* had already indicated the problem here, that the proletariat had little money to purchase art and, as yet, had shown no particular sympathy for expressionism. Although Bender envisioned the dilemma resolved in a utopian perspective, at least one sympathetic artist/critic saw the situation as virtually hopeless. Carl Emil Uphoff, formerly of the Worpswede artists' colony, issued his dire predictions in *Der Cicerone,* a journal generally sympathetic to expressionism and the artists' councils. He warned that there was certainly no money for art since "there are hardly the means for daily bread." Because Uphoff found worth only in artists who had allied themselves with the proletariat, "whose work finds the finest understanding and the most respectful-loving protection in the worker's living room," he did not judge the proletarianization of the artist as necessarily a bad thing. At least it would free art from "the slavery of mammon."[86]

Although the market was in ruins, and artists were calling for an end to its tyranny, the gallery/dealer system endured. In an effort to stay afloat financially, even the artists in the WCA and the November Group continued to sign exclusive contracts and exhibit at private galleries. If the rules of the game had not exactly changed, at least the rhetoric surrounding it had. Cognizant of the prevailing mood, some dealers pursued new strategies to attract artist/clients. In response, some artists altered their allegiances in favor of galleries with a more progressive image. In Berlin at least several artists switched from the "capitalist dictatorship"[87]—as one artist called it—of Herwarth Walden's Sturm gallery to I. B. Neumann's more sympathetic sponsorship of revolutionary artists' groups. Although Walden in *Der Sturm* lamented the lack of institutional reform with the revolution (all that had been accomplished, he wrote, was that a few "genuine Corinths and spurious expressionists" had been purchased by the museums and that the academy had included "a few dilettantes under forty" in their ranks), he was a bitter critic of artists' councils, repudiating what he considered their irrelevant economic demands. "Only the poor can make economic demands," he wrote, "not artists."[88] Walden's apparent hostility towards the artists' councils came at a time when many of them had abandoned his Sturm gallery, perhaps because of his financial difficulties. His gallery and bookstore, overextended in the last years of the war, now faced economic difficulties, and many of the first-line expressionists severed or severely curtailed their relationship with him when he had difficulty meeting contractual obligations.[89]

I. B. Neumann eagerly stepped in to fill the breach and soon became the art promoter in Berlin most closely identified with the revolution. Owner of the *Graphisches Kabinett* on the fashionable Kurfürstendamm, he had been a cofounder in 1917 of *Das Kunstblatt* and was now publisher of *Der Anbruch*, a journal which also promoted expressionism. In early March he published a pamphlet declaring his allegiance to expressionism and the revolution. It began: "In the union of all arts with . . . free socialist society the inescapable conditions of a new human culture must be created. Expressionism, which is no longer just an idea, but a magnificent reality, finds its confirmation in the beginning world revolution."[90] Neumann went further than the usual assertions of the inherently revolutionary character of expressionist art. He now detailed the changes necessary for the dealer of this revolutionary art. He renounced limiting exhibitions in his gallery only to artists represented by him, claiming "artists 'belong' neither to me nor to other art dealers . . . but to humanity."[91] Although there is no evidence to suggest that Neumann suspended contractual relations with artists guaranteeing him a percentage of sales, he quickly gained a reputation as the dealer of the revolution, his gallery becoming a showcase for the most radical art in Berlin, from exhibitions of the Working Council for Art to the first Dada show.

With the setbacks they had experienced, and in the face of increasing political conflict in the country, the Working Council for Art and the November Group had to rethink their strategies, if not their programs. They were faced with a number of difficult questions: What changes were necessary in politics and in the economy to realize their goals? Was the new government a friend or a foe? Was it possible to create a proletarian audience for their art? The responses of the November Group remained inconclusive. Although the guiding principles of the group stated that it was "no economic protective association, no (mere) exhibition association,"[92] the group initially pursued none of the goals of its January manifesto, planning, instead, for its first exhibition. Even here it did not realize its ambitious plans. The group announced its first major exhibition for summer, to include not only works by its affiliated members throughout Germany, but examples of African and South Sea art as well.[93] For whatever reasons, the exhibition never came to pass.

Instead, the group put out a pamphlet entitled *To All Artists!* (An alle Künstler!), which eventually reached a broad audience and came to stand as a summary statement of the goals of modern art with the revolution. These essays pitted artistic and political radicalism against each other and are important for what they reveal about the difficulties the November Group had in reconciling the two. Even more telling, however, is how this indecision could be used to suit the interests of the new government to bolster its revolutionary and democratic claims.

To All Artists! is commonly referred to as a publication of the November Group, and it was perceived as such at the time. Actually, though, it seems to have been sponsored by the Publicity Office, which began soliciting contributions as early as January 1919 and whose torch logo appeared on the lower right-hand corner of Max Pechstein's cover illustration.[94] The pamphlet began with an anonymous essay, "Call to Socialism," reprinted from an earlier Publicity Office brochure.[95] It called for a "spiritual" rather than a "political" revolution and reiterated once more the catchphrase that expressionist art had anticipated the revolution. Still, the author warned of a distinctly political threat to socialism from those who mistakenly called for order from fear of chaos, from "misled bourgeois ambition [which] now still flirts with patriotic death."[96] He lamented, "There were too few flames in the streets, how could the phoenix be born? What we have experienced since November is at most a cliché of a revolution."[97] Still, he asked naively, "Why didn't wine flow instead of blood?"[98]

This political skepticism contrasted with the expressionist writer Bernhard Kellermann's expectation that artists would now be guaranteed absolute artistic freedom and state support, without any reciprocal obligations. In "The Writer and the German Republic," Kellermann primarily attacked the old imperial arts administration. He described the true artist as "revolutionary, anarchic, critical and unbounded," but also "hostile to the state, stateless, and international." What the artist demanded of the state was "freedom, appreciation, and protection of interests." Whether the present government fulfilled these expectations was left unstated.

More than any others the contributions of two November Group members, Max Pechstein and Ludwig Meidner, circumscribed the debate between political and artistic radicalism. A closer look at their essays, and at their artistic activity after 1914, reveal two very different approaches to reconciling revolutionary politics and expressionist art. Pechstein greeted the new government optimistically. His attachment to the SPD was likely a product of his background: the son of a textile worker, he had been apprenticed to a decorator in Zwickau before attending the Dresden School of Applied Arts. Pechstein had first gained a reputation as a member of the artistically radical Brücke and as a cofounder of the dissident New Secession. By 1912, however, he had returned to exhibiting with the more established Berlin Secession and apparently had a degree of success with this more mainstream profile. Franz Marc, for one, thought he had abandoned the modern cause.[99]

Pechstein was in the Palau islands when war was declared and he returned to Germany, where he was drafted in late 1915. After participating in the battle of the Somme, he was given a desk job and finally obtained a discharge in 1917. In 1917–18 he did a series of watercolors and engravings based on the battle of the Somme; and, corresponding to the general war-weariness at the homefront, Pechstein also produced and exhibited numerous escapist, romantic images of the supposedly harmonious and tranquil lives of the native inhabitants of Germany's Palau colonies.

In the first months of the revolution came Pechstein's anti-Spartacist posters for the Publicity Office, followed between January and March 1919 by a number of contributions to the short-lived journal *An die Laterne*. Published by Max Schulz, former chairman of the Berlin businessmen's association,[100] *An die Laterne* generally warned against anarchy and terrorism by the extreme left while promoting the SPD as the protector of socialism. Pechstein's cover illustration for the first issue (fig. 2.6) showed three men with distorted facial expressions holding a fourth to the ground, two of them choking him about the throat, one of them twisting his leg. Another figure points up at a noose-readied lamp post behind them, his arm underlining the text: "To the Lamp Post." Reinforcing this threat of mob violence, the first issue included an attack on Emil Eichhorn, the left-wing USPD police president in Berlin from November until January, which concluded: "If Liebknecht were victorious . . . roaring—murder—madness—plague—decay—chaos."[101] Pechstein also created an advertising poster for the journal

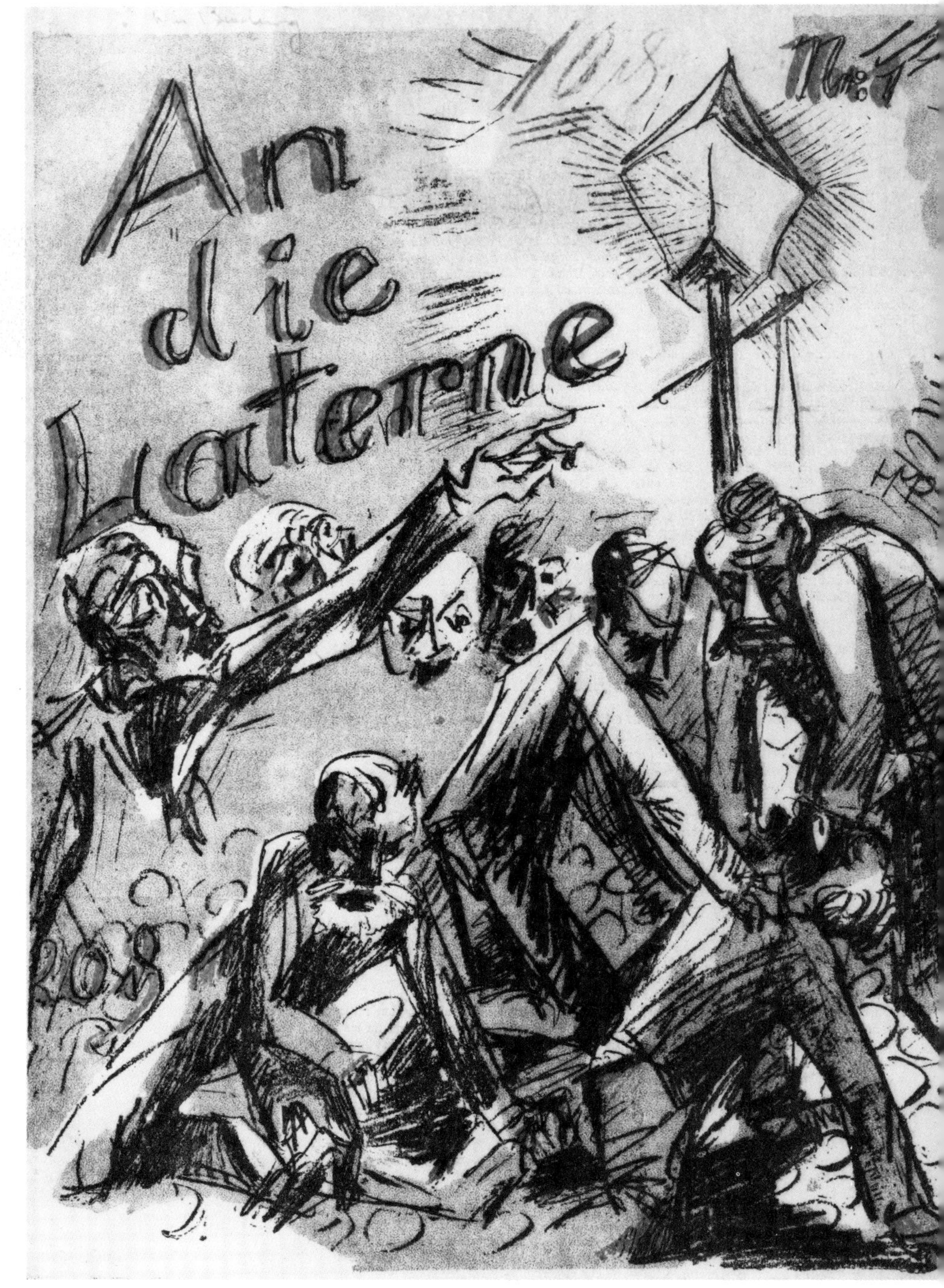

2.6 Max Pechstein, cover illustration for *An die Laterne* 1, no. 1 (1919).

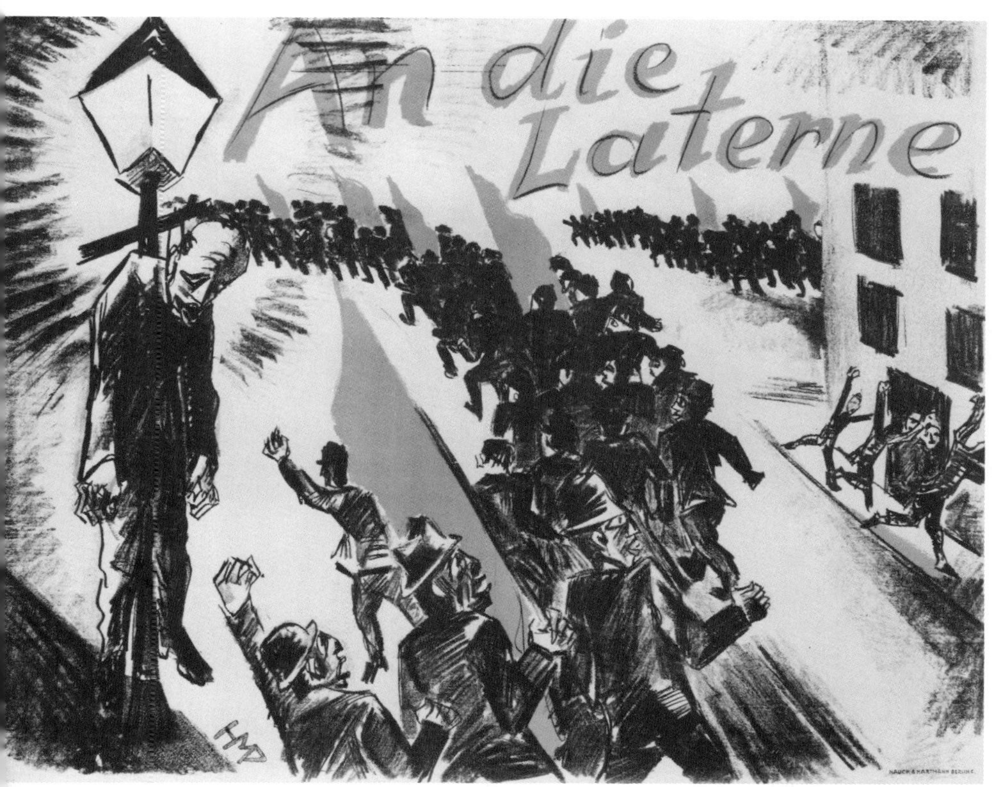

2.7 Max Pechstein, advertising poster for *An die Laterne,* 1919. Color lithograph, 69 x 91 cm. The Robert Gore Rifkind Collection, Beverly Hills, California.

(fig. 2.7) that showed the immediate aftermath of the first cover illustration. A dead body hangs from a lamp post as an angry, threatening procession of clench-fisted figures carrying red flags marches past, and small figures flee in terror. Closest to the viewer, the face of the figure at the rear of the procession displays a prominent "Jewish nose," subtly reinforcing anti-Semitic charges that bolshevism was an alien import to Germany, the result of a Jewish conspiracy. The suggestion of violence in the poster is palpable and heightened by the use of color: the blood-red of the flags and the title are echoed by the fainter red streaks almost surrounding the hanged man and picked up once more in the faces and fists of some of the marchers. Pechstein's advertising poster was also offered as fine art: a limited edition of fifty was available for purchase from I. B. Neumann's *Graphisches Kabinett.*[102]

Pechstein contributed cover illustrations for the remaining eight issues of *An die Laterne* and even lent his earlier art to the political cause of the journal. The fifth issue reproduced one of his Palau drawings with the subtitle "They Also Want to Take This from Us," referring to

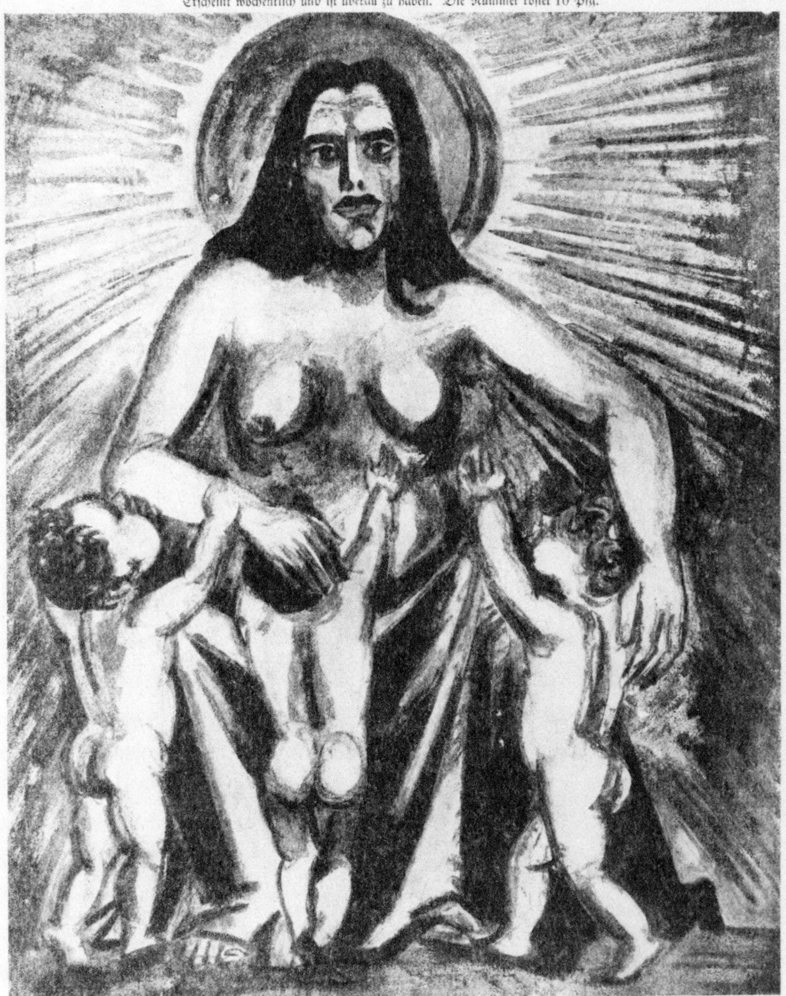

2.8 Max Pechstein, cover illustration for *An die Laterne* 1, no. 6 (1919).

the terms of the peace treaty which deprived Germany of her colonies. His cover for the sixth issue was an adaptation of Daumier's 1848 entry for the Republic competition, in which three children now reached out toward the seated half-nude figure, rather than suckling at her breast (fig. 2.8). Intended to commemorate the February 1919 Second Socialist International in Bern (boycotted by the KPD), the caption read: "Bern: Socialism gathers and nourishes her children." But if the half-nude figure in Daumier had represented the state, by February 1919 the socialist state no longer existed in Germany, nor anywhere except Russia. *An die Laterne* ceased publication in March after only nine issues, the last issue appearing just before the suppression of the so-called Spartacist uprising. With it Pechstein also ceased his partisan pro-SPD, anti-KPD propaganda posters and illustrations.

Pechstein's contribution to *To All Artists!*, entitled "What We Want," assumed the success of the revolution. It was reprinted from the 20 March 1919 issue of the USPD daily *Die Freiheit* and concluded: "The revolution brought us the freedom to give voice to and to realize wishes of years. . . . May the social republic give us trust; we have freedom, and soon flowers will bloom from the dry soil to its honor."[103] In line with SPD promotion of social reconciliation, Pechstein posited a new unified art epoch that would reflect a unified society, a proposition already put in doubt by the violent street fighting only weeks before. This new unified artistic culture was to be achieved through the joining of art and handicrafts. "On the basis of handicrafts," he wrote, "the dawn of the unity 'people and art' shall shine upon us." He continued: "The opportunity to stride further toward art through handicrafts must be offered to the sons of the people. Art is no frivolity, but an obligation to the people. It is a public affair. Those who are left behind are also not then useless drones, but still capable high-quality handicraft workers, who are useful as such to the state."[104] Emphasis on training in the handicrafts had been suggested from all quarters, including the WCA. It was seen as a solution to the problem of the art proletariat, a way to end the privileged exclusivity of art, and a means to equate the artist and the worker ethically. Pechstein placed his faith in the new government to meet this challenge and made only one demand of it: the right of self-determination for artists, which precluded "consultation after the fact" by bureaucrats still remaining from the old imperial arts administration. Disclaiming mere self-interest, he advocated the appointment of a federal arts official with the same "feeling of responsibility" as the expressionist artists.

Ludwig Meidner's contribution to *To All Artists!* could not have differed more in tone. Where Pechstein was optimistic, Meidner was pessimistic. While Pechstein believed the new government was the fulfillment of the revolution, Meidner implicitly criticized its revolutionary claims. Revolution was a longstanding issue with Meidner. It had already been an explicit theme in one of his most important paintings before the war, the 1913 *Revolution (Fighting on the Barricade)* (see fig. 1.1).

When war was declared, Meidner did not enlist. After his closest friend and collaborator died in battle in the first month of the war, Meidner, who had seen no actual fighting, embarked on a series of battle scenes featuring French soldiers. Several, including *French Soldiers* of 1914 (fig. 2.9), which showed the retreat of frightened French soldiers who leave behind an injured comrade, corresponded to the prevailing war propaganda despite their gruesomeness. Such images contradicted the failure of German troops, in the last months of 1914, to gain a decisive victory over the French in Flanders. By September 1915, though, Meidner had apparently turned against the war. A planned cycle of drawings, entitled *Europe 1914/15*, which were never published, included the bitter titles *Dedicated to the Peace Kaiser* (captioned "I no longer see any political parties, now I see only cannon fodder") and *The German Socialists Tear Up the Banner of Humanity*, an apparent attack on the party to which he himself belonged.[105] In the summer of 1916 Meidner was drafted, posted to Sedan, but soon transferred to Kottbus, where he served as a French translator in a prisoner-of-war camp. There he wrote pacifist texts, including *At My Back, a Sea of Stars*, published late in 1918. By 1917, Meidner had abandoned both his apocalyptic cityscapes and his war illustrations and turned to first Catholic, then Jewish religious subjects.[106]

Meidner's long-standing sympathy with revolution became explicit in his contribution to *To All Artists!*, a slightly altered version of an essay that had already appeared in the January issue of the art journal *Das Kunstblatt*, the 5 February issue of the USPD daily *Die Freiheit*, and, in a slightly modified version, the January issue of I. B. Neumann's journal *Der Anbruch*. Addressing himself "To All Artists, Poets and Musicians," Meidner wrote:

> There can be no more exploiters and exploited! It can no longer be that a vast majority must live in the most miserable, shabbiest and most disgraceful conditions, while a tiny minority bestially gorges itself at a table brimming over. We must decide in favor of socialism: for a universal and unceasing socialization of the means of production, which gives to every man work, spare time, bread, a home, and the presentiment of a higher aim.[107]

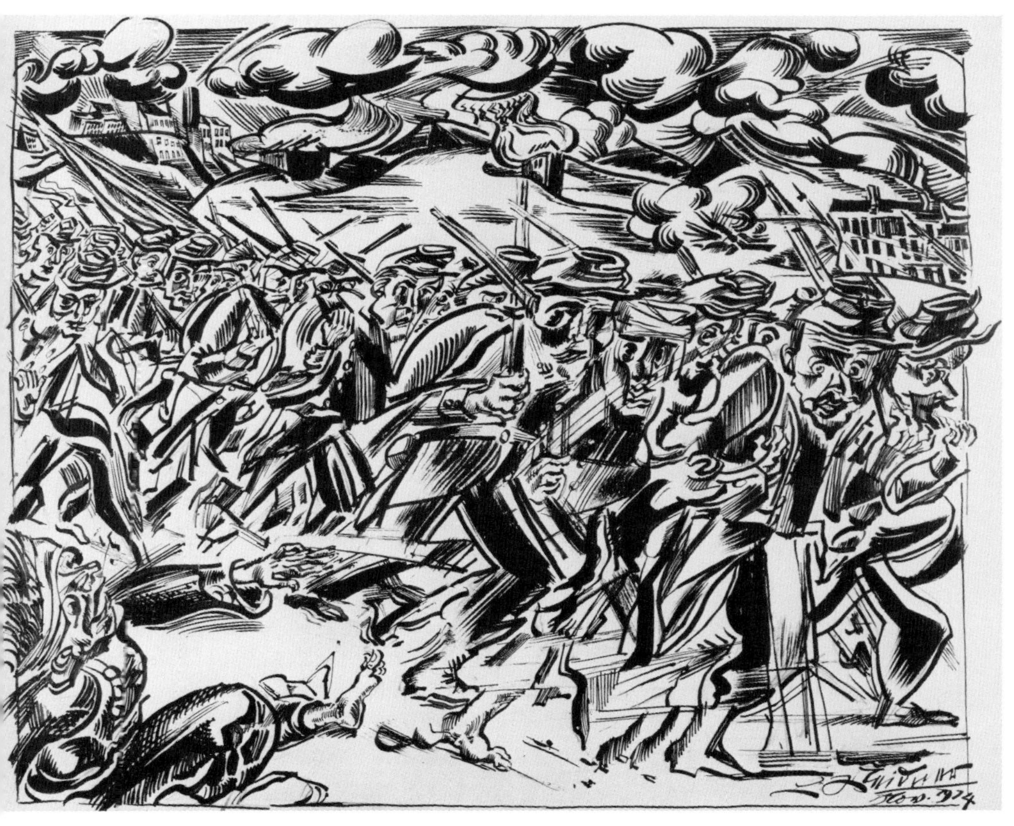

2.9 Ludwig Meidner, *Französische Soldaten (French Soldiers)*, 1914. Pen and ink wash, 42.5 x 63.5 cm. Städtische Kunsthalle Recklinghausen. Reproduced by courtesy of David Meidner, Kibbutz Schluchot, Israel.

His impassioned words further warned against the chicanery of the bourgeoisie, which he believed would try to regain power through "putsches, bribery and unscrupulous election practices."

It was Meidner who identified the artist with the proletarian, based on the precariousness of the artist's economic dependence on a capitalist art market: "We painters and poets are united with the poor in a holy solidarity! Have not many of us known misery and the shame of hunger and material dependence? Do we stand much better or more secure in society than the proletarian?! Are we not like beggars dependent upon the whims of an art collecting bourgeoisie!" [108] He therefore placed his hope in the revolution to radically alter the economics of the art world and to bring art to the "people" as a new clientele. Artists would now find support from the working class, to whom they ultimately belonged. As he characterized it, the worker "respected" true art, while the bourgeois feared it, preferring "frivolities" and "stupidities trussed up aesthetically." According to this analysis, any artist who received high sums for his art was paid with money that was tainted with the "sweat and blood of a thousand poor, overworked men."

Meidner also advocated that artists become involved in organized politics: "We must join the workers' party, the determined, unambiguous party."[109] When Meidner wrote these lines in the early days of the revolution the aims of the socialist parties were generally assumed to be compatible. By spring, however, when *To All Artists!* was printed, the differences had become irreconcilable. Significantly, Meidner now deleted a section from an earlier version which identified him as a member of the SPD for fifteen years;[110] moreover, his reference to the need for "universal and unceasing socialization" now carried with it an implicit critique of the new government. At the same time, though, Meidner struck from the earlier version in I. B. Neumann's *Der Anbruch* a passage about the artist as a revolutionary on the barricades, "with a musket against the enemy," an image borrowed from his own 1913 painting.[111] Similarly, he did not repeat the exhortation to "become communists like me!" from his essay "Brother, Light the Torch: In Remembrance of Carl [*sic*] Liebknecht and Rosa Luxemburg" in the 15 February issue of another expressionist art journal, *Neue Erde*.[112] Even though in that essay his rallying cry called only for "love" as the primary weapon, and "spirit" as the gunpowder, Meidner abandoned all references to street fighting and the KPD after March.

Against the government, but no longer openly sympathizing with the communists, Meidner had no specific political reference point. While decidedly favoring socialism, he no longer mentioned violent upheaval. Despite his revolutionary rhetoric, Meidner had not participated in the turbulent events in Berlin; after his discharge from the army he had gone to his mother's home in Silesia, returning to Berlin only late in 1919. His harsh words for the successful artist, whose earnings were tainted with the blood of the poor, were bound to be read as a self-critique: an exhibition at Paul Cassirer's gallery in January 1918 had brought him numerous sales and an exclusive contract, assuring him a comfortable living for the next several years. Later in 1919 came two successful exhibitions in Hannover and Berlin, and the first monograph on the artist. Revolution did not again figure in his art. Instead, he continued his religious subjects, now calmly posed and carefully drawn prophets.

The careers of Pechstein and Meidner, and their antithetical contributions to *To All Artists!*, indicate the range of responses within the November Group to the revolution. Pechstein sought to update his artistic stance and make it serve a new language of democratic renewal. Meidner doubted the possibility of renewal without radical upheaval, for which he no longer seemed to have the heart.

The other essays in *To All Artists!* were by two politicians, the Prussian *Kultusminister* Konrad Hänisch and the assassinated first Prime Minister of the new Bavarian Free State, the Independent Social Democrat Kurt Eisner. The pairing recalled the coalition of the SPD and the USPD in the November provisional government, now superseded. Hänisch's "The Art Program of the Prussian Government" was reprinted from the liberal *Neue Rundschau* and briefly outlined the broad-based, democratic arts policy that his ministry hoped to pursue, a policy which promised a free path to all artistic directions. As an example of his attempt to reconcile opposing forces, Hänisch cited the planned annual art exhibition, which would now unify the entire art world under one roof. His text, however, mentioned no other proposed changes or reforms and fell far short of the far-reaching demands presented by the expressionists only months before. Even the cited exhibition only projected the appearance of unity, as the left and right wings of the building still would have nothing to do with one another.

Eisner's text was an abridged version of a major speech he had given to the Provisional Bavarian National Assembly on 3 January 1919, only six weeks before he was assassinated. Entitled "The Socialist State and the Artist," it addressed such diverse issues as the nature of art, its economic integration into the production process, and the role of the artist in the socialist state. While Eisner, like Hänisch, wanted artists to remain free of state control, he argued that the artist still incurred obligations toward the state as a member of society: "Art can only thrive in complete freedom. . . . The artist must as an artist be an anarchist and, as a social member, as a citizen, directed toward the satisfaction of the pressing needs of life, a socialist."[113] Further, if art was to be integrated into the production process of a socialist economy, it could no longer have an exchange value. In a key passage he wrote:

> The pictorial artist should only create in the leisure hours of his inspiration; he should not make art a commodity under the force of economic necessities of existence. . . . For that reason I took up the idea whether precisely the pictorial artist should proceed from his own handicrafts; the sculptor, for instance, should work as a stone mason and only create artworks in the leisure time of his inspiration.[114]

Eisner here took into account the severe financial situation of the Bavarian government, which, he pointed out, could not afford large expenditures on the arts.

The pairing of the two articles, one by a prominent member of the SPD, the other by a slain leader of the USPD, was bound to recall the provisional November coalition government and suggest once more socialist reconciliation, a state of affairs that had not existed in Prussia since the USPD left the provisional government. Both authors provided similar assurances of artistic freedom. Yet Eisner's call for a radical economic reorganization of the arts, which not only promised little economic support for artists from the state, but even put in doubt the existence of a separate class of artists, went far beyond Hänisch's modest proposals—and may even have put them in a more favorable light, given the artists' economic uncertainty. Politically significant, however, were the minor abridgements of Eisner's speech, which deleted all references to the specific situation in Munich.[115] For Eisner had spoken not as a member of the USPD, but as the prime minister of the Free State of Bavaria, which had challenged the gradualism of the central government. Moreover, when *To All Artists!* appeared, the first of two radical secessionist council governments in Bavaria had already been declared. Rather than socialist reconciliation, though, the federal government practiced socialist fratricide when it called in Freikorps troops to suppress the second communist council republic in Munich (see chapter 4).

Members of the November Group provided the illustrations for *To All Artists!* Pechstein's cover illustration (fig. 2.10), along with Cesar Klein's illustration *The New Bird Phoenix* (fig. 2.11), were apparently prompted by the introductory essay, in which were found the lines: "There were too few flames in the streets, how could the phoenix be born? What we have experienced since November is at most a cliché of a revolution." Countering this lament, and implicitly supporting SPD claims for the success of the revolution, Pechstein's cover depicted a man striding toward the viewer, his head tilted upward, his heart on fire, flames surrounding his body, his right arm reaching toward the sky. Behind him, in the extreme lower portion of the drawing, are several large buildings topped with smokestacks, identifying them as working factories. Pechstein transforms "flames in the streets," which suggested violent upheaval, into the passionate flames of individual commitment, which do not interfere with the functioning of the factories in the background. Klein's illustration similarly refuted the text: the "new bird phoenix" is born as it recreates itself from the flames. Here the phoenix rises not from the usual altar, but from what appears

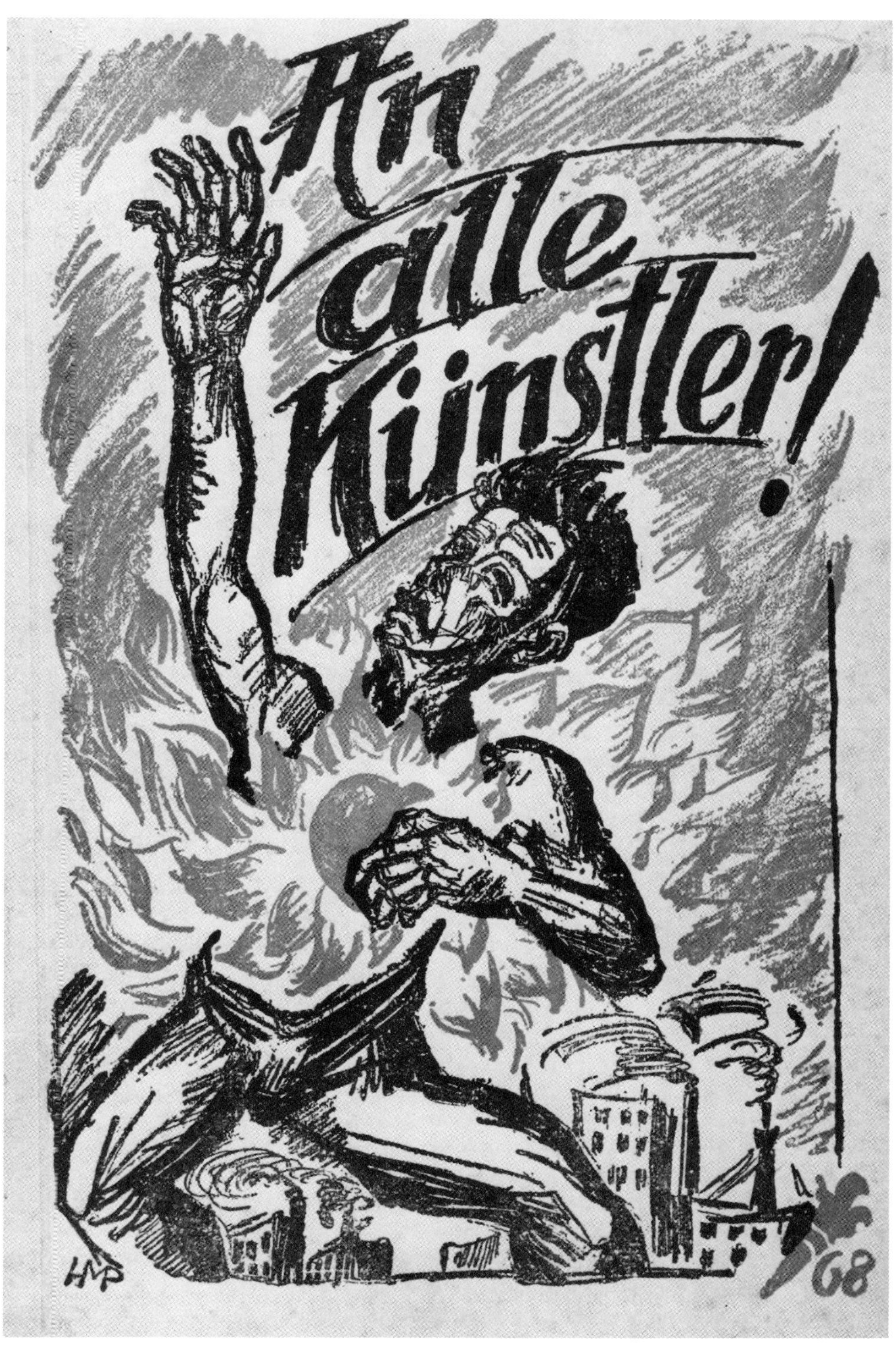

2.10 Max Pechstein, *An alle Künstler!* (To All Artists!), pamphlet cover, 1919. Reproduction of a drawing, 20 x 14 cm. The Los Angeles County Museum of Art; The Robert Gore Rifkind Center for German Expressionist Studies; purchased with funds provided by Anna Bing Arnold, the Museum Acquisition Fund, and Deaccession Funds.

as a war landscape: a few burning buildings, several dead figures lying on the ground, and a lone horse. Also departing from tradition, a man astride the phoenix also ascends, reaching toward the sun, with the moon and a star at his back. In his reach for the heavens and in his uplifted face, the figure recalled Pechstein's cover illustration. Klein here drew on two iconographic traditions. The phoenix as an early Christian symbol of the death and resurrection of Christ promised resurrection and eternal life for the war dead. As a seventeenth-century Dutch symbol of political regeneration, the phoenix here also carried aloft the image of the "new man" rising from the disaster of the war with the dawn of socialism.[116]

What divided the artists and writers contributing to *To All Artists!* was their understanding of the term revolution, whether it was political, economic, or merely artistic. This determined their attitude toward the existing government and their view of the extent to which art would be forced to change. But despite the apparent disagreements and contradictions, in the final analysis the publication of the brochure in itself attested to the incipient success of Hänisch's program: a disparity of political viewpoints, which had as their basic premise a support for the new art, could be successfully brought together as testimony to the democratic forum that now existed for the arts. The various socialist positions could be reconciled in a promotion of modernist art. By 1920 the *Kultusministerium* even sponsored an effort to distribute *To All Artists!* to all art institutions in the country.

In the violent political conditions in Berlin, not only the November Group, but the leaders of the Working Council for Art, too, began to rethink their program. Their deliberations, though, set them on a more radical course than the November Group. Some members increasingly voiced opposition not only to the old imperial art policies, but now also to those of the SPD, jeopardizing group cohesion. On 2 February Walter Gropius, who was becoming more and more active in the WCA, wrote to a friend:

> Here one is totally surrounded by knee-bending "Bürger," among whom it is almost too much for one to remain upright. It only remains to us now to ignore the real world, and to build for ourselves our own inner separated world. . . . For also socialism is so dirtied through this vulgar time, and brought into disrepute to the core, that it will need a long time before it again vindicates its shield.[117]

Another influential member of the group, Adolf Behne, on 20 January lamented in print:

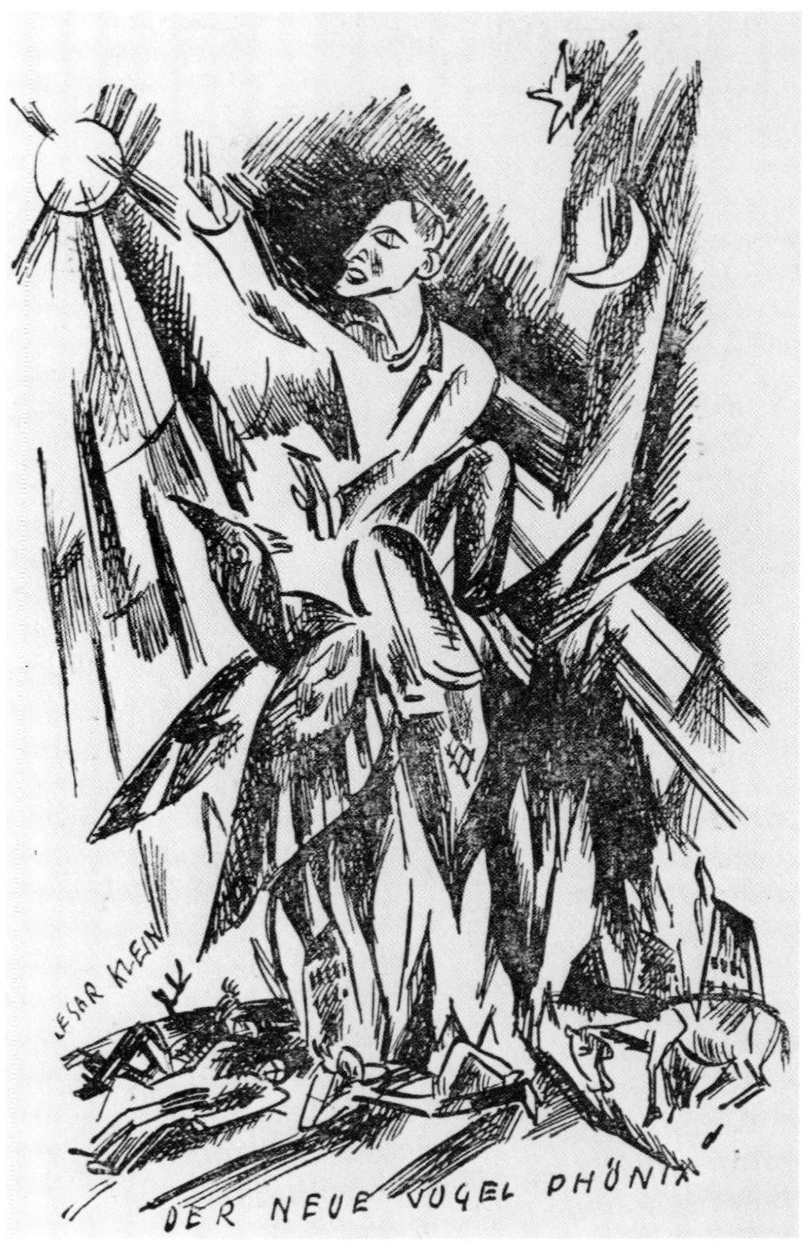

2.11 Cesar Klein, *Der neue Vogel Phönix (The New Bird Phoenix)*, pamphlet illustration in *An alle Künstler*, 1919. Reproduction of a drawing, 19 x 14 cm. The Los Angeles County Museum of Art; The Robert Gore Rifkind Center for German Expressionist Studies; purchased with funds provided by Anna Bing Arnold, the Museum Acquisition Fund, and Deaccession Funds.

We survey the achievements of our revolution with a feeling of sadness and of shame. What has happened in the ten weeks of the revolutionary period? Censorship and the state of siege have been lifted—a foregone conclusion. But otherwise the spirit of the old regime has returned to our people after a few short days of initial enthusiasm. Ideally, they want to set the old machine in motion again, only slightly repainted.[118]

Taut resigned as head of the WCA, apparently pessimistic about the ability of the group to realize its goals given the political setbacks. When Gropius proposed an emergency meeting to try and save the group, the result was that he and Behne took over its administration.

Walter Gropius had been one of the more successful architects of the younger generation before the war, well-known for his innovative Faguswerk factory and his model factory at the 1914 Werkbund exhibition. Unlike Taut, he volunteered for military service with the Hussar Regiment #9, had a distinguished war career, and was awarded the Iron Cross.[119] Nor was Gropius radicalized during his military service; as his letters indicate, he blamed German military setbacks not on the imperial administration or the High Command, but on "Jewish war profiteers."[120]

Gropius abruptly and radically changed his position at the end of the war, when he found himself severely wounded, depressed, close to poverty, with his career in a shambles.[121] Even his personal life collapsed about him as his wife, Alma Mahler, told him that the child just born to them was actually fathered by the writer Franz Werfel. In early December 1918 he went to Berlin "in order to take part in the upheavals,"[122] became radicalized, and found in the WCA an outlet for his new attitude.

Although Gropius was not a member of any political party and did not have a well thought-out political philosophy, he was profoundly affected by the murders of Liebknecht and Luxemburg: "The murder of Liebknecht and Rosa is vulgar, worse than anything the Spartacists have done. . . . These were pure idealists, who lived and died for their idea like few others. Only unfortunately they made the same mistake as their antipodes and also resorted to violence; that is their tragedy."[123] He found identification with neither the KPD nor the USPD, but promoted his own version of bolshevism—actually closer to anarchism—as the only hope of achieving a "true culture." In this he may have been influenced by Taut. Arguing for the dissolution of the state and the rights of the individual, Gropius claimed that true bolshevism, as Lenin defined it, rejected violence.[124] In his correspondence of early 1919 Gropius began to develop the ideas that would preoccupy him for much of the next year and lead to his founding of the Bauhaus in Weimar. Foremost was his dream of a society of artist-craftsmen, modeled on the medieval *Bauhütten*, which would unite artists, sculptors, and architects in work on an ideal building project. This was the romantic notion of recreating the Gothic cathedral in modern times.

On 6 March, Gropius asked Adolf Behne to take over the business affairs of the WCA. With the revolution Behne had resigned from the SPD, joined the USPD, and soon became a resident critic for *Die Freiheit*, the USPD daily. The son of an architect, he had grown up in working-class east Berlin. After studying architecture and art history, and earning a doctorate in 1912 in the latter, he became prominent in SPD circles writing on art for the *Sozialistische Monatshefte* and *Arbeiterjugend* and teaching at the party's night school for workers. He was a long-time friend of Taut's, whom he had met as a member of the Chorin circle, a group of intellectuals who would walk together in the woods and commune with nature.[125] He also became one of the foremost supporters of modern art in Germany, constantly shifting his defense to suit changing political situations. Initially pro-war, he advocated expressionism as the new national art, defending it against charges that it was international and therefore unpatriotic. But when the German art public grew weary of the war after 1916, Behne became less keen on associating expressionism with the war. He soon greeted the Russian revolution, embracing Russian folk art. When expressionism achieved its first financial success during the war and was attacked by some as escapist fare, Behne distinguished between a coopted, pseudo-revolutionary art associated with Herwarth Walden's Sturm gallery ("an art of luxury and pleasure [which] wants isolation, the unconnectedness of art, and assails the joining of art and life . . . and yet does everything humanly possible to meld this art intimately with the better middle class")[126] and a cubist-oriented, progressive expressionist art which had a "constructive" relationship to the world.[127] He continued to promote a cubist-oriented expressionism with the revolution, but for the time being had no comment on the discrepancy between destructive notions of revolution and his own constructive interpretation of cubism.

On 6 March Gropius signaled to Behne his intention to "further radicalize" the group and to "delicately show the door" to those who no longer fit in.[128] In a series of almost identical letters to the leading expressionist artists in Berlin, Gropius attempted to rally a constituency to support his efforts:

On Saturday March 1 at 4 P.M. in the *Deutsche Gesellschaft* a decisive meeting of the WCA will take place, to which we hereby urgently invite you. After initial unclarity the WCA has finally acknowledged that it can only usefully pursue its founding idea if the boundaries between the individual arts—architecture, painting, sculpture—fall away, and a joint, *thoroughly radically oriented work committee* is elected and to begin with carries out preparatory work in quiet, until with a perhaps not too distant second revolution the moment seems propitious to step before the public with the demands of the radical artists. In the meeting on Saturday this working committee will be elected, upon whose composition, naturally, everything further depends. We ask you urgently to take part in this meeting, so that the extreme left wing is manifested without compromise.[129]

Just what Gropius meant by "radically oriented" and "the extreme left wing" is not entirely clear. Did he refer to politics or to art? As in much of Gropius's writing at the time, he seemed to conflate the two. Perhaps the wording of Gropius's letter was intentionally vague to allow for political viewpoints different from his own. One result of the ensuing meeting was that the separate committees for painting, sculpture, and architecture now gave way to a new business committee headed by Gropius, Behne, and Cesar Klein. The inclusion of Klein, who had already produced anti-Spartacist posters, indicates that the interpretation of left-wing was certainly not narrow. On the other hand, a radical artistic style alone did not appear to be a sufficient criterion for inclusion. There are at least some indications that Gropius was looking for those with radical art politics, those who would vigorously support radical change in the art world.[130]

Elected to the new business committee were such luminaries of expressionism as Erich Heckel, Ludwig Meidner, Max Pechstein, Heinrich Richter-Berlin, and Karl Schmidt-Rottluff, along with the architects Bruno Taut and Max Taut, and the curator Wilhelm Valentiner.[131] Also included on the committee were the sculptors Gerhard Marcks and Georg Kolbe. These artists represented a broad political spectrum: Taut, Meidner, and even Gropius stood politically far to the left of Pechstein and Valentiner. At times, these political differences caused conflict. Marcks, for instance, threatened to resign when he clashed with Behne.[132] But Gropius worked hard to paper over these differences and to keep the group together and focused on a joint building project. Of the fifteen members of the new business committee (who were all roughly the same age, thirty-six), several had already worked on joint projects with architects. Cesar Klein and Gerhard Marcks, for example, had collaborated with Gropius at the 1914 Werkbund exhibition. Pechstein had executed murals for the Schneidereith and Wünsche house in Berlin in 1908. Gropius apparently did "delicately show the door" to some of the earlier members of the group;

when the WCA reissued its manifesto in April, many of the original signatories were no longer in evidence. Seven of the members of the new business committee had not signed the original WCA manifesto.[133]

When Gropius assumed leadership of the WCA, he was not particularly sanguine about its possible impact on government art policies. He wrote to a friend, "I am completely clear about the fact that hardly any support worth mentioning for our efforts is to be expected from the present government."[134] His 22 March speech to the membership warned against satisfying themselves with "concessions from the other side," probably referring to the *Kultusministerium*.[135] He contrasted two alternative strategies: practicing art politics in the public arena, or creating a type of lodge, a small minority preparing the ground for an eventual victory of a radical artistic credo. Although the members had previously been split on this issue, Gropius indicated that the recent events dictated that the WCA abandon its more public profile and work instead "in quiet." Just what he meant by this was unclear, for in the coming months the WCA went public with its efforts more than once. Gropius may have been renouncing previously futile efforts to influence government policy. For Behne, at least, the new WCA position meant bypassing government agencies and directly approaching an alternate public: "There is nothing else left for us other than to turn to the proletariat; that is, to those who scorn property, in whom the feeling of the deepest solidarity lives above all boundaries, those without presuppositions, those without prejudice, whose most perfect example is Dostoewski, who described himself as of the proletariat."[136] The proletariat—and Russia—now became the touchstones of the Working Council for Art.

Events in Russia still sparked hope for the triumph of a revolutionary modern art and hardened German artists in their belief that a socialist state could provide them with a living and guarantee them artistic freedom. Knowledge of artistic developments in Russia was still sketchy—contact between the two countries was sporadic—and as yet German artists had no notion of the internal debates that were already dividing the Russian art world. What they did know was that several of the Russian artists with whom they had exhibited in the years before the war[137] had now ascended to the head of the new arts administration and that Moscow was said to be "flooded with expressionism"[138] as the new bolshevik state sponsored colorful street decorations by the radical young Russian painters.

In 1919 contacts between Russian and German artists were largely established by intermediaries and took place against a backdrop of increasingly hostile political relationships between the two countries. The SPD, for its part, propagandized vehemently against the "violent" bolshevik "dictatorship," claiming revolution could never succeed in an economically backward country that had not already experienced the theoretically requisite bourgeois revolution. Since mid-November the Executive Council of the provisional government had used dilatory tactics toward the Soviets, spurning a symbolic offer of food by the Russians for fear of losing Entente food supplies. When the Russians quickly turned toward direct contact with the workers' and soldiers' councils, the Executive Council refused Russian emissaries admittance into the country to attend the Berlin council congress.[139] When martial law was declared in Berlin in March, and Defense Minister Gustav Noske issued orders to shoot anyone armed on sight, Russian officials were accused of fomenting violence and were expelled from the country.

Postwar contact between Russian and German artists seems to have been initiated in January 1919, when the WCA obtained a manifesto from Moscow through Dr. Ludwig Baehr. Baehr was an ex-German army officer and artist who had been attached to the German diplomatic mission in Moscow after the Treaty of Brest-Litovsk. His duties there had been to maintain contacts with the Russian intelligentsia, and by 1918 he had become a close associate of Kandinsky's.[140] On 26 January 1919 Bruno Taut, Walter Gropius, and Max Pechstein, representing both the WCA and the November Group,[141] sent a reply to Moscow "greet[ing] with great sympathy the endeavors of the Assembly of Plastic Artists in Moscow as described by Ludwig Baehr."[142] Two months later, the WCA sent another message to its Russian colleagues. The communiqué came one day after a clandestine meeting between Gropius and a representative of the Soviet government who had remained in Berlin illegally.[143] The opening lines of the WCA text were a reminder of the political nature of the enterprise: "We've wanted to speak to you for months, yet the 'land borders' barred the way. We feel ourselves one with you in the will to do everything on our part to close the fissures that power politics have flung between [our] peoples."[144] Admitting their lack of success in influencing their own government, the German artists of the WCA offered only vague promises that art would bring men together and claimed only that their mission was "to be artists." For the rest, they proposed conferences and exchanges of artists between the two countries.

By March more details about the Russian art world had finally become available. On 15 March, just one day after street fighting ceased in Berlin, Franz Pfemfert's *Die Aktion* published excerpts from Anatoli

Lunacharsky's *Proletkult* program. Lunacharsky, the new Soviet People's Commissar for Enlightenment, had been instrumental in founding the Petrograd *Proletkult,* an umbrella organization of proletarian cultural/educational groups that, until 1920, functioned independently of government institutions. Lunacharsky's text did not outline the specifics of Soviet art policy, but instead offered a more theoretical discussion of the differences between the socialist culture of the future and the proletarian culture of the present. Regardless of these distinctions, his description of the best art of the time read almost like a synopsis of WCA rhetoric: "The solidarity of those who create together on one and the same work; the consciousness of the noble, universal human meaning of this work, the ideal creation, the ethical creation . . . all that fills [the artists'] works with spiritual content."[145]

Most importantly, Lunacharsky addressed the sensitive issue of whether an artist of bourgeois upbringing could be a revolutionary artist. While he insisted that the proletariat itself would be instrumental in creating a proletarian culture, he also described the important role to be played by bourgeois artists who had already energetically broken with their class and who would find their way to an alliance with the proletariat. Although he recognized that the "individualism of the intellectuals" and the "strong lack of education" of the proletariat had kept the two groups apart, he was confident these barriers were artificial and would disappear.

German artists received the first details of the institutional reorganization of the arts in Russia when *Das Kunstblatt* published a report on Lunacharsky's commissariat in the mid-March issue. The reforms bore a striking resemblance to WCA and November Group demands: artists were to be given almost complete control of art institutions, from the new museum for contemporary art to local workshops; art schools were to be "nationalized," with students selecting their own teachers; class distinctions in the arts were to be abolished, with the sculptor equal to the stucco worker. Workshop and exhibition space were to be provided by the state, as would be supplies. A new museum of contemporary art would insure the "complete representation of new painting," as well as emphasize handicrafts.[146]

Expressionist artists may have had yet another source of information on the arts in Russia—letters from their former colleague Wassily Kandinsky. In early April *Die Freiheit* published a letter from Kandinsky to one of his German friends. Kandinsky at that time was active in education and museum reform in IZO NKP, the Visual Arts section of Lunacharsky's commissariat. He was also head of a studio at *Svomas,* the Moscow Free Art Studio, an institution that was charged with reorganizing the system of art instruction. His letter enthusiastically told of plans for a new museum of international modern art, state purchases of work by modern Russian artists, monographs on modern artists already in print, and two new art journals just founded.

Most importantly, Kandinsky authenticated the new alliance between modern artists and the proletariat. He vividly described weekly Sunday lectures on art for workers in Moscow, quoting the appreciative words of a worker who upheld the freedom of art: " 'The working class,' he said, 'only wants a completely free art which serves beauty exclusively. . . . And I as a worker . . . thank from the bottom of my heart artists who enrich my life.' "[147] While all these texts could serve to make German expressionist artists conscious of their own relative lack of success in reforming the art world, they still held out the promise of success in a true socialist state.[148] The example of Russia was clearly before the WCA when they set out to organize their first public exhibition.

The idea behind the first WCA exhibition was a radical one: to present to an alternative public works created by working-class nonprofessionals. Already in January 1919 notices had been placed in the SPD and USPD daily newspapers soliciting architectural drawings from their readers. The plan, however, quickly went awry. When the group received no public submissions they had to turn to their own membership. Max Pechstein sent in a drawing (we have no record of it today) that Gropius, who was on the selection committee, politely returned with the suggestion: "Why don't you make a few sketches completely without architecture . . . of a totally utopian kind, [which] are preferable for the task at hand."[149]

The WCA finally opened their first exhibition, the "Exhibition for Unknown Architects," on 25 March at the I. B. Neumann gallery on the Kurfürstendamm (it ran for a month). In the end, there were a wide variety of drawings exhibited: a limited number of sober housing plans and architectural models, theater decorations, projected new cities with skyscrapers, but also cubist-inspired architectonic drawings, glass pavilions and crystal monuments, fantastic mushroom-shaped towers that defied gravity, and imaginary architectural forms that ignored all rules of static, proportion, and symmetry. The more traditional schemes, some of them already realized projects, were in a separate room and seemed to represent the best of the past. It was the remainder of the exhibition that met few, if any, conventional expectations about architecture.

When the exhibition opened, the visitor to the gallery was greeted not with a catalog, but with a manifestolike leaflet consisting of three statements written by Gropius, Taut, and Behne. Those by Gropius and Taut sounded a common theme: that there was at present no true architecture, that in the "profession today we cannot be creators, but are searchers and callers," that they must "build in fantasy, untroubled with technical difficulties" until a "happier time—which must come" would fulfill their anticipated ideas about building. Taut went so far as to reject all "useful" architecture. Not surprisingly, both authors signaled their approval of the "utopian drawings" on display, most of which were executed by painters. Such views reflected a rejection of the Werkbund aesthetic (designing for industry) and of the materialist culture they held responsible for the war. For Gropius, at least, it was also a rejection of his own past as an architect in the service of industry. Moreover, the statements were symptomatic of political setbacks and economic reality: the WCA had failed to make any inroads in government decision making on architecture, and there was simply no money, or supplies, to build. This is not to say, however, that the only choice for architects was either acquiescence to the needs of industry or recourse to utopia. Other architects (Martin Wagner, for example), put their efforts into forming socialist trade union building guilds to cope with the lack of building materials in an attempt to relieve the desperate housing shortage in Berlin.

With the Exhibition for Unknown Architects the WCA attempted to reach a new public with their art, a public which had the appearance of neglected minorities thus far deprived of culture. Taut advertised the exhibition in an article in the USPD daily *Die Freiheit,* where he called on "representatives of the forwards-striving and revolutionary proletariat, but also women and children" to attend the show. Although the exhibition was held in a fashionable gallery on the Kurfürstendamm, Taut stressed what he considered its proletarian appeal: it was "un-bourgeois" to exhibit "unknown" artists, and the admission was free. In hopes of creating a dialogue, he asked readers to send in to *Die Freiheit* their reactions to the show, so that the artists could know whether they had found the "right language" to bring artists and workers together.[150]

Although we have no catalog of the exhibition, we do know from the reviews several of the works to be seen there. One was Johannes Molzahn's *Architectural Idea* (fig. 2.12), a pencil drawing of a sacred building with a dominating central spire. Molzahn, twenty-seven years old, was a little-known artist and photographer who had exhibited at the Sturm gallery in 1917. He conceived his building as a series of pris-

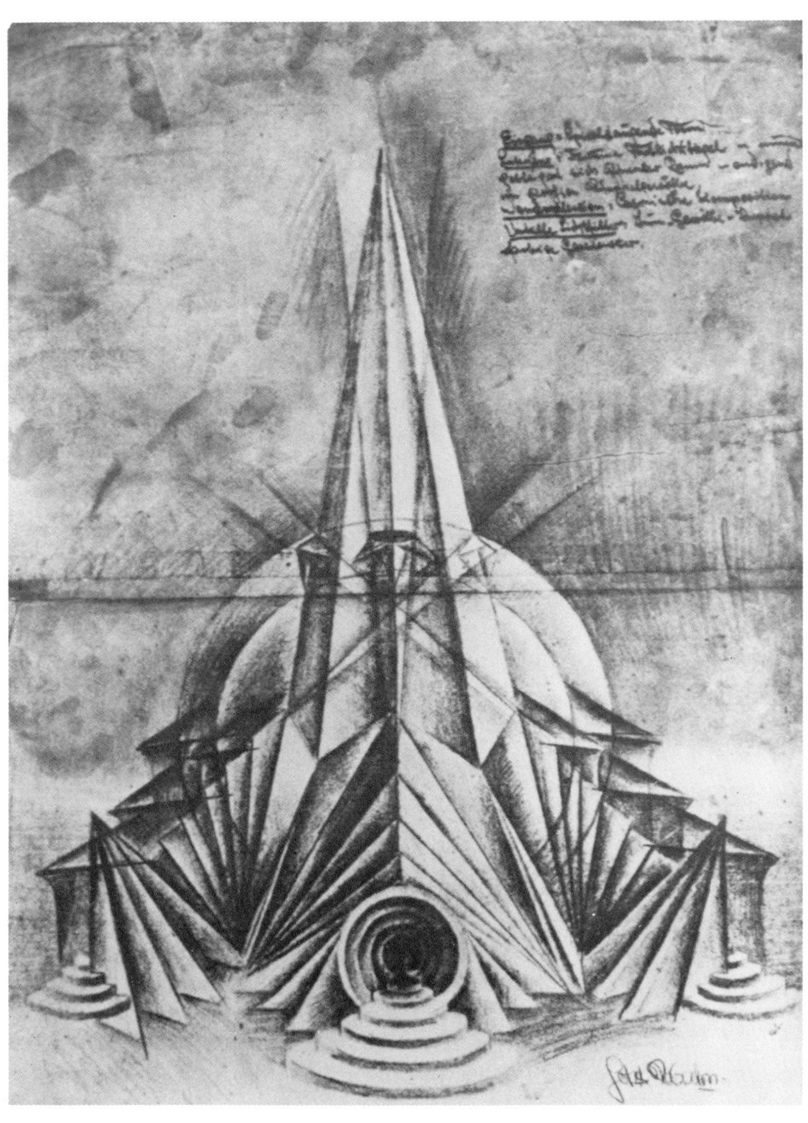

2.12 Johannes Molzahn, *Architekturidee (Architectural Idea)*, 1919. Pencil drawing on transparency, 62.7 x 47 cm.

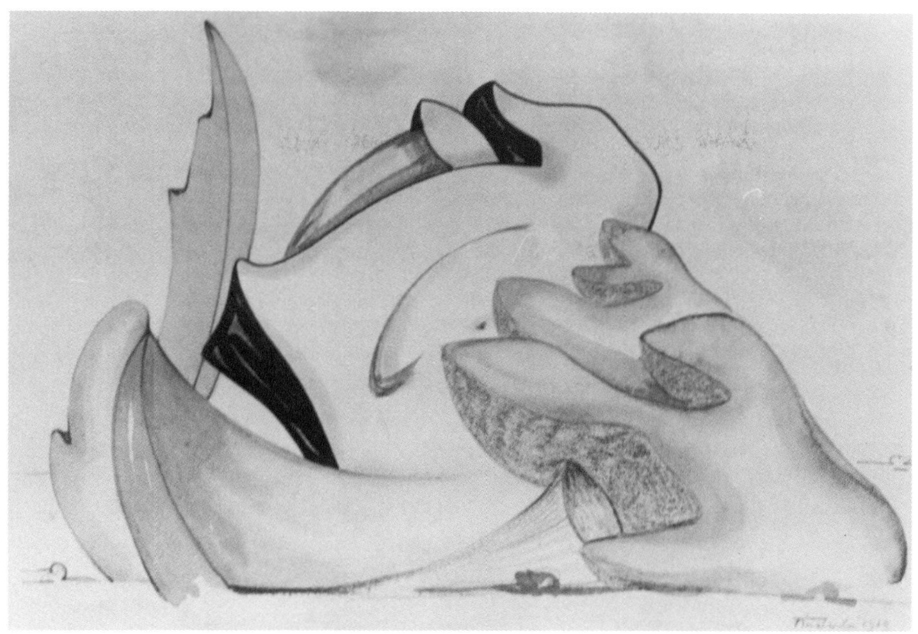

2.13 Hermann Finsterlin, *Phantasie (Fantasy)*, 1919. Watercolor and ink, 20 x 27 cm. Private collection. By permission of Mrs. Gabriele Reisser-Finsterlin.

matic sections arranged in fan shapes. Stylistically, the drawing resembled his earlier cubist-inspired paintings. Although the building was clearly fanciful, the artist provided brief written instructions for interior decoration, including murals and colored-glass windows. Conceptually it owed a great deal to the recently deceased Paul Scheerbart, whose fantasy novels of an earthly paradise of colored-glass architecture were a source of inspiration to many in the WCA. Here Molzahn visualized Scheerbart's ideas in a cubo-expressionist style. A second *Architectural Idea* dissolved the forms of the buildings even further into abstraction, as a central multifaceted star-shape hovered above vertical supports.

Also represented in the show was Hermann Finsterlin, one of the few outside the WCA who had responded to the advertisements for participation. Finsterlin, however, was no layman, but a 32-year-old former science student who had recently begun studying painting at the Munich academy. His architectural *Fantasies* (fig. 2.13), as they were called, consisted of anthropomorphic shapes, which seemed to

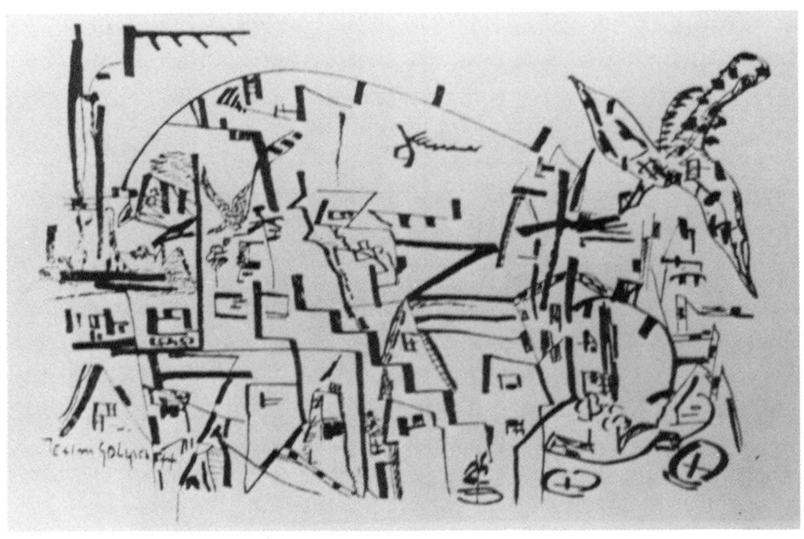

2.14 Jefim Golyscheff, drawing, 1919. Dimensions unknown.

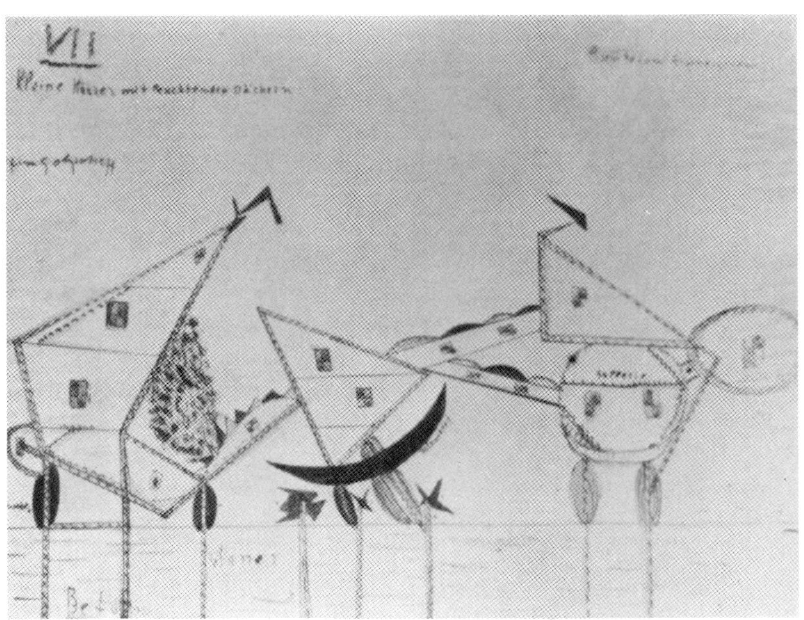

2.15 Jefim Golyscheff, *Kleine Häuser mit leuchtenden Dächern (Small Houses with Luminous Roofs)*, drawing, 1919. Dimensions unknown. Reproduced by kind permission of Verlag Gerd Hatje.

grow organically from the earth. He decoratively filled in the pen drawings with pastel watercolors, creating soft, overlapping polymorphous shapes.

The youngest artist in the exhibition was the 22-year-old Russian musician and novice artist Jefim Golyscheff, who had begun drawing in 1907 under the guidance of his father, a friend of Kandinsky's. One of his drawings in the exhibition suggested some sort of aerial perspective of a city, with a bird swooping down from above, but at the same time alluded to stairways, windows, and roofs seen from ground level (fig. 2.14). In another, he schematically lined up geometrical forms resting on wheels and called it *Small Houses with Luminous Roofs* (fig. 2.15). Small squares suggested windows and sloping lines roofs, but otherwise the drawing did not resemble the houses evoked by the title.

Golyscheff intentionally lacked professionalism in his drawings. Their schematism, their elementary quality, and their never quite filled-in forms were more reminiscent of children's drawings than of architectural perspectives. Children's art had a particularly resonant meaning to expressionist artists. It embodied the idea of spontaneity, of direct expression not subject to the corruption of the culturally conditioned complication of academic art. Kandinsky, who inspired Golyscheff to begin drawing, had been one of the first to promote the art of children, along with that of primitives, as a challenge to contemporary culture.[151] Golyscheff's drawings could be seen as an embodiment of these ideals, a naïve, lay art that rejected convention and offered the promise that anyone could create art. The fact that he was an infant prodigy on the violin seemed to confirm his natural childhood talent, and his Russian origins and connections to Kandinsky conferred revolutionary status on him. Behne was initially hesitant about Golyscheff's contributions,[152] but soon fell into line promoting his art as "intended for the proletariat, to stimulate a desire to produce oneself,"[153] and even began to collect some of Golyscheff's drawings. Gropius in particular was pleased with Golyscheff's submissions and wrote to him: "Let the bourgeois think what he will about them . . . They really are extreme examples of what we want: utopia."[154]

The organizers of the Exhibition for Unknown Architects apparently succeeded in questioning prevailing conceptions of what counted as architecture, who was an architect, how an exhibition was to be organized, and how it was to be advertised. Their open attack on architectural standards and institutions struck a raw nerve with critics, who for the most part were hostile to the works on show, particularly the "misty peaks of extravagant fantasy" reached by Finsterlin and Golyscheff, which to one critic seemed to "sprout from a diseased brain."[155]

Even usually sympathetic critics from the *Frankfurter Zeitung* and *Der Cicerone* demanded a more rational approach to architecture. There is also a record, though, of another response to the exhibition, that of the readers of *Die Freiheit* as transmitted and interpreted by Bruno Taut. The limited responses quoted by Taut do not allow any generalizations as to whether the WCA had found the "right language" to speak to a proletarian audience. In fact, it seems clear that the respondents reacted most favorably to more conventional architectural drawings, with the majority preferring the garden city houses. But Taut also reported that many of the more fantastic drawings found their supporters. He quoted several workers: "Finally something new, finally something original"; and "What pleases me best is the freedom with which each gets his say." He even quoted some of the more sarcastic comments: "With my next lottery winning, the architect Finsterlin should build for us a castle in his manner—the site is on the moon."[156]

If one is to believe Taut, the exhibition encountered two distinct responses: rejection by the educated middle class and its critics, and enthusiasm by the working class. Taut concluded with the words of one worker who wrote of Golyscheff's drawings, "Long live the revolution to all eternity. Amen."[157] The ingredients for a revolutionary art must have seemed possible: hostility from large segments of the bourgeoisie, confirming their antibourgeois status; and the beginnings of interest, and even approval, from the working class, confirming a new alliance.

Yet the text by Behne in the leaflet distributed at the exhibition pointed to another reality, the continued dependence of artists on the capitalist art market. His statement differed dramatically from the euphoric projections of Gropius and Taut, since it was practical and explanatory. Like Taut, Behne hoped that the working class would constitute a new audience for their exhibition. His statements, though, were highly defensive, probably for two reasons. First, the exhibition was being held at an exclusive gallery on the Kurfürstendamm. Second, his disclaimers could not obscure the fact that he was primarily concerned with a buying public, for he announced in boldface type in the opening lines that all the works in the exhibition were for sale. He wrote defensively: "We don't expect that the snob will buy architectonic drawings! . . . It is certain that the interested public and the buyers of our exhibition are totally different than those who previously were found in the salons as buyers."[158] We do not know the prices of the drawings, or whether any of them were sold. But it is uncertain whether a public other than the usual clientele of the I. B. Neumann gallery could afford to "materially support artists through purchases of sketches." For the reality was that these artists were nonetheless financially still dependent on a capitalist art market, the "spineless, passive art consumerism" Behne abhorred.

This same contradiction existed in the reorganization plan of the WCA. On the very same day that Gropius had written to the prominent Berlin expressionist artists to joint the new central committee, he sent out another series of letters, quite different in nature. They were letters seeking financial support from enlightened industrialists who had previously patronized expressionist artists. Among others, he wrote to Walther Rathenau, Robert Bosch, Karl Benscheidt, and Anne Friedländer-Fuld. Benscheidt of the Faguswerk factory gave 200 marks. The Stuttgart industrialist Bosch declined to contribute. Friedländer-Fuld of the coal magnate family, an avid collector of modern art and famed hostess of Berlin soirées, gave 5,000 marks. A Herr Mendel of the firm Fischbein and Mendel gave 1,000 marks. With no government support, with no political base, the WCA had no viable financial support other than that of enlightened capitalists.

The WCA's two-track approach, appealing to both the proletariat and wealthy supporters of modern art, was not hugely successful. Yet its model for alternative working-class exhibitions was to influence others in the art world, largely through the efforts of Taut and Behne. In March, a number of prominent socialist artists organized the Cooperative Society of Socialist Artists (*Genossenschaft sozialistischer Künstler*), among whose most important efforts were art exhibitions in working-class neighborhoods. The Cooperative Society, founded sometime in late March, was organized to bypass the system of dealers, galleries, and state-sponsored exhibitions and to provide in its place a sales cooperative for socialist artists. Much more than the WCA, the Cooperative Society had thought out the economics of their enterprise. Artist members were to receive a standard set price for all works, plus a percentage profit from any sale. All members would share in net profits of the group.[159]

Despite the setbacks to the revolution, the organizers of the Cooperative Society thought it still possible to socialize one segment of the economy: art production. As planned by the writer/editor Friedrich Natteroth, the leader of the group, the Cooperative Society would stage exhibitions in working-class districts with the help of party and trade union organizations. In this the Cooperative Society differed from the WCA, which expected no support from the socialist parties and their organizations. These exhibitions were not only to bring art to the people, but were also to make it possible for workers to buy art at greatly reduced prices, helping to solve the crisis of the art proletariat. After heated debates, it was also decided that a requirement for joining the group was membership in one of the three socialist parties.[160] Membership was based, then, not on artistic considerations (which still seemed to predominate in the WCA), but political ones.

Although we have no membership lists for the group, we know that among its members were Käthe Kollwitz, Heinrich Vogeler (the Worpswede artist who was a member of the Bremen Workers' and Soldiers' Council), Hans Baluschek (a long-standing member of the SPD), Karl Holtz (illustrator for the USPD *Die Freiheit*), and Jefim Golyscheff. Adolf Behne and Bruno Taut were identified in the press as shop stewards (*Obleute*) for the group (although Taut is not known to have been a member of any political party).[161] Their art ranged from Baluschek's genre scenes of working-class life to Golyscheff's fantastic drawings and constructions, and their politics spanned the gamut from Baluschek's allegiance to the right wing of the SPD through Holtz's active participation in USPD politics to Vogeler's commitment to communism.

On 17 April, *Die Freiheit* published the guiding principles of the group, written by Natteroth. Natteroth characterized artists as workers like any others, alienated from their labor by capitalism. Optimistically predicting the downfall of the capitalist economy and the triumph of the proletariat, he called on artists to devote themselves to meeting the artistic needs of the proletariat, from organizing festivals to designing houses, furniture, appliances, and clothing. Rather than calling for artistic freedom like the expressionist artists, Natteroth wanted artists to serve the working class. He also envisioned the economic crisis of art production resolved in a socialist society of the future: the problem would not be that there were too many artists, but that there weren't enough.[162]

Although the Cooperative Society never organized festivals or designed workers' clothing, it did stage its first exhibition in June at the city *Handwerkerschule*. It was an exhibition of graphics designed to decorate both the school and the workplace. The little information we have on the show comes from the local Berlin newspapers. The SPD newspaper *Vorwärts* praised the exhibition and, in doing so, defended the party from attacks on its art policies:

> A socialist pictorial art, as an expression of socialist feelings, exists as yet in its first beginnings—about that we all agree. How should it have been otherwise, since until yesterday a capitalist state and society controlled art. It would also be wrong to declare the newest radical art movements as socialist or communist, although in Russia they were branded the official art of council government by the authority of dictatorship—and not by the will of the people.[163]

By associating expressionism with the Russian revolution, *Vorwärts* only reaffirmed the revolutionary status of that art; at the same time, the review served—whether correctly or not—to associate the more realistic art of such prominent Cooperative Society members as Kollwitz and Baluschek with the evolutionary socialism of the SPD. The exhibition was also praised by the liberal *Berliner Tageblatt,* which, however, vehemently objected to organizing artists on the basis of political affiliation rather than talent. "Fortunately," the critic wrote, "there is no trace of the political intentions (of the artists) in the works exhibited,"[164] thereby contradicting his own fearful assumptions about the type of art socialist artists would produce.

The exhibition traveled to the town hall in Neukölln, a working-class suburb of Berlin—apparently the first art exhibition ever in that part of the city.[165] According to the *Berliner Tageblatt,* almost all socialist political organizations and employee associations visited the show, which was free to the public. The newspaper also reported on the financial success of the exhibition: the city of Neukölln purchased several works and others were sold to the "solvent public."[166] The show then traveled to the hygiene museum in an exhibition sponsored by the factory works council of the giant electrical combine A.E.G. Here the Cooperative Society made inexpensive graphic works available to factory workers, including a lithographic portfolio published especially for the occasion and a one-mark lottery for an original artwork. As reported in *Vorwärts,* about four hundred fifty works were sold.[167] In the following months, the group also held auctions to benefit the metalworkers, whose seven-week strike had ended in failure.

Not surprisingly, stories began to surface in the press about dissension within the group and vague efforts to reconstitute it on a more "democratic" basis.[168] It seemed inevitable that artists from the three socialist parties would clash, particularly since the art several of them produced was politically contentious. Between February and July, for instance, Hans Baluschek published a series of drawings entitled *From the Time of the Revolution in Berlin* in *Wachtfeuer,* the journal of the conservative Society of Pictorial Artists of Berlin. He had been a frequent contributor to the journal since its inception, and now his outright counterrevolutionary cycle on the revolution confirmed the unequivocal patriotic stance of his earlier wartime illustrations for the same journal. In *The Watched Policeman* (fig. 2.16), an armed soldier-representative of a soldiers' council, identified by his arm band, stands next to an unarmed policeman. Baluschek here comments on the Eichhorn affair, when the Prussian government (whose USPD members had just resigned) on 4 January 1919 attempted to dismiss the Berlin police president from his position because of his sympathies with the councils. Eichhorn resisted his dismissal, supported by the leaders of the 5 January demonstration. Baluschek depicts the supposed control of the police by the councils; the irony of his title makes it clear that it is no longer the police who watch, but that they are the ones who are now

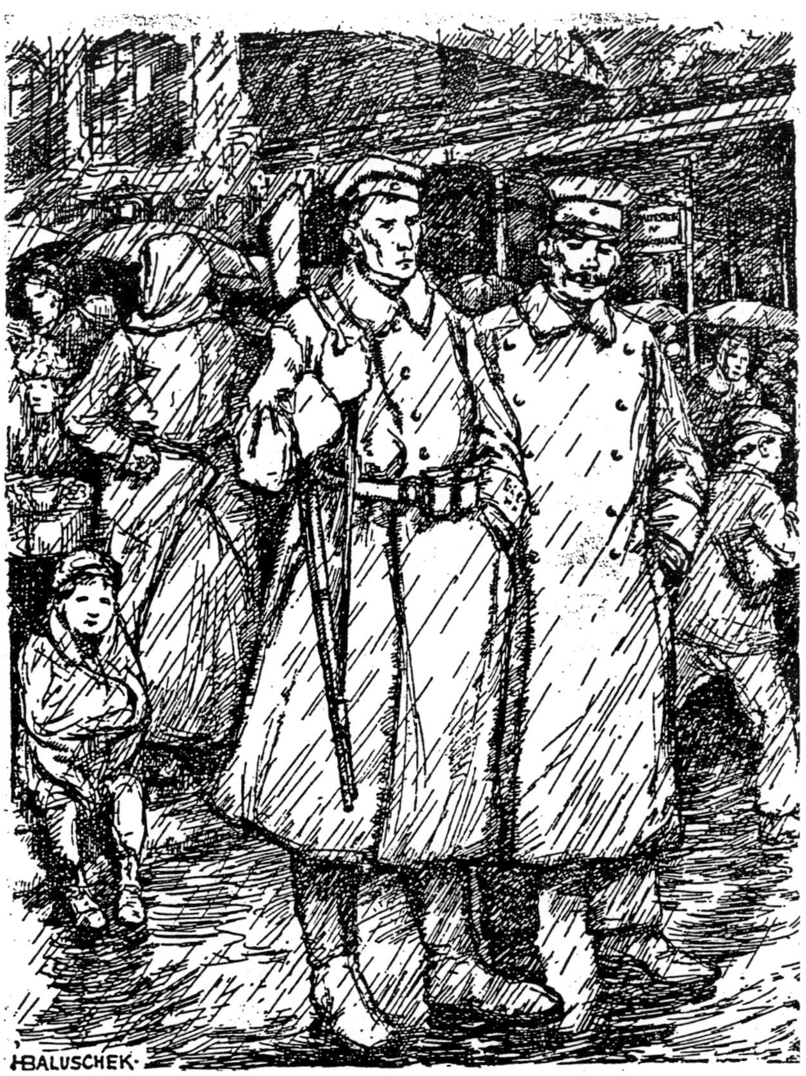

2.16 Hans Baluschek, *Der bewachte Schutzmann (The Watched Policeman), Wachtfeuer,* no. 5 (1919).

being watched. In *Government Troops* (fig. 2.17), the steel-helmeted warrior figures of 1917–18 maintain peace and order. In spite of the warning sign—"Halt! Anyone passing this point will be shot"—not one of the soldiers even has his rifle cocked. One is patiently listening to a woman's inquiry; the other is being admired by two children. The

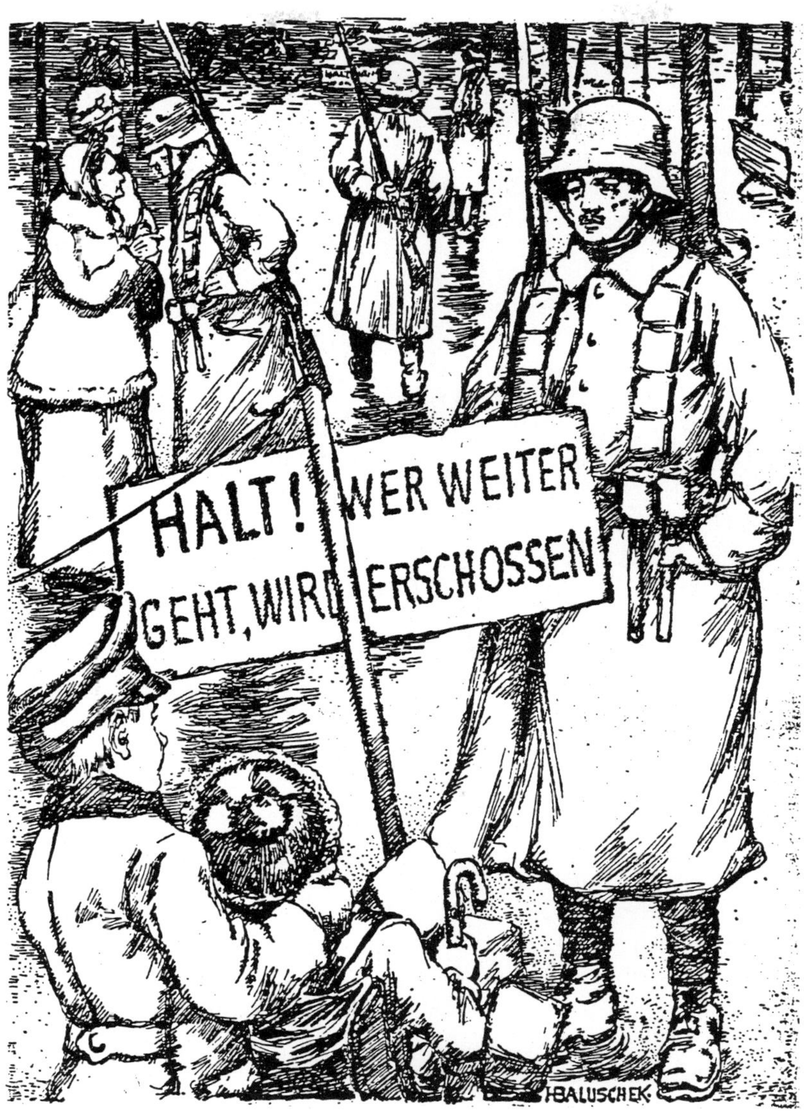

2.17 Hans Baluschek, *Regierungstruppen (Government Troops), Wachtfeuer,* no. 9 (1919).

boy, who wears a miniature uniform indicating his identification with the soldier, gently holds his young sibling back so that the child does not cross the police line. The irony in Baluschek's illustration was that the child would certainly not be shot should it accidently cross the barrier.[169]

Baluschek's partisan graphics were bound to bring him into conflict with Cooperative Society members such as Vogeler, Holtz, Taut, and Behne. Käthe Kollwitz, who, like Baluschek, was loyal to the Majority Socialists, also found herself at odds with the more radical members of the group.[170] Kollwitz had supported the SPD despite certain political misgivings. In her diary entry of 8 December 1918 she had written:

> If the choice were between an Ebert-dictatorship and a Liebknecht-dictatorship, I would certainly choose Ebert. But suddenly, though, it occurs to me what the true revolutionaries have achieved. Without this constant pressure from the left we would not have had any revolution; we would not have extinguished the entire militarism. They [the SPD] wanted always only evolution. And the consistent ones, the Independents and the Spartacists, are also now again the pioneers, they push always *forward,* no matter how things stand. Even if it is idiocy, even if Germany goes to pieces because of it. One will have to muffle them now in order to get out of the chaos, and there is a certain right to that . . . *De facto* one must go with the Majority Socialists.[171]

Although Kollwitz contributed a few drawings to the USPD *Die Freiheit* (for example, of the slain USPD leader Hugo Haase), her allegiance remained with the SPD.

For Kollwitz, the Cooperative Society afforded the prospect of reversing the public for her art. Her sophisticated etchings had previously been reserved for enlightened middle-class patrons. Now she hoped to make inexpensive graphics available to a working-class audience. Her position in the art world, though, was increasingly establishment oriented. Although she initially signed the manifesto of the Working Council for Art and recorded in her diary her sympathy with the group's belief that only the destruction of the old world might pave the way for a "new, naive, creative" world, when the WCA reissued its manifesto in April, Kollwitz's name was lacking. She was not sympathetic to the expressionist style of most of its members[172] and may have been uncomfortable with the steady radicalization of its leadership and their opposition to the SPD. Moreover, in June Kollwitz accepted an appointment to the Prussian Academy, the first woman so honored. Her acceptance came in the face of vehement attacks on that institution by the WCA—and despite the academy's apparent resistance to reform.[173] She had now become a member of the art establishment.

Internal dissension finally caused Natteroth to resign his position as chairman of the Cooperative Society, and in September he organized a new group, the League for Proletarian Culture (*Bund für proletarische Kultur*) modeled on the Russian *Proletkult*. Several Cooperative Society members, including Bruno Taut, joined the new organization, which politically was to the left of the Cooperative Society, although not officially affiliated with the KPD. Kollwitz declined membership in the new organization, writing in her diary:

> Yesterday I was at a meeting of the League for Proletarian Culture, and I have decided not to join. The views which I had on this enterprise were reinforced during the course of the meeting. To begin with, I am opposed to the idea that the League should be established on a party basis. To join would be much the same, as it were, as joining the Communist Party.[174]

Stripped of many of its most active members, the Cooperative Society soon dissolved.[175] The short experiment in socializing art production failed with the lack of socialist unity.

In the eight months following November 1918 little had changed in the art world. The initial hopes for dramatic change, bolstered by the rumors from Russia, had not been realized. Although they had come under fire from many quarters, the old institutions were still in place, staffed in large part by the same bureaucrats. Having met with resistance, and facing economic calamity, many expressionist artists were further radicalized. As the weeks passed, the artists' councils cast about in all directions for solutions. Would the new government act on its revolutionary rhetoric? Could they realize their goals as part of the political opposition? Could they turn to the proletariat for support, both moral and financial? The conflict and confusion in the political sphere compounded their dilemma. With everyone claiming the mantle of revolution, it was difficult to discern where friends were to be found.

This political confusion was nowhere more evident than in the November Group pamphlet *To All Artists*. But it was also to be found in the Exhibition for Unknown Architects and the reorganization of the Working Council for Art. The leadership of the WCA, disillusioned with the government and its agencies, moved to the left. But they brought along with them a group of politically uncertain artists who were not committed to any course of action. Consistency in support of expressionist art counted for more than political consistency. The one serious attempt to socialize the art world, that of the Cooperative Society of Socialist Artists, failed on the mistaken premise that only one segment of the economy could be socialized and that socialist unity was still possible in Germany.

The programs and plans of the artists' councils had been aimed in large part at leading expressionist art out of its isolation and making it accessible to the "people." These plans were based on the conviction that complete artistic freedom could be reconciled with an alliance with the proletariat. However, the contradictions inherent in this position soon became apparent, and artists were faced with a choice between artistic accommodation with the parliamentary democracy or self-defeating opposition.

June–December: Artistic Accommodation

The failure of the revolution left wounds that remained unhealed. The communists never forgave the SPD for the murders of Rosa Luxemburg and Karl Liebknecht, while the SPD blamed the communists for trying to overthrow the democratic republic. The Independents, exasperated by the inability of the SPD to check the counterrevolution, drifted uneasily to the left. Despite the rifts on the left—and the resurgence of the militarist right—the period after June witnessed a growing political stability. The government elected in Weimar had a familiar look: it was basically a reconstructed coalition of the parties that had been in power in October 1918. The signing of the Versailles Treaty (despite the acrimonious debate that led to the collapse of the government) and the approval by the National Assembly of a new constitution were signposts of this new order. To satisfy the left, there were clauses in the constitution permitting socialization and empowering a network of work councils, a legacy of the council movement. But since any significant socialization required a legislative majority, it was essentially a moot issue. And in practice, little power was given to the work councils. Instead, industrialists increasingly took a free hand in the economy, using inflation as a tool for economic recovery.

The increasing stability in both politics and economics carried over into the art world. While political antagonisms continued there as elsewhere, they were now ameliorated by new government efforts. The SPD minister Hänisch had already attempted to join together the various factions in the Berlin art world with the institution of an all-inclusive annual salon. This kind of democratic arts policy, which sought accommodation with the artists' councils, was now more energetically pursued. Its success was helped by a resurgent art market predicated on recovery through inflation.

One of the first signs of this renewed effort by the *Kultusministerium* came in mid-1919 with discussions about a new Gallery of Living Artists, a key demand of the artists' councils. With no money available for construction, the ministry dismissed the idea of a new building and decided instead to use the Kronprinzen Palais to house the new gallery.[176] The new quarters opened in August 1919 with around one hundred fifty works by Wilhelm Trübner, Max Liebermann, Max Slevogt, Lovis Corinth, and other members of the Berlin Secession displayed on the main floor, along with works by French artists such as Edouard Manet, Claude Monet, Paul Cézanne, and Auguste Renoir. On the upper floor works by German expressionist artists were exhibited under state auspices for the first time, either through new purchases or works lent by collectors. Represented were Erich Heckel, Ernst Ludwig Kirchner, Otto Mueller, Max Pechstein, Karl Schmidt-Rottluff, Emil Nolde, Ernst Barlach, Christian Rohlfs, Franz Marc, Lyonel Feininger, Wilhelm Lehmbruck, Heinrich Nauen, Oskar Moll, and Hans Purrmann.[177]

The overhaul of the previous small commission advising on state purchases into an expanded commission of experts facilitated the purchase of these works.[178] Although supporters of expressionism were a distinct minority on the new commission, the majority was considerably less conservative than before.[179] Erich Heckel apparently championed the modern cause on the commission, advised on purchases of expressionist works, and even helped hang the pictures.[180]

Just how the museum director Ludwig Justi actually chose works by expressionist artists for recommendation to the commission of experts remains unclear. It seems likely that the art historian Dr. Walter Kaesbach, a curator at the National Gallery and a close friend and patron of Heckel's, selected many of the works. Regarding the purchase of a work by Feininger for the considerable sum of 5,000 marks, Julia Feininger wrote to her husband on 20 June: "Naturally Kaesbach did the whole affair, and it stands then booked in history as Justi's heroic deed. It really is an obscenity."[181] Heckel and Kaesbach, though, by no means had complete control over selecting works by German expressionist artists and were often forced to compromise. For example, the committee rejected a work by Nolde, and Heckel worried in a letter to Kaesbach that Nolde, along with Rohlfs, might not be represented in the collection at all.[182]

The purchases of expressionist art by the National Gallery fell far short of fulfilling the radical demands for the complete reorganization of the museums under the control of expressionist artists. Still, it signaled the acceptance of expressionism into the cultural policy of the new art administration and its institutionalization in the new parliamentary democracy. Not surprisingly, though, the political debates about expressionism continued. At least one commentator believed the purchases were a concession to radical artists, a form of cooptation, concluding: "Public collections . . . were hastily reordered and expanded so that the radical wing found no cause for opposition."[183]

Other areas of the new art administration now included the expressionists as well. Wilhelm von Bode, director general of the royal museums, soon complained there were now too many people sympathetic to expressionism in the museums; he wondered aloud why people who "wanted to do away with museums" were now so eager to work in them.[184] In July, the *Kultusministerium* held a number of meetings to discuss educational reform and invited Walter Gropius to attend as well as such stalwarts of the pre-war Werkbund as Peter Behrens and Hermann Muthesius. Although Gropius reported to Georg Tappert of the November Group that "the old system still governs" and "the ministry is a hopeless institution," he nonetheless believed the meeting might be a first step and was optimistic about progress.[185] The government also created the post of a federal arts commissioner to regulate the aesthetic quality of new currency, flags, stamps, emblems, and the like following a series of public debates about the suitability of the government's choice for a new emblem.[186] The Werkbund had suggested for the position a number of candidates at least sympathetic to—if not outright supportive of—expressionist art, including the art historian and museum director Edwin Redslob; the Hannover art history professor Ernst Grisebach; Wilhelm Worringer, the author of the influential books *Abstraction and Empathy* and *Form in Gothic;* and Wilhelm Valentiner from the WCA.[187] Predictably, conservative artists objected when Redslob, the former director of the crafts museum in Bremen and current director of the city museum in Erfurt, was appointed to the post. The modern camp enthusiastically supported the appointment, but was disappointed that the new commissioner did not have "dictatorial powers," since he reported to the interior ministry instead of directly to the chancellor.[188] Redslob did not, however, one-sidedly promote the new art, but attempted to carefully balance the interests of all artistic groups. When the expressionist Karl Schmidt-Rottluff designed a new Reich eagle emblem, for example, Redslob praised his effort publicly, yet another more conservative design was eventually selected.

A resurgent art market also fostered the accommodation of expressionism. By September 1919, *Kunstchronik und Kunstmarkt* could point to a slow but steady improvement in art sales and to the reappearance of significant art auctions.[189] Three months later the journal *Der Kunsthandel* marveled at the exceptionally strong market for art[190] and by early 1920 *Kunst und Künstler* could report:

> Feverish movement reigns on the art market. Works are bought almost sight unseen, and everywhere there is a lack of merchandise. Whither with the paper money? . . . Then one remembers that paintings, graphics, books and antiquities are objects of value. To be sure of fluctuating exchange value, but for the present of increasing art value. . . . In the exhibitions every third picture boasts a "sold" sign. And since there is no longer a reactionary art, since everyone paints and draws in the modern style, the expressionist who was yesterday still derided becomes overnight an artist with a public and a capitalist. Now it is he who grumbles about the paper money, fears the capital levy, looks to buy houses or farmsteads, and becomes cautious about selling his works.[191]

The sarcastic description of the capitalist expressionist was meant to confirm *Kunst und Künstler*'s earlier skepticism about the revolutionary nature of their art, as well as to deride it as modish and transitory. Yet its description of the art market was undoubtedly accurate. With the acceptance of the Versailles Treaty, the change of government in June (Gustav Bauer formed a new coalition of SPD and Centre), and the suspension of the blockade, Germany began a period of tentative political stabilization and economic recovery. The government's commitment to a capitalist economy was signaled not only by the weakening of the factory work councils, but by the resignations on 12 July 1919 of the SPD economics minister Rudolf Wissell and his undersecretary Wichard von Moellendorff, whose modest socialization plans were considered too extreme. Industrialists now gradually began to realize that they could use inflation to rebuild, virtually extinguishing the national and corporate debt, while gaining a distinct export advantage (the external value of the mark dropped faster than the internal value).[192] By the end of 1919 the mark was worth less than one-third of its 1914 value, and those with money sought to safeguard its value through the purchase of real property, including artworks. Since foreign bidders dominated the market for older art (despite outcries that Germany was losing her artistic heritage, the government did not discourage art exports because it brought in needed foreign currency), modern German art flourished on the domestic art market. When in 1920 an official of the Bavarian Ministry for Social Welfare reported on the general trend toward the "Proletarianization of the Intellectual Worker," artists were for the most part excepted:

Art dealerships are springing up like mushrooms, the "new" friends of art are more numerous than the old. Understandably: they prefer to hang their life-insurance, the value of their stocks, their war- and revolution-profits on the walls in the form of artworks, before they are completely depreciated by the paper money catastrophe. . . . The newest art, say a Kirchner, valued at 300 marks two years ago, today brings 10,000 marks.[193]

Whether prices had generally increased as much as 3,000 percent in two years is doubtful, but it seems clear that the major expressionist artists enjoyed dramatically increased sales during the second half of 1919, a turnaround from the earlier part of the year. As late as March 1919 Lyonel Feininger, a member of the WCA, had been despondent about his economic prospects. An exhibition of his work in February and March at the Osthaus Museum in Hagen had been highly disappointing. None of the twenty-odd paintings had been sold—only three watercolors and four woodcuts, for a total of 1,008 marks.[194] By June, however, the situation had reversed itself. Feininger's one-man exhibition at the I. B. Neumann gallery in Berlin brought 23,800 marks, with one painting sold to the Stettin Museum for 6,000 marks, an increase of 50 percent in the price asked for the most expensive picture exhibited in Hagen just four months before.[195] His total income for June, which included the 5,000 marks paid by the National Gallery for his painting *Gelmeroda,* was roughly four times that of a Berlin university professor's income for an entire year.[196]

A new clientele had supported expressionism in the final years of the war, when it was advertised as spiritual refuge in the midst of catastrophe. This same clientele, it seems, was now prepared to accept the revolutionary claims of this art. Unlike the lower middle classes, which feared proletarianization with the revolution, members of the enlightened bourgeoisie proved themselves among the most able supporters of the republic—and its revolutionary rhetoric. Bourgeois politicians and representatives of industry developed a greater political flexibility than could have been anticipated in dealing with the revolutionary threat.[197]

The sales successes seem not to have been limited to the first rank of expressionist painters. Sales at the annual state-sponsored Berlin art exhibition in 1919 were the best in years, as were sales during the second half of the year at the smaller *Badischer Kunstverein* in Karlsruhe and at exhibitions at the Museum for Arts and Crafts in Weimar. The 1919 show in Karlsruhe included the most works ever shown and the most works ever sold, with no reduction in the average price.[198] An art proletariat still remained (287 Munich artists alone needed financial assistance from an artists' relief association in 1919),[199] and the Economic Association of Pictorial Artists gained steadily in membership as artists pressed for tax and other relief. But the success of expressionism was attested to by the huge numbers of imitators who now began to paint in that style.

Government policy encouraged this free market economy for art despite the residue of socialist rhetoric. This was evident in a report by *Kultusminister* Hänisch in early 1920 on "The Distress of the Intellectual Worker." Although much of the report focused on the supposed achievement of bringing the workers to power with the revolution, and on the pressing need to reverse the trend toward the proletarianization of many intellectuals, solutions, where offered, eschewed state support. Hänisch instead praised such efforts as those by the staunchly conservative Düsseldorf art academy to raise millions of marks privately from "wealthy 'friends and patrons.' "[200]

The first real test of how well the government succeeded with its new broad-based arts policy came with the annual Berlin Art Exhibition, held from 24 July through 30 September 1919 in the Glass Palace. Despite the rhetoric of unity, the exhibition was really a series of separate shows held at the same time in the same place. There was not one commission, but separate ones each for the Association of Berlin Artists, the Berlin Secession, the Free Secession, and the November Group (with the last two cooperating to some degree).[201]

The exhibition finally opened on 24 July after several delays. With works hung from the baseboards to the rafters, the exhibition assumed its traditional look. The Association of German Artists exhibited almost seven hundred fifty works by some three hundred fifty artists in seventeen rooms, while the other groups shared ten rooms, where they exhibited some five hundred thirty works by almost two hundred thirty artists. The November Group section alone contained one hundred eighty-two works by seventy-nine artists. Most of the better-known expressionist artists chose to exhibit with the juried Free Secession, including Georg Kolbe, Otto Mueller, Karl Schmidt-Rottluff, Ernst Ludwig Kirchner, Oskar Kokoschka, and Gerhard Marcks. Erich Heckel exhibited with both the Free Secession and the November Group. Besides Heckel, the only well-established expressionist artists exhibiting in the unjuried November Group section were Ludwig Meidner and Max Pechstein, along with Paul Klee. The rest were mainly younger, lesser-known artists, ranging from the *Die Aktion* contributors Karl Jacob Hirsch and Max Burchartz to the Sturm gallery artists Oskar Fischer and Rudolf Schlichter. Many of the members of the November Group and WCA, who had vocally opposed the jury system in the opening days of the revolution, now chose to place their work in a juried section of the show. Both the November Group and the

Free Secession solicited works from artists outside Berlin: the latter included the Dresden Secession Group 1919 in their rooms, while the former invited affiliated artists from all over Germany. The November Group also devoted two of its rooms to the work of the Russian artist Marc Chagall.

When the show opened the reaction was violent, and this grew in intensity throughout the duration of the show. The first review by the critic Fritz Stahl in the *Berliner Tageblatt* on the day the show opened immediately pointed out the charade of the exhibition: there was no unity in the Berlin art world. He reserved his most vehement comments for the November Group rooms, likening them to a "lunatic asylum" and criticizing the artists for the mistaken idea that "in politically wild times art [must also be] for its part wild."[202] Stahl was also the first of many to comment on the derivative, imitative nature of much of the November Group art; the majority of the young artists, he claimed, were only "malingerers who reproduce traits of strange madness with cold method."[203] Another conservative critic described the exhibition as a scene of "tumult" and mocked the November Group rooms for their incomprehensible art. The typical viewer, he wrote, saw specks of color on the canvas, turned the pages of the catalog in search of explanation, and despairingly read the seemingly unrelated titles. His list of fictitious titles (including *The Sex Murder, The Step into the Uncertain, The Drunkard I, The Drunkard II, Madness and Suicide,* and *The Deranged Philistine*) presented an image of the November Group artist as degenerate.[204]

Even *Das Kunstblatt,* the staunch promoter of expressionism, voiced disappointment at the November Group rooms. Alluding to the decision of many major expressionists to exhibit with the Free Secession, the critic Walter Ley wrote:

> One awaited with interest the first public appearance of the November Group. After all, the alliance of all fresh and lively artistic powers had long ago become urgent for Berlin. The November Group is not this alliance. It was not able to bring around the spirits who appear as the true representatives of the development. Instead, irresponsible fellow-travelers grow wild in it, to whom there was no necessity of providing broader propaganda possibilities.[205]

Paul Westheim, the editor of *Das Kunstblatt,* had early on opposed the annual salon as a relic of the past. Now he, too, called the November Group artists "fellow travelers," characterizing the entire show as a "falsely understood notion of democracy" where the number of adherents was prized above quality.[206] The reality of the exhibition was that the November Group rooms included many young artists who only recently had adopted expressionism, including a number who imitated Kandinsky with their abstract compositions. Even the most sympathetic critics had to agree that the works were for the most part weak and derivative and that the contributions of the more-established expressionist artists were not their best efforts.[207]

By September, though, the criticism had changed dramatically. It no longer centered on artistic merit but rather on political persuasion, taking on a more aggressive and hostile tone. Curt Glaser, a conservative member of the new commission advising on state purchases, wrote in *Kunstchronik und Kunstmarkt:* "One stands as before a fate and asks oneself if it had to come to this, if our time is condemned to destroy the forms of the old art, just as the bolshevists in Russia smash the forms of social life and claim that today that is only what matters, but that reconstruction is a question of a future time."[208] Glaser characterized expressionism as destructive and not so subtly equated the shattering of old forms in art with the reputed violence of the bolsheviks. Such assaults now transpired not only in the press, but at the exhibition itself. As reported by a Berlin newspaper, a representative of the Anti-Bolshevist League appeared regularly in the November Group rooms inveighing against the "art which brings down and dishonours [the] fatherland," warning that the "nihilism which topples everything previously established in art also brought about the upheaval in public life."[209] The SPD newspaper *Vorwärts* also reported on the "intolerant heresy and abusive language" at the exhibition, which reminded the author of a "tumultuous [political] gathering." He pleaded, "Above all in an art exhibition one should look, not debate."[210] The resident art critic for *Vorwärts,* John Schikowski, defended the November Group, even maintaining in the face of these attacks the original claims of the WCA and November Group to mass accessibility. Ignoring those who found the art incomprehensible, he still believed expressionism was destined to become "an art for the great masses." Only the lack of an adequate "cultural level" among the masses, he wrote, prevented expressionism from being "a true people's art"—a problem that would be remedied under socialism.[211]

The verbal assaults soon escalated into physical ones. At least one sculpture was damaged, and the November Group commission announced that it could no longer guarantee the safety of the exhibited works. The general exhibition committee even recommended that November Group members patrol their own rooms, particularly during peak visitation hours—a suggestion rejected by the group. The sculptor Georg Leschnitzer removed his work from the exhibition, and several others threatened to follow suit.[212] *Kunstchronik und Kunstmarkt* commented on this turn of events:

> One party attempts to ascribe the cause for these incidents to the other, and the whole affair is played over again into the political sphere. One speaks of agents of counter-revolutionary groups who incite the public through adept agitation. It also herein appears that the attempt is made on the one side to use art as a means of political struggle, on the other to exploit the revolutionary boom in order tendentiously to bring the latest manifestations in the cultural realm into contact with the party groups which stand furthest to the left—as was already successfully attempted in Russia. But what was attained in Russia by means of dictatorship must fail deplorably here by means of the majority will, as the attitude of the Glass Palace public now glaringly shows.[213]

The criticism in *Vorwärts* and *Kunstchronik und Kunstmarkt* represented the contradictory claims made about expressionism. Certainly expressionism had reached no mass audience, but neither had it been accepted by the extreme left nor had it taken over the cultural institutions of the new republic. Although government policy and a resurgent art market facilitated an accommodation of expressionism, the ideological debate about the new art continued unabated.

This debate took place not only in the press and at the annual salon, but in the new Prussian provincial parliament (*Landesversammlung*) as well. In December 1919, on the occasion of the annual submission of the program of the Prussian *Kultusministerium*, the various parties put their divergent views on expressionism on the record. The delegates of the Centre Party, the German National People's Party (DNVP), and the German People's Party (DVP) all, to a greater or lesser degree, attacked expressionism. Dr. Ritter of the DNVP denounced the new art as an international art, a conspiracy of the press, and "like all decadence, condemned to extinction."[214] He excitedly warned against differentiating art on the basis of class (singling out the Cooperative Society of Socialist Artists and the League for Proletarian Culture for "artificially rousing class antagonisms") and even opposed a democratic art policy on the basis that "democracy in art is certainly not suitable; it's just that here the aristocratic principle undeniably goes."[215] Delegate Garnich of the DVP, if more cautious, was still critical. Declaring that her party had always preferred a democratic arts policy that favored all directions, she continued nonetheless:

> We must hereby give expression to the fear that unfortunately yet again a kind of official art seems to prevail, only from the other direction. . . . Today to our regret indications make themselves noticeable that an artwork is judged only by which political position its creator adheres to. . . . There is only art as such,

that is good or bad art . . . but there is no proletarian art and also no capitalist art . . ."[216]

Although Garnich conceded that a completely impartial policy might include state purchases of expressionist works for the Gallery of Living Artists, she added, "Such pictures also do not need to be procured in excess."[217]

On the other side of the debate the USPD representative vigorously defended expressionism and just as forcefully rejected the idea that art was apolitical. The USPD delegate Henning proclaimed:

We can state at once that the revolution changed nothing in the fact that there are art-poor, culturally propertyless classes, the mass of the people at the bottom . . . Because we do not have a unified body of people we self-evidently also have no unified art life. . . . Because we live in a fermenting—socially fermenting—time, the same is the case for art. . . . We find that embodied, for example, in both artistic directions in painting, which we can describe . . . as on the one side the defenders of that which exists, and [on the other] those who we address as expressionist, who form the new, who express through art a formation of the will of society . . . , who want to place art in the service of the new social forms. . . . The artistic and intellectual youth are on our side, on the side of the working class . . . [218]

Thus, the USPD, out of power now, rejected conciliatory SPD policies that promoted a unified German culture. Instead, it described expressionist art as politically revolutionary, aligned with the working class, and inherently opposed to the status quo, confirming its revolutionary claims in spite of its incongruity with the actual state of affairs. For expressionism had certainly reached no mass audience; rather, its acceptance had come with a resurgent art market supported not by the "mass of the people at the bottom," but by the culturally propertied classes the USPD spokesman opposed.

Representing the government in the debate was the SPD delegate Frank, who conceded that artists still suffered under "art capitalism and the system of exploitation," but boasted that "the revolution had destroyed the hard shell of militarist-imperialist censorship" so that "art today can travel freer and better paths."[219] He continued, "The artist is still today dependent on the bourgeoisie; that is, citizens well provided with capital. But my friends in the party are of the view . . . that art should not be only an art for the shallow and perverse Kurfürstendamm public, but much more an art for the broad masses of people, a healthy people's art."[220] Art, he seemed to guarantee, was like the economy on the evolutionary path toward socialism. But he proposed no immediate measures to bring these changes about. Instead, he defended Hänisch's program, which aimed at a democratic arts policy while limiting state expenditures. This evenhanded policy extended to the specific artists cited in his speech, from the neoclassicist sculptors Franz Metzner and Louis Tuaillon to the expressionist painters Lyonel Feininger and Oskar Kokoschka. Praising the inclusion of the expressionists in the annual salon he noted:

> No one requires that you love these people [expressionist artists]; but there are those who do not bother to understand these artists only because they are something novel, because they are revolutionaries of art. That is absolutely false. If you give these artists so much social compassion, so much love, that they can at least live, then you will see what is achieved. In every revolution a somewhat bold gambol to the left or the right is sometimes made; that just logically follows from every revolution. Whether it happens in art or politics is all the same.[221]

Unlike Hennig, Frank presented the depoliticized version of revolutionary art, ameliorating any negative connotations.

The lack of socialist unity on cultural policy in Prussia was clearly evident. The USPD, out of power, unequivocally rejected the idea of a unified German culture and promoted expressionism as the art of the revolutionary working classes, thereby confirming the revolutionary claims made for the new art in the first days of the revolution. Although the USPD representative gave expressionism the strongest endorsement of any party, he also ignored the economic realities the SPD delegate implicitly acknowledged: expressionism had reached no mass audience, and its recent success was dependent on the capitalist art market. The SPD, on the other hand, accepted the revolutionary claims for expressionist art, but depoliticized such claims and pledged to continue its even-handed policies, to which most expressionist artists had begun to accommodate themselves. The discussion of expressionism in the Prussian Provincial Parliament continued the ideological debate about the new art, one in which all parties assumed expressionism was revolutionary in one sense or another.

The dilemma of claiming revolutionary status for their art while increasingly enjoying the benefits of an antirevolutionary government and economy was evident not only at the annual Berlin salon and the debate in the Prussian Provincial Parliament, but in a special December 1919 issue of the Dresden expressionist journal *Menschen* devoted to the November Group. Adolf Behne's introductory essay is of particular importance for its almost desperate insistence on the revolutionary nature of expressionist art in the face of increasing cooptation by a bourgeois public.

Behne's explanation of the revolutionary character of the November Group fell back on its name, which to him signaled an "avowal of socialism and the revolution." He was anxious to separate the group from the "November socialists," opportunists who supported the revolution in its earliest days but had no true commitment to socialism. Yet he was at a loss about how to do so. In the body of his essay Behne attempted to explain the apparent contradiction of a revolutionary art eagerly embraced by the bourgeoisie:

> There are still art-loving burghers who are unsympathetic to placing the two things—expressionism and world revolution—in relationship to one another. They find it not to the point to name the things in the same breath. . . . They have come to terms with the liberating energies of the new art, but in no case do they want these energies, here perceived as interesting, to have an effect beyond the picture frame. The effect is to remain limited to the circle of connoisseurs as an aesthetic one. . . . Art has nothing to do with politics. . . .
>
> If now the same art-loving burghers have begun to buy and collect expressionist art, then they again self-evidently conclude a compromise. They do not perceive the spiritual in the new art, which is hostile to their spirit, but see exclusively the surface, to which their eyes are not accustomed, which they enjoy as the attraction of surprise. The compromise consists in that in their minds they degrade a cultural movement to a fashion—so that they can share in it.[222]

In this scheme it was not the artists, but their patrons who performed the dreaded compromise. Behne's summation was no less uneasy. Reviewing the activities of the group since its inception, he could name no concrete effort to form an alliance between expressionist art and the proletariat; although he cited the group's bylaws that it was no "mere exhibition group," its only activities thus far had in fact been exhibitions.

It was indeed a "mere exhibition group" that the November Group ultimately became, and a highly successful one at that, lasting until 1933. The discrepancy between its original revolutionary ambitions and its eventual cooptation was commented upon already in 1920, on the occasion of the opening of the annual Berlin salon, as no less than President Friedrich Ebert toured the Glass Palace. An angry critic on the left observed that as long as a single "member of an artists' group toadies before Fritz Ebert, the authorizer of death sentences . . . and personification of bourgeois indolence, it has damned little right to call itself radical or even revolutionary."[223] Describing the behavior of the November Group leaders as Ebert toured their rooms, this critic continued:

[They] lead him [Ebert] with deferential smiles and friendly bowing before the parade of young, radical, revolutionary art. Yet the much-tested one does not lose his form and while somewhere in the Ruhr the command "fire" resounds, he also seeks to do justice to the radical revolutionary art. Still: stifled laughter shakes the elegant waistcoat of the sovereign and doing justice clearly is not easy for him. The expressionist leader who guides him submissively explains, as if he were dealing with a brewer art-patron; the band of small expressionists listens intently.[224]

The following year the occasion of the third annual salon brought an end to any remaining revolutionary ambitions. In a controversial move, the leadership of the November Group bowed to pressure from the *Kultusministerium* and the titular head of the exhibition, Max Schlichting, to remove two offending works by the Dadaists Rudolf Schlichter and Otto Dix (Schlichting threatened to call in the public prosecutor). Outraged, the left wing of the group resigned in protest, publishing an "Open Letter to the November Group" in the communist-oriented *Der Gegner.* While these artists acknowledged that the group may have had revolutionary aspirations at the moment of its founding, they lamented that the leadership had abandoned these goals as it sought to "raise themselves to a better class of bourgeois artists" and gain public recognition by "wooing the goodwill of a government held in the halter by Ludendorff, Kapp and Stinnes."[225]

Unlike the November Group, the Working Council for Art continued, for a time, its tenuous efforts to enact its program, including coming up with an ideal building project and addressing a working-class audience. These two goals preoccupied the group for the better part of six months after its reorganization, a process that once again revealed the lack of political or institutional—and therefore economic—support for their efforts.

When the WCA reissued its New Artistic Program in April, it was illustrated with a woodcut (probably done by Max Pechstein) (fig. 2.18) that depicted three figures—an architect holding a protractor, a painter with palette and brush, and a sculptress with hammer—actively at work on a large building block inscribed "Arbeitsrat für Kunst." The figures tower over the already completed section as they work under a star-filled sky. The woodcut was meant to represent the new reorganization of the group, as well as its goal: the separate committees for painting, architecture, and sculpture that had previously made up the group had now given way to a central committee whose primary task it was, according to the final paragraph of the manifesto, to pursue an ideal building project embracing all the arts.

Given little hope of state support, various members of the WCA

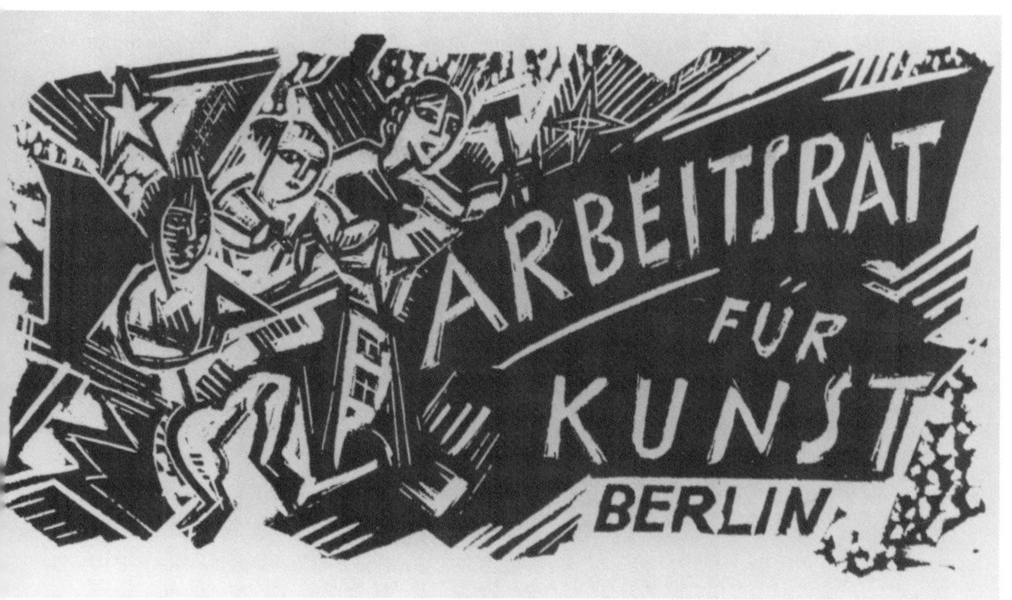

2.18 Max Pechstein, illustration for program of the Working Council for Art, 1919. Woodcut, dimensions unknown.

attempted to devise a building project the group could carry out independently. Gropius apparently suggested the first such project in April;[226] the membership rejected it, although the reasons—and the exact nature of the project—remain unclear.[227] In the following months, WCA members, many of them painters and sculptors, filled their correspondence with elaborate proposals for building projects. As early as March the sculptor Rudolf Belling sent Gropius a clipping from the *8 Uhr Abendblatt* that reported on plans to eventually spend some fifty million marks on building projects in Berlin in an attempt to relieve unemployment. Belling enthusiastically suggested WCA involvement, proposing they immediately contact trade unions and building officials. But Belling's conception of the role to be played by the WCA undoubtedly clashed with the views of other members of the group, including Gropius and Taut. Adopting the conservative line argued in the *8 Uhr Abendblatt,* which blamed the lack of economic recovery on workers' strikes and wage demands, Belling believed the WCA could be the perfect intermediary to convince the workers that they "hurt themselves with their absurd wage demands, hinder culture, and cause great damage to artists who really represent their interests."[228]

The plan that found the greatest response among the membership concerned the rebuilding of areas of northern France and Belgium in response to the provisions of the Versailles Treaty and was developed by Bruno Taut and the Swiss architect/sculptor P. R. Henning. According to Section VIII of the Entente response to Germany's proposed schedule of reparations payment, Germany could in certain cases pay reparations in practical work. By September, the German government had indicated its intention to rebuild areas of northern France and Belgium with German labor and materials.[229] Taut and Henning's ambitious plan, presented at the 18 November meeting, concerned housing for German workers on foreign soil, calling for the erection of workers' communities for 100,000 German workers over a ten-year period. They saw this as an ideal experiment: housing would be secondary to the building of a central "people's building," which could inculcate a new sensibility among this geographically isolated community of workers. The focus of the WCA's thinking, then, was not so much on the rebuilding of northern France and Belgium, but on influencing the German worker through architecture. Just how this plan was to be financed was unclear: Taut claimed he was "indifferent to how things stood politically and what the government had planned" and suggested perhaps the Werkbund would defray the costs. Yet at the same meeting, Gropius' proposal that the WCA join the Werkbund had met with strong opposition from those who were suspicious of the latter's conservative politics. Other tactics called for the group to approach the National Assembly for financing, or to bring their sketches and models directly to the working class, which could then demand of the government that they be carried out.[230] Although the members enthusiastically planned to meet again in two weeks with sketches, there is no evidence that such a meeting took place or that the proposal was explored further.[231]

It is not surprising that the WCA never developed its ideal building project, for it had neither political nor financial support for such an endeavor. At least one member of the leadership had already drawn these conclusions. In March Gropius had taken up duties as head of the unified College of Fine Arts and the School of Arts and Crafts in Weimer, now known as the Bauhaus.[232] He had entered into negotiations for this position as early as January 1919 and concluded the agreement on 20 March 1919.[233] Negotiations for a position in a state institution dependent on a Social Democratic provincial government, then, occurred simultaneously with his active participation in the founding of the WCA; he had accepted the position only days after the suppression of street fighting in Berlin. Gropius may already have concluded that the WCA had little chance to enact its programs without state financing. Now he hoped to carry out the program of the WCA, particularly the reform of art education and the unification of the arts under architecture, at the Bauhaus. In the end, Pechstein's illustration on the new WCA manifesto might have better served on the first Bauhaus manifesto. As it turned out, Lyonel Feininger's woodcut for the latter (fig. 2.19) featured the ideal goal of a building project embracing all the arts modeled on the Gothic cathedral, rather than the artists themselves actively engaged in work.

One of the more successful ventures of the WCA, at least in terms of reaching a wider audience, was the publication of *Yes! Voices of the Working Council for Art* (*Ja! Stimmen des Arbeitsrates für Kunst*) in December 1919. This book contained responses by twenty-eight of the group's members to a questionnaire distributed the previous April concerning everything from the reform of art education, to the role of the artist in a socialist state, to whether artworks should be exhibited anonymously.[234] Many of the questions, most likely written by Adolf Behne, were vague, particularly in their political reference points; for example, several of the questions addressed the role of the socialist state, without, however, defining whether it referred to the present government or to a hoped-for one. Of the twenty-eight responses published, five were from architects, nine from painters, six from sculptors, and eight from a cross-section of nonartists including critics, museum people, and teachers.[235]

The greatest accord in the answers—and the most extensive commentaries—concerned the reform of art education. Many of the respondents favored spontaneity and direct expression rather than the overbearing academic training and the imitative art instruction provided in the schools. For example, Behne wrote, "We have no better regulations to offer in the place of the old regulations, but rather our and the people's artistic spontaneity. . . . Here our task is: destruction of education."[236] George Tappert added:

> Abolish and reorganize previous drawing instruction. Complete allowance of childhood fantasy in children's homes and schools up until the age of about 10. . . . The teachers should encourage childlike expressive drawings; it should not be the task of the teacher to correct the drawings for correctness, technical neatness, and such things. It must be the task of the teacher to stimulate the fantasy of the child . . . [237]

Wilhelm Valentiner responded, "The most fundamental reform would be achieved through the (at least temporary) abolishment of all schools. Perhaps art becomes better if it once again grows wild, as it was in the beginning of all things when a naïve art developed."[238] The exaggerated demands for an end to all art schools was not only a challenge to the art

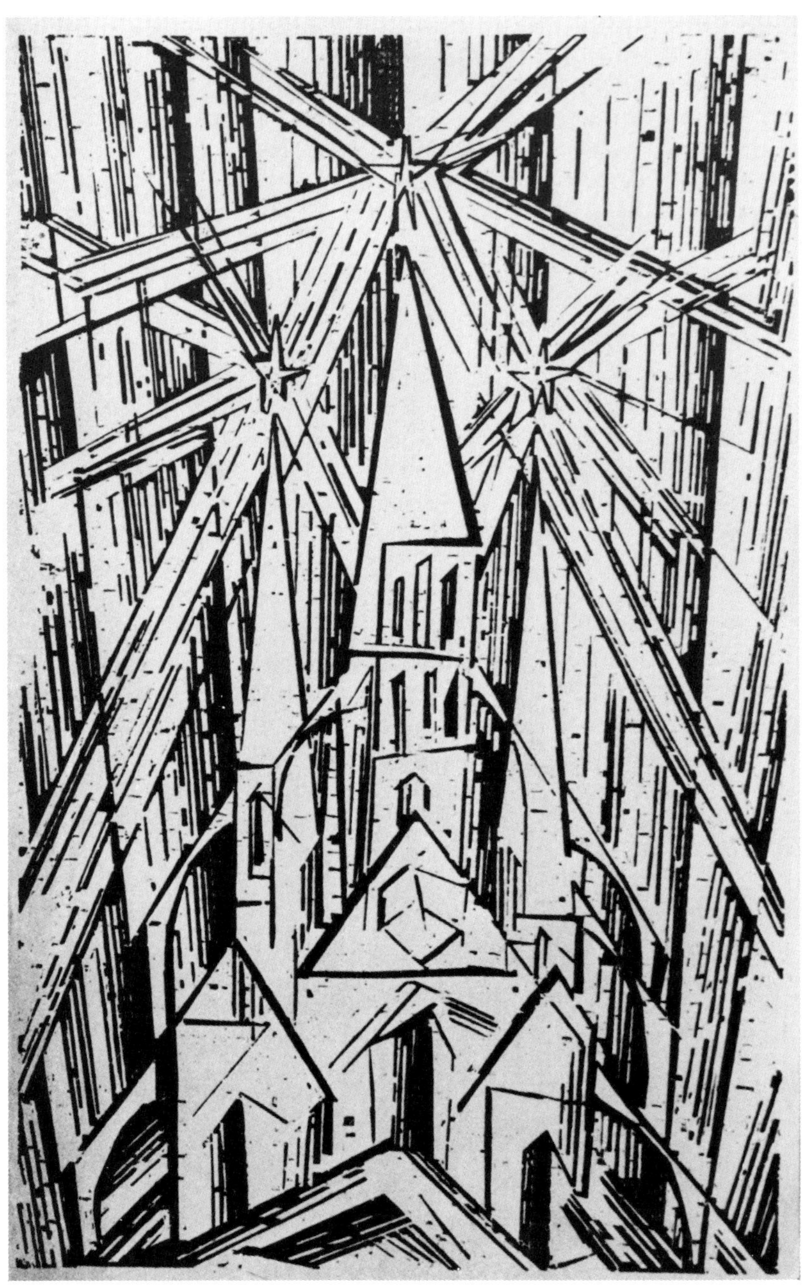

2.19 Lyonel Feininger, *Kathedrale (Cathedral),* cover illustration for the *Bauhaus-Manifesto,* April 1919. Woodcut, 30.5 x 18.7 cm. The Los Angeles County Museum of Art; The Robert Gore Rifkind Center for German Expressionist Studies; purchased with funds provided by Anna Bing Arnold, the Museum Acquisition Fund, and Deaccession Funds. © 1989, copyright by Cosmopress, Geneva.

and art education of imperial Germany, but also to the persistent lack of change since the revolution. Several of the respondents, though, already occupied teaching positions at state institutions, including Georg Tappert at the State Academy for Art Education in Berlin and Walter Gropius at the state-sponsored Bauhaus in Weimar. Gropius, not surprisingly, devoted most of his answer to the reform of art education based on the handicrafts and work on an actual building project, the bases on which he hoped to develop the Bauhaus curriculum.

When it came to the issue of the role of the state in artistic matters, the three dominant spokesmen for the WCA differed from much of the membership, particularly from the painters. The responses by Taut, Gropius, and Behne shared a common thread: hostility toward the state. Behne insisted, "The state according to its essence is hostile to art."[239] Gropius, despite his appointment to a state institution, explained, "Art and the state are irreconcilable notions."[240] Articulated even more bluntly, Taut concluded, "The state must be totally ignored."[241] Distrust of state interference was now directed not at the Wilhelmine past, but at a present coalition government that had not met the demands of the group.

More fundamentally than Gropius, Behne and Taut confronted the consequences of the rejection of all state support, including state purchases, state museums, and state sponsored exhibitions. Art would now be dependent on the support of the masses, who, according to Behne, would be approached directly in the factories and on the streets. Behne redefined the social position of the artist in terms of a worker, to be paid according to the same daily wages and to be employed by a joint commission of workers and radical artists to paint workers' apartments, union halls, and the like. Taut, too, envisioned workers' patronage—as opposed to state patronage—for modern art. Financing would come from the work councils at the factory level, the only remaining vestige of the council system by mid-1919. Taut also insisted that the artist was a worker, like any other. Going even further than Behne, this meant for him that the artist would only create in his leisure time. Despite his usual high-flown rhetoric, Taut's response confronted the contradictions inherent in many of the conflicting demands made by the group. In rather pragmatic terms, he also acknowledged the failure of the revolution and the limited possibilities for change in the near future.

Representative of the painters' responses, on the other hand, were those by Cesar Klein and Georg Tappert, who still expected state support for expressionist art. Although Klein began his answer with a key demand of the left—"Socialization. Art must be socialized."[242]—this meant for him only institutionalized state support for the new art. Thus all state projects "belonged" to the new art, to be produced in state-supported workshops. Klein also wrote of expanding the base for "radical, modern, good" art through such measures as illustrated supplements in working-class newspapers, exhibitions in working-class areas, and guided tours on Sundays by trade unions. In doing so, he assumed an identity of interest between the current government and the working class. Tappert, too, placed extensive demands on the state, which was to provide free workshops and exhibition space for all artists. Although he sought a broader public for modern art, he rejected any preferential treatment for socialist artists' organizations (probably referring to the Cooperative Society of Socialist Artists), as well as close contact with the traditional socialist organizations. The first he opposed on the grounds of artistic freedom, the second purportedly for tactical reasons. Rather than expanding the public for expressionism through workers' organizations, he placed his hopes on a generational change: the WCA must educate the young, so that they will "carry the efforts of modern artists into the circle of the family and into workrooms and workshops."[243] In a similar vein, Moriz Melzer, another leading figure in the November Group, distrusted any involvement with politics, and the painter Arnold Topp questioned whether modern artists really even wanted the support and approval of the masses. Only one respondent suggested a specific political course of action: the stucco worker and part-time artist Oswald Herzog advocated protests against the activities of the current government and an unconditional alliance with leaders of the USPD and the KPD.

In the introduction to the volume, Behne had indicated that with the questionnaire the WCA had sought to define a unified basis for action. The unified basis, which was in fact achieved, seemed to extend only to agreement on the reform of art education, the importance of the handicrafts, and the need to unify the arts under architecture. Yet another, less apparent, agreement existed, both in the formulation of the questions and in the answers. That was the inability to make explicit the contradictions upon which the WCA now operated. The questions took for granted a politically undefined socialism, as did most of the answers. Those who demanded state support for expressionism assumed an identity between the interests of the government and those of the working class. Those who opposed state intervention ignored the inability, and the seeming unwillingness, of the working class to support expressionism. And while almost everyone at least implicitly opposed the capitalist art market, they were all still counting on it. Even the format of *Yes! Voices of the Working Council for Art* spoke to that contradiction: fifty-five copies of a deluxe edition on handmade paper, with an original woodcut by Lyonel Feininger, were available for collectors.[244]

Soon after the publication of *Yes! Voices of the Working Council for Art,* the group made one last stab at an exhibition designed for the proletariat. Perhaps following the example set by the Cooperative Society of Socialist Artists to which Taut and Behne had belonged, the WCA in November planned an exhibition of expressionist art in the working-class district of East Berlin. The sponsor was the Free Youth (*Freie Jugend*), a socialist youth organization funded by the syndicalist Free Workers' Union of Germany. The exhibition opened on New Year's day 1920 in the rooms of the Petersburgerstrasse commune organized by the group's leader, Ernst Friedrich, an actor by training who had been active in the Spartacist uprising.[245] Friedrich was also a partisan of expressionism, who had provided simple explanations of that art in the pages of his journal *Freie Jugend,* equating "radical" artists with the "radical" youth movement.[246]

Behne advertised the small exhibition in an article in the USPD *Die Freiheit,* rehearsing once again the WCA views on art exhibitions. "The WCA did not want to imitate art salons in their exhibitions," he wrote. "It also did not want to string together pearls of expressionist masterworks."[247] Instead, the exhibition included works by WCA members, members of the Free Youth, and children's art. Elementary expression, which asserted itself despite "all restraining influences," according to Behne, became the theme of the exhibition. The message was that anyone could create art.

Among those contributing to the exhibition from the WCA were the architects Bruno and Max Taut; Lyonel Feininger; Arnold Topp, a painter connected with the Sturm gallery; the Hannover expressionist Max Burchartz; and Albert Klawon, a stucco worker and fledgling artist. Also participating was the Russian Marc Chagall.[248] Many of the works were exhibited anonymously. The exhibition also launched the artistic careers of the 25-year-old Otto Nagel, who had studied at the city's night school, and Paul Eickmeier, who, like Nagel, was a member of the KPD. They were joined in the show by Felix Gasbarra, a member of the anarcho-syndicalist Communist Workers' Party (KAPD) (and later a producer for Erwin Piscator), who exhibited wood sculptures.[249]

According to a WCA report, attendance was brisk and sales were good. An ingenious arrangement was worked out whereby a representative of the WCA would negotiate a sales price with the artist, taking into account the purchaser's age, profession, and ability to pay.[250] Coordinated with the exhibition were twice-daily guided tours by Ernst Friedrich and lectures by Behne on expressionist art and Taut on architecture. Also planned in conjunction with the exhibition were Sunday lectures in the town hall and a memorial tribute to the slain anarchist leader Gustav Landauer, who had promoted expressionist art during the council republic in Munich.[251]

The exhibition, though, came to a precipitous and rancorous end four weeks after it had opened when a local court issued an order to close it. A formal complaint, registered by the landlord of the building, cited misuse of the rooms, which were supposed to be used for the Free Youth press and not for exhibitions. The lawyer for the landlord described the exhibition and lecture evenings in his legal brief as an "innocent false front for bolshevist agitation."[252] Political tensions in the city were high, and the dispute had followed shortly after a mass protest in front of the Reichstag in which forty-two demonstrators were killed.

Following the sudden closing of the exhibition, a debate ensued about the relationship between expressionism and socialism in the *Freie wissenschaftliche sozialistische Agrar-Korrespondenz,* an obscure periodical with a limited readership. Still, the positions staked out were indicative of persistent contradictions and misunderstandings inherent in bringing expressionist art and the masses together. A number of workers had apparently complained in the *Agrar-Korrespondenz* about the overemphasis on expressionism in the East Berlin WCA exhibition.[253] One author now took issue with Behne's lecture on expressionism, in which the latter had dismissed naturalist art, still popular with large segments of the proletariat. Chiding Behne he concluded:

> A word still on your claim, unproven and yet apodictically made, that socialism and expressionism belong together. . . . It [expressionism] is in the final analysis totally exclusive, aristocratic, solitary, uncooperative [*ungenossenschaftlich*]. Where is the relationship with socialism? Are not socialism and revolution here confused with one another? . . . For where does it [expressionism] have its primary partisans? In Berlin WW, Kurfürstendamm, where the November-socialists and salon-Spartacists sit![254]

Complicating the debate was the fact that the writer in the *Agrar-Korrespondenz,* while defending as true socialist art Heinrich Zille's working-class genre scenes, attacked bolshevism as "asiatism and despotism." Behne stepped in to defend bolshevism, claiming that such a negative characterization came from the same narrow-mindedness that had caused the courts to close the WCA exhibition. Ironically, the success of expressionism with a bourgeois public now caused some on the left to attack it as being nonsocialist, while WCA members such as Behne were among the few still openly defending bolshevism.

The Working Council for Art sponsored one more exhibition, "New Building," which opened on 3 May 1920, at the I. B. Neumann gallery. By this time, however, internal dissension began to surface within the group. In June 1921, its finances depleted and its members scattered, the WCA made its dissolution official.[255]

The November revolution had begun with high expectations on the part of artists, who envisioned in a socialist state not only an end to the discriminatory imperial art practices, but complete artistic freedom and a renewed social relevance for their efforts. These artists believed expressionist art to be politically progressive and lyrically envisioned its ultimate success and appreciation alongside socialization, workers' control, and an era of human brotherhood. Their dreams were strengthened by initial support in the socialist press and rumors of the triumph of modernist art in Soviet Russia. But, from the start, what everyone called "the revolution" was ambiguous—revolution from above as well as from below. With the murders of Liebknecht and Luxemburg, the suppression of the Spartacist uprising, and the events of March, artists' expectations began to prove illusory. Although such creeds as complete artistic freedom may have been laudable, they were vague and devoid of practical consequences. The revolution had failed, and expressionism was still indissolubly linked to a capitalist economy, which is what Germany remained.

What must be kept in mind, however, is the complex and confused state of the art world at that time, which made political distinctions less clear-cut than they appear retrospectively. There was, for one thing, still a difference between the November Group's unbending belief in the revolutionary nature of expressionism no matter what the political outcome and the Working Council for Art's constant efforts to adopt new strategies in the face of political setbacks, opposing first imperial and then SPD art policies. Moreover, artists often received contradictory signals as the process unfolded. Who could have predicted that the promotion of expressionist art in *To All Artists!*, for example, would be utilized so successfully to buttress SPD claims to progressive art policies? Even the eclecticism of *Yes! Voices of the Working Council for Art* succeeded in emptying the discussion of art and revolution of its politically inflammatory content, effectively neutralizing it. The reconciliation of disparate political viewpoints in these publications seemed, in the end, adequate proof of a democratic forum for the arts. Further complicating the picture was the mixed political reception accorded to expressionist artists from both the left and the right. Their economic success (at least after June) had to be defended, on the one hand, against charges of cooptation. On the other hand, the hostile response to the November Group rooms at the annual salon in 1919, or the rabid denunciations by the DNVP and DVP in the Prussian Provincial Parliament, seemed to confirm their revolutionary claims. Similarly, SPD policies toward the expressionists could be used to buttress their revolutionary rhetoric—or prove their antirevolutionary stance.

One piece of criticism stands adequately for the dilemma. It was published in Franz Pfemfert's *Die Aktion,* which after November 1919 stood closer to the KPD than ever before. After a year's absence of commentary on art and the revolution (most of the column inches were now devoted to the SPD "betrayal" of the revolution), *Die Aktion* printed an article on 29 November 1919 titled "Pictorial Arts and the Revolution." Written by a Dr. Heinrich Stern, it attempted to define a revolutionary art, but one which emphatically placed art at the service of the revolution. At this late date Stern still argued that expressionism was this art—if it fulfilled its potential to provide "direct access" to human emotions through form, a "direct access" denied under capitalism. But for Stern the majority of expressionist artists had not fulfilled this potential; their art "found no object," remained "utopian," "classless," "rooted with no movement in real life." Only by placing expressionist art at the political service of the revolution could it achieve its full potential:

> The revolution, though, will force the expressionist artist down to earth and impart to his style something of the heavy tread of the proletarian revolutionary masses. It will take away from him the dangerous longing for hothouse spirituality and will allow him to gain, through the consciousness of being a comrade-in-arms in the ranks of the revolutionary proletariat, the genuineness of feeling after whose expression he strives.[256]

But if Stern confidently postulated expressionism as the art of the revolution, and believed that the proletariat would come to support it, he was nevertheless at a loss to specify just how it was to change. Typical of much of the critical writing on expressionism and revolution, he cited no works of contemporary German artists who approached his ideal. His formula, like that of so many others, remained abstract. Did forcing the artist down to earth mean a personal political commitment to proletarian revolution? Did lending his style "something of the heavy tread of the proletarian revolutionary masses" mean a change in the way that art was supposed to look? These questions were left unanswered.

DRESDEN 3

November–April: Revolution or Reform?

Saxony, of which Dresden was the capital, was historically one of the most significant socialist strongholds in Germany. In the last Reichstag election before the war, nineteen of twenty-three Saxony constituencies returned socialists.[1] Yet relatively little attention has been paid to the history of socialism in Dresden and even less to the revolution there. Those accounts that do exist are more tendentious defenses of the communist party than histories documenting the actual course of events. The firebombing of the city in the Second World War and the attendant destruction of archival materials make the task of reconstructing the actions of artists during the revolution even more difficult. Still, differences from events in Berlin become apparent almost immediately, differences which have to do both with the previous history of expressionist art in Dresden and the course of the revolution in Saxony.

In Dresden, the unity that characterized the "people's revolution" in Berlin was threatened almost from the start. The rival socialist parties did not immediately join together. Rather, on 9 November two rival workers' and soldiers' councils declared themselves governing bodies in Dresden, one dominated by the SPD, the other by the USPD.[2] Although one day later they merged and established parity in the leadership (despite a clear SPD majority in the councils), by 16 November radical USPD leaders led by Otto Rühle resigned after their proposals, which included arming the proletariat and immediate socialization, were rejected.[3] Council elections on 24 November resulted in forty-seven seats for the SPD and only three for the USPD. In late December Rühle and his followers helped found the Communist Party in Dresden.

In contrast with the local Dresden soldiers' and workers' councils, the USPD overwhelmingly dominated councils elsewhere in Saxony.[4] Representatives of these councils elected Richard Lipinski, the Leipzig USPD leader, former Reichstag deputy, and outspoken critic of the SPD, chairman of the Provisional Council of People's Representatives for Saxony.[5] Thus while the SPD dominated the local Dresden government, the rival USPD controlled the provisional provincial government, seated in the same city. This discrepancy—a more radical provincial government, a more moderate city government—was to influence the formation of the artists' councils in Dresden and where they looked for support and encouragement.

By 16 November two rival artists' councils had already met in Dresden, which posed the alternatives of radical change and moderate reform. One was called the Provisional Revolutionary Council of Artists and the second, more simply, the Council of Artists. The first demanded a new economic footing for the arts and proclaimed "death to all the old academic systems."[6] The other "greeted the socialist republic"[7] in its first public meeting. Walter Gasch, a relatively unknown 32-year-old artist returning from two and one-half years at the front, became the primary spokesman for the Provisional Revolutionary Council.[8] (Gasch later became a prominent figure in the Dresden art world under the National Socialists.) At a well-attended meeting he demanded the overthrow of the academy, reform of exhibition policies, abolishment of the Academic Council governing artistic affairs in Dresden, control of state funds for art by the Provisional Revolutionary Council, and guarantees of a minimum income for all artists. In place of the capitalist "parvenu" art patron he suggested an alliance with the "people." As reported in the SPD *Dresdner Volkszeitung*, Gasch's style was that of the revolutionary firebrand: "Down from the thrones with the old autocratic art popes! Down with all academicism! . . . Away with all medals and secret titles!"[9] At the same meeting, another speaker was greeted with tempestuous applause when he declared that a complete reorganization of economic and social relations was a necessary prerequisite for the reform of art. He continued, "It is no honor for artists that they left it to the workers and soldiers to overthrow existing conditions. Artists would not forget what they had achieved for them!"[10] Unlike artists in Berlin, the speaker did not assume that a revolution in art had preceded and prepared the ground for political revolution, but rather the other way around.

Meanwhile, the Council of Artists, denounced by some in the Provisional Revolutionary Council as a clique, released its first public statement on 19 November:

[We] greet the new socialist free state and the united German republic which is forming . . . [We] hope that the reorganization and liberation from brutal powers will at the same time purify the world from the materialism of the past epoch and thereby will also make art more intimate and sublime. The assembly . . . views itself as spokesman and essential representative of Dresden artists, all the more as the impetus for it came from the younger artists, and as it contains no personality that is not willing to keep in step with the artistic youth and with all demands of the time. The artists assembled here will never be the hiding place of an artistic or other reaction.[11]

Their model for art was intimate and sublime, not public and practical. Nor did the group elaborate any specific demands, either political or artistic, but rather claimed legitimacy from the cooperation of the younger Dresden artists and vaguely hinted at progressive politics. Like the Working Council for Art in Berlin, the Dresden Council of Artists at its inception represented a broad spectrum of the Dresden art world, from the academy professors Otto Gussmann, Otto Hettner, and Robert Sterl to the expressionists Conrad Felixmüller and Oskar Kokoschka. Paul Adler, the Fontane prize-winning author with ties to the expressionist camp, was named business leader of the group. Perhaps because the Provisional Revolutionary Council nowhere mentioned the new art, the expressionists were more attracted to the Council of Artists.

Almost immediately efforts began to merge the two groups. Gasch prepared a program for discussion at a 5 December meeting of all Dresden artists' groups that insisted, among other things, on financial assistance for artists returning from the front, social welfare insurance for artists modeled on that for civil servants, increased government spending on art, election of a unified artists' council, reorganization of competitions and exhibitions, reform of art schools, and protection of public monuments and collections.[12] Many of these demands centered on economic questions and addressed the growing ranks of the art proletariat. On 14 December, efforts to merge the two groups were successful, and the Provisional Revolutionary Council joined representatives of all Dresden artists' associations in creating a new unified Council of Artists.[13] Gasch's more radical demands, however, were no longer in evidence. In fact, a secret report to the mayor of Dresden several months later insisted the new unified council "comprises *not* pre-eminently the extreme elements; rather, their efforts from the beginning were to create a counterweight to the radical intentions and proclamations of . . . Gasch's group which emerged in the first days of the revolution. This radically oriented group was, as it seems, taken into the Council of Artists by an adept counter-move of its founders."[14]

When the new Council of Artists drafted its provisional statutes, Gasch's economic concerns were not even addressed. In response to the problem of the art proletariat, the group did not propose a guaranteed income for all artists, but sought rather to limit the number of artists, first by excluding craftsmen from the Council of Artists, and second by establishing stringent membership requirements, including having participated in at least two juried exhibitions.[15] These two elements alone distinguished the Council of Artists from the Working Council for Art in Berlin, among whose most adamant demands had been an end to juried exhibitions and an emphasis on the handicrafts. Further, the new unified council had little to say about existing art institutions; for example, it proposed only to enlarge the Academic Council governing the academy. This was reform rather than revolution, consensus politics rather than confrontational tactics. The eleven-man governing committee of the new Council of Artists reflected the broad spectrum of support, from the academy professors Otto Gussmann and Otto Hettner to the expressionists Conrad Felixmüller and Otto Schubert.[16]

The ground for this cooperation had been prepared well before November 1918. Unlike Berlin, where the Association of Berlin Artists and even the Berlin Secession had at times blocked participation by expressionist artists, the Dresden art establishment had long been more forthcoming in its relationship with the avant-garde. The academy had long ago accepted impressionism, and the liberal Artists' Union, to which many of the academicians belonged, included in its annual exhibitions during the war relatively unknown young expressionists such as Felixmüller, Constantin von Mitschke-Collande, and Peter August Böckstiegel, along with the *Brücke* painter Max Pechstein.[17] The consolidation of the artists' councils was also not surprising given the political climate in Dresden. A strong leftist political opposition never established itself in the city and, therefore, offered no political base, whether real or imagined, for a more radical group. And it was unclear what support, if any, could be expected from the more radical provisional government of Saxony.

Only in early January did the provisional government indicate its position on the institutional reorganization of the arts. The USPD leader Richard Lipinski, by virtue of taking over the portfolio of the interior ministry, now became a member of the Academic Council in Dresden, which supervised the academy and advised on state purchases of art.[18] On 4 January he wrote to the Council, which had been the target of criticism in the years before 1918 for its conservative policies, particularly in purchasing art. Although he did not propose the immediate dissolution of the Academic Council, an action favored in November by Gasch's group, he suggested that substantive reform of both the Academic Council and the academy might well be in order. Asking its members to clarify their positions, he briefly outlined his own and distinguished between two types of demands made by artists. The first "are in part economic, and aim at an assurance of the economic existence of the artist; to that extent only the question will arise for the state whether, and in what way, *self-help* of the artist—as it say develops in the Artists' Aid League—can be furthered and perhaps . . . supported."[19] Lipinski thereby envisaged no financial support for artists along the lines proposed by the Provisional Revolutionary Council of Artists. On the other hand, he favored a more thorough examination of "art-political" demands that challenged the authority of the existing art institutions, citing as the two most urgent areas for reform the academy and the Academic Council. For the rest, he criticized the existing institutions for discriminating against the "most viable contemporary art efforts"[20] and endorsed self-governance by artists. In this he went beyond the modest demands of the new Council of Artists.

One week later Lipinski was no longer in office. On 10 January the League of Red Soldiers organized a mass rally at the Sarrasani Circus in the Dresden Neustadt that was attended by more than five thousand people. It turned violent when participants marched on the SPD *Dresdner Volkszeitung* building on Wettiner Platz. Otto Rühle, now the leader of a group of syndicalist-oriented independent communists,[21] had warned at the rally against the march on the SPD newspaper headquarters, which had already been occupied by the military for several days. Although the marchers were unarmed, Saxony government troops opened fire, killing fourteen and wounding fifty. Rühle and ten other KPD leaders were arrested, and all KPD gatherings were temporarily banned in the city. The three USPD members of the Saxony government resigned their positions in protest, basically renouncing political responsibility.[22] These events radicalized a few expressionist members of the Council of Artists; still, the more moderate consensus-oriented reform movement maintained the upper hand in the Dresden art world.

Although the expressionist artists were well represented in the Council of Artists, late in January several of them decided to establish their own separate organization, which they called the Secession Group 1919. The choice of name was telling: the association was not with the council movement or with the revolution, but with a long line of secession movements in the German art world beginning in 1892. The driving force behind the group was the 22-year-old expressionist painter Conrad Felixmüller, the son of a factory blacksmith, who had already achieved considerable success as an artist after leaving the Dresden academy in 1915. In later years he often styled the founding of the group as an outgrowth of his own political commitment to the Communist Party, which he joined sometime in 1919. In a retrospective letter in 1971, for example, Felixmüller claimed he wanted to convince his fellow expressionists "that it was now necessary to be organized in the most determined party, namely the KPD."[23] Similarly, in an unpublished autobiography he described his attempt to ally the Secession Group 1919 with "political organizations"—although here he deleted from an earlier draft the statement that it was tied to the KPD.[24] Felixmüller had participated in the 10 January protest demonstration in Dresden, recording the event months later in a woodcut, a lithograph, and a painting. Yet the statutes for the Secession Group 1919 drafted by him only nineteen days later certainly betrayed no partisan political commitment. Jotted hastily on the back of a leaflet from the Socialist Group of Intellectual Workers, to which Felixmüller also belonged, they read in part:

> 1. The Secession "Group 1919" is composed of a number of artists who have in mind for their art ideal undertakings, which necessarily separates them, and their art, from previous artists. Fundamental principles are: Truth—Brotherhood—Art. The elan of the time has produced the group, and the coming [elan] can destroy it: we will contribute in that we will prepare the way for those who come, because we are the way already.
>
> 2. New members can only be admitted by unanimous vote of all of the group; decisive in every case is courage and the inner urgent conviction which speaks to us from the works of the applicant. It is not permitted to belong to the Dresden Artists' Union; membership in out-of-state groups only by common decision. . . .
>
> 4. Exhibitions in Dresden will only be organized as a group; in special cases exceptions can be made by resolution. All members of the group will jury [works] together.[25]

These statutes, along with the name of the group, suggest it was originally conceived as an exhibition association along the lines of the established secession movements in Berlin and Munich, intended to promote expressionist art in Dresden. Nowhere did Felixmüller mention the revolution, economic reorganization of the arts, contact with the "people," or even reform of art institutions. Nor did he include any of the ubiquitous catchphrases of the revolution ("Proletarian, intellectual worker, unite!") that appeared on the verso of his draft for the Secession Group statutes. In fact, the statutes' bureaucratic rules and regulations, along with restricted, juried exhibitions suggested continuity rather than a break with the past. Of the five artists who signed the statutes along with Felixmüller, three of them were currently students at the academy: Otto Schubert, twenty-seven years old; Wilhelm Heckrott, twenty-nine years old; and Otto Dix, twenty-eight years old. They were joined by the 35-year-old Constantin von Mitschke-Collande, a former student at the Dresden academy, and the Lithuanian Lasar Segall, twenty-eight years old, who had studied at the Berlin and Dresden academies. Also signing the statutes was the architect Hugo Zehder. Added to the group shortly thereafter were Felixmüller's brother-in-law, Peter August Böckstiegel, a student for two years at the Dresden academy; Otto Lange, another former academy student, now a teacher at the School for Arts and Crafts in Bromberg (and, at forty, the oldest member of the group); and the sculptress Gela Forster, daughter of the well-known architect Bruno Schmitz and the only woman in the group.

The radical reputation of the Secession Group rests largely on Felixmüller, the most committed of its members politically, who sought to balance his communist sympathies with his devotion to expressionist art. Well before 1919 he had perceived tension between these two, and by 1920 he considered them to be in open conflict. As he wrote in a thinly veiled autobiographical statement for *Die Aktion* in 1920:

> The proletarian son [Felixmüller] was promoted, patronized, and succeeded in the "upper social class" which took him up and made him, the talented one, their artist . . . The previously unknown luxury . . . , the discussions of "the new poetry," "abstract art," "expressionism," staggered the rising son of the poorest, hard-working people . . . , so that in the midst of the "bourgeois" he sank in art . . . With that the proletarian son betrayed his origins and became an artist . . .
>
> In this time of ecstatic enthusiasm the war broke out . . . Visionary he saw the stooped masses of the entire world in a struggle for their existence; he saw them now also in the war as a mass, as cannon-fodder. Here he felt again like one of them, as a comrade-in-arms . . . felt as a traitor and rebelled . . . Each day and each hour distanced him from the "upper" [class], which he saw and hated as criminals . . . ; hated just like the artistic bluff in contemporary art, which now tortured him and appeared as a shame . . . His will was against the war; fervently he refused military service . . .
>
> He opposed himself to the moloch of war and militarism, to the district commanders and psychiatrists . . . , and endured with strong silence and strong, resolute will imprisonment and confinement to a mental asylum . . .
>
> At this time a secret league existed, primarily consisting of literati. They discussed all through the nights. They made anarchistic plans, revolutionary poems, passed around forbidden texts, wanted to support refusal of military service and help prepare strikes. Finally the thing ended as a literary venture,

became a fine gesture which remained empty, became snobbish. That was the break . . .

As is generally known, the revolution was betrayed and bloodily suppressed . . . Crimes against brave revolutionaries depressed Pönnecke [Felixmüller] so much that he ceased to work. It was clear to him: there is no other task than to be a revolutionary . . . If the proletariat has the political power, the power that it needs to develop itself, it will create from this tradition of struggle and of final victory its culture and its art: the art of simple men, devoid of luxury; the art of love, of human relation.[26]

In this text, Felixmüller resolved the conflict between art and politics by seemingly opting for the latter; in reality, however, the choice was not as clear-cut for him before 1920, when he tried to reconcile the two, or at least believed expressionist art could be politically progressive. His autobiographical account was part truth, part fiction. Felixmüller had indeed become a successful artist, but not before the war, as his account would have the reader believe, only during it, as part of the upsurge in the market for expressionist art. His radicalization, like his success, coincided with homefront war weariness late in 1916. Although he was introduced to Franz Pfemfert in 1915, it was not until February 1917 that he broke with Herwarth Walden's apolitical *Der Sturm* and began to contribute graphics to the anti-war *Die Aktion.* Among his contributions was a portrait sketch of the socialist leader Franz Mehring, just released from prison.

Sometime in 1917, probably around May, Felixmüller was drafted.[27] His autobiographical account of 1920 suggested that he became a draft-resister, resulting in imprisonment and confinement to a mental asylum. These claims may have been exaggerated; he apparently performed some sort of alternative service as a military hospital orderly in Arnsdorf, where the mental asylum had been converted into a hospital.[28] His experiences there, however, intensified his opposition to the war and found their outlet not only in *Die Aktion,* but in the "Expressionist Working Group of Dresden" (*Expressionistische Arbeitsgemeinschaft Dresden*), a group that, working out of Felixmüller's atelier, not only promoted expressionist poetry, but also circulated among its members Spartacist letters and the resolutions of the Grunewald Conference. This was the combination of "anarchist plans" and "revolutionary poems" to which the artist referred in 1920. Felixmüller also became active in the journal *Menschen,* which promoted the ideas of the Expressionist Working Group, an amalgam of pacifism, radical politics, and a belief in the potential of the new art to transform humankind. The editors were careful to distinguish their effort politically from the two best known expressionist journals: "Far from all infatuation in ecstatic rapture, the struggle against self-sufficiency is taken up; no more flight into another land that cultivates fantastic-poetic mirages, no storm of actions ["Sturm von Aktionen"] that break down in poisonous polemics of resentment, but joint attack, challenge, and promise."[29] They repudiated any spiritual comfort for the miseries of war proclaimed for the new art in the apolitical *Der Sturm,* as well as Franz Pfemfert's intransigent personal politics in *Die Aktion,* which deterred united action.[30] Among Felixmüller's anti-war contributions to *Menschen* were a text and a lithograph prepared for the May 1918 issue. In "Military Hospital Orderly Felixmüller XI Arnsdorf," the artist described a dream in which he identified himself with those who had lost their lives and limbs during the war. In an indictment of those who had not prevented the war and allowed it to continue, he pleaded: "All [the wounded and mad] would immediately be healthy and happy if one said to them: 'the war is over.' "[31] In the accompanying lithograph, *Soldier in the Lunatic Asylum* (fig. 3.1), the return address on the envelope the soldier clutches reads "Felixmüller." The other hand grasps the imprisoning bars as the artist identifies with those whose salvation he demands. Although Felixmüller in 1920 reported that the Expressionist Working Group ended as an empty, snobbish literary venture, his affiliation with its journal *Menschen* continued well into 1919.

Simultaneous with his anti-war activities, Felixmüller began to meet with financial success in an art market heated by war profits. By 1918 the Dresden dealer Emil Richter signed him to a contract for his graphics promising 1,200 marks per year (the contract was soon extended for three more years).[32] He also found patrons in the Elberfeld banker August Freiherr von der Heydt, the sculptor Bernhard Hoetger, and the Wiesbaden collector Heinrich Kirchhoff, the latter of whom signed a 1918 contract of first refusal for his paintings, assuring Felixmüller another 3,000 marks per year.[33]

With the revolution, Felixmüller began the transition in his art and writings from anti-war outrage to sympathy with the revolutionary events. In his own personal politics he moved steadily toward the left. He confided his antipathy for the SPD and his disappointment at the failure of the revolution in a January 1919 letter to his brother-in-law Böckstiegel, who had not yet returned from the front:

> A worse military dictatorship than before 9 November rules. The heroes of the revolution sit again in fortresses; the workers in Berlin and other cities have attempted armed rebellions, but after initial splendid victories (all newspapers, arsenals, police headquarters, market-halls, railway stations) were clubbed down by (!) front soldiers. Russian comrades supplied the workers money and

> weapons, fought with them—now they are arrested, shot; Liebknecht and Rosa Luxemburg are also dead! Here in Dresden there was also machine gun fire, on proletarians and soldiers who were demonstrating; our comrades were arrested; fourteen dead, sixty wounded—I escaped with my life. The proletarian bleeds like never before—the bourgeois rejoices.[34]

The problem for Felixmüller was how to resolve his political commitment with his participation in the Dresden Secession Group 1919. At

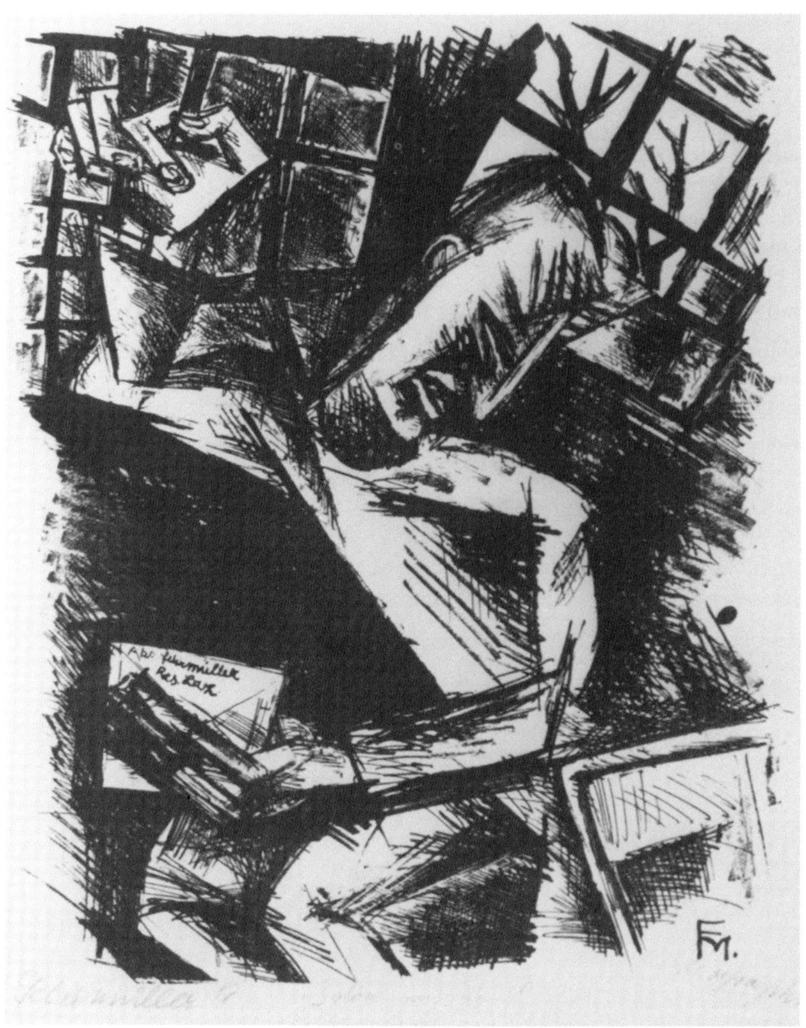

3.1 Conrad Felixmüller, *Soldat im Irrenhaus (Soldier in the Lunatic Asylum)*, 1918. Lithograph, 40.5 x 31 cm. Photo courtesy of Titus Felixmüller.

its founding the aims of the group were for the most part undefined. If Felixmüller had conceived it as a radically oriented group politically, it was nowhere evident in the group's scarce public statements, including a March circular that claimed little more than artistic ascendency through rejection of past art and an emphasis on individual expression. The question was whether the 22-year-old artist could press his political views on its members. Yet it was not Felixmüller who created a public profile for the group in its early months, but instead the *Neue Blätter für Kunst und Dichtung,* a publication of the Emil Richter Gallery.

The *Neue Blätter* had begun publication the previous May under the editorial guidance of Hugo Zehder, an unemployed architect turned editor who was one of the cofounders of the Secession Group 1919. It promoted a broad range of expressionist art featured at the Richter gallery, including the work of Felixmüller, whom Zehder praised in the July 1918 issue as the only legitimate inheritor of the "disturbing, oppositional" *Brücke* heritage in Dresden.[35] With the revolution the journal initially promoted the ideas of the Socialist Group of Intellectual Workers, another of the countless intellectual councils established throughout Germany in the early days of the revolution. The stated goal of the group was to influence "through their social situation and their ideology" that segment of the bourgeoisie which leaned toward socialism, as well as "intellectual workers" in general.[36] Unlike the workers' and soldiers' councils, the Socialist Group addressed itself not to the working class, but to the middle class. That the group embraced socialism as a conciliatory doctrine that united, rather than divided, all classes was clear from an early pamphlet, on the verso of which Felixmüller had written the statutes of the Secession Group:

> What is socialism not? . . . Socialism is not the abrogation of individualism . . . Socialism is not the rule of a class. The victory of the working class is the means (whose necessity we have seen) but not the aim of socialism. Victorious socialism brings . . . the dissolution of all class consciousness in a feeling of commonality and at the same time a feeling of freedom . . . Socialism according to its essence is not irreligious, for it demands the freedom and independence of religion.[37]

The "utopian socialism" of the group, as one of its members called it in the *Neue Blätter,* equally dismissed the SPD (indissolubly tied to capitalism), Christian socialists (mere social reformers), and the Spartacists (extremists endangering the revolution).[38] Both Zehder and Felixmüller initially joined the twelve-man propaganda committee of this Socialist Group, despite the latter's sympathy with the Spartacists.[39]

Zehder soon announced that henceforth the *Neue Blätter* would "place itself at the service" of the Secession Group 1919. In describing their art he wrote: "From deep reconciliation, following the struggle, a new beauty rises."[40] The key term was "reconciliation," which linked it to the ideology of the Socialist Group. Although for some the idea of reconciliation had been put in doubt by the street fighting in January and the withdrawal of the USPD from the Saxony government, it was nonetheless utilized to argue against the need for further revolt. In these circumstances the new art was now accorded an affirmative power, in which it alone provided the necessary impetus for social change. Zehder no longer dwelled on the "disturbing, oppositional" characteristics of expressionism, but on its affirmative, spiritual values. Also indicative was Zehder's use of the word "community" (*Gemeinschaft*), which increasingly in 1919 became ideologically redefined to signify the cooperation of all segments of society, over and beyond political divisions, to preserve national unity.

Nowhere did Zehder explicitly mention the revolution, nor did he elaborate any specific demands for the group—political or otherwise. Neither did the first comprehensive essay on the Secession Group 1919 in the March *Neue Blätter* written by Will Grohmann, a Dresden high school teacher who became the most important publicist for the group (and the most influential promoter of expressionist art in Germany after the Second World War). Grohmann's laudatory essay nowhere mentioned reform of the art world, the economic organization of the arts, or even the revolution. Rather, his terms—"transcendental content" and "heightened spirituality"—recalled the characteristics successfully used to promote expressionism during the war.[41] Historical relevance was of no importance for Grohmann, whose closing words—"without beginning and end"—typified his claims for the immanent development of modernist art for years to come.

Essays such as Grohmann's were undoubtedly designed to promote the young expressionists to an enlightened bourgeois public to which the Socialist Group also hoped to appeal. At least initially such efforts may have been successful. A January exhibition of expressionist graphics, in which at least four members of the Dresden Secession Group 1919 participated, resulted in sales for many of the better-known artists, including Erich Heckel, Max Pechstein, and Karl Schmidt-Rottluff from the Brücke, Paul Klee from the Blaue Reiter, and Felixmüller.[42]

By February, though, a small note of dissatisfaction with the pace of reform in the Dresden art world crept into the pages of the *Neue Blätter.* Zehder published the "Call of Russian Progressive Pictorial Artists to their German Colleagues" and applauded such reforms in Russia as the transformation of academies into artists' ateliers, the founding of a museum for contemporary art, the creation of state art workshops available to all, and the abolition of class distinctions in the arts (such as those between artist and craftsman)—all of which had as their goal bringing art to the masses. Although the *Neue Blätter* never explicitly stated that the art of the Secession Group was directed at the proletariat, it now believed that events in Russia were proof that those who prophesied the end of art with the disappearance of rich patrons were mistaken.[43] The article concluded: "While German artists' councils rather helplessly fumble about, Russia's young artists have resolutely embarked on (a new road)."[44] The complaint remained for the time being politically unfocused. Indeed, the *Neue Blätter* still maintained its utopian socialist stance by ascribing the success of modernist art in Russia to those who had "returned from scientific socialism to utopia."

If the inclusion of the Russian manifesto in the *Neue Blätter* signaled a dissatisfaction with the pace of institutional reform, the Dresden Secession Group nonetheless followed a path of compromise within the Council of Artists. Felixmüller, a member of the provisional executive committee of the council since December, was formally elected to the new executive committee in March. In an effort to gain more of a voice for expressionist artists, he set about regularizing the relationship between the Secession Group 1919, the Council of Artists, and the liberal Artists' Union. In negotiations with Otto Gussman, a professor at the academy and a member of the executive committee of the Artists' Union, Felixmüller declared his willingness to allow the Artists' Union to represent the "young art" on the Council of Artists—if it would share its building and exhibition space with the Secession Group 1919 (the arrangement never materialized).[45] Felixmüller also worked within the Council of Artists to assure adequate representation for the members of the Secession Group. A partial draft proposal suggests he at one time envisioned a two-thirds majority for the "young" artists on the executive council, although he probably eventually proposed parity.[46] Here he was more successful.

When the statutes of the Council of Artists were formalized in March, there was no longer even any mention of the "socialist republic":

> The Council of Artists was founded in order to expose the causes of grievances in the art life of the land, to investigate the possibilities for improvement, and to propose the ensuing reforms to the administrative authorities for their introduction. It is composed of artists of all directions and can already today be considered the representative body of the entire artistic profession.[47]

Among the subsections of the statutes were calls for protecting artworks from confiscation by the "enemy" and preserving monuments of "high artistic value" whose "removal could be demanded for political motives." Such an exemption of art from political challenge was very different from the Working Council for Art's iconoclastic calls for the removal of all war monuments. While the statutes promised to investigate academic reform and state exhibition policies, no specific measures were indicated. A section on art economics admitted that "socialism demands a limitation on personal property in artworks," but rather than calling for an end to the capitalist art market, the statutes concluded: "The interest of artists strives for a share in the increase in value of sold works, which expresses itself in the course of time in the fine art trade."[48] This was a demand frequently made at the time—that artists participate in the price increases of their works after having sold them. It was a far cry, however, from abolishing the entire market system. Two hundred fifty individuals and organizations were listed as members of the Council of Artists, with the executive committee split almost evenly between members of the academy and younger expressionist artists.[49] This must have seemed a major achievement to the young artists, particularly when compared to the situation of their colleagues in Berlin. There, expressionists still met with resistance from most institutions, and their antipathy for the policies of the government seemed to grow day by day. In Dresden, on the other hand, expressionist artists had achieved parity in the key artists' group, assuring them a strong voice in governance of the art world.

The expressionists must have been encouraged as well by the actions of the Academic Council and the Academy of Fine Arts. When the Academic Council responded to the inquiries of the interior ministry concerning reform (more than a month after Lipinski had resigned) they wrote, "The Academic Council cannot conceal that the reorganization of political relations will also have to react upon the competence and composition of the Academic Council itself."[50] They announced a number of changes in the governance of the academy, among them consulting students in the decision-making process and giving professors more control of the teaching program (including authority over students, a prerogative previously maintained by the Academic Council).[51] While they did not suggest eliminating the Academic Council, they did advocate expanding its membership to include two more academy professors, the head of municipal building in Dresden (the architect Hans Poelzig), and three independent artists, including the best-known expressionist painter in Dresden, Oskar Kokoschka.[52]

The academy, too, while not conceding any substantive changes, tried to encourage the expressionists. Unlike Berlin, the main cause for dissatisfaction in the Dresden art world was not the academy. Almost all the members of the Secession Group had received academic training, and three were still students there. Although Felixmüller could privately admonish his brother-in-law Böckstiegel in 1917 not to listen to his former teacher Otto Gussmann—"that old, timid ass,"[53] and Dix, enrolled at the academy, could complain in a letter to a friend that "the academicians are philistines,"[54] the Dresden academy was in no way as opposed to change as its Berlin counterpart. The professors set up committees to consider reform proposals, including one drafted by the students[55] and one by the Association of Dresden Women Artists, who demanded admittance and equal rights for women in the academy.[56] Significantly, the theme for the annual competition at the academy in 1919 was "Revolution." Although there were strong voices which opposed reform, they came mostly from outside the institution itself.[57]

Just how far the Dresden academy would go to integrate expressionism into its curriculum was seen at a 26 March 1919 faculty meeting. The professors voted unanimously to offer a teaching position to Max Pechstein.[58] This was to be the first appointment of an expressionist artist to a major academy in all of Germany. A departed native son, Pechstein was the least radical of the Brücke artists stylistically, given his inclination toward somewhat more classical figures and large decorative forms. Moreover, he had achieved a certain establishment reputation with his decision in 1912 to exhibit with the Berlin Secession rather than the New Secession. With this nomination, the academy signaled its intention to recognize expressionism in its teaching curriculum. Still, the suggested reforms in no way considered altering the basic structure of artistic training, for example, to emphasize the handicrafts or to unify the arts under architecture, as the WCA in Berlin had demanded.

The apparent success of the Dresden Secession Group 1919 culminated in their first exhibition, which opened on 5 April 1919 at the Emil Richter gallery on the fashionable Prager Strasse. The group had drawn up a contractual agreement with Richter valid for one year (1 April 1919–1 April 1920) that, among other things, assigned all entrance fees for the exhibition to Richter and stipulated that the dealer would receive forty percent from the sale of all graphics and watercolors, twenty-five percent from that of all paintings and sculptures.[59] Participating in the exhibition were Felixmüller, Böckstiegel, Heckrott, Lange, Mitschke-Collande, Segall, Schubert, Forster, and Dix. Missing was Oskar Kokoschka, who had accepted honorary membership in the group late in March.[60]

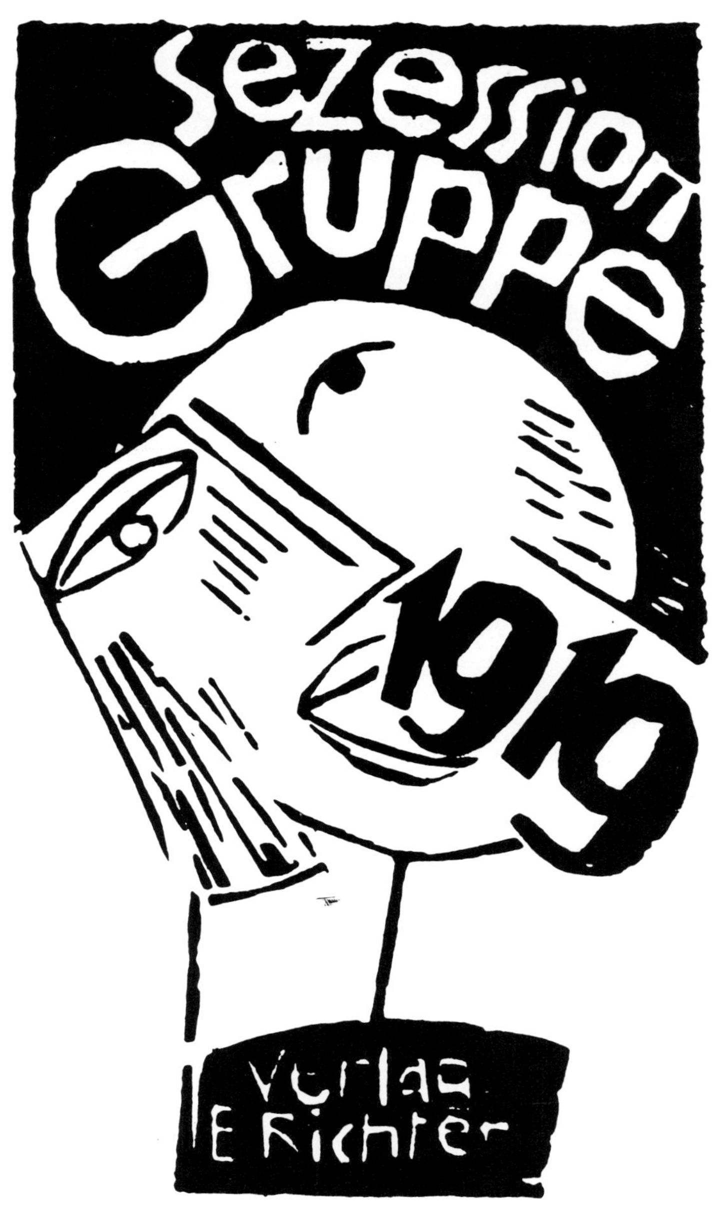

3.2 Conrad Felixmüller, cover of the Dresden Secession Group 1919 exhibition catalog, 1919. Woodcut, 26.5 x 15 cm. The Los Angeles County Museum of Art; The Robert Gore Rifkind Center for German Expressionist Studies; purchased with funds provided by Anna Bing Arnold, the Museum Acquisition Fund, and Deaccession Funds.

The catalog had on its cover a woodcut by Felixmüller (fig. 3.2), a rounded head, extremely simplified, whose open mouth seemed to announce the year—1919. Following a list of members was the March manifesto and then an essay by the expressionist author Walter Rheiner, in which he linked the formal characteristics of the new art both to oppositional destruction ("they fell that which falls") and to constructive rebirth ("a new cosmos forms, the spirit"). Significantly, he titled the essay "The New World." The works in the exhibition for the most part fell into certain predictable categories: nudes, nudes in landscapes, and portraits.[61] Although the show included a few timeless scenes of sorrow, including Segall's *Kaddish (Mourner's Prayer)* (fig. 3.3), a much more upbeat, optimistic imagery dominated, with regeneration of one kind or another a ubiquitous theme. In this category were oil paintings by Felixmüller (*Pregnant Woman in the Autumn Forest*), Heckrott (*Queen of May (Madonna)*), and Schubert (*In the Forest*) [fig. 3.4], along with Heckrott's woodcut *Harvest Dream*, Gela Forster's sculpture *Conception*, and even Otto Dix's erotic charcoal drawing of 1917, *Fruit Bowl.* The paintings by Heckrott and Schubert, with their elongated, angular nudes in landscapes and their expressive colors, were variations of Brücke imagery and suggested continuity with the expressionist heritage in Dresden.

The only works in the exhibition in clear-cut response to the revolution were by Constantin von Mitschke-Collande and Otto Dix. Mitschke-Collande exhibited six woodcuts, illustrations to Walter Georg Hartmann's short story "The Inspired Way," a parable devoted to "the dead, living, and future heroes of the legitimate revolution." Hartmann's story allegorically recounted from the perspective of a young soldier the political events in Berlin, from the proclamation of the revolution to the funeral of Karl Liebknecht. Hartmann's central concern was the question of whether violence was justified in the cause of revolution. In the story, the soldier experiences the betrayal of the revolution ("Is that your entire revolution, placing yourselves on the empty thrones?") and reluctantly takes part in the street fighting, in which he dies. His spirit cannot rest, though, and he travels the city observing the brutal suppression of unarmed "workers, poets, students, doctors, women and those in rags"; the capture of a revolutionary leader by three soldiers; his torture by an angry mob; and his death by shooting. Although clearly sympathetic to the revolutionary left, Hartmann envisaged a utopian resolution to the dilemma of armed resistance. The soldier's spirit confronts the three soldiers responsible for the death of the revolutionary leader, convinces them to repent, and instructs them to proselytize in the name of "love" and "human broth-

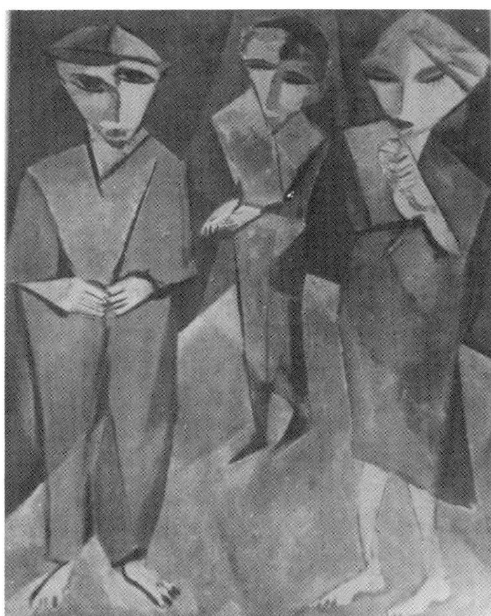

3.3 Lasar Segall, *Kaddisch (Totengebet)* [*Kaddish (Mourner's Prayer)*], 1917–18. Painting, 97 x 80 cm. Museu Lasar Segall, São Paulo.

erhood." At the funeral of the revolutionary leader, the soldier's spirit appears, and as the crowd admits they have erred in trying for "too distant a goal" too soon, the spirit admonishes them to "prepare humanity." As the throngs respond favorably, his soul is released and ascends to heaven, departing with the words: "the time is ripe." As political allegory, "The Inspired Way" argued against the need for further armed revolt to achieve the goals of the revolution.

Mitschke-Collande was, like Felixmüller, a member of the KPD. In his woodcut illustrations he featured not the revolutionary action, nor suppression of the revolutionary forces, but the implicit religious salvation promised in Hartmann's text. The cover illustration depicted a resurrecting nude figure, arms extended, head tilted upward, rising from the dark toward the light (fig. 3.5). His illustration *You Have Killed Your Brother* (fig. 3.6)—the phrase with which the spirit admonished the soldiers who had killed the revolutionary leader—combined the religious imagery of apocalypse and the promise of resurrection typical of expressionist religious imagery since 1917. Mitschke-Collande here combined scenes from Christ's crucifixion and the Revelation of John. At the top, two of the horsemen of the apocalypse (one indicated with the head of the horse and an arm holding a bow at the right; the other joining the rider of death and the rider holding the scales on the left) charge in from either side. Below, the soldiers, indicated by the steel helmet of the nearest figure, stand in the position of the tormentors of Christ, while the nude body of the slain leader lies in the position of Christ descended from the cross, surrounded by mourners. The final image, *The Time Is Ripe* (fig. 3.7), repeated the rising figure from the cover, now atop the sun in the heavens. In his woodcuts Mitschke-Collande extended expressionist religious imagery to provide the promise of salvation after the horrors of the revolution.[62]

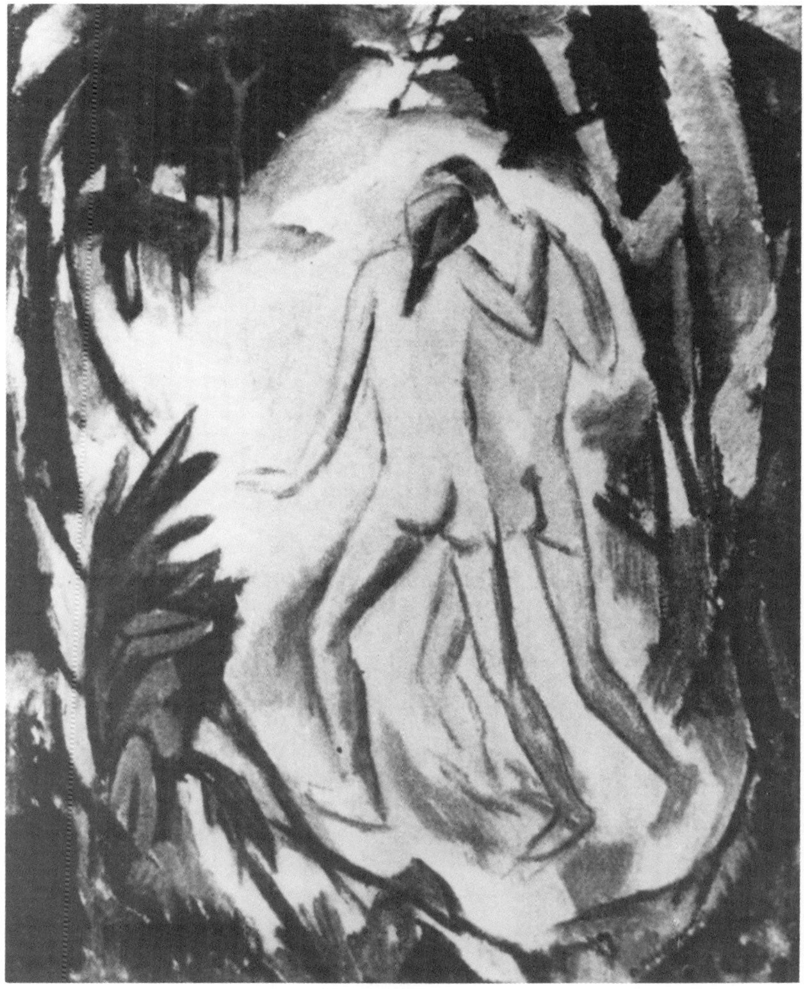

3.4 Otto Schubert, *Im Wald (In the Forest)*, oil on canvas, dimensions unknown.

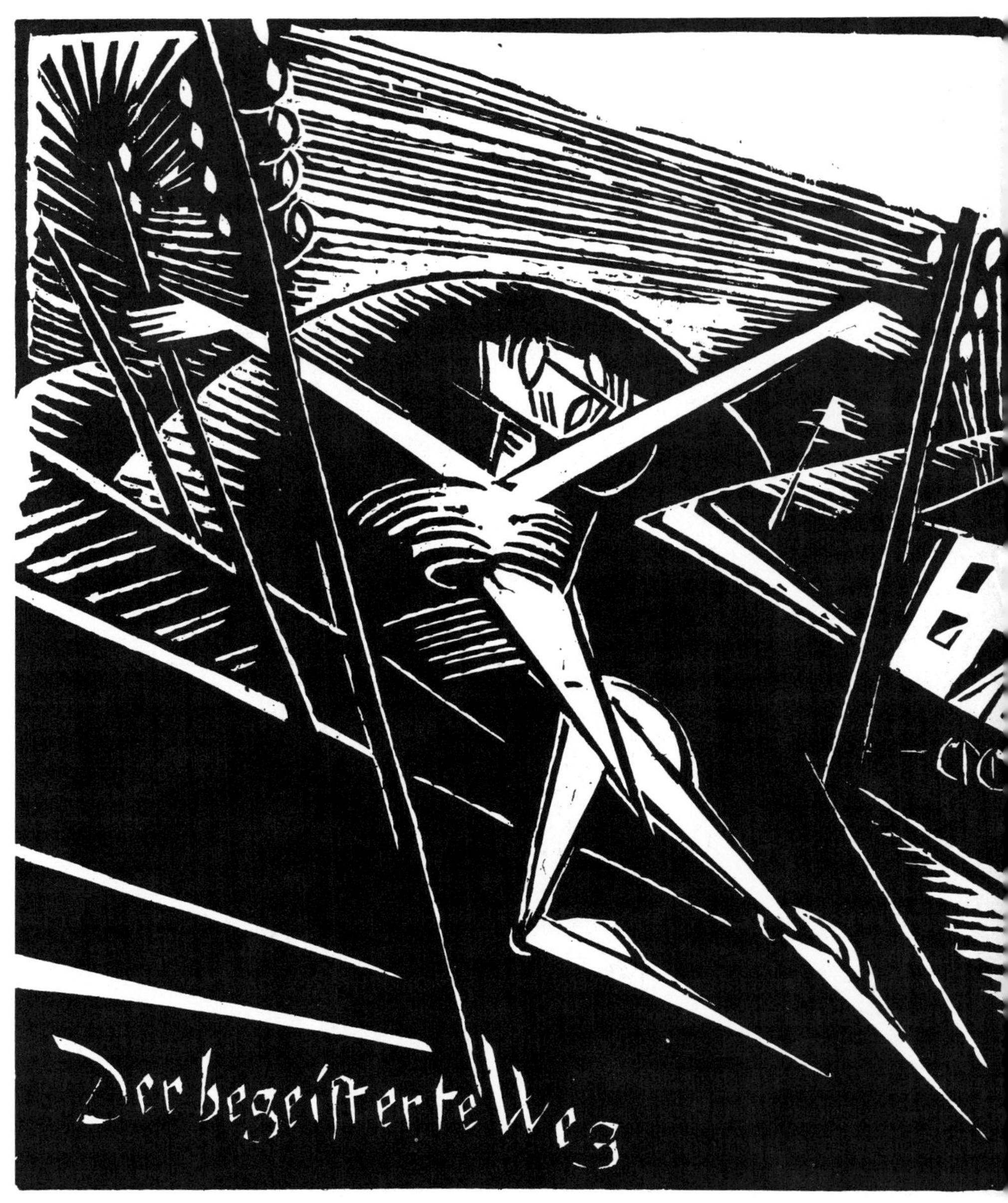

3.5 Constantin von Mitschke-Collande, *Der begeisterte Weg (The Inspired Way)*, plate 1 from *Der begeisterte Weg*, 1919. Woodcut, 34.3 x 29.8 cm. The Los Angeles County Museum of Art; The Robert Gore Rifkind Center for German Expressionist Studies.

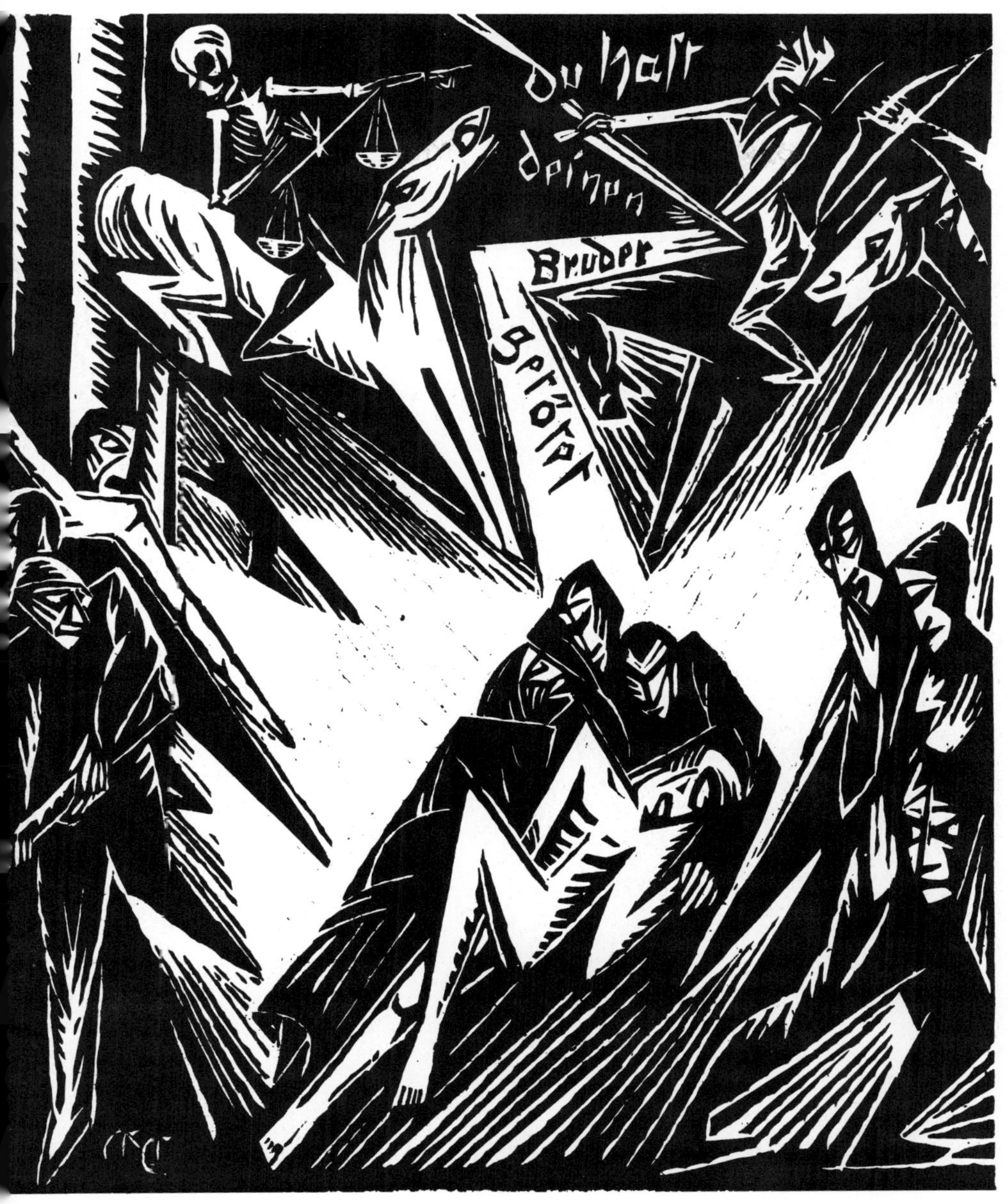

Constantin von Mitschke-Collande, *Du hast deinen Bruder getötet (You Have Killed r Brother)*, plate 4 from *Der begeisterte Weg (The Inspired Way)*, 1919. Woodcut, 34.5 .7 cm. The Los Angeles County Museum of Art; The Robert Gore Rifkind Center German Expressionist Studies.

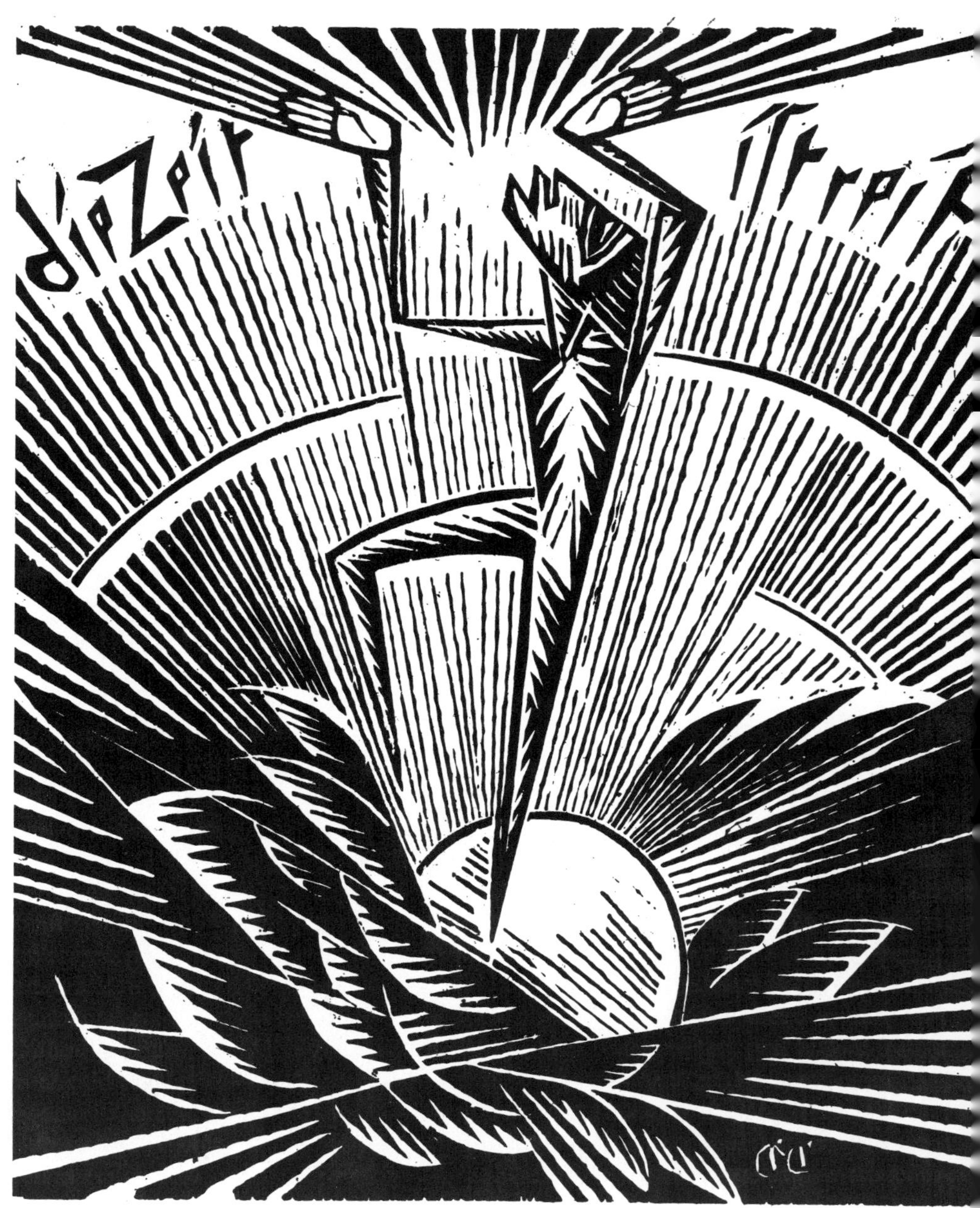

3.7 Constantin von Mitschke-Collande, *Die Zeit ist reif (The Time Is Ripe)*, plate 6 from *Der begeisterte Weg (The Inspired Way)*, 1919. Woodcut, 35.2 x 30 cm. The Los Angeles County Museum of Art; The Robert Gore Rifkind Center for German Expressionist Studies.

Also in the show was Otto Dix's *Felixmüller Family* (fig. 3.8), which depicted Felixmüller in the double role of revolutionary and family father. The two had met after Felixmüller saw Dix's work at the Arnold gallery and invited him to join the Secession Group 1919. Dix, like Felixmüller, came from a working-class background. Unlike his new mentor, though, Dix had enthusiastically volunteered for military service in 1914, serving at the front for most of the war as a machine gunner and later training as an airman. He eventually achieved the rank of master sergeant and received both the Iron Cross and the Friedrich-August medal after he was wounded by grenade fragments. At the end of the war he returned briefly to his parents' house in Gera, and then in February 1919 he resettled in Dresden and enrolled in the academy. The works that may have attracted Felixmüller to Dix were most likely his 1917–18 graphics of the war done in an expressionist style. Dix,

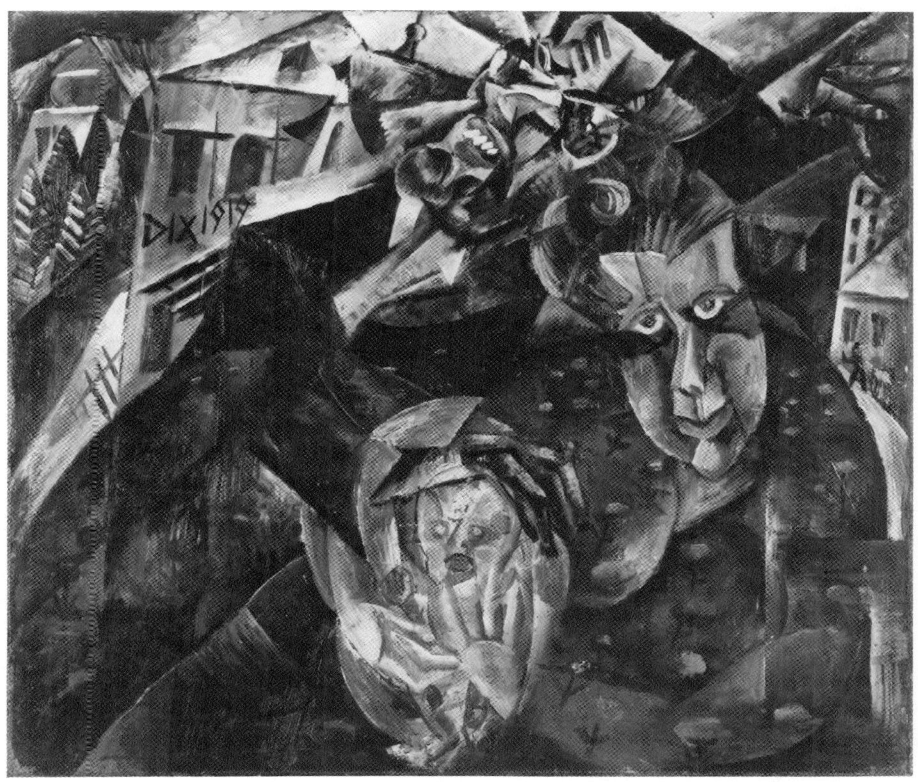

3.8 Otto Dix, *Familie Felixmüller (Felixmüller Family)*, 1919/10. Oil on canvas, 30 x 36 inches. The Saint Louis Art Museum, bequest of Morton D. May.

probably aware of the success of religious imagery in those years, had tried his hand at a number of drawings of apocalypse and resurrection. Felixmüller now commissioned the impoverished Dix to paint the portrait of his family, which stood in sharp contrast to Felixmüller's own family portrait in the show (fig. 3.9), where he depicted himself as solicitous father beside his wife Londa, who protectively held their child. Dix's portrait was a wild cubo-futurist depiction of Felixmüller, his wife, and child set against the streets of the Klotzsche suburb where they lived.

In general, the local Dresden newspapers responded favorably to the show, with any political discussion of expressionism virtually absent. The national-liberal *Dresdner Anzeiger* praised the effort, while softening any possible connection with the revolution by concluding that "all in all the exhibition shows that the storm of our days did not bring this creation as something . . . new to light, but the germ and beginnings began to develop already years before the war."[63] The connection to the present was thus discarded for an origin in the past. The Social Democratic *Dresdner Volkszeitung,* which in February linked the new art to the proletariat,[64] now no longer mentioned the public for this art.[65] None of the critics discussed Mitschke-Collande's woodcuts or Dix's portrait of Felixmüller. The show was an apparent critical success, based on the promotion of expressionism as an affirmative, spiritual art.

The expressionists in Dresden had played the game of consensus politics and could consider their efforts rewarded with their slow but steady integration into the institutional art world. This acceptance came with the confident projection of their art as part of an affirmative culture of reconciliation in journals such as *Neue Blätter* and in their first exhibition. Another Dresden art journal, though, briefly put forward another view of expressionism, one which tried to link it politically with the far left. Rather than gain widespread support among the expressionists, it essentially reflected the concerns of only one member of the Secession Group 1919—Conrad Felixmüller.

Although not formally tied to the Secession Group 1919, the journal *Menschen* conspicuously featured graphic contributions by its members. In November 1918 *Menschen* split into two different publications, one subtitled *Monday Paper: Politics, Public Life, Art, Culture,* and the other *Journal for New Art, Literature, Graphics, Music, Criticism, Politics.*[66] Both represented political views different from those put forward in the journal during the war. They were published after January by the 25-year-old writer Heinar Schilling, who also edited the *Monday Paper.* Schilling summed up the general political orientation of the

Monday Paper in an ecstatic declaration in the first advertising sheet: "O, what friend of mankind would not be a socialist?"[67] Schilling's socialism was defined only as an expression of the "spirit." In art, he took for granted the link between expressionism and socialism, with art assigned a pivotal role in changing human consciousness. This was a far cry from the savage anti-war rhetoric of the wartime journal and a

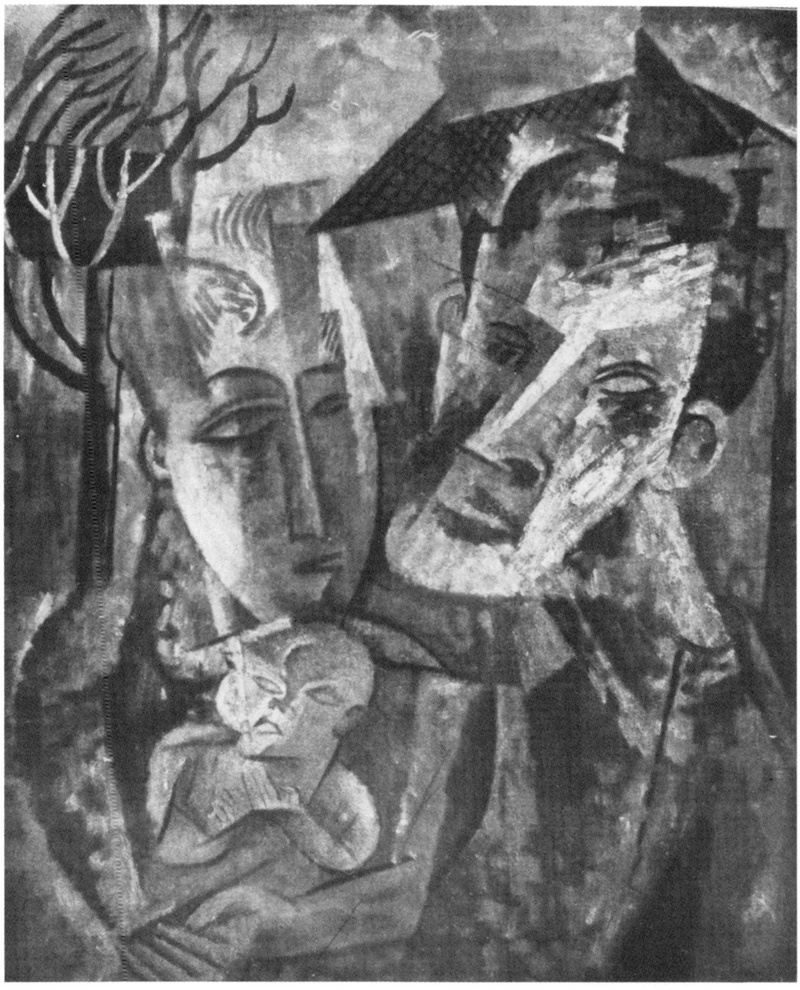

3.9 Conrad Felixmüller, *Familie (Family)*, 1918. Oil on canvas, 90 x 75 cm. Formerly in Gemäldegalerie, Dresden, now lost. Photo courtesy of Titus Felixmüller.

reversal of its skepticism about the spiritual in art as part of an escapist bourgeois culture.[68] Not surprisingly, the *Monday Paper* was also loosely affiliated with the Socialist Group of Intellectual Workers, to which Schilling, too, belonged.[69]

The art journal *Menschen,* though, cautiously moved to the left of the *Monday Paper* despite the fact that Schilling became its publisher (replacing Felix Stiemer) in January. This radicalization occurred under the editorship of the 24-year-old expressionist author Walter Rheiner, a friend of Felixmüller's and frequent contributor to *Die Aktion.* At first Rheiner, too, repeated the standard claims for the generalized revolutionary significance of expressionism. In his first issue as editor he posed as an alternative to materialism a "fundamental idealism," which, in art, he called expressionism and, in politics, "*a-national socialism,* which is demanded *unconditionally* and *radically, not only in the spirit, but in reality!*"[70] "A-national socialism" was probably a reference to Franz Pfemfert's attempt to form an "A-National Socialist Party" in Berlin. First announced in November 1918 in *Die Aktion,* the A-National Socialist Party was a brief—and unsuccessful—attempt by

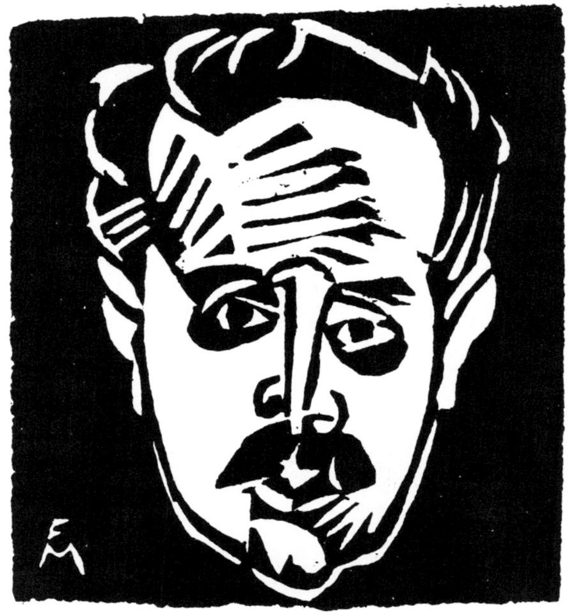

3.10 Conrad Felixmüller, *Karl Liebknecht,* 1916. Woodcut, 8.3 x 7.5 cm. Staatliche Museen zu Berlin, Kupferstichkabinett / DDR Nationalgalerie. Photo courtesy of Titus Felixmüller.

Pfemfert to organize a party that was politically close to the syndicalist International Communists[71] and may thus indicate a possible link between Rheiner's views and Otto Rühle's International Communists in Dresden.

After the use of Saxony government troops against demonstrating workers and soldiers in Dresden, the arrest of Otto Rühle, the ban on KPD meetings, and the murder of the communist leaders Karl Liebknecht and Rosa Luxemburg in Berlin, Rheiner took an outright leftist stance in *Menschen* and for a time decisively abandoned art for politics. Surrounding a woodcut portrait of Karl Liebknecht by Felixmüller[72] (fig. 3.10) in the 15 January issue was the following statement:

> Karl Liebknecht and Rosa Luxemburg were the only ones who held the flag of revolution high these four years. Today they were murdered by the measures of the "revolutionary" government. The beast triumphs over the spirit of socialism! The venal newspapers rejoice over 480 corpses and 1,000 wounded, fighters for an idea who are true to their convictions.
>
> HUMAN BEINGS!
>
> The government is guilty of multifarious murders! The human butchers of militarism are their hired executors. Honour and glory to their slain opponents! We bend down before them to the earth.
>
> Explain! Speak! Talk! Shout![73]

In the 15 February 1919 issue Rheiner again attacked the government for the murders of Liebknecht and Luxemburg and decried the "class justice in Berlin-Moabit" that condemned communists to prison while the murderers went free. Rheiner asked, "People, proletarians, workers! And you, the 'intellectual-workers-councils'! How much longer do you want to tolerate something like this?"[74] His blunt attack on Schilling's politics with his veiled reference to the Socialist Group of Intellectual Workers led to an open split between the two. In the 1 March issue Rheiner sarcastically announced that the word "politics" had been eliminated from the subtitle of the journal, since he and Schilling were so at odds, and that from now on all political contributions should be sent to the *Monday Paper.*[75] As if in defiance, though, he published the communiqué of the Russian revolutionary artists to their German colleagues. By the following issue Rheiner had resigned, replaced as editor by Schilling.

In only five issues Rheiner had not really succeeded in joining together radical politics and expressionism in any meaningful way. Except for Felixmüller's portrait of Liebknecht, none of the numerous expressionist graphics in *Menschen* bore any apparent relationship to the political texts they accompanied. Significantly, Felixmüller was the only Dresden expressionist to contribute to *Menschen* between January and March.[76] Still, the juxtaposition of the new art with texts taking an outright political stance sympathetic to the KPD seemed to confirm its revolutionary status and to promote its oppositional, rather than affirmative, spirit. By late March, though, the political tensions that had provoked Rheiner's outcry in *Menschen* had lessened significantly in Dresden. When on 2 March Otto Rühle called for a strike to protest the betrayal of the revolution, he found little response.[77] Even the intersocialist rivalry temporarily ended when on 23 March the USPD leaders Geyer and Lipinski rejoined the Saxony government.[78]

The episode in *Menschen* seemed a brief departure. More than almost anywhere else in Germany, the expressionists had gained concessions from the art establishment in Dresden with relative ease: Max Pechstein had been nominated to the academy, the Academic Council conceded the need for reform, students had gained a voice in the academy, and the first exhibition of the Secession Group 1919 was a critical success. But the political climate in Saxony soon grew radical once more, and in its wake some artists in the Secession Group, dissatisfied with the pace of reform, moved further to the left. As they did, the art establishment reciprocally began to warn against the revolutionary aspirations of the expressionists.

April–August: Dissatisfaction and Resistance

On 12 April 1919 several hundred soldiers and war cripples demonstrated at the war ministry in Dresden to protest a reduction of their allowances. When they elected a delegation to negotiate with the Saxony government, they were turned away. Several soldiers forced their way into the building, seized the war minister, tossed him into the Elbe, and shot him.[79] At the demand of the federal government in Berlin, the SPD leader of the Saxony government, Hermann Gradnauer, proclaimed a state of siege for all of Saxony. General Maercker and his federal and Freikorps troops entered Dresden the next day.[80] Leipzig, still a USPD stronghold with an active workers' and soldiers' council, refused to apply the state of siege. On 11 May the federal government used this refusal as formal grounds to intervene; federal and Freikorps troops under General Maercker entered Leipzig, and the city surrendered without a fight.[81] USPD and KPD leaders were arrested and their newspapers were banned.[82] These events soon spurred a return to a more radical rhetoric in the Dresden art world and to a closer questioning of the meaning of the revolution for expressionist art.

On 23 April, ten days after the imposition of the state of siege, the Academic Council wrote to the interior ministry warning that the Council of Artists should be recognized by the ministry only as long as it represented the entire body of artists of Saxony, and only as long as the "more moderate elements" prevailed in the group. They also argued against any official appointment of members of the Council of Artists to the Academic Council.[83] One week later, the interior minister Schmitt wrote to the Council of Artists. While he praised the formation of the group as an "important step forward," he also wrote that in order to maintain its "complete freedom," the Council should not be officially connected with any governmental body—thereby denying it representation on the Academic Council. Schmitt, following the Academic Council, apparently feared that the more moderate elements might not prevail in the group. Thus, he wrote to the Council of Artists that "no one will doubt that in no sphere is an over-extension of the democratic principle less suitable than in that of art."[84] This echoed the rhetoric and sentiment of the most conservative forces in the Dresden art world. Further, he warned that the Council of Artists would lose its influence if it submitted to the "one-sided dominion of particular directions," undoubtedly referring to the expressionists.[85] These letters pointed to a new resistance to reform on the part of the government.

Soon the *Neue Blätter* published the first far-reaching public criticism of the lack of reform in the Dresden art world. The May issue had already included two essays indicating a new political perspective on the arts reprinted from a Moscow journal published by Lunacharsky's commissariat. In them the author forthrightly admitted that "still nothing is known about art under . . . socialism," but nonetheless rejected all idealist notions of beauty, criticized artistic inspiration as a fiction, questioned the need for a separate class of artists, and refused potential bourgeois objections to the concept of an art for the masses. Under socialism, he concluded, a "higher taste will cease to be the privilege of a group of usurpers and become the property of the masses."[86] The identification between art and the proletariat expressed here had not been heard in Dresden since the early days of the revolution. Now, in June, Hugo Zehder questioned the achievements of art with the revolution. His reservations were apparent in an "Open Letter to the Ministers of the Republic of Saxony," which, however, recognized the legitimacy of the current government, challenged by the USPD and the KPD since the state of siege: "Through the will of the majority of the people and their parliamentary representatives you [government ministers] have been called to lead the reconstruction of the republic of Saxony." He continued:

> It is to be assumed that you view the young, progressive art as a cornerstone of the great building which you are thinking of erecting, for you do not have the intention to use old and already worn-out material for it. The repugnance . . . among the supporters of the New Art is strong . . . to the previously practiced system of bureaucratic tutelage, practiced by those unjustified to make judgments, and to the preference—which cannot be justified on any objective grounds—for an art which is no longer sustained by the rhythm of the present.[87]

Fully eight months after the revolution, Zehder apparently referred still to the old imperial arts administration. The measures upon which he now insisted, though, applied as much to the position of the interior ministry as articulated in its letter to the Council of Artists as to the imperial government. He advocated abolishing the Academic Council (whose very existence he now found "superfluous"), purchasing expressionist works for public collections, and appointing a "people's commissioner for art." He may also have implicitly criticized the Dresden Secession Group—with which he now had fundamental disagreements[88]—when he concluded: "The extremely rich proposals of the artists' councils which were formed in other places . . . (also the organizing activity of the commissariat for art in Russia) should also have served as a basis [for reform]."[89] He did not comment on the changes necessary in either politics or the economy to enact these reforms.

Zehder repeated many of the demands made by the Working Council for Art in Berlin. Missing, however, was any criticism of SPD policies, as well as any mention of the academy, the institution which came in for the harshest criticism from the WCA. The exemption of the academy from his attack may have been because of its concerted attempt to appoint an expressionist painter as professor. After a long period of negotiation, though, Max Pechstein declined the offer. Quickly, the faculty voted in July, with six in favor and four abstentions, to hire Oskar Kokoschka, who was backed by the students over other candidates.[90] The 33-year-old Kokoschka had studied at the Vienna school of arts and crafts and had worked at the famous Wiener Werkstätte, the pioneering Jugendstil studio of design. Since 1910 he had been a member of the Sturm circle, creating a stir with his expressionist portraits and provocative expressionist plays. In 1914 he volunteered into the Austrian cavalry and was seriously wounded. After a period of convalescence, he returned to the Italian front as an observer, but soon suffered shell shock. He spent most of the remainder of the war in a Dresden sanatorium, where he worked behind the scenes to secure an appointment to the academy.[91]

In proposing Kokoschka to the minister of the interior, the professors of the academy described his art and personality as rooted in

> that which one calls . . . "modern," in the problematical. Sensitive and spontaneous to the extreme in technique, exclusive in the direction of taste, his art is to be sure not accessible to everyone. However it contains in its remarkable and composed nature, in its ingenious lustrous coloration, its unusual mystical pensiveness, values that are lacking to the students in this form and that constitute a necessary and valuable complement to the rest of the faculty.[92]

The academy professors, in describing Kokoschka's art as "exclusive" and "not accessible to everyone," contradicted those who called for the creation of a new proletarian audience for expressionist art. Kokoschka's art had been described quite differently in the 19 January 1919 issue of *Menschen* (*Monday Paper*). There the expressionist writer Walter Hasenclever commented on the coincidence of the events in the streets with the opening of an exhibition of Kokoschka's work on the fateful day of 9 November 1918 at the Paul Cassirer gallery in Berlin:

> On these pictures one saw a range of people, again and again painted afresh with exciting tenacity, whose expression seemed to bind them in some kind of mysterious relationship with those who cried out on the street. It was as if a movement of the heads and hands on the canvas emanated to the great sites where the spectacle of the world came to pass . . . For the faces, which were confined in the chamber of horrors, today run about on the streets![93]

Hasenclever here forcefully reiterated the generalized claims about the anticipatory status of expressionist art, literally describing Kokoschka's art as an embodiment of the revolution.

Although Kokoschka's work could still engender outrage,[94] he was not all that controversial a candidate. Even the conservative *Dresdner Neueste Nachrichten*, while rejecting academic reform, had suggested him as a candidate for professor.[95] He was not among those who denounced academic training and, despite Hasenclever's essay, he had in no way openly supported the revolution. A lithograph titled *The Principle* (fig. 3.11), presumably dating from November/December 1918 but published only in 1919 in Paul Cassirer's graphic portfolio *Die Schaffenden*, attests to his attitude. It shows a woman's head in three-quarter view, a distortion of the French *Marianne*, the female personification of the revolution since 1848. A few strands of hair, the lip, and the right eye were tinted red, as well as an inscription in the base that changed the motto of the French revolution to read: "Liberty, Equality,

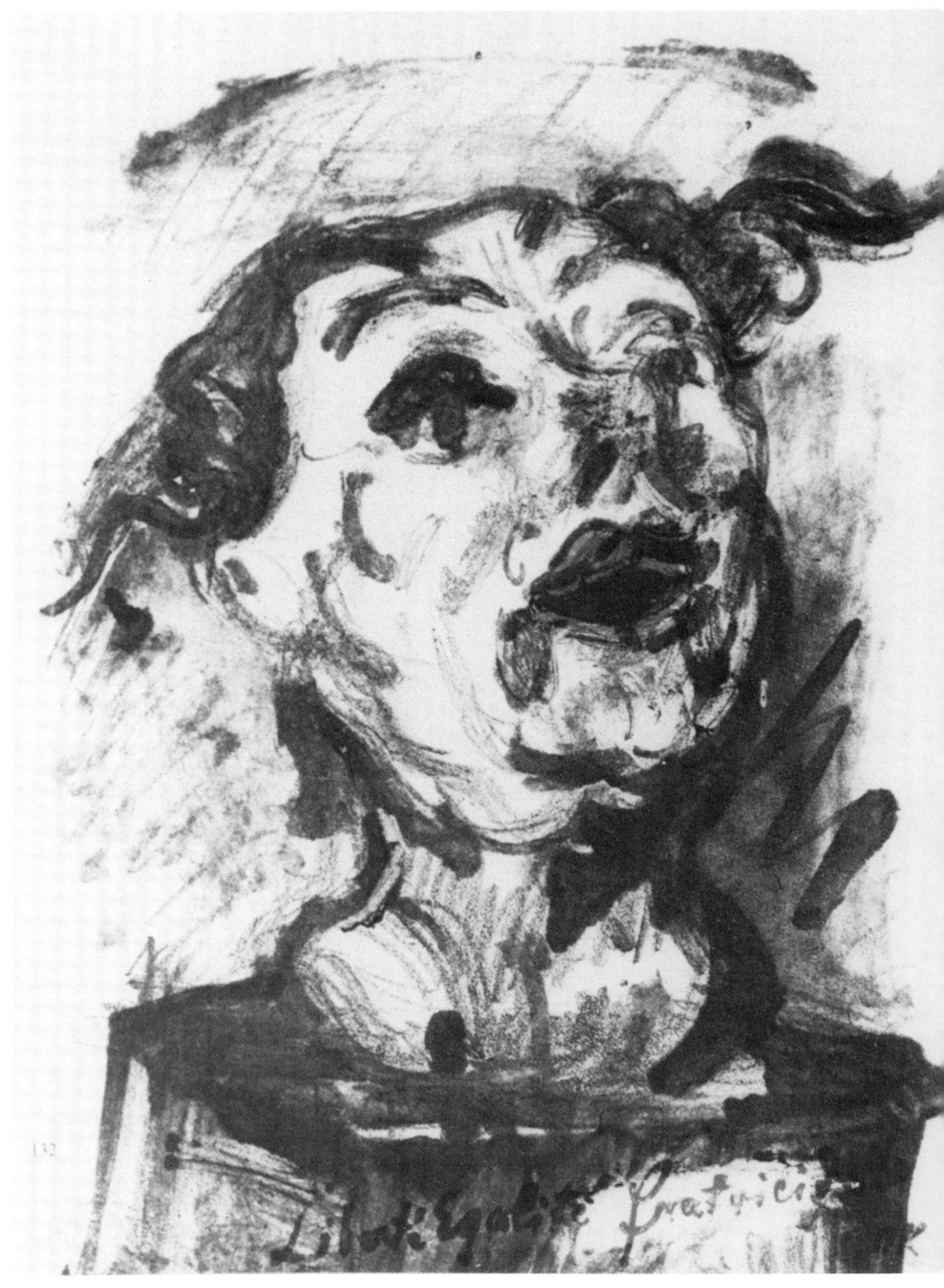

3.11 Oskar Kokoschka, *Das Prinzip (The Principle)*, 1918. Color lithograph, 34 x 24.5 cm. © 1988, copyright by Cosmopress, Geneva.

Fratricide." Since Kokoschka had at an earlier date drawn the same bust without the touches of red or the inscription, the impression was now of the artist smearing his earlier work with blood. Its 1918 date precludes any interpretation of the lithograph as a comment on the "fratricide" committed by the SPD after January and points much more to a reading that for Kokoschka the "principle" of revolution inevitably resulted in "fratricide." He may even have contributed a lithographic poster to the Association for the Fight Against Bolshevism in 1919.[96] Kokoschka was eventually approved and the Dresden Academy of Fine Arts had its first expressionist professor.

Instead of the academy, the primary target for the expressionist artists in Dresden became the museum. In July, Felixmüller and Lange, in the name of the Secession Group 1919, wrote a scathing attack on the administration of the Dresden Gallery that was printed in both the *Dresdner Neueste Nachrichten* and the *Dresdner Nachrichten*. At that time, the modern wing of the Dresden Gallery contained only one expressionist work by Max Pechstein, which, however, had been purchased not by the museum, but by a private support group.[97] Protesting the persistent exclusion of expressionist works from new acquisitions, they argued that the "people" had a right to be able to acquaint themselves with the new art. To this end the Secession Group had begun offering art courses to and working with an organization called the Dresden Worker-Art-Association. Lasar Segall wrote instructional guidelines for this group emphasizing spontaneous expression over technical expertise, a seeming rejection of academic standards and practices.[98] Felixmüller and Lange were no doubt angered when the Dresden Gallery failed to act on the rumored purchase of a painting by Segall from the Secession Group exhibition. Still, Felixmüller and Lange did not argue for fundamental reform of the administration of public museums or of the art market. It was not the system they blamed, but individuals. In fact, they held up the private collector of expressionist art as a model for how the state could acquire good art at a reasonable price. It was not enough, they wrote, that

> a few museum directors who until now offered very little or no interest in the new art now buy modern pictures. Does the understanding of modern art come so suddenly? We believe that fashion is conformed with only superficially and that there is no question that any kind of personal feeling prompts the valuation.[99]

They wanted instead to install one of their own at the Dresden Gallery and offered four candidates. Three of them had little or no museum experience. They were the art historian and critic Wilhelm Hausenstein, the socialist-leaning art editor of the *Münchner Neueste Nachrichten;* the art historian and critic Paul Erich Küppers, editor of the expressionist *Das Kestnerbuch* in Hannover; and Theodor Däubler, the expressionist poet and art critic, who had written on Paul Klee for the *Neue Blätter* in 1918. The only candidate with museum experience suggested by Felixmüller and Lange was Hans Friedrich Secker, director of the Provincial Museum of Arts and Crafts in Danzig, who probably appealed to them because of his interest in Gothic art and his experience in a museum featuring the crafts.

Almost immediately the *Dresdner Nachrichten* published an angry response to these proposals by the art historian Dr. Wilhelm Junius, who denied that the "people" wanted their museum to become a "playground for artistic experiments and extravaganzas." "The people," he wrote, would surely "pass the most derogatory . . . judgments on certain pathological abuses and childish symptoms of regression of the most modern and most revolutionary art."[100] Typically, the expressionists' fascination with the art of children and the insane was turned against them. Added to the list of derogatory terms was now "revolutionary." In any event, the Dresden Gallery continued much as it had before. Although the royal museums were renamed the "state collections," no personnel changes were made, and even the members of the gallery commission remained in place and pushed the old policies.[101] When the 1919 purchases of paintings for the contemporary wing of the Dresden Gallery were announced in August, no expressionist works were included. Instead the commission preferred paintings by artists such as the academy members Otto Gussmann and Richard Dreher and the Berlin impressionist Lovis Corinth.[102]

Although purportedly aimed at bringing art to the "people," Felixmüller and Lange's attack on the directors of the Dresden Gallery seemed to have more to do with the placement of people sympathetic to expressionism in decision-making positions. The Secession Group 1919 could consider it a partial victory, then, when the art historian Paul Ferdinand Schmidt, a prominent supporter of the new art, was appointed director of the City Museum in July.[103] But even here it seems that little could be accomplished; due to a general lack of finances in Saxony, the budgets for the Dresden museums remained restricted, particularly when compared with other cities in Germany.[104]

With the growing dissatisfaction in the Dresden art world after April, some of those who defended expressionism began to distrust the affirmative characterizations of the new art advanced with the revolution. This was nowhere more evident than in the July issue of *Menschen,* which was devoted to the fate of art after the suppression of the revolution. Even Heinar Schilling, now editor and publisher, adopted a more radical profile. On 1 June he took the unusual step of socializing his press, making it a cooperative venture with its writers, including Felixmüller, Zehder, and even Rheiner, with whom he had feuded earlier.[105]

Schilling now presented in *Menschen* a broad range of opinions on art and the revolution, from a defense of art as revolutionary, separate, and distinct from any political considerations, to a critique of the revolutionary claims made for culture. A number of the authors in the issue now went back on the constructive, affirmative characterization of the new art and returned to a definition of avant-garde art as subversive resistance against bourgeois authority. Thus one author attacked bourgeois society as "philistine," challenged its claims to art based solely on patronage, and concluded: "Art exists not for, but against society."[106] Similarly, the writer Will Erich Peuckert in "Majority and Spartacus" projected an art which undermined society, citing Ibsen as a precursor. Peuckert told the apocryphal story of a Spartacist brought before the court, who was asked during the course of the trial whether he was aware that the majority of the people did not stand behind him. In his defense the accused quoted Ibsen: "The majority never has right on its side."[107] Caricaturing the bourgeois philistine, Peuckert had the state's attorney proclaim that "for the most part the blame must be meted out to the aforesaid author, who undermines society with such bohemian teachings and causes all bases of the state to totter."[108] In this tale both sides of the political spectrum testify to the subversive, revolutionary potential of art: the Spartacist quotes Ibsen as his authority, and the attorney equally assigns the power to topple the state to the playwright.

The most intransigent leftist critique in the issue belonged to Felix Stiemer, the former publisher of *Menschen*. He wrote his "Determination of Limits" from Berlin, where he had taken refuge in the wake of the suppression of the second council republic in Munich. He now advocated what amounted to communist demands: a six-hour day, workers' ownership of the means of production, and a council system of government. These, he declared, would not follow from a spiritual revolution, but were presuppositions for it: "As long as men are strained in the Taylor system, hence [as long as] relationships are not changed, a change of men cannot be spoken of . . . As long as interests are not satisfied, any 'ideal' remains idle talk . . . Where economic preconditions are not fulfilled, any other possibility remains cut off."[109] Stiemer thus put into question the very notion of art precursing revolution, suggesting much more that any preoccupation with purely artistic concerns actually thwarted political goals—and was therefore reactionary. Attacking "aristocrats of the spirit" who believed in their own leadership, Stiemer was ready to renounce art altogether for politics.[110]

The July issue of *Menschen*, however, concluded with two essays on the pictorial arts that preserved a revolutionary potential for avant-garde art. The term revolution itself occurred only once, in the title of an article by Walter Georg Hartmann, "Revolution, its Artists and Comrades!!" Hartmann, author of "The Inspired Way" (which Mitschke-Collande had illustrated), asserted the close relationship between the artists he addressed in *Menschen* and the revolution: "Decades long you created, helped in the very late rebellion, rumbled, called, threw together, and now?"[111] The question "and now?" referred to the unfinished business of the revolution:

> On the thrones in our lands the puffed-up princes still sit and deceive the obedient people with their spiritual-traps, their art-swindle, their patron-gestures. Now it is time to make a clean sweep of all simple deceit, to give all compulsory liars the finishing stroke . . . Down with the falsifiers, who in the pose of the spirit betray the spirit![112]

For Hartmann, it was a matter not only of principle, but of economic self-interest as well: "Should [those] who receive gold for our work throw pennies to us?"[113] He therefore called on artists to "smash in the windows of the art manufacturers," to put an end to "art racketeers," "purse-paunch" art dealers, and "art middlemen." But if Hartmann implicitly attacked the capitalist structure of the art market, he never addressed the contradiction of an art he himself associated with revolution and its dependence on that market.

Finally, in an essay on Karl Schmidt-Rottluff, Felixmüller sought to preserve the designation of expressionism as revolutionary by emphasizing the negative, destructive characterizations of that art projected in the pages of *Menschen* during the war. In writing about Schmidt-Rottluff, he focused on the oppositional, culture-critical aspects of his friend's art:

> His language is against our time, his form is above it . . . Two of his naked men tread the miserable, laughable ballast of our centuries old "culture": aesthetic [is] dead. With him there is nothing "aesthetically-beautiful" . . . Ruthlessly Schmidt-Rottluff trampled down all systems which surround us, which sit on us, grind down, assert, oppress, keep blind and deaf.[114]

Felixmüller, though, concluded on an upbeat note, describing Schmidt-Rottluff as the harbinger of a spiritual alternative: "Schmidt-

Rottluff is the manifestation of our will and [our] goal: liberation from the lot of slaves, living men—the godlike essence of world creation—for the intensity of his body and [his] spirit in freedom."[115]

Menschen had begun publication during the war, promoting the ambivalent claims of expressionism to destroy the old and build the new, where the old was known but not clearly circumscribed and the new was unknown and hence utopian. In the early days of the revolution its editors had repeated the standard claims for the revolutionary significance of expressionism. With the murders of Liebknecht and Luxemburg, and the suppression of revolutionary activity in Dresden, Walter Rheiner had steered the journal from concerns with art toward a commitment to radical politics. Now, with the suppression of the revolution in Saxony, Schilling, too, became radicalized. The revolutionary claims made for expressionist art, however, still predominated in the July issue of *Menschen*. Although many of the authors revised the affirmative characterization of the new art advanced with the revolution, they returned to the definition of avant-garde art as a subversive resistance against authority that the journal had promoted during the war. Ignored in the process was the intervening history of expressionism, its simultaneous association with the idea of revolution and its dependence on the capitalist art market. Only Stiemer, now absent from Dresden, put in question the very notion of revolutionary art, renouncing art in favor of politics.

After April, Felixmüller, too, became radicalized, producing a number of partisan graphics for Franz Pfemfert's *Die Aktion* that took as their subject events and personalities of the revolution. In all likelihood Pfemfert commissioned these works directly, either by telegram from Berlin or during a brief stay with Felixmüller in Dresden when he was in hiding from the Berlin authorities.[116] Among them were the woodcuts *The Murdered Man* (fig. 3.12), *The Revolutionary (Long Live the World Revolution)* (fig. 3.13), and *People Above the World* (fig. 3.14). *The Murdered Man*, published in the 3 May 1919 issue, shows the defiant, erect torso of a man who has been shot and who has blood streaming down his body from his temple. *The Revolutionary* and *People Above the World* appeared in the 5 July 1919 memorial issue for Rosa Luxemburg and Karl Liebknecht. In the first, a man charges toward the viewer down a city street, arms raised, one fist clenched in the communist salute. His gesture seems enough to topple the building behind him. In the second print, Felixmüller presented the communist leaders Liebknecht and Luxemburg arm in arm, ascending to heaven over the city of Berlin like Christian martyrs. The Christian context of Felixmüller's commemoration still tied in with the spiritualization of

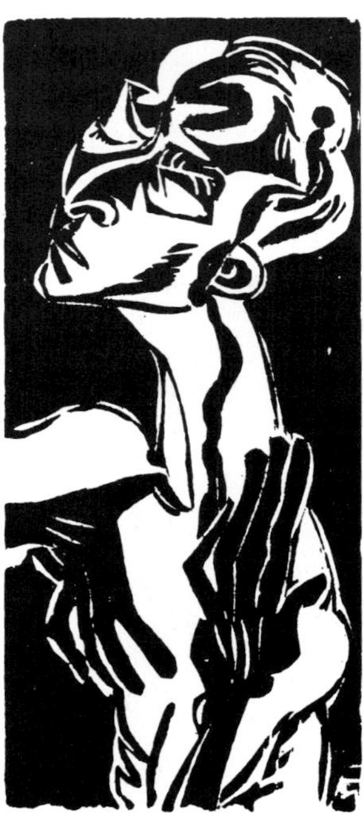

3.12 Conrad Felixmüller, *Der Ermordete (The Murdered Man)*, 1919. Woodcut, 16.5 x 7.5 cm. Staatliche Museen zu Berlin, Kupferstichkabinett / DDR Nationalgalerie. Photo courtesy of Titus Felixmüller.

expressionism, as did the accompanying text by Iwan Goll, "Litany to Liebknecht's Death," a poem in the form of a rogation with the refrain "Ave Liebknecht."

Felixmüller published only one of his partisan leftist graphics in Dresden, the portrait woodcut of Liebknecht for the 15 January 1919 issue of *Menschen* protesting the murders of the communist leaders. Nor did he exhibit any of them with the Dresden Secession Group 1919—possibly because he considered these overtly political works unsuited for his Dresden audience. Enlightened patrons elsewhere in Germany, however, applauded these efforts (the majority of his patrons came from outside Dresden). The banker Baron August von der Heydt, who in 1918 donated a Felixmüller painting to the Elberfeld Museum, praised his "deeply affecting revolutionary pathos as a symbol of our excited epoch."[117] Dr. Hans Koch, associated with the von Bergh and Co. Gallery in Düsseldorf, successfully promoted Felixmüller's work during these months. Just five days after *People Above the World* appeared in *Die Aktion,* Koch wrote to congratulate Felixmüller, calling his work "the strongest hope of German art of TOMORROW."[118] Outside Dresden, Felixmüller confidently promoted his own

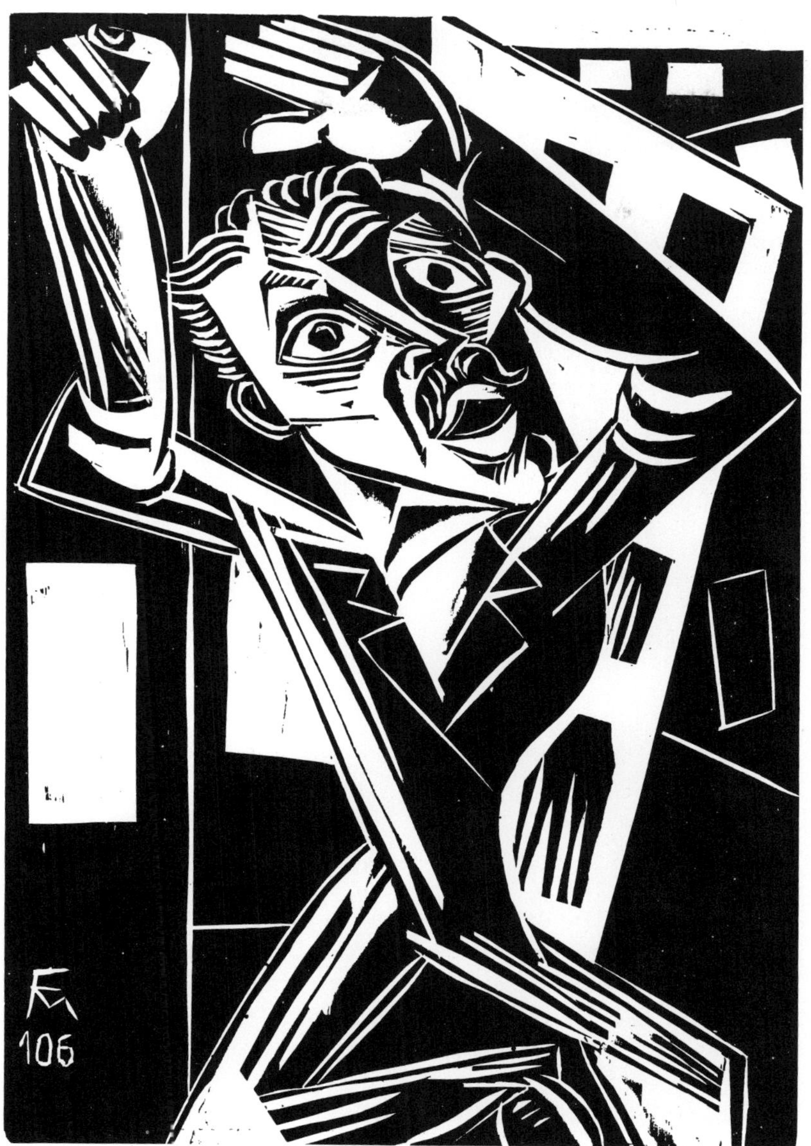

3.13 Conrad Felixmüller, *Der Revolutionär (Es lebe die Weltrevolution)* [*The Revolutionary (Long Live the World Revolution)*], 1919. Woodcut, 24 x 16.8 cm. Kunstmuseum Düsseldorf.

art as politically radical. In P. E. Küppers' *Das Kestnerbuch,* published in Hannover, he argued that his art was

determined by the spirit-era of our times . . . : velocity, mechanics; politics, religiosity; luxury, war; our war; our high-speed railways, airplanes, autos, mil-

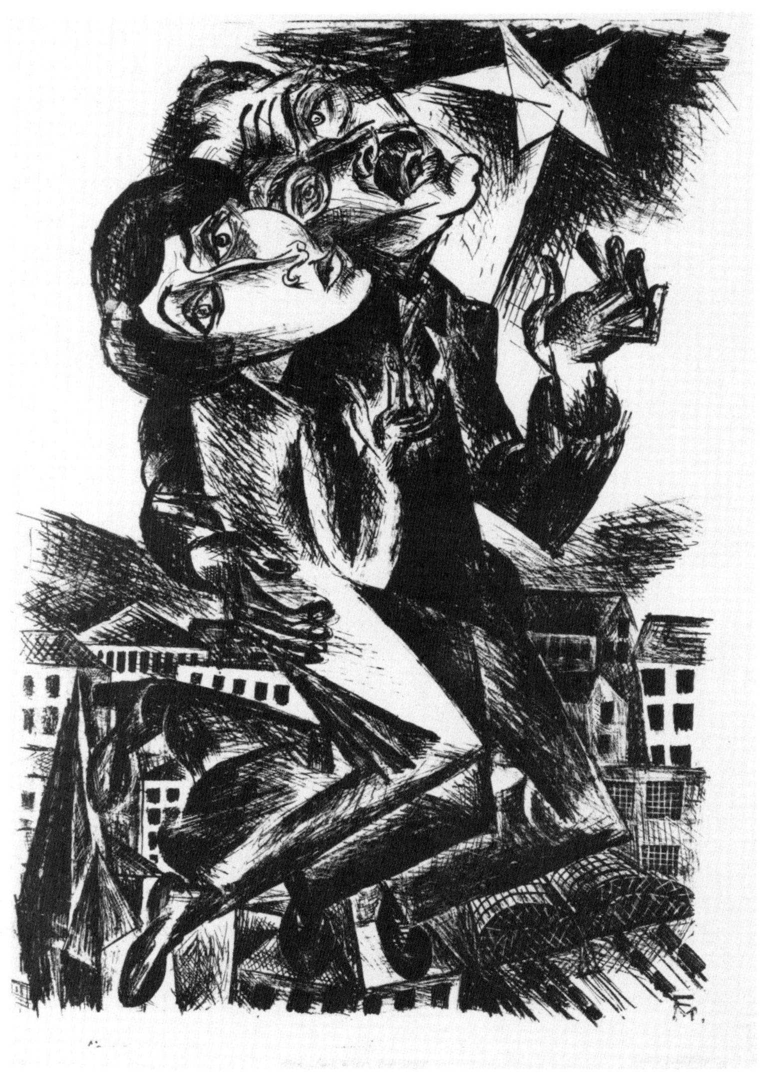

3.14 Conrad Felixmüller, *Menschen über der Welt (People Above the World),* 1919. Lithograph, 69 x 50 cm. Staatliche Museen zu Berlin, Kupferstichkabinett / DDR Nationalgalerie. Photo courtesy of Titus Felixmüller.

itary hospitals, street battles—the revolution of men . . . Not the individual—but what is nearest him, the masses. The art of the masses, for them, as product of the masses from the human being/artist, the representative of the masses, who perceives the desire and torment of all as his own desire and torment . . .[119]

Felixmüller illustrated this text with his lithograph *Dead Comrade* (fig. 3.15), which commemorated the January street fighting in Dresden that he had witnessed firsthand. A slain protester, viewed from above as he lies with his head down on the cobblestone pavement, holds aloft the flag, defiant in the face of death.

Felixmüller's public profile in the nine months after the revolution was often contradictory. He was the committed communist artist producing partisan graphics for *Die Aktion* and the revolutionary artist of choice for enlightened segments of the bourgeoisie; he was a voice of protest against the museums, but one willing to accede to its bureaucratic structure; he was the driving force and leading artistic personality in the Secession Group 1919 and a key member in the moderate Council of Artists.

Perhaps because of Felixmüller's aggressive politics, perhaps because of the general tension in the Dresden art world, the public response to the Secession Group underwent a dramatic shift. This was most noticeable in the critical response to the second exhibition of the Dresden Secession Group, which opened scarcely two months after the first show had closed. This time the exhibition had competition: it was only one of two important shows to open late in June, the other by the Artists' Union. The reception that greeted the two exhibitions, and the artists who took part in them, indicated the terms on which the Dresden art world was willing to accept expressionist art.

The second Dresden Secession Group exhibition also took place at the fashionable Richter gallery. Beside the Dresden Secession Group members (who had expanded their ranks to include the Leipzig expressionists Rüdiger Berlitt and Max Schwimmer),[120] invited guests participating in the exhibition included, among others, such established expressionist artists as Lyonel Feininger, Georg Tappert, and Karl Schmidt-Rottluff, along with a number of young, unknown newcomers.[121] Rudolf Probst, who had lectured on expressionism at the first exhibition, wrote the introductory catalog essay, which challenged the audience not to be seduced by traditional art forms, "not to be confused by the precious play of beautiful form."[122] Rather, he called for an art appropriate to the times, which he described as follows: "Now everything that was seems radically blown apart—in between gapes the terrible abyss, in which all previous value is irretrievably lost. Existence

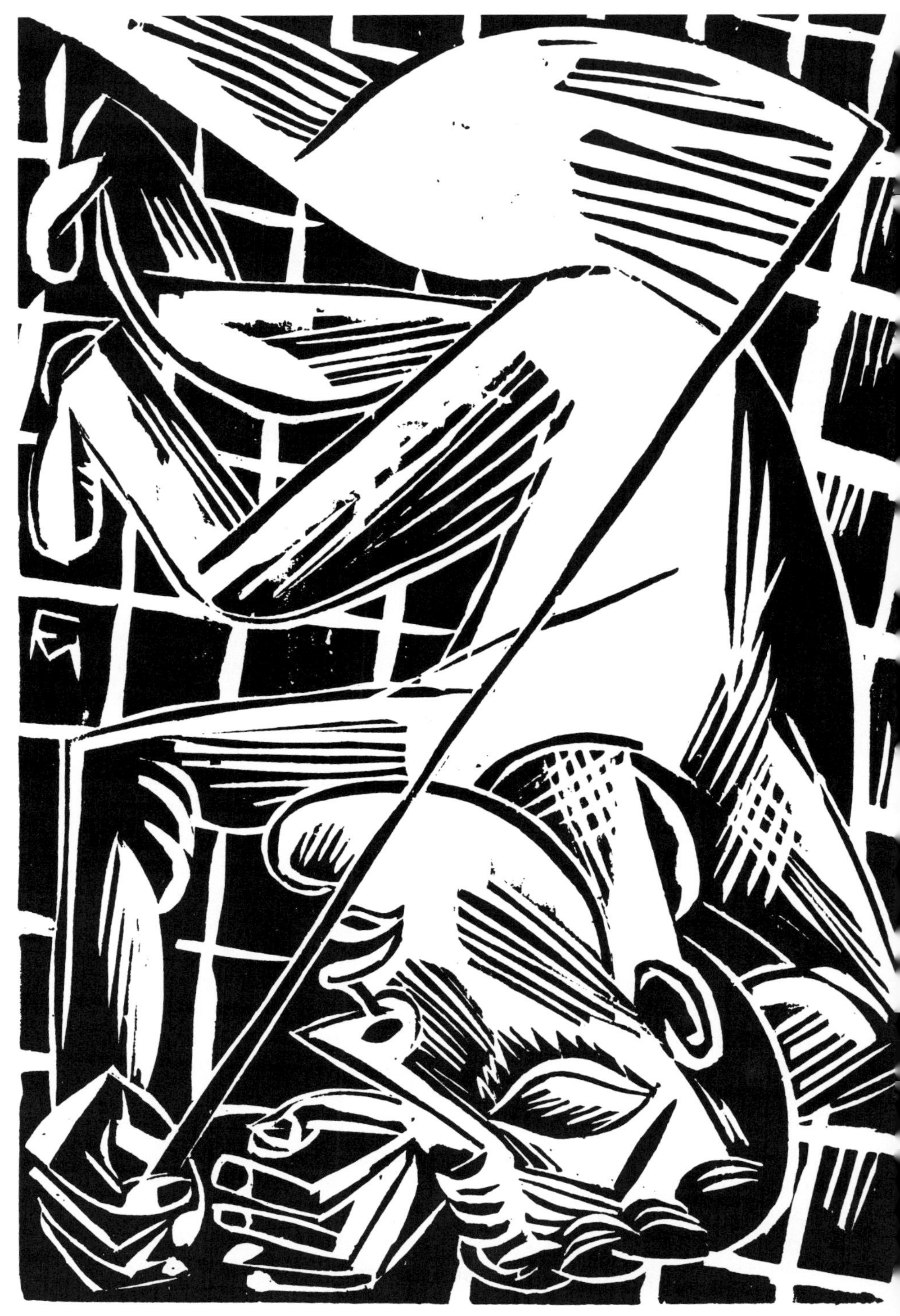

3.15 Conrad Felixmüller, *Toter Genosse (Dead Comrade)*, 1919. Woodcut, 24 x 16.8 cm. Kunstmuseum Düsseldorf.

itself is split open as in puberty. Do you all sense the development of a new time in your own blood? A new consciousness of humanity struggles forth."[123] Probst now repeated once again the ambivalent claims of expressionism to destroy the old and build the new, which Felixmüller had also reconfirmed in the July issue of *Menschen*.

Unlike on the occasion of the first Secession Group 1919 show, the local critics were now decidedly hostile. They unanimously questioned the quality of the works shown. Complained the critic for the *Dresdner Anzeiger:* "the numerical extension [of the participants] . . . brought no enrichment."[124] The critic for the *Dresdner Neueste Nachrichten* seconded this opinion, and added that "most [of the works] . . . are still the feeble work of followers."[125] The vehemence of the reaction seemed overblown. While it was true that the exhibition included the work of numerous latecomers to expressionism, it also included such established and well-respected artists as Schmidt-Rottluff and Feininger. Moreover, the first exhibition of the group had also clearly been the work of a second generation of expressionist artists, many of them still students.

Surprisingly, it was Felixmüller who now disappointed the critics. Although only two months before the critic for the *Dresdner Neueste Nachrichten* had singled Felixmüller out as the leading personality of the group, he now pointedly remarked that "a leading personality of the group is in general lacking."[126] Ignoring Felixmüller's more standard expressionist graphics in the show, the critics zeroed in on his most recent work *The Family of the Art-Metal Worker Georg Mendelsohn, Hellerau* (fig. 3.16). The critic for the SPD *Dresdner Volkszeitung* wrote of the painting: "For the most part everything is still so unclarified in conception and so affected and tortured in the presentation . . . that a deeper absorption becomes quite impossible."[127] The critic for the *Dresdner Anzeiger* considered it a step backward in Felixmüller's career,[128] and the critic for *Dresdner Neueste Nachrichten* described the composition as awkward, noting that the painting might be more convincing "if the painter could free himself more from his far-fetched theories."[129] Just what these theories were the critic never made clear.

In this painting Felixmüller depicted his friend Georg Mendelsohn, founder of the Hellerau Workshop for Metal-Work, as a simple yet dignified man, surrounded by his six family members, in a bare interior. With his overly large, serious face, seated stiffly in his Sunday best, Mendelsohn was the central focus of the composition. The portrait appears as an idealization of the artisan and of the handicrafts, corresponding to the notions of the Working Council for Art in Berlin and the founding program of the Bauhaus. The painting signals a change

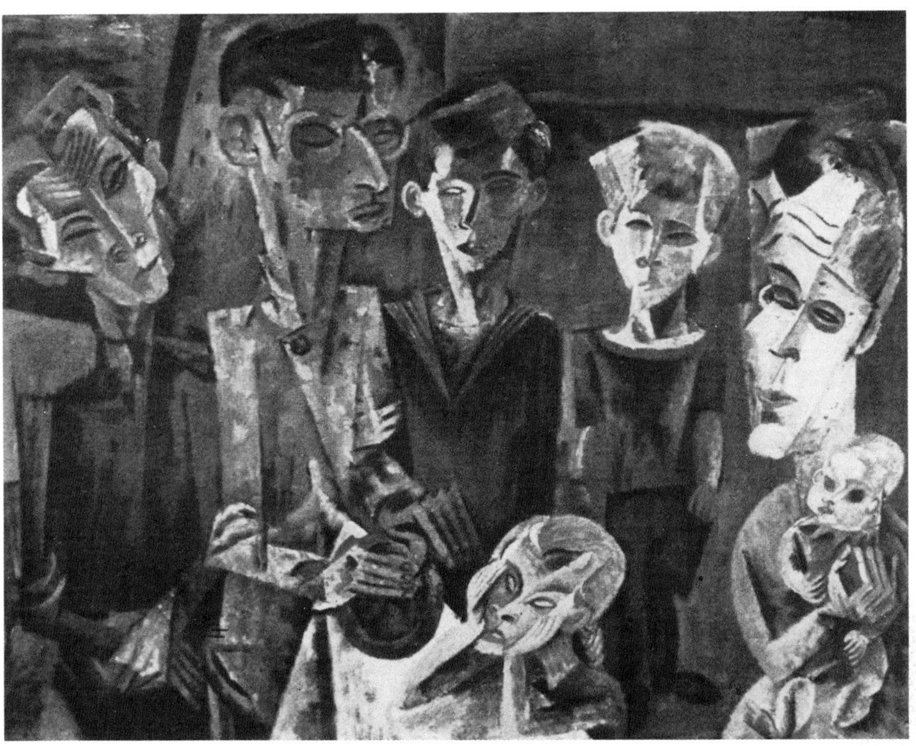

3.16 Conrad Felixmüller, *Die Familie des Kunstschlossers Georg Mendelsohn, Hellerau (The Family of the Art-Metal Worker Georg Mendelsohn, Hellerau)*, 1919. Oil on canvas, 130 x 160 cm., original now lost. Photo courtesy of Titus Felixmüller.

in Felixmüller's position, in which the handicrafts are now presented as an ideal for the expressionist artist. The critics clearly perceived the family portrait as different from his earlier work, which they had often praised.

The critics were also upset by Otto Dix's recent work. Dix was represented in the show with three of the paintings he had completed in rapid succession around March, along with three drawings and graphics from the war years with themes of apocalypse and resurrection. His poster for the second Secession Group show (fig. 3.17) was a reworking of one of these, the 1917 chalk drawing *Wounded in the Evening* (fig. 3.18). Whereas the 1917 drawing of resurrecting figures reaching toward the sun provided solace for death in war, the figures now aggressively clawed their way upward. Dix had converted the empty eye sockets and curving fingers into staring eyes, bared teeth, and grasping hands. The effect was no longer yearning, but aggression.

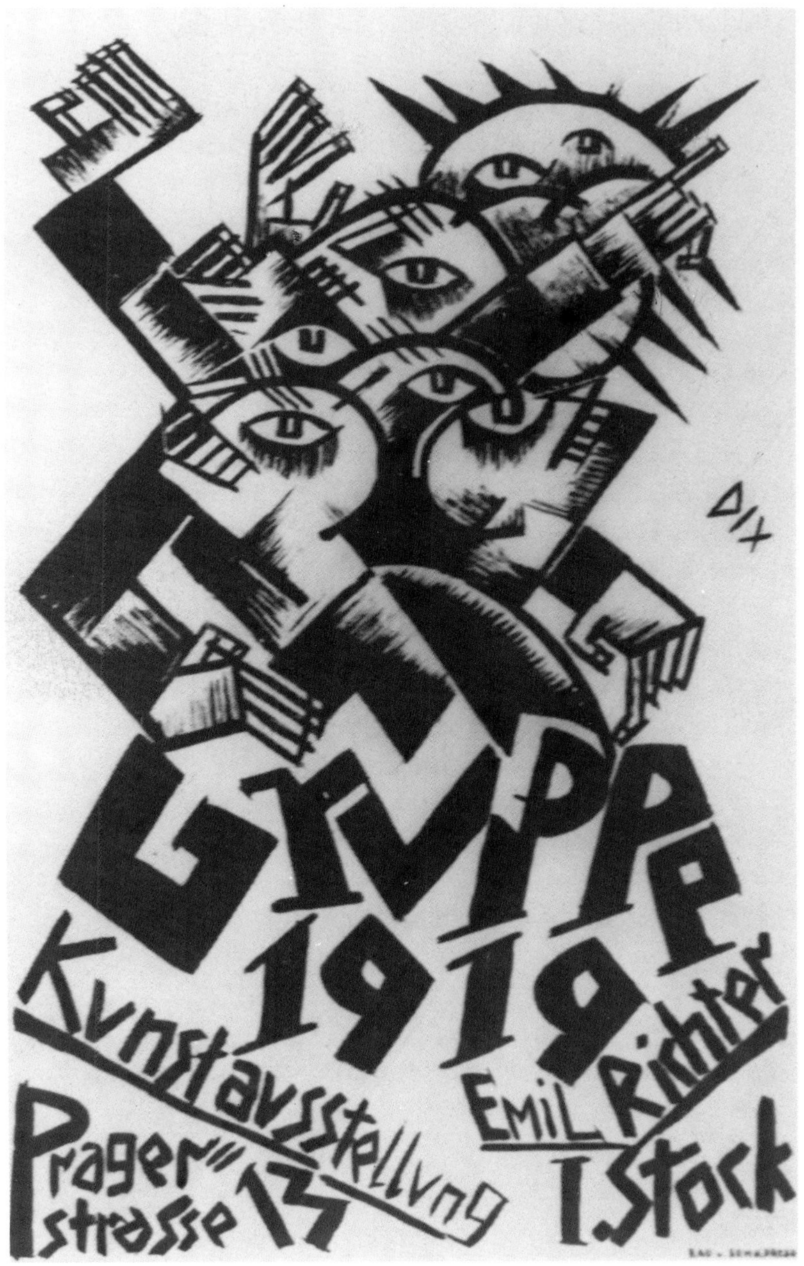

3.17 Otto Dix, cover of the second Dresden Secession Group 1919 exhibition catalog, 1919. Lithograph, 90.6 x 58.3 cm. Staatliches Lindenau-Museum, Altenburg.

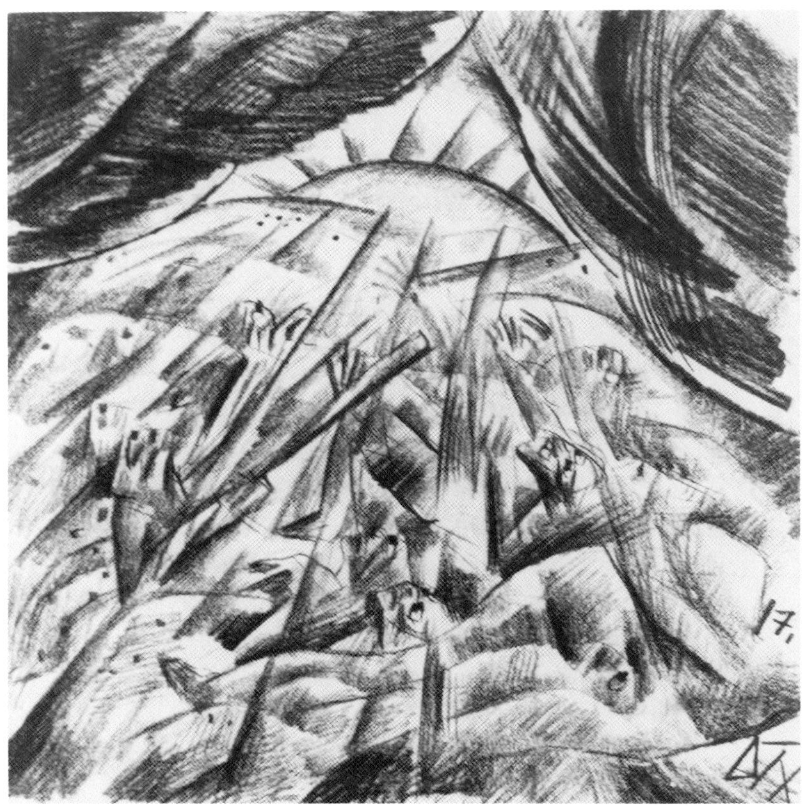

3.18 Otto Dix, *Verwundete am Abend (Wounded in the Evening)*, 1917. Chalk drawing, dimensions unknown.

The critics now ignored his earlier expressionist graphics, turning their attention to his more recent paintings. The comments by the critic for the *Dresdner Nachrichten* were typical:

Otto Dix suddenly hit upon the idea that instead of painting colorful fragments [he would paint] for a change bubbles, spherical jelly of bloated bodies which glow red or blue and have dancing stars around them. This is a totally arbitrary artists's joke—which can convince no one of its inner necessity—carried out in its particulars in a childish playful way. Such atelier jokes harm the reputation of the new art.[130]

The same critic linked Dix to the Hannover artist Kurt Schwitters, whose collage of streetcar tickets, pieces of newspaper, postcards, and other shreds of everyday life pasted on canvas he claimed "had nothing more to do with painting." Another critic found the "affected symbolism" of Dix's paintings "quite insignificant."[131] Here, too, the critics responded to a change in Dix's art: his newest paintings, including *Moon Wife* (fig. 3.19) and *Transitoriness* (fig. 3.20), now bordered on caricature, which on balance gave them a mocking anti-expressionist aspect. Dix's new interest in caricature probably derived from an informal Dada group he had joined. The Prague composer Erwin Schulhoff had brought the Dada manifesto from Zurich to Dresden, where it found a receptive audience among a number of students at the academy, including Dix.[132]

The aggressive alternatives to the spiritualization of expressionism put forward by Felixmüller and Dix, discrepant as they might be, clearly provoked part of the hostile response accorded the second Dresden Secession Group exhibition. It also seems likely that the group's growing public criticism of the Dresden art establishment had inflamed some of the critics against them. The critic for the *Dresdner Neueste Nachrichten* even argued that there was no need for the Secession Group 1919 (as, he conceded, there was for the Brücke in 1905) when established groups such as the Artists' Union "behaved rather liberally toward artistic progress."[133] When the Secession Group 1919 show closed in September, Lyonel Feininger wrote to his wife that although "the interest awakened in art circles has been exceptionally strong," there were "no sales worth mentioning up to now."[134] Whether this was the case for other participants is unclear.

Simultaneous with the Secession Group show was an exhibition sponsored by the Artists' Union, which had invited the Secession Group 1919 to participate. Although the Secession Group had declined (following their statutes), a number of first-rank expressionist artists were represented, including Emil Nolde (who had his own room with thirty-four works), Max Pechstein, Otto Mueller, and Ludwig Meidner; these artists now exhibited alongside the academy professors Otto Gussmann and Robert Sterl.[135] Even more significantly, Oskar Kokoschka, an honorary member of the Secession Group 1919, and Will Grohmann, their chief publicist, opted to exhibit with the Artists' Union. Not only did the inclusion of expressionist artists in the show seem to confirm the liberality of the Artists' Union (a point emphatically stressed in the introduction to their catalog),[136] but a number of more traditional artists even tried their hand at the new style (Otto Hettner and Hans Blanke met with the disapproval of the critic of the *Dresdner Neueste Nachrichten* for their efforts).[137] In comparison with the Dresden Secession Group exhibition, sales were apparently brisk, with numerous purchases announced in the local newspapers well before the exhibition closed on 24 August.[138] Dresden had proven its ability to accommodate the new art, but within the parameters of the Artists' Union rather than within those of the Secession Group, given the questionable revolutionary politics of its leader Felixmüller and the provocative imagery of its *enfant terrible* Dix.

September–December: Cooptation and Disillusionment

By late September, the prospect of a successful revolution in Saxony was further off than it had ever been. Although as late as 6 September

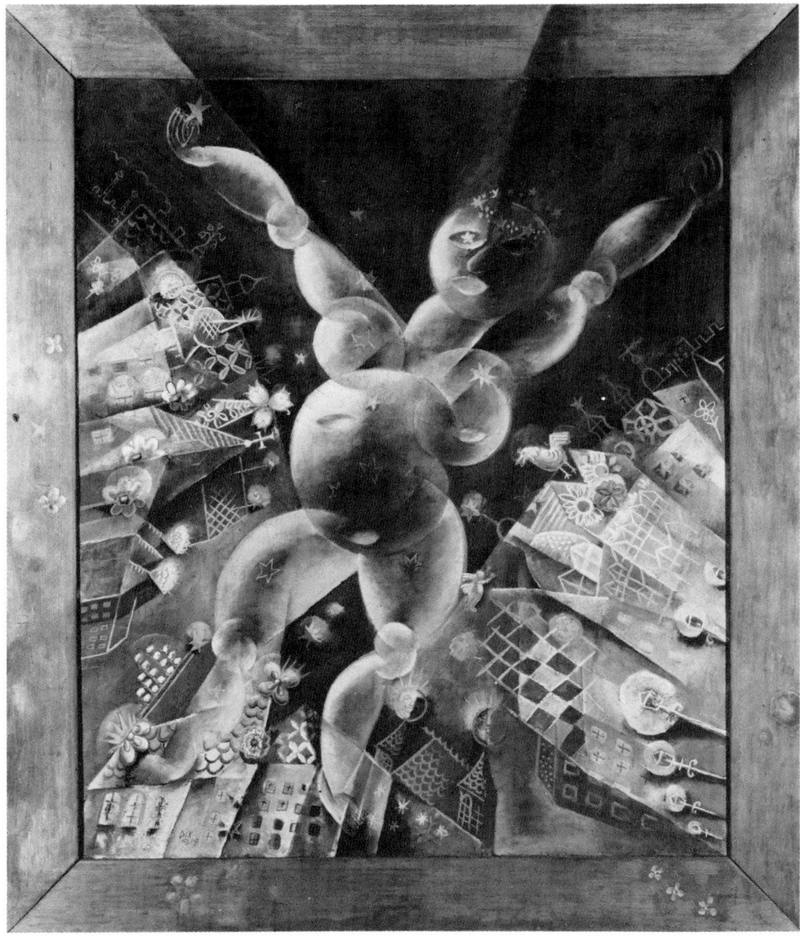

3.19 Otto Dix, *Mondweib (Moon Wife)*, 1919. Oil on canvas, 120.5 x 100.5 cm. Staatliche Museen zu Berlin / DDR Nationalgalerie.

3.20 Otto Dix, *Vergänglichkeit (Transitoriness)*, 1919.
Oil on pasteboard, 70 x 48 cm.
Private collection, Rome.

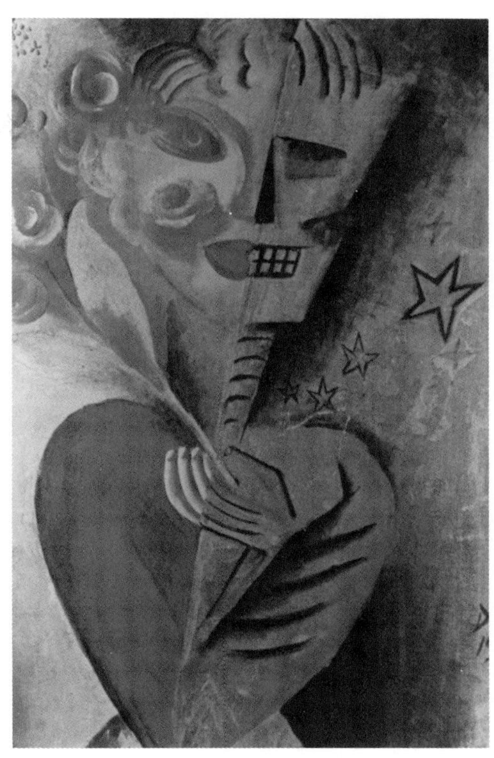

1919 the USPD leader Curt Geyer had predicted in the *Leipziger Volkszeitung* that the revolution would "undoubtedly come in months, or perhaps even weeks,"[139] by late September the USPD officially abandoned any hope of forming a government of socialist unity in Saxony and thereby regaining power; it went instead into parliamentary opposition. As expressionism was gradually incorporated into the mainstream art world, as in the Artists' Union exhibition, many of those who had championed the new art began to worry about its cooptation—and entered into their own kind of opposition to the republic. Among them was Hugo Zehder. In January 1919 Zehder had promoted expressionism as an affirmative art of socialist reconciliation. In June he had recognized the legitimacy of the SPD government while lamenting the lack of reform favoring expressionism. Zehder once more shifted his defense of art to suit the changing political situation. Now, he abandoned expressionism for its betrayal of the revolution. In the September issue of the *Neue Blätter* he promoted Otto Dix's art as a radical challenge to expressionism.

For Zehder, expressionism's practitioners had betrayed the revolution for pecuniary reasons. Rather than renounce art altogether, as Felix Stiemer had done, he promoted a new opposition found in the art of Otto Dix, whom he differentiated from his fellow members of the Secession Group:

> "How do I paint expressionistically?" Otto Dix never asked himself this question, posed by those who are inadequate or came too late, to whom the doubtful fortune falls of profiting from the embourgeoisement of a radical art movement. . . . Naturally it did not occur to Dix to perceive the call to freedom as a new command to march in rank and file, as permission to carry out the revolution according to order with the great followers of those who readjust their ideas so readily. His glorious temperament does not allow itself to be invited to a walker's step, which carries with it in the rucksack all kinds of family friends, considerations of a regular circle of cronies, and the famous "eternal ideals" and "holiest goods" as good ballast. He is an Indian, a Sioux chief. Always on the warpath. He swings his brush like an axe and every blow is a cry of color.[140]

Dix, he argued, was still an opponent of the system. Ignoring Dix's initial war enthusiasm and his 1917–18 quasi-religious expressionist experimentations, Zehder described him as a "totally undivided and indivisible human being" who "lay in wait" during the war for the "great rush forward," the revolution. Reproduced in the September issue were his most recent works, including two of the paintings (*Pregnant Woman* and *Moon Wife*) Dix had exhibited with the Secession Group 1919. Zehder perceived a critical edge to these pictures, perhaps based on the coexistence in them of expressionist and caricatural elements, which on balance gave them an anti-expressionist, anti-bourgeois aspect.

Zehder, however, was not so concerned with Dix's art as with making a case against expressionism. Thus he caustically mocked "dogmas of the catechism of expressionist painting, which shortly will appear in a popular edition," and " 'modern' art officials" who deliver "sermons . . . on a new world consciousness, expressionist religiosity, and the cosmic revolutionary, not without flattering connections to a past that differentiated itself from the present most profitably through the fact that it needed no thought-out references for its self-assertion."[141] Zehder thus renounced his own earlier position, and by implication the Secession Group 1919 from which he had resigned the previous month.

Another prominent writer in Saxony came to similar conclusions. Writing in the Leipzig journal *Der Cicerone,* the Worpswede artist/critic Carl Emil Uphoff had earlier commented extensively on the relevance of the revolution for the artist in straightforward economic terms. In one article he had demanded that art be incorporated into the production process as a whole, a process which was to be socialist.[142] Given the economic crisis in defeated Germany, though, he predicted that art would be forcefully decapitalized: as luxury items, who could afford artworks when "there are hardly the means for daily bread?" By December, though, Uphoff no longer wrote of the socialization of art, but withdrew to a position of opposition to authority. He now embraced an anarchist posture, characterizing the artist as a revolutionary in opposition to a state that was "a result of error," a "derailment of man from the path toward the perfect, world-embracing individuality to the path of impersonal herd instinct."[143] Uphoff, like Zehder, withdrew to a notion of the oppositional personality in response to the failure of the revolution. Once the historical course of events had disproved their hopes for the revolution, writers such as Zehder and Uphoff now hardened to outright subversive concepts of resistance against the state.

After July *Menschen* ceased regular publication, appearing only at irregular intervals with special issues, promotional efforts on behalf of expressionist artists' groups throughout Germany, including Forces (*Kräfte*) in Hamburg, the November Group in Berlin, and the Secession Group 1919 in Dresden. The issue on the November Group featured Adolf Behne's almost desperate insistence on the revolutionary nature of expressionist art in the face of increasing cooptation by a bourgeois public. In an attempt to explain the apparent contradiction of a revolutionary art eagerly embraced by the bourgeoisie, Behne claimed it was not the artists, but their patrons who performed the dreaded compromise. In a special September issue of *Menschen* devoted to the Dresden Secession Group 1919,[144] Grohmann skirted the same issue. He defended the group against mounting charges of cooptation:

> Expressionism—for many only a style compulsion of the time, third-hand experience and for that reason [merely] aesthetic. Seldom was a word so quickly discredited. Now the chorus asks: where is the ecstasy, the vision, the spirituality; where does the secret wonder remain? . . . What does spirit concern me? I'd rather have bread.
>
> Certainly, you'd rather have bread. Let us not think of the maker, not of the word. Look and test. For the sake of a few righteous the others were allowed to live on.[145]

Grohmann here defended the "few righteous" (presumably the artists represented in the issue) against the charges of both the right and the left, claiming that the best of the new art still promised the rehabilitation of mankind. It was Grohmann who was still largely responsible for promoting the new art in speeches throughout Dresden as the affirmative response to a "materialist-unspiritual epoch," which restored not only "mystical and cosmic powers to mankind," but "the possibility of expression to the German soul."[146] Nowhere did Grohmann even mention the revolution, as if it had nothing to do with the expectations of and disappointments in the new art.

Eventually even the socialization of Schilling's press proved not quite what it seemed: Schilling loaned the cooperative 100,000 marks at six-percent interest, demanded a fixed salary, decided unilaterally about the inclusion of new authors, and stipulated that the cooperative would be dissolved upon his death.[147] In only a few months time the press merged with another publishing house, and there was no more discussion of a publishing cooperative. By January 1920, Schilling renounced political engagement in the pages of *Menschen,* "in more than one sense 'leave-taking' from the great time."[148]

The Dresden Secession Group 1919, too, languished. Although the special *Menschen* issue on the Secession Group 1919 featured reproductions of some twenty-five graphics by seven members of the group, conspicuous through his absence was Conrad Felixmüller, who sometime late in 1919 resigned from the group. His reasons remained unstated, but may have had something to do with his growing political radicalization. At least this is what Felixmüller claimed many years later, when he wrote about his failure to enlist the other members of the group in the KPD:

> Otto Lange declined: he was organized in a trade union and was an opponent of the KPD. The same with Otto Schubert—he had been at the front for five years—now he wanted to have a rest. Heckrott declared he had been an officer and the KPD was out of the question for him. Segall [said] he was a Jew and a Pole, a foreigner—for that reason he could belong to no German party. Dix [said]—leave me alone with your stupid politics—I'd rather go to the brothel. Only Constantin von Mitschke-Collande joined the KPD.[149]

Poor reviews of the second show provided little incentive to stay, particularly since he had successfully established a reputation independent of the group. Certainly some of his oldest friends and influential supporters did not encourage him to remain with the group. The dealer Dr. Hans Koch wrote to Felixmüller in August expressing disappointment with the Secession Group, whose art he was to present in Düsseldorf: "The exhibition will hardly be significant . . . I am quite certainly not emphatically linked with this Secession as such. With Felixmüller, so to speak, the cream is skimmed off the top."[150] Koch also reported to Felixmüller the expressionist painter Heinrich Campendonk's poor opinion of the group.

With Felixmüller's resignation the Secession Group lost its best and most prominent member. Böckstiegel left the group along with his brother-in-law, followed shortly thereafter by Schubert. Four new members took their place: the sculptors Eugen Hoffmann, Christoph Voll, and Ludwig Godenschweg, along with the painter Walter Jacob. None, however, ever achieved the reputation of Felixmüller, and the Secession Group 1919 remained essentially a local phenomenon. When their contract with the Richter Gallery expired in April 1920, the group moved their third show to the rival Arnold Gallery, where it received lackluster reviews. Even Paul Ferdinand Schmidt, the newly appointed director of the City Museum who was sympathetic to expressionism, found the show a disappointment and admitted the group no longer had a "real program."[151] By 1922 the Secession Group dissolved, its members successfully integrated into the mainstream Dresden art world, among those honored by the academy with state prizes.[152] There was little reason anymore for a separate expressionist artists' group.

The momentous shifts and dizzying reversals that characterized the Berlin art scene after November were not as evident in Dresden. Berlin was a kind of crucible for the expressionists, the center of debate, protest, and reaction. When they made their peace with the republic, whether through choice or adept countermaneuver on the part of art institutions, it came after serious efforts to remake the art world in their own image. They had at least discussed, if not tried to put into action, an end to the capitalist art market, to academies, and even to museums as they were previously known. Through a number of exhibitions they had tried to approach the proletariat with their work. In Dresden, though, expressionist artists had not pursued the same program. When Gasch and the Provisional Revolutionary Council of Artists made their more radical demands in the first days of the revolution, they found little, if any, support from the expressionists—perhaps because expressionism was never mentioned in the group's program, which was more concerned with reversing the economic status of the art proletariat. Because of the previous history of the avant-garde in Dresden, and possibly because of the marginal status of the city as an art center, the expressionists found others in the art world more willing to compromise than they were elsewhere in Germany. The Brücke may have fled the city almost ten years before for lack of support, but by 1912 at the latest expressionism was slowly but inexorably incorporated into the mainstream Dresden art world. Still, there were certain parameters for this acceptance: expressionism could fit neatly into the pluralism of the Artists' Union, but was frowned upon when its rhetoric became too radical, as in the second Secession Group exhibition.

The most complex and compelling figure in the Dresden art world was undoubtedly Felixmüller, only twenty-two years old when he founded the Secession Group and became a key player in the Council of Artists. Whether he envisioned the Secession Group 1919 as the inheritor of the Brücke mantle or as a group of communist artists—or both—is still unclear. He was certainly unsuccessful in convincing his fellow Secession Group members to commit themselves to the far left politically—if he ever really tried. Still, in the heady first days of the revolution it might have seemed possible for Felixmüller to think he could. On the one hand, there was no one on the far left in the city to dictate to these artists what might constitute a communist art; the possibilities for expressionism seemed as open as anything else. On the other, lack of a strong leftist presence in Dresden offered no concrete support for such efforts—as the USPD had in Berlin. In the end the artists in the Secession Group 1919 either faded into the comfortable acceptance of the Dresden art world, or, like Felixmüller and Dix, soon chose outright political opposition.

MUNICH 4

November–March: Rival Artists' Councils

Traditionally conservative Bavaria, the most agrarian and least industrialized German state, seems at first glance the least likely locale for violent revolutionary struggle. Yet the susceptibility to revolution in Bavaria was already so pronounced in the summer of 1918 that both the ministers of war and of the interior warned that open rebellion could probably no longer be prevented.[1] Earlier and with more intensity than almost anywhere else in Germany, Bavarians had become disillusioned with the war effort. Fostered by the Bavarian press, the suspicion grew that the war was being fought not in the interest of all Germans, but only in the interests of German industrialists in the north and their puppet Prussian politicians.[2] Even the King of Bavaria was accused of war profiteering and subservience to Prussia. As early as 1 August 1915, the first anniversary of the outbreak of the war, the military had to suppress sporadic strikes and protests of food shortages. In 1916 there were organized demonstrations, and in January 1918 came strikes at the munitions factories that had been built in and around Munich during the war. Much of the skilled work force in these factories came from outside Bavaria; remaining in Munich after the war, it constituted a significant militant core for revolutionary activity.[3]

On 7 November 1918 Bavaria anticipated the rest of the country when hastily improvised workers', soldiers', and peasants' councils declared a separate "Free People's State of Bavaria." The anarchist Erich Mühsam was the first on the spot to proclaim publicly the abolition of the German monarchy as Ludwig III fled the capital. The Social Democrats, who only days before had favored a preemptive "revolution from above," now joined with the Independent Social Democrats in a provisional council government headed by Kurt Eisner, the USPD leader of the January strike movement who had only recently been released from jail.[4] Revolutionary sentiment was on the rise since late October, fueled by the threat of foreign troops occupying Bavaria and widespread rumors of impending air attacks.[5] News of the proclamations of republics in Vienna and Bucharest furthered these expectations, while the continued pressure of virtual martial law magnified ordinary grievances. For these reasons Eisner's government began with widespread support, as even the middle classes and the conservative peasantry had little sympathy left for the monarchy or for Prussian domination. Indicative was the cover illustration for the first November issue after the revolution of the famed Munich satirical journal *Simplicissimus,* which had been a bulwark of nationalism all through the war. Now it, too, greeted the new provisional government, presenting a drawing after Thorwaldsen's *Ganymed with the Eagle* with the words: "Hope—the German eagle will drink new powers from the fountain of youth of freedom" (fig. 4.1). Yet despite the initial acceptance and even enthusiasm for the new government, the question mark was still the extent and timing of revolutionary change. For the peasantry and middle classes, the end of the war and the overthrow of the monarchy had already fulfilled most of their aims. But for a growing number of returning soldiers and unemployed workers the goal was no less than council government and the socialization of major industries.[6]

As in Berlin and Dresden in November, Munich artists constituted their own organizations vaguely modeled on workers', soldiers', and peasants' councils. Eleven days after the republic was proclaimed, eleven existing artists' groups, representing the academy to local illustrators, joined together in the "Council of Artists."[7] Shortly after its inception two other groups signed on, the New Secession, which had seceded from the Munich Secession in 1913, and the Group of 100, a hastily organized group numbering far fewer than its name would suggest and consisting mainly of New Secession members.[8] These two groups represented the newer tendencies in the Munich art world, from the Cézannesque biblical paintings of Karl Caspar to the abstractions of the former Blaue Reiter artist Paul Klee. Still, the New Secession largely signaled continuity with the past and even a certain distance from the extreme of pre-war expressionism in Munich. Kandinsky and Marc had never joined the group, and its public profile during the war was decidedly patriotic, as the group defended itself against accusations that its internationalism in art was politically suspicious. Still, with the participation of the New Secession and the Group of 100, the Council of Artists could claim to represent the entire spectrum of the Munich art world. Its earliest public statement, published in the 22 November

A. g. XIII

ünchen, 12. November 1918

23. Jahrgang Nr. 33

SIMPLICISSIMUS

spreis vierteljährlich 6 Mark

Alle Rechte vorbehalten

Begründet von Albert Langen und Th. Th. Heine

Bezugspreis vierteljährlich 6 Mark

Copyright 1918 by Simplicissimus-Verlag G.m.b.H. & Co., München

Hoffnung

(Th. Th. Heine)

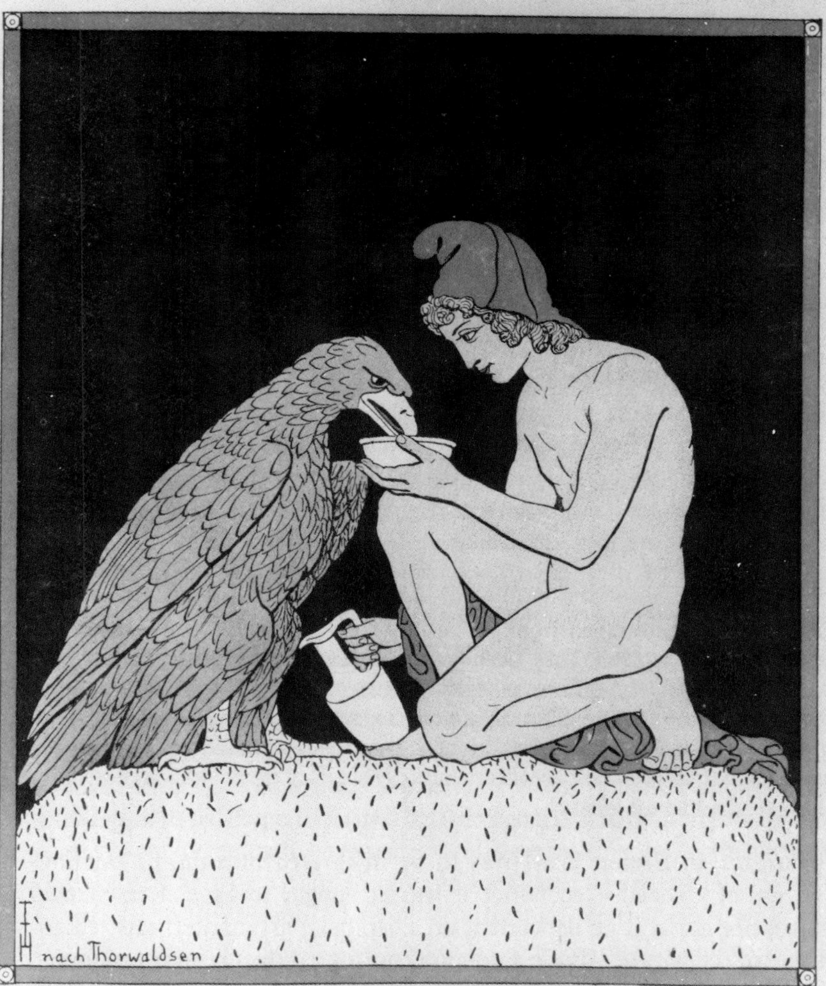

Aus dem Jungbrunnen der Freiheit wird der deutsche Adler neue Kräfte trinken.

Thomas Theodor Heine, cover illustration for *Simplicissimus* 23, no. 45 (November 1918).

The 12 January elections brought increasing polarization as revolutionary workers and soldiers sought both to maintain the advisory status of the councils and to extend their power by creating factory councils. For its part, the leadership of the SPD sought to disband the councils. Dissension also grew within the art world over the timing and pace of change and over the question whether the Council of Artists would or could accommodate its younger, more artistically radical members. Although expressionist art had achieved a level of success elsewhere in Germany, it still had not made significant inroads in Munich, where it was hampered by political attacks in the right-wing press. At its extreme was the *Bayerischer Kurier*, which attacked expressionism with the epithets "un-German," "Jewish," and "Slav," and declared that "corrupt," "Berlin" art was not only tantamount to, but essentially responsible for, political bolshevism.[13]

The bellwether for promised change quickly became educational reform. As in Berlin, modern artists regarded the academy as the bastion of conservatism in the arts. In Munich the situation was even more acute, since not one of the fifteen professors at the academy was younger than fifty years (six had already taught there for twenty years or more), and all considered impressionism the extreme of modern art.[14] The sculptor Edwin Scharff, a prominent academy-trained member of the New Secession recently influenced by cubism in his work, antagonized fellow members of the Council of Artists executive committee in January when he suggested dismissing all academy professors and turning their ateliers over to promising young artists.[15] Members of the Group of 100 pressed their leadership to accelerate demands for academic reform. They supported a broad range of proposals, from abolishing the academy outright to merging the Academy of Fine Arts with the School of Arts and Crafts (thereby creating aesthetic and institutional parity for the fine and applied arts).[16] The idea behind unifying the two schools originated in 1917 with Richard Riemerschmid, director of the School of Arts and Crafts since 1913. Although the academy had declared itself against his plan already in the summer of 1918,[17] it was now resurrected once more. The students, too, expressed a desire for reform, encouraging the academy to hire professors sympathetic to more recent trends in art. On 1 April they listed their preferences: the Frankfurt expressionist Max Beckmann, Karl Caspar from the Munich New Secession, the Dresden expressionist Oskar Kokoschka, Max Pechstein from the Brücke, and the impressionist Max Slevogt, who had departed Munich some twenty years before.[18] Yet the reform proposals finally submitted by a special commission of the Council of Artists essentially left the academy intact. Any reforms, it became clear, were meant merely to preempt more vocal discontent. One proposal, written by the academy professor Hugo von Habermann, included a sharp attack on expressionist art, which ridiculed calls to alter the student/professor relationship and subtly implicated expressionism as a temporary political symptom of the revolution:

> I come now to the . . . most intensive opponents of the academy, the representatives of the most recent direction of all, whom I here for the sake of convenience want to call *expressionists* or *futurists*. Logically they must in principle reject every kind of educational establishment, even the so-called workshop system, because the relationship of the student to the adept is settled for them primarily by the fertilization of fantasy and with a general aesthetic appreciation of the work or with an art-historical exchange of ideas; this kind of education can be settled on a walk or in a cosy chat with much more modest costs. . . .
>
> [As I understand it,] . . . one would impose on oneself a heavy responsibility . . . if one were to draw into artistic matters external circumstances—for example the momentary distribution of political power factors—as a means for coercion for achieving artistic aims.[19]

Although members of the New Secession and the Group of 100 were frustrated in their attempts to reform the academy and were confronted with consistent efforts to marginalize them through recourse to political name-calling, many still found themselves politically, if not artistically, content within the Council of Artists. Their political orientation was expressed most directly in a new art periodical, the *Münchner Blätter für Dichtung und Graphik,* to which several prominent members of the New Secession and the Group of 100 contributed, including Edwin Scharff, the author of the plan to dismiss academy professors; Max Unold, another academy-trained painter only recently influenced in his work by Cézanne; Richard Seewald, a contributor to the pre-war journal *Revolution;* and Paul Klee, the Blaue Reiter artist associated with fairytale and childlike themes. In a programmatic statement in the first issue the managing editor warned against a precipitous embracing of the revolution in general, and rejected bolshevism in particular. "For us," he wrote, "only one thing remains: to be on guard and believe in the spirit. For that is our fate."[20] Such statements were undoubtedly meant to refute such generalized criticism as that in the *Bayerischer Kurier,* which sought to implicate expressionism in revolutionary politics. They also repeated the by-now-familiar catchphrase "spirit," which was used to promote expressionism during the war.

While members of the New Secession and the Group of 100 continued to work within the Council of Artists for change, dissidents on the political left began to organize against its nonrevolutionary stance. On

23 December 1918 many of them attended a meeting of more than four hundred artists in the Deutsches Theater at which Eisner previewed the speech on art that he delivered to the Provisional National Assembly. The meeting dissolved in confusion as artists on the left and right hurled accusations at one another. The *Bayerischer Kurier,* once more fostering negative racial and political stereotypes, reported on the meeting as follows:

> The Jewish-Polish expressionist [Stanislaus] Stückgold read out a doctrinaire-fanatic creed full of heavy, dark mythological words . . . [Another painter] who was closely connected with futurism [said]: the Council of Artists is not in accord with the new times . . . Those with titles and offices should no longer have a say . . . A third speech by the sculptor [Theodor] Pilartz, profusely saturated with political-revolutionary views . . . vehemently reproached the "court painters" who were not to be allowed to thrust themselves forward in the new government.[21]

Sometime in late February, Pilartz and Stückgold were among a handful of relatively unknown young Munich artists and writers who constituted their own artists' organization to the left of the Council of Artists, calling it the Action Committee of Revolutionary Artists (*Aktionsausschuss revolutionärer Künstler*). Pilartz was a young Munich sculptor loosely affiliated with the expressionist camp. Stückgold, who began to paint only at the age of thirty-eight and was largely self-taught, painted in an expressionist-tinged symbolism.[22] Stückgold had a history of political activism: a Polish Jew, he had taken part in the failed 1905 revolution in Russia and had spent time in a Russian prison.

There are no records documenting the founding of the Action Committee of Revolutionary Artists, no complete list of membership, and, with only one exception, there are no minutes of its meetings. For the most part we are left with its public record. Already in January several of the artists and writers who were to form the Action Committee coalesced around a new periodical, *Der Weg,* whose pages offer an insight into their political perspective. *Der Weg* was yet another of the many expressionist journals founded after November; it differed from a number of others, though, in its juxtaposition of artistic contributions (both literary and pictorial) with political glosses. Included in its pages were apolitical essays on individual artists, discourses on the ethical responsibility of the individual, and tracts expounding the necessity of proletarian dictatorship, many of them influenced by reformist anarchism.[23] Their position was grounded in a profound anticapitalism that, however, rejected the centralization and economic determinism of communism and any abridgment of individual freedom. Many of the authors in *Der Weg* were influenced by the ideas of the anarchist writer/philosopher Gustav Landauer, who had argued in his writing for changed human consciousness as a precondition for revolutionary socialism. Now *Der Weg* struggled to reconcile this call for changed consciousness, necessarily a lengthy process, with the fact that a political revolution had already begun.

The "path" of the journal's title was summed up in a programmatic essay in the first issue:

> Our path is traveled by each one who believes in mankind. Perhaps this alone is revolutionary conviction: to believe in mankind.
>
> It is beside the point to tear the hood off the bourgeois, academics, reactionaries; but also of the radicals from prudence, the anticapitalist economists. . . .
>
> There is one path, and we all traveled it: the road from the simple "I" to the loving "I."[24]

Individual consciousness was emphasized as the most significant means to a revolutionary end. Discounting class struggle, the author opposed not only antagonism toward the oppressing class ("bourgeois, academics, reactionaries"), but internecine warfare on the left as well ("radicals from prudence, anticapitalist economists"). The rejection of class warfare as the primary means of struggle was seconded in a gloss by Eduard Trautner, a former political science instructor at a Munich Gymnasium and future member of the Action Committee, who edited the literary and political contributions to *Der Weg:*

> If one exterminated all members of a class today, the gaps would soon be filled and re-established by the growth of another class. Existing classes are grown and are comprehensible from the species of existing men. Class destruction would tear a wound for which healing could only be expected in approximate restoration of the previous condition.
>
> Before one erects the other society, one must have other men to compose it with. Here is the presupposition of all success, and fulfillment must be striven for all the more ardently and fanatically, the more human and deeper understanding and forbearance are opposed to contemporary chronic ill health.[25]

Accompanying these texts was an outright expressionist art, culled from a number of artists associated with the Hans Goltz gallery, the premiere modern gallery in Munich. The similarities between expressionism and reformist anarchism—however superficial—were deemed self-evident: rejection of art dogmas could be equated with rejection of authoritarian power and the emphasis on personal expression likened to insistence on the rights of the individual. Four of the six graphics in the first issue were by the 30-year-old art editor of *Der Weg*, Fritz Schaefler, whose apartment served as editorial offices. His full-page cover woodcut for the first issue (fig. 4.2) showed a figure gesturing at a spiral path leading through the mountains to the dawning sun, signaling, no doubt, the ascent of the individual to a new society. Schaefler was a recent convert to expressionism. As a student at the Munich Polytechnic and the School of Arts and Crafts before the war he became acquainted with several members of the New Secession, but his own work—both naturalistic paintings and *Simplicissimus*-like caricature—remained for the time being unaffected.[26] It was only during the last year of the war that he turned toward expressionist art, while recuperating from serious head wounds received in action on the western front. These were religious etchings, whose emphasis on resurrection and redemption was part of a general turn by expressionist artists to religious themes as a response to increasing disillusionment with the war.

Schaefler also contributed graphics to another Munich journal, whose eclecticism far surpassed that of *Der Weg*. This was *Süddeutsche Freiheit*, which under the editorship of Gustav Klingelhöfer consistently featured expressionist graphics on its cover.[27] Klingelhöfer, a member of a Munich soldiers' council who had switched party allegiance from the SPD to the USPD with the revolution, proclaimed as the goal of *Süddeutsche Freiheit:*

> . . . the national greater-German federal republic. The national and socialist people's state. Overcoming of imperialist capitalism. The national and international working partnership of the peoples.
>
> Our path: the overcoming of Prussian power centralism. Fight against every dominion by person or class. Education of all to political and social responsibility. Cultivation of the international solidarity of the spirit.[28]

Federalism, anticapitalism, socialism, and anti-Prussianism were all tenets of Eisner's political philosophy in the early days of the revolution, as were the anticommunism and opposition to one-class rule also espoused in *Süddeutsche Freiheit*. In this it also followed the precepts of Landauer, who was called by Eisner to Munich to participate in the revolutionary government. Klingelhöfer's utopian socialism was even more expansive, however, joining together contributions from Christian socialists, anarchists, SPD and USPD theoreticians, and even anthroposophists. Schaefler's cover woodcut for the 13 January issue (fig. 4.3) was indicative of the inclusiveness, simultaneously evoking revolutionary exhortation and religious admonition. A crowd gathers in a city street, proclaiming: "Brothers—do your duty for humanity." Schaefler drew on two earlier graphic works for his woodcut, the 1918 etching *Golgotha* (fig. 4.4) and a woodcut of the same year titled *Proclamation of Freedom* (fig. 4.5). The figures resemble the exuberant,

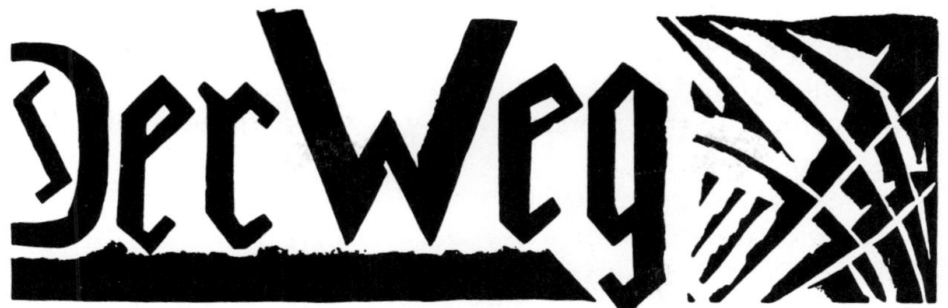

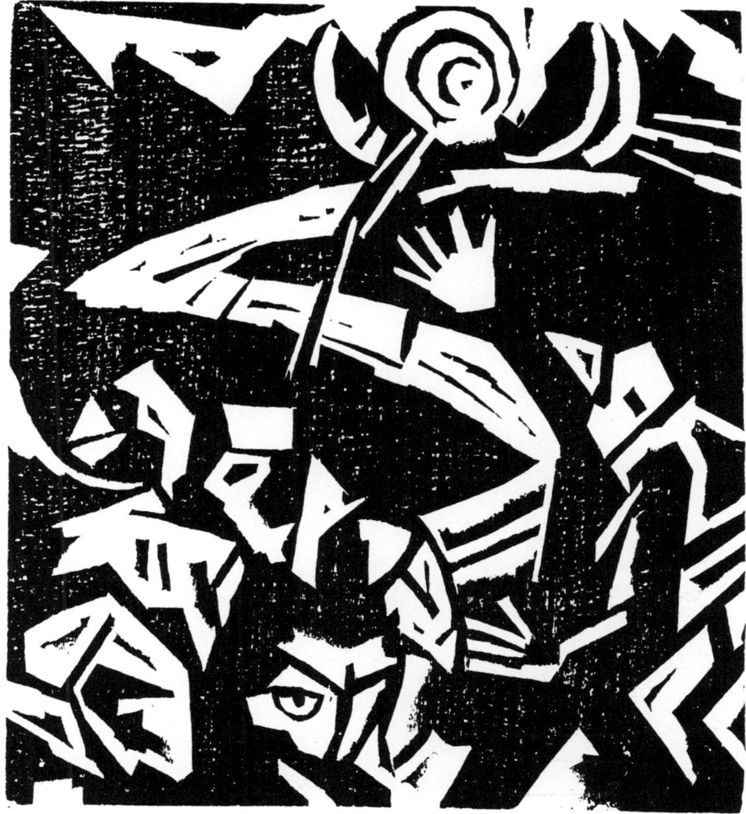

4.2 Fritz Schaefler, cover illustration for *Der Weg* 1, no. 1 (1919). Woodcut, 46 x 32 cm. © Anne Gold, fotografin.

united marchers from *Proclamation of Freedom,* which was one of Schaefler's first woodcuts celebrating the revolution. Compositionally the *Süddeutsche Freiheit* cover resembles *Golgotha,* the rising sun replacing Christ's head and the text forming the horizontal axis of the cross.

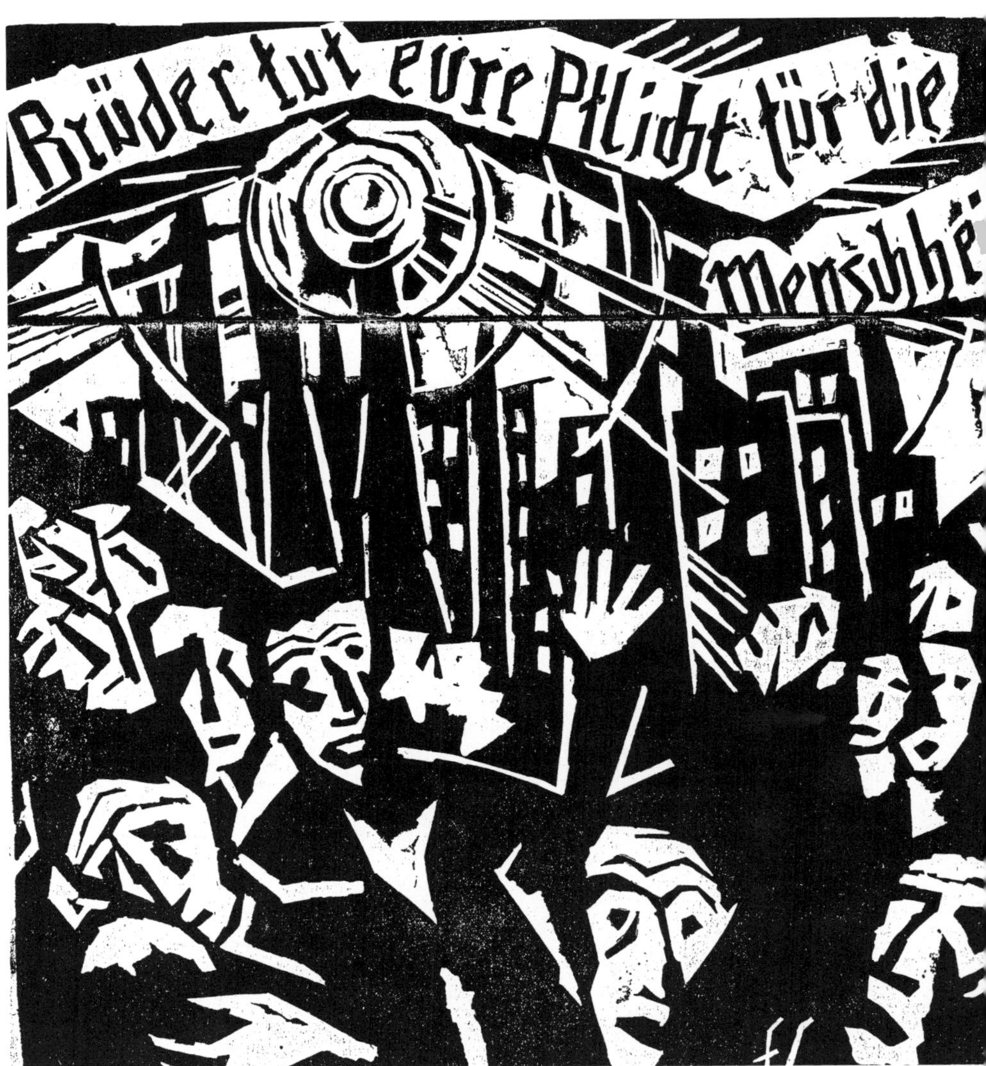

4.3 Fritz Schaefler, cover illustration for *Süddeutsche Freiheit* (13 January 1919). Woodcut, dimensions unknown.

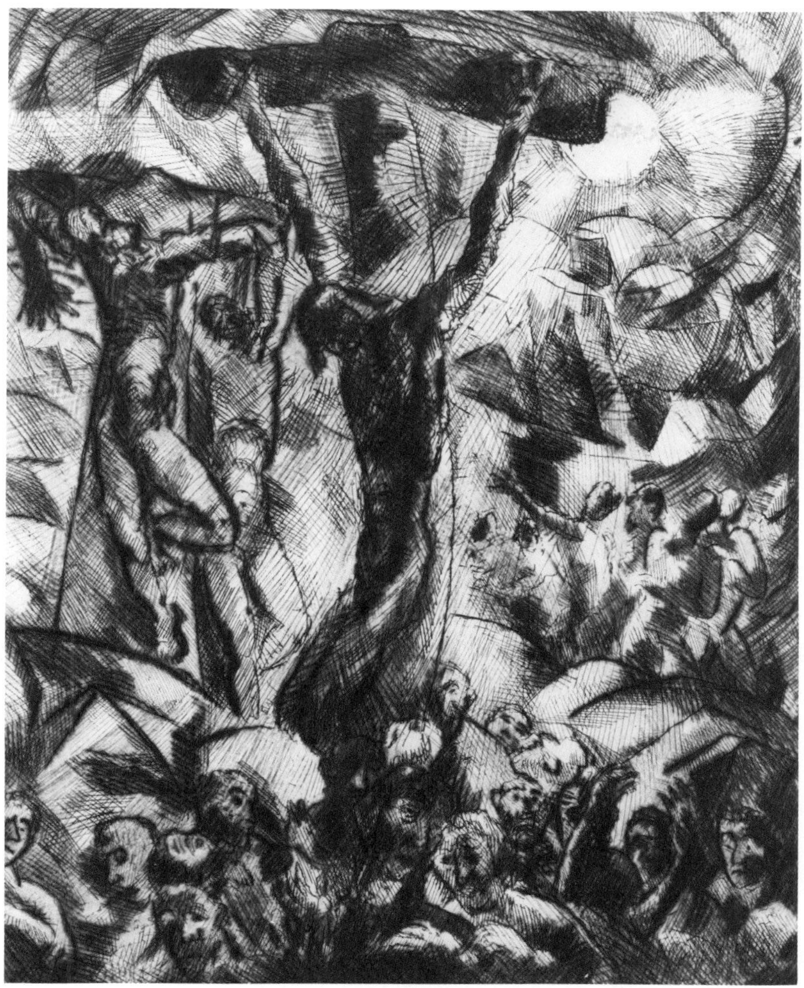

4.4 Fritz Schaefler, *Golgotha,* 1918. Etching, 28.7 x 22.8 cm. © Anne Gold, fotografin.

These were the heady days of the revolution, when Trautner, Schaefler, Klingelhöfer, and others could still imagine an ideal union of socialism, religion, and expressionism based on an altered human consciousness. Almost immediately, though, one of Klingelhöfer's coworkers questioned one element in that equation, the comprehensibility of expressionist images for a proletarian audience. Klingelhöfer defended the prominence of expressionist graphics in *Süddeutsche Freiheit* as follows:

You ask me if it is absolutely necessary that the title page of *Süddeutsche Freiheit* displays an expressionist image "that no one understands." Yes, it is necessary. For these images proceed from the same revolutionary spirit from which the content of our newspaper is born. The proletariat previously had too little time to bother with things that were not immediately connected with questions of its existence. The revolution has created a remedy for this, and now the prole-

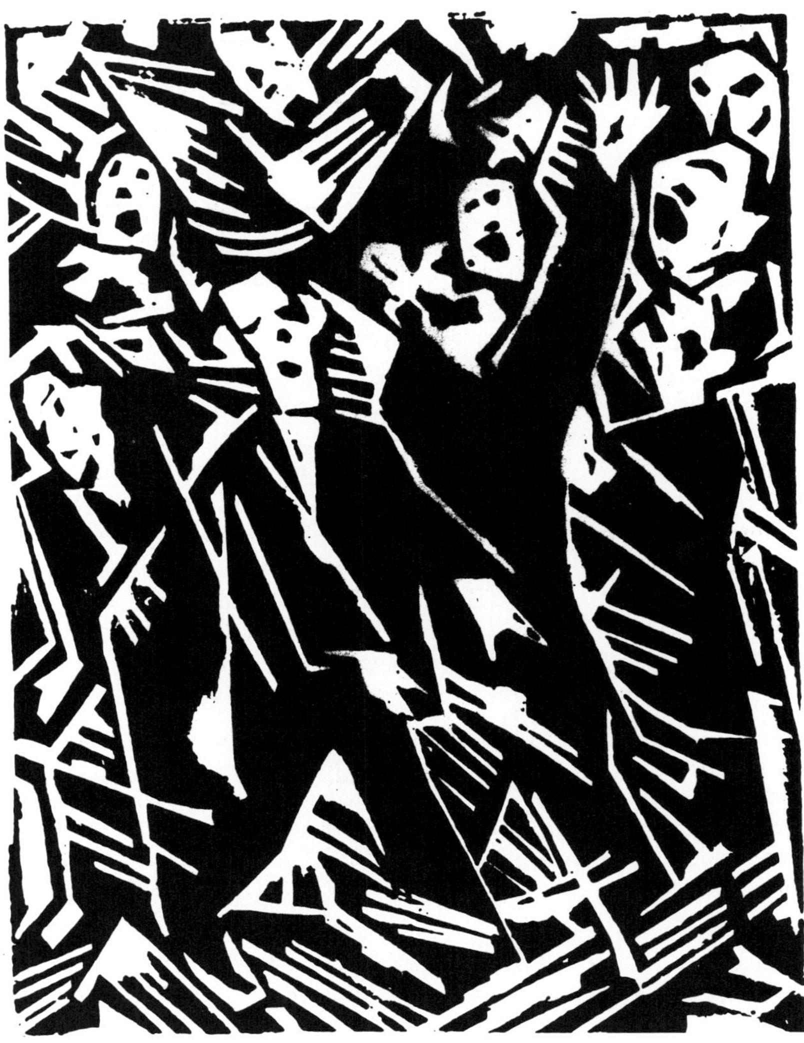

4.5 Fritz Schaefler, *Ausruf der Freiheit (Exclamation of Freedom)*, 1918. Woodcut, dimensions unknown.

tariat is obliged to concern itself somewhat more with questions that did not interest it before. The proletariat should deal with the new art, for it is revolution as well.

The artists who sketch our title pages are mostly from the proletariat, or in any case are closely connected with it in conviction. . . . And the proletariat is obliged to at least try to understand the new art. Just as it demands from the bourgeoisie that they understand the revolution.[29]

Klingelhöfer thereby reasserted once more the generalized claims for the revolutionary nature of expressionism and envisioned the dilemma resolved simply by goodwill on both sides. This goodwill, though, was more difficult to find in the coming weeks, when the issue of whether the proletariat could understand expressionism surfaced yet again.

In the wake of the January election defeat of the USPD, the contributors to *Der Weg* and *Süddeutsche Freiheit* were forced to reassess their views. The second issue of *Der Weg*, which appeared after the elections, still held steadfast to its idealized view of revolution, but nonetheless signaled in several critical contributions a move to the left. Trautner's monthly gloss no longer emphasized reconciliation, but warned in cryptic words of the threat to the revolution from all sides: "New grown interest discovers the proletariat . . . Often fear (fear of the slaveholder) and mistrust call themselves love of mankind . . . efficiency scents business (proletariat = possibility of activity if overseas is closed)."[30] This was not the threat of suppression, but of cooptation of the revolution. Trautner was equally wary of self-aggrandizing political parties and the proletariat, criticizing the former for only "labor[ing] to sharpen differences" and as a result "divert[ing] aspirations," and the latter for concern only with wage issues. The provocative concluding essay in the issue, written by Kurt Bock, took an even more radical line:

It is time that the revolution create a revolution, a reformation. The hour cries for the politics of fact. It is a doubtful thing to believe in the self-acting force of the spirit and to trust that appeal, program, and idea must triumph through evolution. . . . The politician of the spirit is a fruitless notion; dictatorship . . . alone enforces true politics. . . . One may stand in whatever camp it might be, under the stormy pressure of necessity he will not escape socialism.[31]

Bock's language carried unmistakable political code words: "dictatorship" rather than "evolutionary" socialism, "action" rather than "spirit." This was in contradiction to the *Münchner Blätter,* with its fear of bolshevism and its antithetical warning not to confuse "spirit" with "action." It was also a response to prominent intellectuals in Munich, such as Heinrich Mann and his Progressive Council of Intellectuals, who, although ostensibly socialists, opposed radical change under the banner of the "radicalism of the spirit."[32]

The art-critical contributions to the February issue of *Der Weg* similarly responded to the changed political situation. An essay on Paul

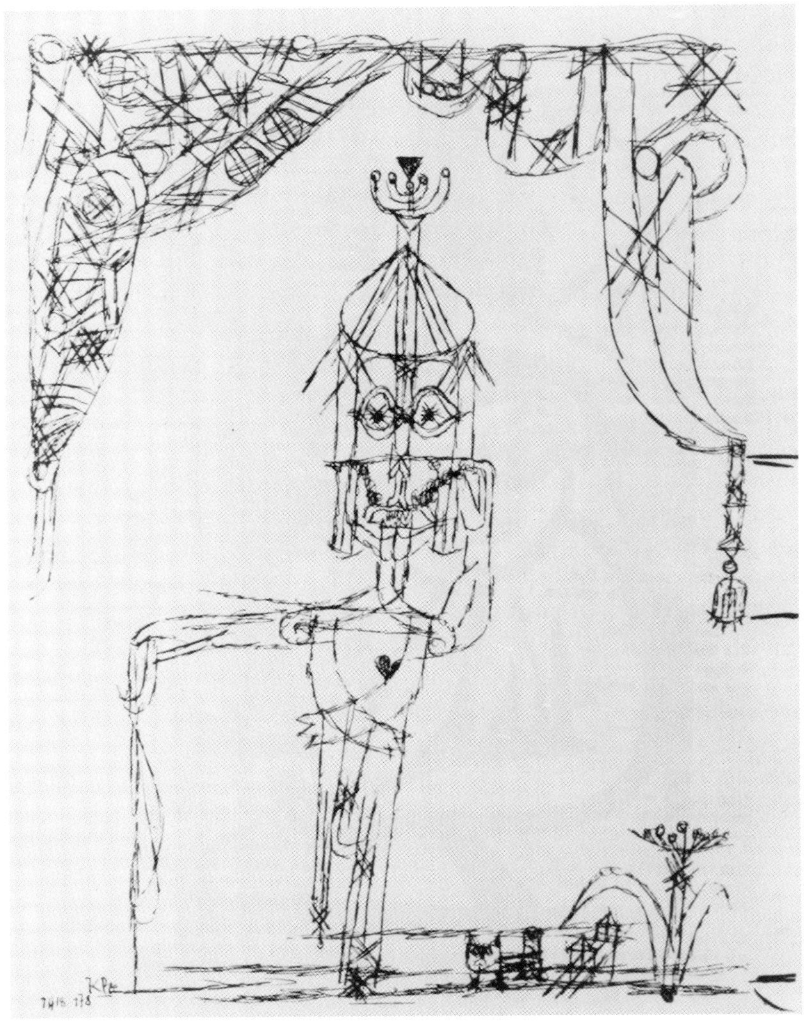

4.6 Paul Klee, *Der Feldherr (Commander-in-Chief)*, 1918. Pen and ink on linen paper, 29.5 x 22 cm. Cabinet des Estampes, Strasbourg. © 1989, copyright by Cosmopress, Geneva.

Klee that avoided any mention of political significance for his art, for example, was illustrated with one of his more explicit political caricatures of Kaiser Wilhelm II (fig. 4.6), the embodiment of philistine taste and artistic repression. Even more significant was Trautner's review of the January graphic exhibition at the Hans Goltz gallery. Rather than praising all the expressionist art on display, Trautner distinguished—if somewhat inarticulately—between two groups of artists, expressing disappointment in the "merely aesthetic" works of Josef Eberz and H. M. Davringhausen while praising works by the Berlin artist George Grosz and the young Munich expressionists Fritz Schaefler, Georg Schrimpf, and Aloys Wach. The distinction between the two groups was a subtle one. Eberz, with his ecstatic religious graphics, and Davringhausen, with his *Valori Plastici* influenced work, were less "classic" expressionists in the sense that their images were less fragmented, more plastic and readable. The distinction, though, may have had more to do with political affiliation than aesthetic merit: at that moment Schaefler, Schrimpf, and Wach were involved, along with Trautner, in the radical Action Committee of Revolutionary Artists. Trautner probably knew that the Berlin Dadaist Grosz had recently joined the Communist Party. Eberz, on the other hand, apparently declined to join the Action Committee, as did Davringhausen.

At its peak the Action Committee of Revolutionary Artists numbered no more than twenty-five or so members; the Council of Artists, by comparison, boasted more than two thousand members from eighteen different groups by late January, and on 21 February, it was recognized by the Bavarian *Kultusministerium* as the official advisory body on artistic affairs.[33] Yet it was the Action Committee of Revolutionary Artists that was to play the critical role in the Munich cultural scene in the coming months. For on the day the Bavarian *Kultusministerium* recognized the Council of Artists, the day the Bavarian constituent assembly was set to meet for the first time, Kurt Eisner, his resignation as prime minister in his pocket, was assassinated by a right-wing extremist, and the real crisis of the Munich revolution began.

7 April–13 April: Revolutionary Expressionism and the First Council Republic

When news of Eisner's murder reached the public, one of his supporters rushed to the opening session of the constituent assembly and shot and wounded Erhard Auer, Eisner's SPD rival. The meeting dispersed in panic, and the workers' and soldiers' councils interceded to fill the political void. They called a general strike to protest Eisner's murder and bourgeois opposition to the revolution, and they formed a Central Committee to supervise a new coalition socialist government headed by Johannes Hoffmann, a member of the SPD. But leftist impatience with the Hoffmann government increased with the proclamation on 20 March 1919 of a soviet republic in neighboring Hungary, with rumors that Austria was headed on the same path, and with reports of a successful miners' strike in the Ruhr. In order to forestall the re-assembly of the Bavarian parliament, on 7 April 1919 several Independent Socialist politicians, most of them members of the Central Committee, along with several leading leftist intellectuals, proclaimed a council republic in Munich. Bavaria now had two rival socialist governments as the Hoffmann government fled to Bamberg and requested aid from the central government in Berlin. The Munich USPD, as the largest party to support the council republic, received five of the eleven seats in the new cabinet, which was led by the 26-year-old pacifist dramatist Ernst Toller, Eisner's successor as head of the party. Also influential in the new government was Erich Mühsam, who had organized the anarchist Gruppe Tat in 1909 and contributed to the journal *Revolution* in 1913. He now nominated for Commissar for People's Enlightenment (as the minister in charge of education and culture was now called) the 48-year-old anarchist Gustav Landauer, who had delivered the eulogy at Eisner's funeral. The participation of the anarchist Landauer in the government was a political landmark. Anarchist antiparliamentarism had heretofore precluded any direct participation in the political life of Germany. Landauer's position in the Munich council republic—however short-lived—was the first time that an anarchist took political office in Germany. Skeptical that the time was propitious for seizing power, the communists remained outside the government.

These dramatic events did not take long to reverberate in the expressionist camp. Following Eisner's murder, the mood was somber. The third issue of *Der Weg* documented the increasing tension between the utopian dreams for a brotherhood of mankind and the brutal realities of Munich politics. Fittingly, the issue was devoted to the slain Eisner, prophet of the journal's guiding philosophy. Featured was a poem by Trautner that simultaneously expressed lamentation and hope for the future; the poet's faith in the transition from "chains" to "victory" was at once recognition of political crisis and a means of conjuring it away. It was the only contribution in the March issue to bring about this reconciliation. The other essays in the issue were discrepant with one another, either steadfastly adhering to "faith in mankind" or moving

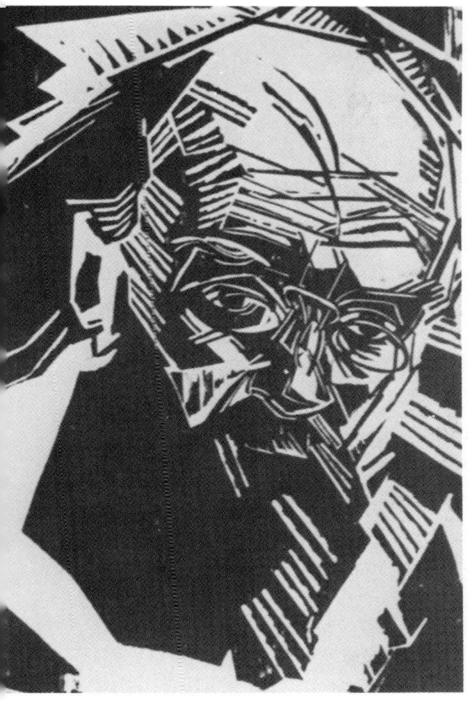

Fritz Schaefler, *Kurt Eisner*, 1919.
·dcut, 32.2 x 22.4 cm.

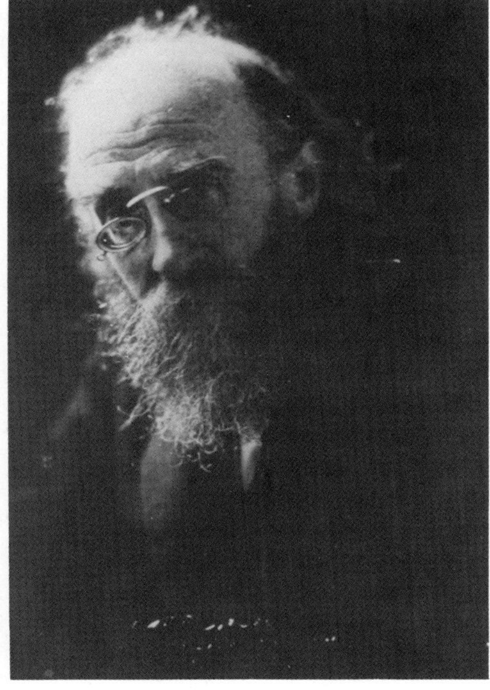

4.8 Germaine Krull, photograph of Kurt Eisner, 1918.

toward communist rhetoric. Most prominently featured in the March issue was a full-page woodcut by Schaefler of Kurt Eisner (fig. 4.7) based on a well-known official photograph of Eisner taken in 1918 by Germaine Krull, which had been widely circulated as a postcard[34] (fig. 4.8). The journal thus upheld Eisner as a leading figure in spite of his defeat in the election and murder, thereby combining antiparliamentary sentiment with expressionistic hero-worship.

Süddeutsche Frieheit, too, gradually altered its political line. By March it was publishing essays that sought to convince its readers that democracy and council rule were not mutually exclusive. On 10 March 1919 *Süddeutsche Frieheit* also published an expressionist woodcut portrait of Eisner by Schaefler based on another Krull photograph (fig. 4.9). This woodcut, however, was even closer to the original photograph, perhaps to make it more understandable to a wider audience not initiated in expressionist art. *Süddeutsche Freiheit* offered for sale signed copies of the woodcut priced at twelve marks each, considerably higher

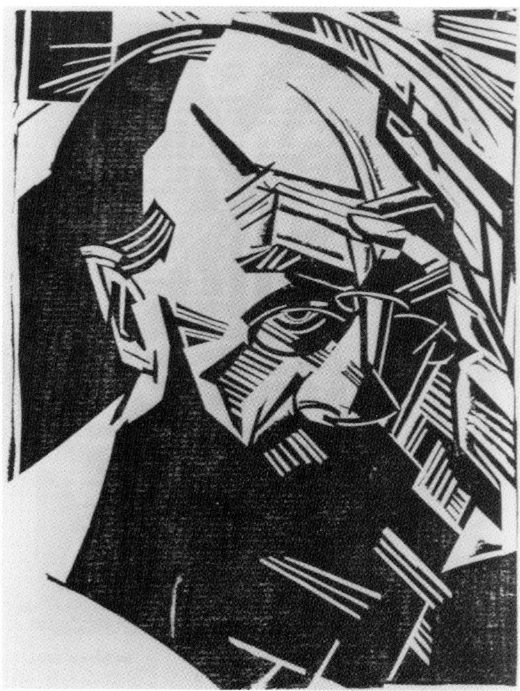

4.9 Fritz Schaefler, *Kurt Eisner,* 1919. Woodcut, 45.5 x 30 cm.

than the three-mark postcard photos of Eisner. Directed at a middle-class audience that supported expressionism, the difference in price between the woodcut and the postcard illustrated the class divisions that still existed between expressionist art and photography. It was precisely the accessibility of the new art that was to be questioned time and again in the coming weeks.

When Landauer became Commissar for People's Enlightenment, he chose as the group to implement his cultural program not the Council of Artists (which had more than two thousand members), but the smaller, more radical Action Committee of Revolutionary Artists. This choice confirmed the ideological convergence between Landauer's anarchism and the program espoused by Action Committee members in *Der Weg*.

Despite Landauer's political isolation before the revolution (or perhaps because of it), he exercised a great deal of influence on a younger generation of artists and writers, particularly those who became involved in the Munich revolution. From the memoirs of Ernst Toller, the new head of the council republic, and those of the expressionist writer Oskar Maria Graf, a member of the Action Committee, we know that Landauer's 1911 *Call to Socialism* played an important role in shaping their political consciousness.[35] What Landauer outlined in this book was an elaborate model for anarchist settlements based on Pierre Proudhon's and Peter Kropotkin's ideas of decentralization and mutual aid, which were to prefigure a future socialist society brought about not simply by political and economic liberation, but by spiritual renewal as well. With its erudite style, it was directed not so much at the working class as at intellectuals, including artists, promising them a central role. Indeed, Landauer's early anarchist efforts involved several artists and writers, including his 1901 attempt to establish a mutualist community. His utopian vision of a distant socialist society, and his recourse to intellectuals and artists, was, however, also a result of his political weakness, most significantly his exclusion from the Anarchist Federation of Germany, whose main weapons—class struggle and the mass strike—he vigorously opposed.

Landauer's impact reached its nadir on the eve of the war (the circulation of his journal *Der Sozialist* had sunk below two thousand and ceased publication in 1915; his Socialist League, which at its height had only 150 members, did not even meet in 1914).[36] With increasing disillusionment in the war effort after 1916, though, he began to attract a wider audience. Although he had opposed the war from the beginning, he was mindful of censorship and refrained during the war from explicit discussions of politics, writing and lecturing instead on literary and philosophical issues. Landauer's retreat from active political involvement had as its corollary an increased preoccupation with the role of art in bringing about social change. Munich artists and writers could read his essay "From Unstillable Desire" in the Munich journal *Zeit-Echo;* although heavily censored, his repudiation of the state and his promotion of the "spirit" as a guiding force in a restructured society were still discernible. "The Path of the German Spirit," published in the 6 February 1916 *Frankfurter Zeitung* and rewritten for *Die Weissen Blätter* in June 1916, lamented the isolation of art and the artist as a sign that "spirit" was lacking in German society, predicting that revolution alone would make it possible for "spirit" to reassert itself once more. He now assigned to art a critical function in achieving revolutionary change, concluding: "The consequence of poetry is revolution." With no political outlet for his own pacifism, artistic activity took the place of political action.

Despite the fact that the first edition of his *Call to Socialism* had a print run of only 250 copies and that it was censored in 1915,[37] it had created enough of an impact that by July 1916 Landauer received daily requests for copies.[38] By 1917 he had received so many requests that he was planning a new edition, which finally appeared early in 1919.[39] His description in *Call to Socialism* of an economy based on mutual aid, favoring the handicrafts, and his high praise for the integration of the arts in medieval society, seemed to anticipate the new manifestos of radical artists' groups, which also proposed an end to the isolation of art as a luxury commodity through the intermediary of the crafts. His writings offered artists and intellectuals opposed to the war a vision of a socialist future, achieved without violence, where spiritual and economic renewal were inseparable, guaranteeing social significance for their efforts without, however, jeopardizing artistic and intellectual freedom. Yet Landauer had in no way forecast the November revolution, and only traveled to Munich from his home in Krumbach after having been summoned by Kurt Eisner. Once there he did not join Eisner's cabinet, but joined the Revolutionary Workers' Council and the Central Workers' Council. Landauer, who had previously argued that revolution would only occur in a far-distant future, was now faced with the discrepancy between his own projections and the rapidly moving political developments. Still, when he reissued his *Call to Socialism* in January 1919 he held fast to his earlier positions: he was still anticentralist and anti-Marxist, and still insistent on Kropotkin's model as the path toward spiritual socialism. He concluded: "The transformation of society can only come in love, in work, in quiet."[40] Yet even Landauer soon recognized the threat to peaceful transformation; precisely at the time his book was reissued, he found himself moving toward the left. He disagreed with Eisner's call for elections to the constituent assembly and viewed this act as a concession to the right.

When Landauer took over the department for culture in the council republic he brought with him an established agenda for change. During the war he had developed ideas on restructuring education, particularly university education.[41] One of his first acts as Commissar for People's Enlightenment was to comply on 8 April with a demand by several members of the executive committee of the Council of Artists to suspend all professors at the Academy of Fine Arts. This was apparently an effort by the Council of Artists to forestall more radical demands made by the Action Committee. The majority of students signaled their approval, forming their own students' council. Landauer had also long been involved with plans for reforming the theater to make it more accessible to the working class. He had served for years on the board of the Berlin *Volksbühne* and shortly before the end of the war he had concluded negotiations with the avant-garde Dumont-Lindemann theater in Düsseldorf to take over as artistic director (a position he was never to assume). Already on 8 April he held a meeting with actors in the Wittelsbach Palace to discuss plans for their self-governance of Munich theaters, a plan he had already anticipated for the Düsseldorf theater.[42] Two days later the Action Committee announced in the *Münchner Neueste Nachrichten* Landauer's approval for converting the Prince Regent Theater into the "first true theater of the people of Bavaria."[43] Landauer also considered appointing Bruno Taut of the WCA in Berlin—who had strong ties to the anarchist movement—to the building ministry.[44] Above all else, though, Landauer wanted to reform the Munich press. In a 30 December 1918 speech to the provisional national assembly he had argued:

> This is no press freedom that we have. On the contrary, I declare, we are in a revolution, we are in danger, the republic is in danger through this propaganda . . . With the help of so-called public opinion again and again counterrevolutionary putsches are being prepared.[45]

In this speech he singled out for special criticism Munich's two largest bourgeois newspapers, the *Münchner Neueste Nachrichten* and the *Bayerischer Kurier.* On 8 April, the Action Committee assumed control of both these papers.[46]

Landauer's choice of the Action Committee of Revoltutionary Artists to enact his cultural program was not a foregone conclusion. For one thing, Landauer had never been an outspoken supporter of expressionism, distrusting " 'ism' mania."[47] His own taste in the visual arts apparently ran more toward the socially committed realism of Käthe Kollwitz.[48] Yet there is evidence to suggest Landauer considered expressionism—at least expressionist drama—the art of the future, even if for the time being it remained obscure to a general audience. By 1918 he had become a committed supporter of Georg Kaiser's expressionist dramas, recommending his play *Gas* to both the *Volksbühne* and the Dumont-Lindemann theater.[49] When Kaiser arrived in Munich in late December 1918, Landauer was immediately in touch with him.[50] Kaiser soon joined the Action Committee, where he was only one of the personal links between Landauer and the group. The journalist Titus Tautz, who became editor of the *Münchner Neueste Nachrichten* during the council republic, knew Landauer through his father's participation in the anarchist *Neue Gemeinschaft* group. Another member of the Action Committee, the writer Alfred Wolfenstein, had corresponded with Landauer throughout the war.[51] Oskar Maria Graf and the Munich expressionist painter Georg Schrimpf had belonged to Erich Mühsam's Gruppe Tat group before the war, an offshoot of Landauer's Socialist League, while another Action Committee member, Max Bethke, had belonged to a Berlin chapter of the League. Landauer may also have known Fritz Schaefler through their mutual friend Mühsam. Landauer, then, was personally acquainted with many of the members of the Action Committee, making their selection over the Council of Artists to enact his cultural program even more likely. What Landauer now offered these writers and artists was an opportunity to end their isolation and assume control over the institutional art world.[52] With the selection of the Action Committee Landauer apparently overcame his trepidations about expressionism.

The cover pages of the *Münchner Neueste Nachrichten* and the *Bayerischer Kurier* on 8 April 1919 left little doubt that the Action Committee promoted expressionism as the art of the radical council republic. On them were emblazoned expressionist woodcuts by Aloys Wach, whose art came to be more closely identified with the council republic than that of any other member of the Action Committee. Wach, like Schaefler, was a little-known artist who had exhibited in group shows

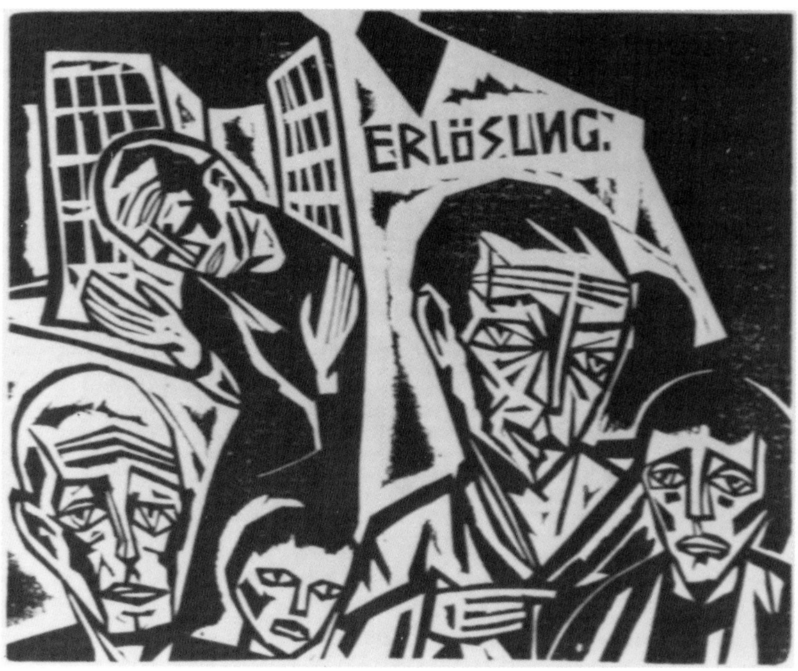

4.10 Aloys Wach, *Erlösung (Redemption)*, 1919. Woodcut, 32.2 x 24 cm.

at Goltz's gallery during the war while serving in a press and propaganda division of the royal Tirolean fusiliers. He was drawn to Munich after the war by his friend Egon Wertheimer, private secretary to Eisner's minister of finance,[53] and soon became friendly with Schaefler. The Wach woodcut in the *Bayerischer Kurier* (fig. 4.10), with its characteristic exaggerated, overly large, worried physiognomies, had appeared already in the February issue of *Der Weg*. In the dramatic black and white contrast of the raw woodcut technique, Wach juxtaposed two scenes, joined together at the seam. In the first, a figure retreats forlornly, while in front of him two faces stare out at the viewer. In the second, a man points at the youth beside him, with the word "Redemption" inscribed above. In *Der Weg* the woodcut had appeared in the same issue as a text calling for the building of a new community to end the isolation of the individual. As with Landauer, the process of escaping from "private self-centeredness" to "comradeship" (which the author of the article described as "redemption") necessitated a political commitment as well. Wach's woodcut depicted this redemption: from dejected isolation on the left to the beginnings of comradeship on the right. Surrounding Wach's woodcut in the *Bayerischer Kurier* were the slogans "Long live the council republic," "Proletarian and peasant unite," "Prohibition against child labor," and "All protection and rights to working women." Wach also provided two woodcuts for the 8 April *Münchner Neueste Nachrichten*. The first, subtitled *Brotherhood* (fig. 4.11), presented a man's head, with furrowed brow and somber expression, and a city visible behind him. The other (fig. 4.12) depicted a barefoot man with a similarly worried physiognomy, gesturing toward the empty ground beside him. Behind him is a jumble of tilted buildings. Its subtitle, *Confiscation of Bourgeois Apartments*, referred to the government's new policy of confiscating private houses to relieve Munich's housing shortage and thereby suggested the worried man was a homeless worker. Wach had been concerned with the homeless, the poor, prostitutes, and the hungry since a stay in Paris in 1913–14, when a delay in receiving money from his family caused him to wander the streets homeless and hungry.

Published under the aegis of the revolutionary government, the meaning of these woodcuts was now supposed to become true. Yet the downcast eyes, furrowed brows, and slumped shoulders of Wach's figures anomalously undermined their appeal, suggesting not salvation, but misery. His woodcut of the homeless revealed only the pathetic symptoms; it was the subtitle, probably not provided by Wach, that indicated both the cause (bourgeois greed) and the solution (confiscation). Furthermore, a woodcut such as *Redemption*, which required for

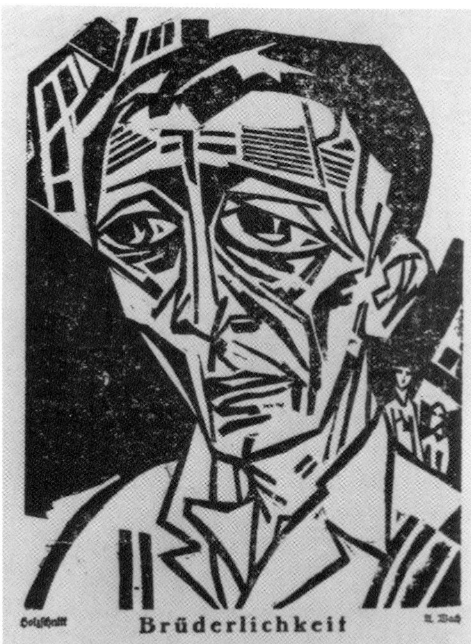

4.11 Aloys Wach, *Brüderlichkeit (Brotherhood)*, illustration for the *Münchner Neueste Nachrichten* (8 April 1919).

its understanding the accompanying text, now stood alone, as if its meaning were self-evident. As reported retrospectively by a member of the Action Committee, the woodcuts, with their intransigent expressionist style, enraged many workers. When one group complained to Landauer, he reportedly counseled patience, assuring them that the artists represented their cause, and advised them to familiarize themselves with the new art before condemning it.[54]

Wach's woodcuts continued to appear in the *Münchner Neueste Nachrichten* and the *Bayerischer Kurier*, accompanied by revolutionary slogans, for two more days and then ceased. For the next several days, however, the *Münchner Neueste Nachrichten* prominently featured in a series of articles the most lengthy, explicit, and public discussion of expressionism that had ever taken place outside an art journal. The first such text was written by a member of the Action Committee, the art critic Ludwig Coellen:

Before there was the political revolution there was the revolution of art. Long before the end of the world war cleared the way politically for the spirit of the new time, this spirit had come to be alive in the new art. This is what today

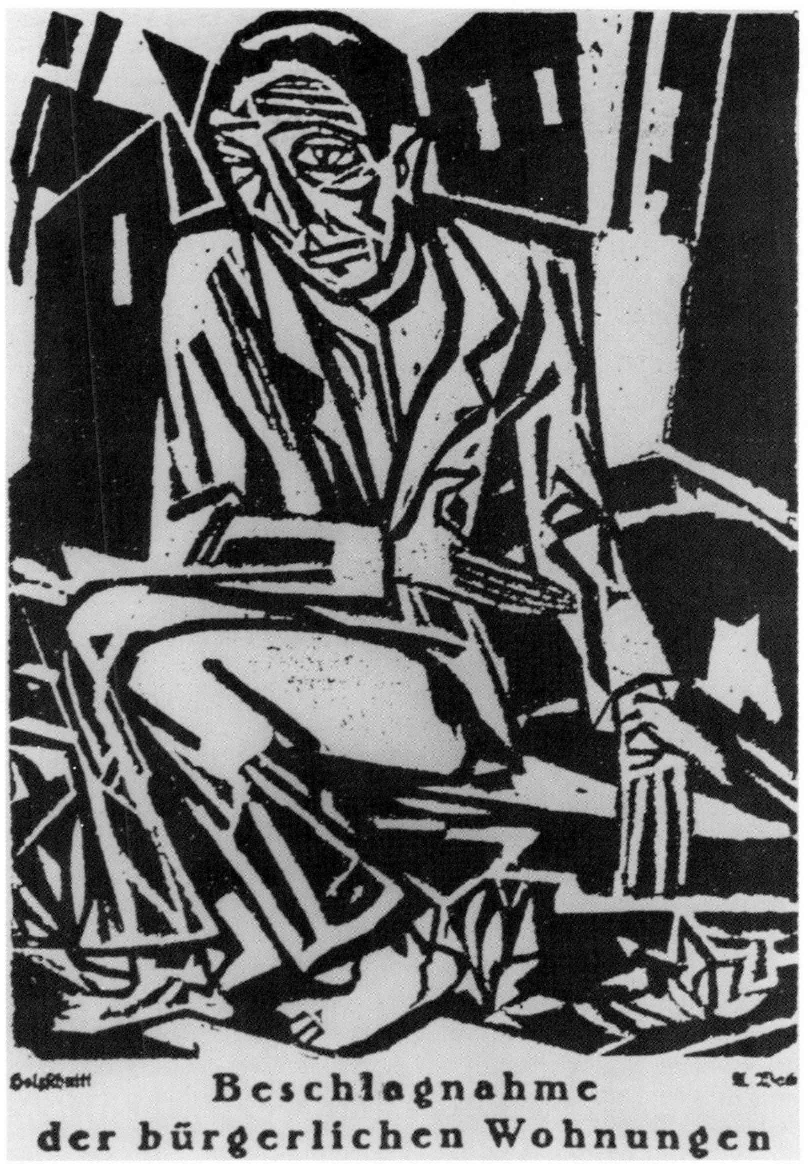

4.12 Aloys Wach, *Beschlagnahme der bürgerlichen Wohnungen (Confiscation of Bourgeois Apartments),* illustration for *Münchner Neueste Nachrichten* (8 April 1919).

the working people must know: that the young artists and the young art are its allies. It is the spirit of the brotherly, of the all-embracing community, it is the spirit of the living mass movement which produced this art, which gives birth to its forms and shines through it. . . .

Precisely because the new art, according to its spirit, completely set itself in opposition to the dominant tradition, its form is also something completely new, something foreign, which still seems strange to people, which many people, who have not seen this art grow, do not yet recognize as belonging to them. . . .

It [the new art] wants to show the working people that it works for them and is of one mind with them. Soon the time will be there when each countryman feels: that is my art, that is the art of the people. Have a little patience and you will love these forms which appear strange . . . The new art cheers the world revolution. It knows that now the day of its own victory has also come.[55]

Echoing nineteenth-century utopian socialist art theory, Coellen also described the task of the artist as expanding art into everyday life, giving artistic shape to everyday objects. In this essentially pleading text, Coellen repeated what was by then the avant-garde version of the affinity between art and revolution, namely that the artistic revolution had presaged the political one. Proof was offered by analogy and in the negative: the form of the new art was opposed to the "dominant tradition." Coellen was equally vague about whether the new art represented an all-embracing "community"—thereby harmonizing class conflict—or only the interests of one class.

In the same issue of the *Münchner Neueste Nachrichten* was a position paper on "Art and the Proletariat" signed in the name of the Action Committee by Titus Tautz. Unlike Coellen, Tautz never mentioned the new art by name. Rather, he was more concerned to justify the importance of art—and the artist—in the new political situation:

[Art] has no end in itself. It must serve the new life—which should be a true community—summon it and incite it. It must make men mature and give them the conscience and the pure beauty which shall from now on actively determine all human relationships.

Finally the artist proceeds to the position which is due him, at the center of and in fruitful connection to the . . . significant plan of general work. . . . Only he has a right to call himself an artist whose work is . . . necessary and good for men, so that he is conscious of his worth as a person, can comprehend his human task and aspire more strongly and self-assuredly to perfection.

Art is neither luxury nor amusement.

Art is bread; the oppressed, suffering man who finally liberates himself is hungry for truth and beauty. Only that which stills this hunger is art. Art is to be made accessible to all men. It is to be kept pure from the empty, superfluous . . . and contaminated products of the old society.[56]

Dramatizing its significance with the phrase "art is bread," Tautz claimed a privileged role for art as an instrument to revolutionize human consciousness, much as Landauer had during the war. Tautz's vague notion of integrating art into a "significant plan of general work" still sidestepped what had been the central concern of Eisner's artistic program, namely the economic basis of art production.

In the following days other writers repeated similar convictions in the same passionate, exhortative language. Another author envisioned a "revolutionized" art education as the key to creating a revolutionary consciousness. In words similar to Tautz's he explained: "Everyone who knows how dependent the final and true accomplishment of the socialist idea is on a fundamental transformation of the human psyche must understand that artistic education is something which is as necessary as bread."[57] Hans Theodor Joel, an editor of *Der Weg*, sought to link the visual appearance of expressionism to this transformation, insisting that expressionism involved "the search for the proper expression of a vigorous personality, the struggle of the spirit against the exterior fetters of an only apparent world. . . . The ethical goal of this art . . . is educating [people] to humanity."[58] Yet another article examined the political significance of expressionism, summing up the view of the Action Committee:

> It is natural that this generation of artists had to become political (as opposed to previous ones, which allowed the exterior world to act on them like an instrument)—specifically socialist-revolutionary, for the sole expressionist-political program has as its goal to give form to the exterior world according to a human inner one, to make human beings masters and organizers of matter. . . . The greatest announcers of expressionist politics are Plato and Christ, the radical promoters not of the objective/accidental, but of the spiritual/eternal.[59]

These were still the spiritual claims for expressionism promoted during the war, now vaguely linked to revolutionary politics. Incorporating the buzzwords of political and religious renewal, the articles in the *Münchner Neueste Nachrichten* passionately assumed the ability of art and artists to lead the way to revolutionary consciousness. Many of these artists and writers had ties to the pre-war anarchism of a journal such as *Revolution*. But their optimistic proclamations now had little of the biting rhetoric of explosive violence and sexual license characteristic of pre-war anarchism in Munich.

To further educate the readers of the *Münchner Neueste Nachrichten* and *Bayerischer Kurier*—the only two newspapers published during the council republic besides the USPD *Neue Zeitung*—the Action Committee also announced public lectures on the new art by its members, in addition to Stanislaus Stückgold's continuing lectures and drawing instruction for the proletariat.[60] These, too, were attempts to broaden their appeal and influence. Like artists in other German cities, they also pointed to events in Russia to bolster their claims. In the 9 April *Münchner Neueste Nachrichten,* the Action Committee published the text of a communiqué from the NARKOMPROS in Russia, as well as their own reply. The Russian artist D. P. Sterenberg reported on the triumph of modern art in revolutionary Russia and seemed to confirm Coellen's opinion when he wrote: "Only the new creative work which arose shortly before the convulsion of the world can agree with the rhythm of the life which develops anew."[61] The Action Committee responded: "With the proclamation of the Bavarian Council Republic we want to create the possibility to realize our plans, which completely coincide with yours."[62]

Surprisingly, none of the essays on the new art in the *Münchner Neueste Nachrichten* was written by the socialist-leaning art editor of the newspaper, Wilhelm Hausenstein, who had been one of the earliest supporters of expressionism in Germany. A member of the SPD since 1907 and a former instructor in socialist evening courses, Hausenstein had attempted in his early writings to develop a sociological approach to art based on the writings of Marx. In *Der nackte Mensch in der Kunst aller Zeiten und Völker* (1913) he promoted modern art as the art of a coming socialist society, without, however, elaborating on the political life or economic organization of such a society. By early 1918, though, he had become increasingly disillusioned with expressionism, suggesting in speeches that its innovative phase had passed, that its increasing subjectivity threatened comprehension, and that it was degenerating into an "expressionist academy."[63] He also became disillusioned politically, leaving the SPD in 1919 because, as he later wrote, "it seemed to me to stand in an impossible compromise with the right. For a while I was at the point of becoming a communist."[64] These sympathies may have prompted Ernst Toller in early March 1919 to write a memorandum to the provisional council government—one apparently never acted upon—proposing "comrade Wilhelm Hausenstein" as "art commissar" to work under the auspices of the *Kultusministerium.*[65] Yet Hausenstein, arguably the most influential critic in Munich, played no role in the council republic, and in an April essay presented a position counter to that of the Action Committee of Revolutionary Artists. In "Art and Revolution," published in a supplement to the journal *Neue Merkur* and in the catalog *Easter 1919* celebrating the reopening of the Alfred Flechtheim gallery in Düsseldorf,[66] he explicitly rejected any precipitous link between art and politics. He insisted that true art was in and of itself revolutionary, but for that very reason should shun potentially harmful political alliances:

> Art can gain decisive meaning in the long run only from its own artistic actuality. The path of political insinuation gives art itself no legitimacy, and it is completely indifferent whether this path emanates from reaction, from war, or from revolution. Art rests in itself, not in its connections to power.[67]

Although in large part a scathing attack on the pre-war official arts administration, official monuments, and art academies, Hausenstein's "Art and Revolution" opposed artists' councils and, therefore, any direct political activism on the part of artists. He advocated instead individual freedom to the point of anarchism—what he termed "consistent anarchy." His rejection of any fundamental link between art and the political revolution reflected a profound disillusionment developed during the course of the revolution, which, he wrote, lacked "revolutionary fruitfulness." His concluding words expressed his hope that a new state might produce a "new collectivity" that would provide "a quiet state of affairs for those who create" rather than "revolutionary gestures."

In fact, little was accomplished in the first days after the Action Committee assumed control under Landauer, even though the decentralized plan of Landauer's ministry probably gave them extensive authority. For one thing, there is reason to believe the Action Committee had not yet worked out a program of its own. A student who visited one of their meetings on 5 April recorded in his diary: "The Action Committee of Revolutionary Artists are just big talkers; they may be good painters and musicians, but that's the size of it. Again there's just no unity, everyone is doing his own thing . . . Sad but true!"[68] For another, they still had to contend with the Council of Artists, whose modern wing sought to gain the upper hand in the group and to "strengthen the representation of progressive forces" by adding seven members of the New Secession to the executive committee.[69] It was four members of the Council of Artists who, for whatever reason, had taken the initiative in seeking Landauer's authorization to suspend the professors of the Academy of Fine Arts.[70] Going beyond the demands of the Council of Artists, on 11 April the Action Committee also demanded the immediate closure of the School of Arts and Crafts, the dismissal of its professors, and a reorganization under the supervision of the Action Committee and a group of revolutionary students; no action was immediately forthcoming, though.[71] A measure of their uncertain control was an announcement in the April 12/13 *Münchner Neueste Nachrichten* of the first unjuried Munich exhibition in the Glass

Palace. Rather than an exhibition devoted to the new art, one half of the show would be controlled by the conservative Artists' Guild and Munich Secession, the other by the Council of Artists, a compromise worked out the previous February by the Council of Artists and the government.[72] This was similar to the compromise concluded for the annual exhibition in Berlin. The rivalry between the Action Committee and the Council of Artists became explicit in a contribution to the April issue of *Der Weg* written by the architect Hans Hansen, a member of the radical Cologne artists' group associated with the Marxist-oriented journal *Der Ventilator* who probably came to Munich during the first council republic.[73] In "Revolutionary Artists" he charged that the designation revolutionary had been usurped by artists who in the new political circumstances sought merely public recognition and the economic benefits accompanying it. In a not-so-veiled attack on the Council of Artists he wrote: "To you revolution and art is a state of business like every breath of your sorry life."[74] He further criticized those who sought merely compensatory measures in reforming the art world by showing disdain for "making revolutionary ministers out of royal lackeys."[75] But he was also skeptical of the views of some of his fellow members of the Action Committee. In what sounded like a response to insistent calls for artistic freedom, he pointed out the political danger in such claims:

> Expressionism—the revolutionary art as the bourgeois revolutionary understands it, is the revolution on the palette and in the inkwell. The magnificent and best in it is that it obligates to nothing. The artist can as an artist confidently be an anarchist. Anarchist art is paid for. It can live with it; it serves capital and the bourgeoisie as before.[76]

Hansen opposed any self-sufficient concern with art on political grounds. Likewise, he attacked the proposition that expressionist art had anticipated the revolution. Those who claimed this, he wrote, subscribed to a "bourgeois falsification of history." His own solution for preventing bourgeois cooptation of expressionism had at its center a monumental precedent, the remodeling of Paris after the French revolution. Artists councils, likened by Hansen to the 1793 commission of artists of Paris, would design a large-scale project to transform the total environment. Left unspoken was how such a project could be financed. Although he argued against any self-sufficient concern with art, his alternative envisioned the revolutionary artist leaving art in its traditional sense behind and moving into reality—but only to give it artistic shape.

The writers in the pages of the *Münchner Neueste Nachrichten* and the *Bayerischer Kurier* called upon art to reconstruct a world that had been destroyed and rhetorically equated the style of expressionism with the ability to end oppression and master material reality. In a language which often mixed religion and politics, they called upon the new art to revolutionize human consciousness, ostensibly as a precondition for the success of the revolution. It was this premise that allowed them to maintain the claim to complete artistic freedom. But revolution for them was still based on a fictitious notion of community, of the willing cooperation of all segments of society to realize these goals. After only six days, though, the first council republic came to an abrupt end. Before dawn on 13 April, Palm Sunday, detachments of the republican security forces, directed by the government in exile in Bamberg, secured the rail terminal and stormed the Wittelsbach palace, the seat of government. Reinforcements failed to arrive and Munich workers successfully repulsed the attack. Seizing the moment, the leaders of the Communist Party in Munich, Eugen Leviné and Max Levien, declared a communist council republic. The justification for their new willingness to assume power was the rumored capture of members of Toller's government and the new readiness displayed by the workers to defend council rule with force. The Action Committee of Revolutionary Artists now confronted a radically altered political landscape. Rather than a government that sympathized with their reformist anarchist leanings, they were faced with a communist government under military siege.

13 April–1 May: Revolutionary Expressionism and the Communist Council Republic

Despite serious misgivings, Landauer at first publicly supported the communist council republic. He was not offered any significant role in the new government, though. By 16 April he had sent a private letter to the communist leadership expressing his dismay at the course of events. He wrote:

> Socialism, which becomes true, makes all creative powers immediately alive; in your work, though, I see . . . that you do not understand the economic and spiritual spheres. This note remains on my part utmost private; far be it from me in the least to disturb the difficult work of defense that you are conducting. But I lament most painfully that it is only still the smallest part of my work which is now defended, a work of warmth and progress, of culture and regeneration.[77]

In the power vacuum that ensued the Action Committee of Revolutionary Artists retained the authority given it by Landauer. On 15 April the following notice appeared in the "Communications of the Executive

Committee of the Factory and Soldiers' Councils," the official newspaper of the new government:

The Action Committee of Revolutionary Artists hereby explains that it alone is to be considered as the representative of the artists' community of the city of Munich and of all Bavaria. It places itself on the basis of communist principles and recognizes the dictatorship of the proletariat as the true and only way to the realization of the proletarian council republic and of communism.[78]

The following day, however, the statement was modified:

We explain: We are not the "representatives" of Munich, or Bavarian, or any other artists who belong to the capitalist age. We are the representatives and authorizing body of an idea, and our aim is to assist practically in the building of a new community and its ideal development.[79]

It remains unclear as to who was responsible for the first announcement. The political issue in dispute was representation versus minority leadership or even dictatorship. Signing the 16 April statement in the name of the Action Committee were Titus Tautz, the former spokesman for the group as editor of the *Münchner Neueste Nachrichten,* and the Dada artist Hans Richter. Richter's name first appeared in association with the Action Committee when he was listed as a signatory to the 9 April appeal to Russian revolutionary artists. During the second council republic he was to become the acknowledged leader of the group.

Richter's first success as an artist came with the politicization of expressionism by Franz Pfemfert in *Die Aktion,* where it was presented as a radical challenge to the prevailing wartime culture. In 1916 Richter was also featured in an exhibition at the Hans Goltz gallery in Munich, where his own catalog essay advanced a trenchant critique of artistic resignation in the face of the war, while at the same time confidently promoting the liberating potential of expressionist art—although not in explicitly political terms.[80] Richter went to Zurich for medical treatment of war injuries later that year and participated in two discrepant artistic ventures that eventually posed the first significant challenge to his conception of the political significance of his art. The first was a three-month collaboration with the expressionist writer Ludwig Rubiner on the Munich pacifist/anarchist journal *Zeit-Echo,* now published in exile in Switzerland. Rubiner, a friend of Landauer's, devoted the journal to anti-war activism as well as to the projection of an alternative society described in the anarchist rhetoric of freedom, universal brotherhood, and communal ties. In this context he called on artists to pro-

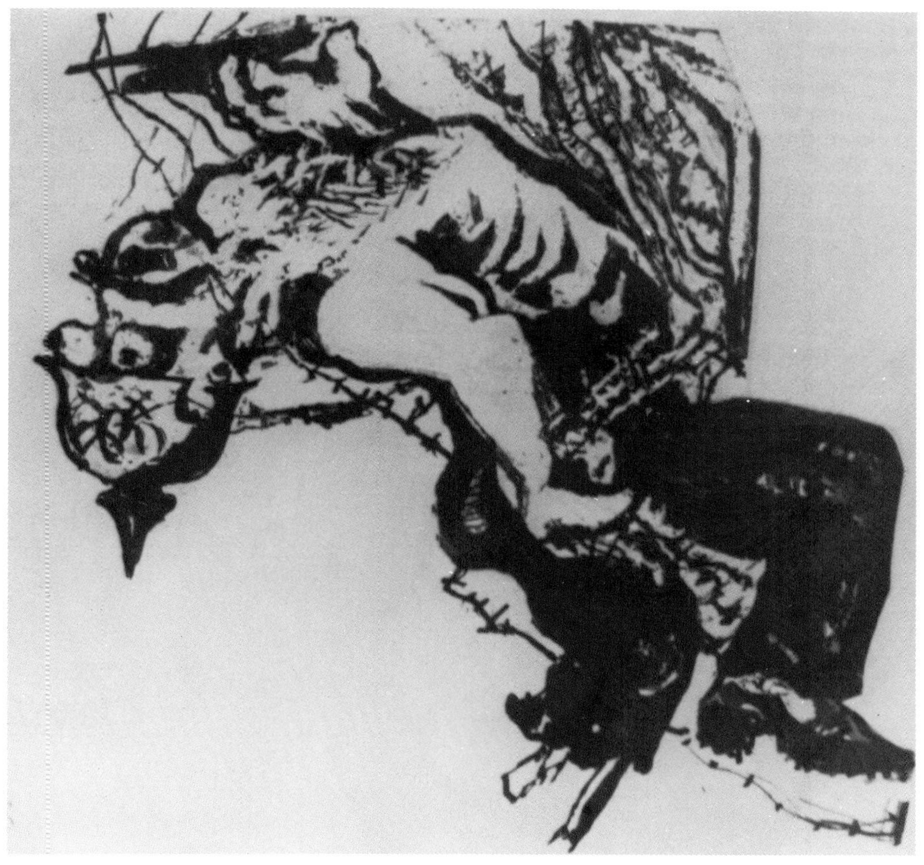

4.13 Hans Richter, *Im Felde der Ehre (On the Field of Honor)*, 1917. Pencil on paper, 20.7 x 22.9 cm. Kunsthaus Zürich, Graphische Sammlung.

duce an explicitly anti-war art, accessible to the masses. As the sole illustrator for the journal, Richter responded with a number of large-scale, realistic, brutally unambiguous anti-war drawings (see fig. 4.13) and with a programmatic statement that called for a committed art against the war. He repudiated autonomous easel painting and sarcastically criticized "isms," thus questioning his own previous artistic production.[81]

Simultaneously, though, Richter collaborated with the Dada artists associated with the Cabaret Voltaire, who by 1917 had turned from the aggressive, anti-art attacks on bourgeois culture of the cabaret performances to the promotion of modernist art in a series of exhibitions. Here

Richter exhibited *Visionary Portraits* (fig. 4.14), small-scale artistic experiments in chance, painted at dusk, when he chose from memory the paint on the palette. The portraits soon gave way to another rapid stylistic shift, the *Dada Heads* (fig. 4.15), semi-abstract portraits of friends that soon left any portrait elements behind and became exercises in

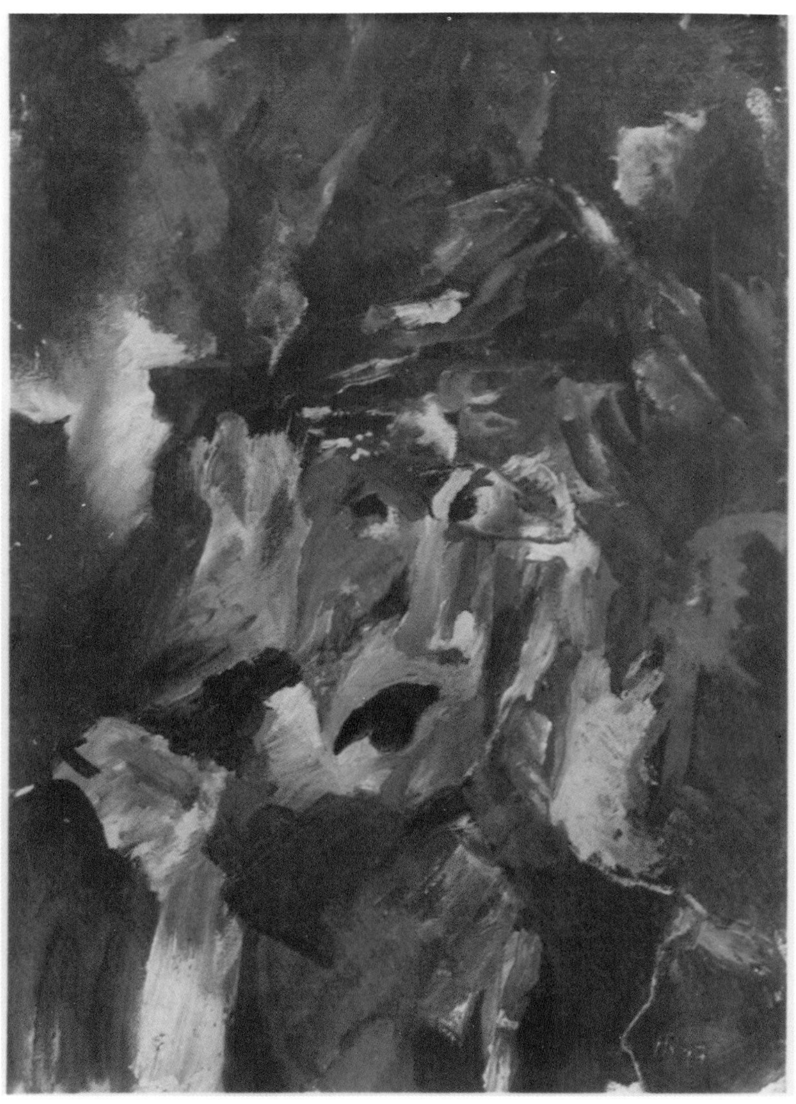

4.14 Hans Richter, *Visionäres Porträt—Makabres Porträt (Visionary Portrait—Macabre Portrait)*, 1917. Oil on canvas, 53 x 36 cm.

abstract composition. These efforts soon led to a break with Rubiner, who implicitly challenged this art on political grounds.

Despite the political challenge to modernist art, which Richter experienced firsthand, he persisted in advancing the revolutionary potential of modernist art, both in his own work and in his art-political ac-

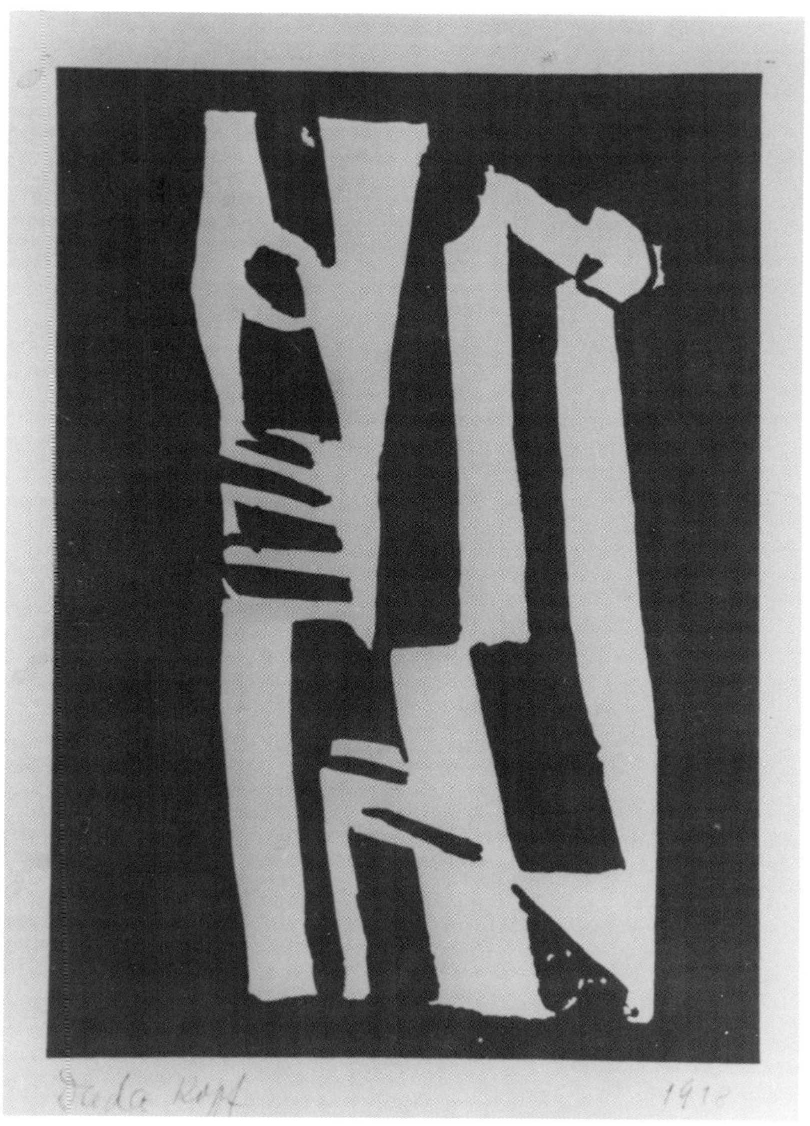

4.15 Hans Richter, *Dada Kopf (Dada Head)*, 1918. Linocut, 26 x 21 cm.

tivities. Revolution appears as the subject of a number of drawings and linocuts, which began as rapidly sketched, expressionistically distorted drawings based on firsthand observation of a socialist-sponsored antiwar rally (fig. 4.16) and which he subsequently transformed into more abstract compositions such as *The Speaker* (fig. 4.17), implying the revolutionary significance of abstraction.

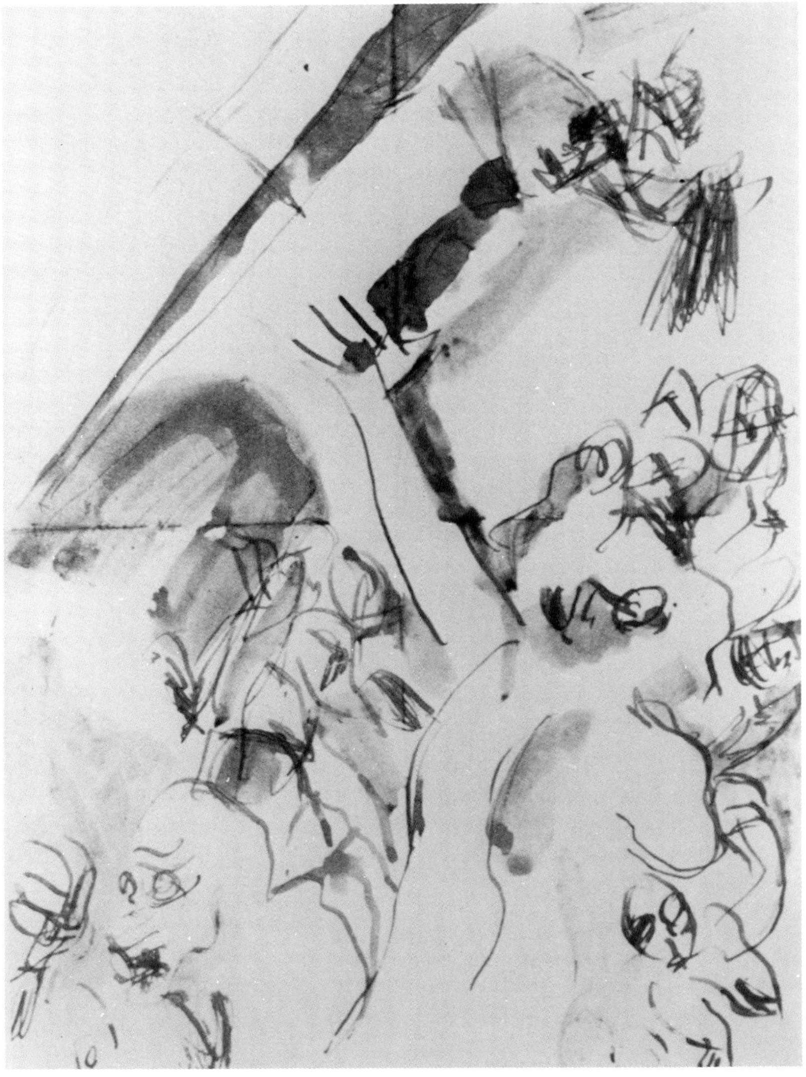

4.16 Hans Richter, *Revolution*, 1918. Pen drawing, 27.7 x 21.8 cm.

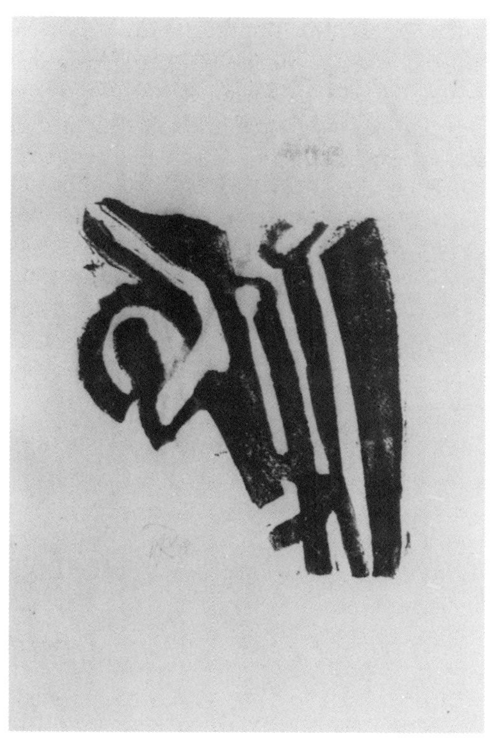

4.17 Hans Richter, *Redner (The Speaker)*, 1918. Linocut, 26 x 18 cm.

Richter probably first came in contact with the Action Committee during an early March 1919 trip to Munich. He had traveled there after attending the Second Socialist International in Bern, where Kurt Eisner had been the most celebrated—and controversial—speaker. Most likely he knew several members of the Action Committee already, including the writer Alfred Wolfenstein, who like Richter had contributed to Rubiner's *Zeit-Echo*. Richter, too, had read Kropotkin and Landauer during the war (possibly under Rubiner's tutelage) and had frequented meetings of a small Swiss anarchist group led by Luigi Bertoni, a Bakunin student and an editor of the Geneva anarcho-communist periodical *Le Réveil*.[82] By early April Richter had returned to Zurich to take part in the eighth—and last—Dada Soirée, when he received a telegram from his "art-political friends" in Munich, urging him to return immediately: a council republic had been proclaimed.[83] Richter's aggressive Dada stance may not have been his only calling card; as several drawings attest, he already knew at least one of the major political actors on the Munich scene, the communist leader Max Levien (fig. 4.18).

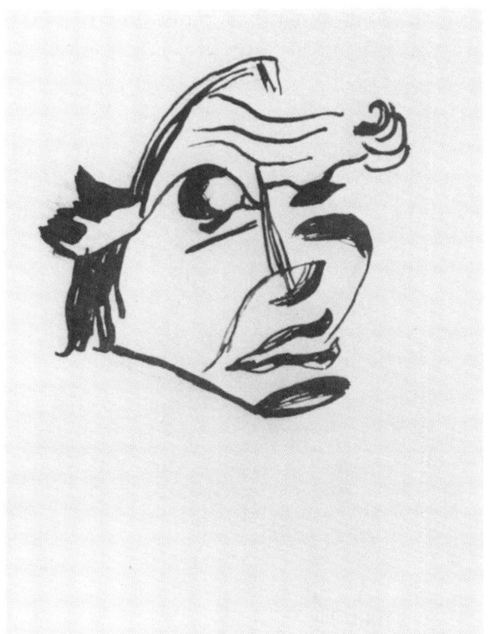

4.18 Hans Richter, *Dr. Levi[e]n*, 1917. Pen drawing, dimensions unknown.

Munich and the Action Committee of Revolutionary Artists seemed to offer Richter propitious circumstances for realizing his own conception of a politically progressive modernist art, which he had developed inconsistently since 1916. He had pursued these concerns once again in early April 1919 when—along with the Swiss Dadaists Viking Eggeling, Marcel Janco, Hans Arp, and others—Richter organized the Zurich "League of Radical Artists," whose manifesto read in part:

We artists, as representatives of an essential part of the total culture, want to place ourselves "in the middle of things" and help take over the responsibility for the coming, ideal development in the state. . . . We announce that the artistic law of movement of our epoch already is at hand in a comprehensive formulation. The spirituality of an abstract art (see program) means the huge extension of man's sentiment to freedom. The aim of our belief is brotherly art: the new mission of man in the community. Art in the state must mirror the spirit of the entire people's body. Art compels toward clarity; [it] should form the foundation of the new man; [it] should belong to every individual and to no class.[84]

The thrust of the manifesto, from the claim that modernist art had anticipated the revolution, to the postulate of art for the masses, to ideas of classless community, recalled not just the plethora of revolutionary art manifestos already published in Germany, but even more specifically the numerous articles in the Munich newspapers sponsored by the Action Committee during the first council republic. What was new was the advocacy of a specifically abstract art identified with political freedom. Munich, as opposed to Switzerland where revolutionary activity had been suppressed almost immediately after the war, offered Richter greater promise for the realization of these goals.

By 19 April Richter listed himself as chairman of the Action Committee in correspondence to friends in Switzerland.[85] On 22 April six members of the group met in the Landtag to formalize a program. Attending were Richter, Schaefler, and Pilartz, along with the abstract painter Walt Laurent, the American artist Hermann Sachs, and the actor Ado von Achenbach. According to the minutes of that meeting—apparently the only extant record of their meetings—they proposed a radical program: the selling off abroad of major state-owned monuments and collections to raise money for social welfare programs (including furnishings of the royal palaces and confiscation of the Nymphenburg porcelain factory, the Schack gallery, and the Villa Stuck).[86] These proposals represented a shift in the group's thinking toward more pressing economic needs. The members further discussed health and welfare insurance for artists and plans to meet the following day with the strongest political authority in Munich, the factory councils, presumably in order to present their program. Richter also submitted the manifesto of the Zurich League of Radical Artists for discussion at the next meeting, possibly as a model for the group. The notation "revolutionary, radical or not" recorded in the minutes already indicates what the parameters of the discussion were to be.[87] They also established a number of "art commissariats" with the following members:

PAINTING: Richter, Schaefler, Klee, Eggeling, Campendonk, Laurent, Holzer
ARTS AND CRAFTS: Schrimpf, Sachs
SCULPTURE: Pilartz
EXHIBITIONS: Stückgold
ARCHITECTURE: Hansen, Janes[88]

Commissariats for "museums" and "social welfare" remained unfilled. These provisional committees included not only those already publicly associated with the group, but a number of newcomers as well. Prominent among them were two members of the New Secession, who were among the best-known and most successful expressionists in Munich: Heinrich Campendonk and Paul Klee. Also listed was Viking Eggeling,

Richter's friend, who still resided in Switzerland. In the cases of Campendonk and Eggeling it is uncertain whether they expressed any interest in joining the Action Committee. This was not the case with Paul Klee, who the group voted to "coopt" into the Action Committee at its meeting.

On 12 April, as republican defense troops unsuccessfully laid siege to Munich, Klee had sent the following brief note to Schaefler:

> The Action Commiteee of Revolutionary Artists may completely have at its disposal my artistic energy. That I consider myself belonging to it goes without saying, for already many years before the war I already produced in the manner which shall now be placed on a broader public basis. My work and my other artistic energy and knowledge are at your disposal![89]

Klee, the creator of childlike cosmic fantasies, had declared his sympathies with the more radical of Munich's two artists' groups. It had not always been so, for if anything, Klee had been cautiously to the right of the Action Committee in both his private views on the revolution and his public art political stance. Already on 30 October 1918, in the closing days of the war, he had expressed in his diary his fears of the revolution:

> What a moment this is—the Reich stands all alone now, armed to the teeth and yet so helpless! Will the hope also be shattered that inner dignity will be preserved and that the idea of destiny will keep the upper hand over common atheism? We would now have an opportunity to be an example of how a people should endure its downfall. But if the masses go into action, what then? Then the usual things will happen, blood will flow, and still worse, there will be trials! How banal![90]

In the early days after 9 November, Klee maintained this aloof tone, awaiting his discharge from the airbase at Gersthofen where he was stationed. Upon his return to Munich, however, he immediately plunged into Munich art politics. First, he joined the editorial board of the *Münchner Blätter* and followed its consistently anti-communist line in a series of graphic contributions. (He contributed to the journal steadily during its twelve-month existence.) In his capacity as secretary of the New Secession, Klee must have joined the Council of Artists.

It remains unclear what precipitated Klee's switch to the more radical Action Commiteee, whether dismay at the pace of reform within the Council of Artists or a more fundamental concern with the course of the revolution and its implication for the arts. Because he joined the Action Committee at such a late date, he had little chance to participate actively in any of its propaganda efforts or behind-the-scenes politicking at the art schools.

Such politicking preoccupied the Action Committee during the Second Council Republic, particularly regarding reforms for art education. Richter now took the lead in that fight. He hoped to appoint two of his colleagues from the Zurich League of Radical Artists to professorships at the academy,[91] whose director had now gone into hiding.[92] At least one scenario for the reorganization of the School of Arts and Crafts envisioned the new Action Committee member Paul Klee as a graphic instructor there.[93] On 24 April, in response to a motion by Richter, the teachers of the arts and crafts school were effectively suspended pending a "revolutionary" restructuring to be worked out by the Action Committee and the students at the school.[94] Once again the Council of Artists interceded, presumably to forestall more radical action. Hermann Esswein, art critic for the SPD *Münchner Post*, reported on the general confusion at a 26 April meeting at the school attended by teachers, students, and representatives of the rival artists' groups. Esswein ridiculed the spokesmen of the Council of Artists, the "leader of the aristocratic-exclusive New Secession" Edwin Scharff, and the "bourgeois-portly [Walther] Püttner" for their unlikely "role as executors of a proletarian-revolutionary" direction. He continued:

> The broad jolt to the left, the communist government, also brought into ascendancy the most radical wing of the body of artists debating in Munich at the present time, and I must openly confess that the spokesman of the communist artists' commission—as I understand it a Mr. Richter from Zurich—pleased me better than the previously elucidated group [Council of Artists]. A clear standpoint, a distinct yes or no is worth gold, and if there is still no cause to discuss before the public certain demands and plans of Mr. Richter, his like-minded friend H. C. Pillarz [*sic*] and their employers, still the main point, in whose name the men have come, deserves a word of explanation. The men spoke in the name of expressionism, advanced the claims of the New Art and the young, spiritual-revolutionary generation captured by it.[95]

Esswein considered Richter and the Action Committee tantamount to representatives of the communist government and expressionism its artistic style. Two days after this meeting a newly formed Council of Specialists and Action Committee of the School for Arts and Crafts announced a new commission to reorganize the school composed of teachers, students, and representatives of the Action Committee of Revolutionary Artists.

Although Esswein assumed an identity of interest between the Action Committee and the communist government, there is little evidence to suggest the group received any concrete support or encouragement from the government, which was more concerned for the time being with the defense of Munich than with a reorganization of the arts. On the contrary, the limited evidence indicates the government responded at best with apathy, at worst with antipathy. According to the minutes of the 22 April meeting, an attempt by Richter to meet with Levien was unsuccessful, despite the fact that Richter was acquainted with him personally. Efforts to gain the support of the factory councils may have been equally disappointing. There is a telling account of Richter reading the program of the Action Committee to an assembled gathering of supporters of the communist council republic on 28 April. He was met with open hostility, and a long-time working-class activist rejected what he called Richter's "sermon." One commentator lamented: "The evening accomplished nothing positive—not through the fault of the proletariat, but due to the self-seeking of the 'spiritual workers.' "[96]

On yet another front an attempt was made to influence the communist government in favor of the new art. Despite the fact that he no longer held a ministerial post, and despite the fact that Leviné only grudgingly acceded to his participation, Gustav Landauer began work on a long-range program for the reorganization of the arts and education, along with a communist party member who went by the pseudonym "Fidelis."[97] In their joint proposal, the section on art began with architecture:

> The new era of human history has to find its expression in the monuments and public buildings that are erected from now on. At all times young artists are also to be called upon when it comes to state commissions; this holds true for all the arts. Painting and sculpture are from the beginning to be incorporated into architecture.[98]

The emphasis on public buildings—unifying the arts under architecture—and on young artists recalls the manifesto of the Working Council for Art. In fact, Landauer had already considered appointing Bruno Taut to the building ministry during his brief tenure as Commissar for People's Enlightenment. Further, although his comments on painting and sculpture were exceedingly brief in comparison with the sections on educational reform, they seemed unequivocally to side with the new art: "Painting and sculpture: promotion of living artists and modern directions through state purchases. Establishment of a museum for modern art. The state makes state buildings available for exhibitions and provides for touring exhibitions."[99] The latter provisions, particularly the use of the phrase "touring exhibitions" (*Wanderausstellungen*), may likewise have come from the program of the Berlin Working Council for Art.

When Fidelis submitted Landauer's proposal to the communist government, however, he apparently deleted all references to modern art from the original text, changing "establishment of a museum for modern art" to "founding of new museums" and omitting the reference to "young artists" in the section on architecture.[100] Despite these changes, Fidelis's own commentary, which accompanied it, was itself a defensive plea for the revolutionary nature of expressionist art. He described, as an example,

the splendid horse of a Colleoni or an animal figure of an "impressionist" sculptor such as Gaul. Both adhere to the external [appearance]. One may want to mount Colleoni's horse; one may want to stroke Gaul's figure of an animal. That of an expressionist is totally different; say an animal of Marc's. In his horses is contained the "original" horse. That is no longer whatever horse, but is simply *the* horse.

These examples may suffice. They also suffice in order to clearly recognize the essential. The others cling to the figural, these approach the "communal," the "generally valid." In every point, in every line, in every surface, just as in every color the struggle of the new artists expresses itself. The figural, as in Kandinsky's art, can completely disappear in the process. The artists' community, and with it the masses, strives toward spiritual-religious intensification—the not-satisfied, not-bourgeois-like masses. . . . The new art will be an art of the proletariat.[101]

Obviously well-versed in contemporary writings on expressionist art, Fidelis summoned up the current arguments for its revolutionary character. What is striking is the allusion to the visual appearance of this art—even abstraction—as revolutionary in and of itself. Of particular significance is the confident repetition of pre-war assessments of expressionism by writers such as Wilhelm Hausenstein, suggesting that this art movement was the harbinger of a collective culture that would overcome the subjective and individualistic nature of other art. Preempting the criticism that the masses did not accept the new art, Fidelis implied that the "true" masses, uncorrupted by "bourgeois" modes of thinking, already shared its goals. To bolster his arguments, he quoted from Lunacharsky's *Proletkult* program.

With his deletions and his own commentary, Fidelis may have sought to take the edge off Landauer's known support for expressionism, since Landauer was not particularly in the good graces of the communist government. As Fidelis reported it, though, Leviné was not convinced and rejected the program outright as "too much fixed in the traditional, too much fixed in the bourgeois."[102]

May–December: The "Murder of Modernism"

On May 1 and 2 Freikorps and federal troops brutally suppressed the second council republic of Bavaria. They arrested Toller and Leviné (Levien escaped to Austria, whose government refused to extradite him), as well as Gustav Landauer, who had gone into hiding at the home of Eisner's widow, some distance from Munich. Landauer was taken to the Stadelheim prison, where Freikorps soldiers cold-bloodedly murdered him. Artists and writers associated with the revolutionary government were also tracked down. At least seven members of the Action Committee were arrested: Hans Richter, Alfred Wolfenstein, Georg Schrimpf, Ado von Achenbach, Theodor Pilartz, Oskar Maria Graf, and Eduard Trautner. A court sentenced Richter to five years imprisonment, but released him after two weeks through the intervention of influential family friends; he was expelled from Munich under a 21 May decree ridding Munich of undesirable non-Bavarians.[103] Schrimpf, Achenbach, Pilartz, and Graf were soon released.[104] An officer who recognized Wolfenstein secretly released him, whereupon he spent several days in hiding at a friend's. Later he was repeatedly subjected to house-searches for weapons and incriminating literature or letters.[105] Trautner initially fled to Berlin, but returned to Munich where a court sentenced him to five months in prison for his role as a medical orderly for the Red Army and for providing the fugitive Ernst Toller with his identification papers.[106] Schaefler fled to Passau,[107] where, relatively safe, he wrote on Trautner's behalf to the Munich court, claiming that although Trautner was a "socialist from conviction," he had "nothing to do with the council government" and had often expressed his belief that the "terror" of the "communist government" was "inhuman."[108] Wach fled to Lainbach, where a friend, a former officer of the Tirolean guards, warned him that White Guards in Munich were still searching for him. En route to Braunau-am-Inn, where he eventually settled a few months later, he spent a nervous nine days in jail in Simbach after being arrested for an irregular passport. The authorities there cabled Munich for information on Wach, but released him when the requested information still had not arrived after more than a week.[109] As late as 11 June Paul Klee left for Switzerland after Ernst Toller was discovered hiding in the same building in which he rented an atelier. Less than two weeks later police searched his house.[110] Munich remained under martial law until 1 August 1919.

After the suppression of the council republic recriminations filled the pages of Munich's newspapers and art journals. The press now generally took for granted the political radicalism of expressionism and described the Action Committee with epithets such as "radical," "bolshevik," and "dictatorial." Conservatives sought to defame the council republic through an aggressive attack on expressionist art. The book *München auf dem Kopf,* rushed to press as an "illustrated history of the revolution," facetiously labeled Wach's woodcuts as heroic depictions of worker-revolutionaries. *Simplicissimus,* which had turned rabidly anticommunist since January, parodied the political implications of expressionist art with a cartoon (fig. 4.19) the caption of which read: "The curve, the primary form of capitalism, is overcome. The new day dawns. Threateningly, the cubes march through the universe." A *Kladderadatsch* cartoon modeled after a work by Franz von Stuck described the threat to art from bolshevism (fig. 4.20), and *Feurjo* compared a healthy German art ("immer Dürer") to a degenerate, "bolshevik" Wach woodcut ("immer dürrer") (fig. 4.21). More seriously, the mili-

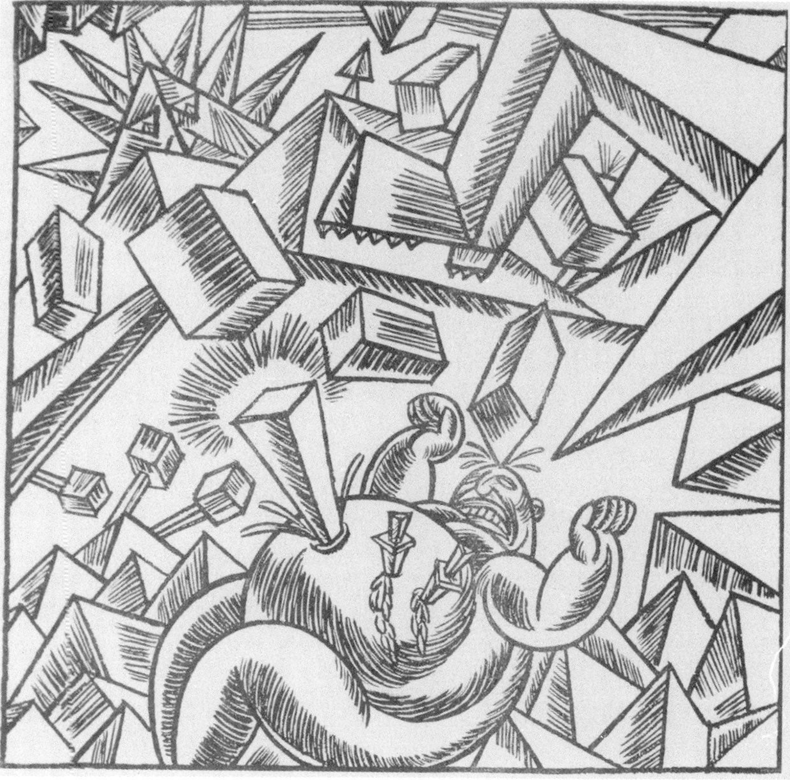

4.19 Cartoon, *Simplicissimus* (1919).

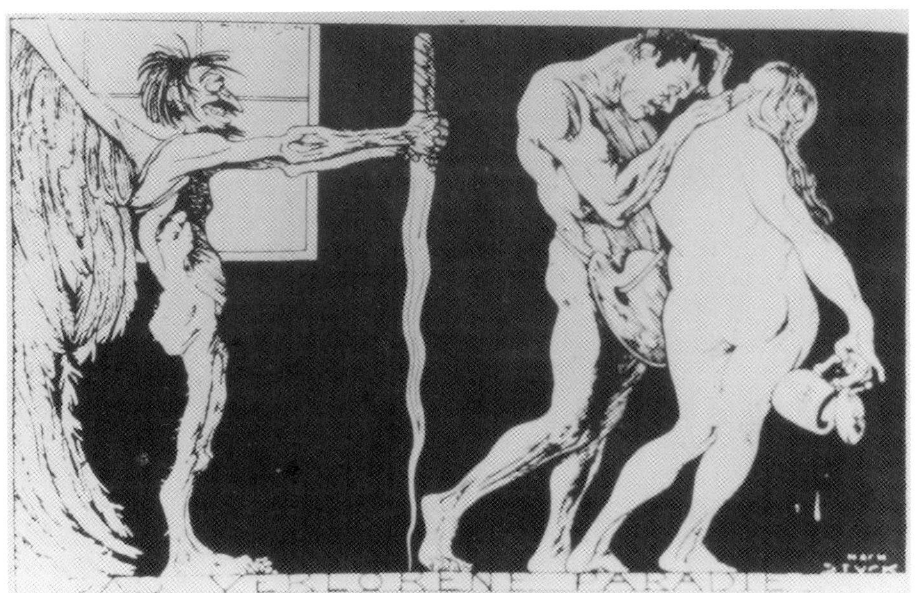

4.20 Cartoon, *Kladderadatsch* (1919).

tary administration, as part of its secret political surveillance of the city, undertook to investigate the Radical Movement of Intellectuals in Munich, including artists. As if to point up the threat of such persecution, *Der Weg,* its editorial operation now located in Berlin, published the following anonymous postcard it had received:

From a German! Woe to you, filthy Jewish swine! You Spartacists! Incompetents! Speculators! Dogs! Scoundrels! Woe to you, who are ruining the German fatherland and German art! . . . The same scoundrels as Mühsam, Levien, etc. Kokoschka! Heckel! Kirchner! Eberz! Unold! Seewald! Dawringhausen [*sic*]![111]

Linked in the same breath were anarchists, communists, Berlin and Dresden expressionists, and liberal members of the Council of Artists. However crude, the political accusations could not have been stated more clearly. Although the language was more moderate, the implications were the same as four members of the Council of Artists sought to clear their own names in the affair of the closing of the art schools. As the charges and countercharges raged in the pages of the *Münchner Neueste Nachrichten* and the *Münchner Post,* one of the four, Hermann Urban, insisted:

It was known to the Council of Artists that an Action Committee of Revolutionary Artists had formed which was waiting for the proclamation of the coun-

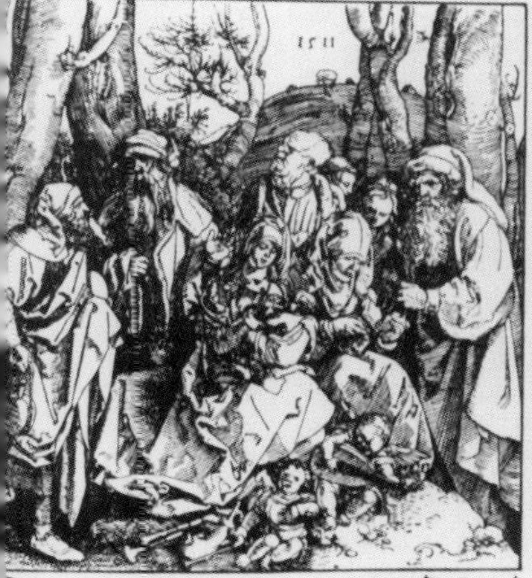

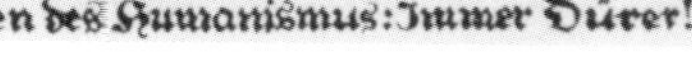

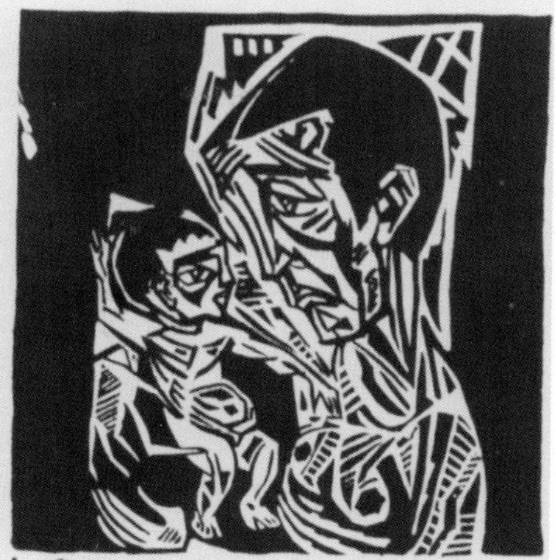

4.21 Cartoon, *Feurjo* (1919).

cil republic in order to immediately advance the most radical measures. The tendency of this Action Committee was oriented toward the Moscow artistic program, to pave the way immediately for the socialization of art under the dictatorial leadership of the artistic direction which is summed up by the name expressionism.[112]

Urban conveniently failed to distinguish between the two council republics, and tarred the Action Committee with the explosive code words "Moscow" and "dictatorial."

Despite these protestations, the conservative elements in the Council of Artists used the affair of the closing of the art schools to discredit the Group of 100 and the New Secession. The Group of 100 and the so-called "action committee" of the Council of Artists, dominated by New Secession members, still tried to promote academic reform, endorsing Richard Riemerschmid's plan for a unified art school with a loose workshop structure, a plan which did not even mention expressionist art, much less give any preference to it.[113] By discrediting them politically, though, the conservatives effectively blocked any lingering efforts at academic reform. On 16 May, the executive council of the Council of Artists passed a vote of no confidence against the "action committee" of the group, precipitating the withdrawal of the Group of 100 and the New Secession.

In response to these events, the defense of expressionism took two forms. First, a number of expressionists now sought to divorce themselves and their art from the revolution. Responding to Esswein's report on the 26 April meeting at the school of arts and crafts that suggested he was a representative of the communist government, Pilartz in a public statement now denied any affiliation with the communist party and proclaimed: "I belong to no political party at all and pursued purely artistic aims as a member of the revolutionary artists' council."[114] Writing in the May issue of the *Münchner Blätter für Dichtung und Graphik,* the critic August Mayer argued vehemently in an essay entitled "Revolution and Art" that the term revolution in art had nothing to do with that in politics.[115] While admitting that the revolution "was influenced and prepared by art," he turned the particular into the general: art was always revolutionary and artists the greatest revolutionaries. The revolution Mayer envisioned, though, was confined to culture and barred from politics. He presented the model of a timeless and classless humanity described in cosmic terms, which he advanced against any political claims in the revolutionary concept of art. Thus the most revolutionary artists, according to Mayer, did not oppose the social order. On the contrary, in discussing the succession of revolutionary artists stretching from Pisano, Giotto, and Michelangelo to Manet, van Gogh, and Cézanne he commented: "Nevertheless it is noteworthy that the majority of these artists as men stood completely on the base of their respective social orders; they were correct, almost stolid bourgeois."[116] Defending expressionism against the rabid attacks in the conservative press, the October *Münchner Blätter* featured an article with the ominous title "Murder of Modernism," which insisted that the "negative, destructive aims" of expressionism had nothing to do with politics.[117]

Even more significantly, with the suppression of the council republic the dealer Hans Goltz's house-organ *Der Ararat,* which had appeared twice as a sort of nationalist pamphlet opposing harsh reparations terms, went to extreme lengths to repudiate the revolution and separate "true" art from its stigma. His inflammatory conservative rhetoric was all the more surprising considering that most artist-members of the Action Committee had exhibited with him regularly—or were under contract to him. Contributing to the tense political atmosphere Goltz argued:

Is the 16–30-year-old metal worker who earned up to 1,000 marks per month and who in the years 1917 and 1918 drank champagne from litre mugs . . . a proletarian? Is a District Judge, who with a wife and four children from 1915 to 1919 had to consume his tiny fortune so that his loved ones would not go hungry, a bourgeois?[118]

He described revolutionaries as "psychopaths," "convicts," and a "den of robbers" and the Freikorps and federal troops as "clean shaven," "well-bred" "rescue troops." The tone could not have contrasted more sharply with an appeasing statement in the *Münchner Neueste Nachrichten* only days before by, among others, Wilhelm Hausenstein, the brothers Heinrich and Thomas Mann, and Rainer Maria Rilke warning against the use of force and urging the bourgeoisie to remember that its own fate was tied to that of the working classes.[119]

In keeping with his extreme conservative line, Goltz in the same issue of *Der Ararat* distanced himself from the proclamations of the Action Committee ("worded in foul German language") and, without mentioning him by name, Wach's illustrations in the Munich press ("a novice of the new art," he called him, although Wach's first public success had come at his own gallery). The current state of affairs, in which "not the inability of the anaemic government" and "not the apathy of the bourgeoisie," but "only the new art" was blamed for the "Munich misery," he dismissed as yet another of the "persecutions," "defamations," and "denunciations" to which the new art had been subjected over the years. Standing his ground ("we will remain"), Goltz styled a true art, separate from politics, which was exclusive and democratic at the same time:

The path to the temple [of art] is steep and rocky. It is too narrow for processions and mass migration. But open for each one, whether in workers' clothes or in cutaway. . . . Art is indeed not for the people, but stands open to each one from the people who wants to seek it out not from curiosity, but from the passionate need of his or her heart.[120]

While the *Münchner Blätter,* Hans Goltz, and others reacted to the suppression of the council republic by repudiating any relationship between art and the revolution, some former members of the Action Committee responded with a cautious measure of outrage and defiance. *Der Weg,* published in exile in Berlin, opened its May/June issue with the poem "Released Prisoners" by the imprisoned Ernst Toller, who awaited trial in Munich. It also featured a lengthy piece by Trautner, entitled "Terror," detailing the repressive measures of the military authorities in Munich. He charged, "They kill someone and 'prove' afterward that he was a murderer."[121] Against the brutality and violence he steadfastly maintained the vision of the slain Landauer: "One could ask: is it necessary that the state behaves this way?—Yes! It is necessary! It is not only necessary, but self-evident, as long as 'state' is identical with 'domination' and not with 'community.'"[122] In the July issue, Felix Stiemer, the former editor of *Menschen* in Dresden who was expelled from Munich in May, affirmed as a necessary presupposition for a spiritual revolution "everything that is called a communist demand": the council system, a six-hour day, and socialization of not just ripe, but all industries.[123] Other expressionist journals loosely associated with the Action Committee were equally bold at turns. *Die Bücherkiste,* founded the previous March, included in its May issue a woodcut portrait of Lessi Sachs—an artist and secretary of the Schwabing KPD—by her fiancé Otto Urbas, a member of the KPD propaganda division. Sachs had just been arrested and was soon sentenced to more than a year in prison for her role in the second council republic.

When it came to art-critical essays in these journals, however, the editors carefully sidestepped any mention of the revolution or politics. About the closest *Der Weg* came in its May/June issue to a political perspective on the arts was an article that attacked "self-satisfied," "hedonistic," philistine bourgeois art appreciation. Uncharacteristically for *Der Weg,* that same issue included not a single essay or gloss on a Munich artist (other than the deceased Maria Uhden, who was married to Georg Schrimpf), featuring instead expressionist artists unconnected with the events in Munich. Even the August/September issue that featured the Berlin Dadaist and KPD member George Grosz made no mention of his politics and was accompanied by two prerevolutionary graphics. (Grosz was under contract to Hans Goltz.) In the same issue were two religious woodcuts by Aloys Wach and an essay by the artist Hans Reichel, who had been arrested for hiding the fugitive Ernst Toller in his atelier and subsequently sentenced to four months imprisonment. Reichel fell back on the line of the rival *Münchner Blätter,* arguing for the separate realm of the spirit.

After June, *Der Weg* became, in effect, just another expressionist art journal, publishing a broad range of work from Dada caricatures, to expressionist religious woodcuts, to abstract graphics. For a time it had attempted, however inconsistently, to bring to bear on its discussions of art and of art politics a commitment to socialist revolution, however naïvely or vaguely defined. It could be argued that the careful avoidance of political discussions in relation to art after the suppression of the second council republic was basically a defensive gesture, meant to deflect political persecution. In any case, though, the editors' vague faith in the revolution as a means of leading art out of its isolation as a luxury commodity and into some meaningful alliance with the proletariat had met with failure. Their myths of community, individual freedom, and spirit had been met with the murder of their sponsor, Gustav Landauer. The tenuous nature of their project was reflected in the uncertain, confused, and defensive articles now published on expressionist art. Symptomatic was a review of the New Secession exhibition in the July issue. Not surprisingly, the critic tried to counter the prevailing conception of expressionist art as "merely revolutionary," as an expression of the "complete destruction of the old forms of life." In praise of the work of four New Secession members (including Klee and Campendonk, whose names had been associated with the Action Committee), he found no convincing words to challenge such a negative reading other than what he called their "inner prophecy." His concluding paragraph was an ironic reversal of earlier calls for a more accessible art, warning against the "false popularity" of a "pseudo"-expressionism. His elaborate refutation of the critique leveled at expressionism concluded that "life almost overnight [*had*] caught up with . . . art."[124] Once again expressionist art was promoted for its anticipatory status—not as the constructive harbinger of revolution, but as an art shattered to pieces before life itself had become that way.

One newspaper in Munich dealt openly with the confusion between artistic and political radicalism. This was the *Neue Zeitung*, the organ of the Independent Social Democratic Party. Unlike the Berlin party, which promoted the new art in *Die Freiheit* (and spoke on its behalf before the Prussian Provincial Assembly), the Munich USPD had been conspicuously silent on the subject. When Wach's woodcuts appeared on the covers of the *Münchner Neueste Nachrichten* and the *Bayerischer Kurier* in early April, the *Neue Zeitung*, the only other newspaper granted permission to publish, did not follow suit. Nor did it publish essays on the new art. After the suppression of the revolution, in an anonymous 26 June 1919 article, the *Neue Zeitung* distanced itself from the idealism of Landauer and the Action Committee:

> The artist who continues to create in the old traditions of his profession can be just as politically radically minded as the one who artistically seeks new paths can stand under the charms of the harshest capitalism. It was a misplaced attempt in the first days of the council republic to want to stamp a certain artistic direction as the art of the revolution. . . . For we are dealing here certainly not with a people's art, but with an artistic direction which thus far is cultivated in circles that offer mostly mighty little understanding to popular sentiment.[125]

The article openly advanced the discrepancy between political and artistic radicalism and the undeniable ties between expressionist art and capitalism. These harsh judgments were directed against what current Munich USPD leaders considered the dilettantism of Landauer and others loosely associated with the party during the revolution. Still, the party did not call for a specifically class-conscious art, but merely embraced the idealist separation of art and politics, so that art might be "an oasis in a life all-too-much governed by politics."

It was not until the December issue of *Die Bücherkiste* that a political reckoning with the Munich experience finally appeared in a Munich art journal. This was a short political gloss entitled "Gustav Landauer" by Felix Stiemer, the former editor of *Menschen* who had participated in the Munich revolution. His essay was at once paean to the slain leader and sober political assessment. "Gustav Landauer was a prophet, the last prophet of a great style in our time," Stiemer wrote. But, he continued:

> If he said that socialism was not a science but an art, then it must be demanded from his followers that they reassess the notion 'art' just as Marx renewed the notion 'science.' We must demand that the communist economy is put in place before the communist spirit: before that we have no right to spiritual demands on the proletariat.[126]

Stiemer reversed the privileged role assigned to art by Landauer and the Action Committee as an instrument to revolutionize human consciousness, insisting on the priority of revolutionary economic and political change.

By December 1919 authorities no longer saw expressionist artists as posing any direct political threat. The report to the military administration, "Radical Movement of Intellectuals in Munich," observed that "relatively little remains of revolutionary aspirations" at the Munich academy and that "the coloring of political convictions by artistic radicalism has taken place in only a few cases."[127] From surface indications it appeared that revolutionary expressionism had been successfully eradicated in Munich: the academy had returned to its status quo, choosing as the subject of its annual competition "Peace," and the rump Council of Artists, boycotted by the New Secession and the Group of 100, had reconstituted itself the previous June as the Working Committee of Munich Artists, severing any vestige of a connection with the revolution and its councils. In reality, though, expressionism was not formally or systematically excluded—now that it had generally retreated from political commitment. The New Secession boycott of the Working Committee of Munich Artists, for instance, was sufficient grounds for the government to deny the new organization exclusive recognition.[128] The Munich Artists' Society (*Künstlergenossenschaft*) and the Secession were still denied complete control over the annual salon, with a portion of the Glass Palace set aside for the first time for an unjuried exhibition. (In this the government adhered to the plan worked out by the Council of Artists and the *Kultusministerium* the previous February.) As late as November 1919 the *Kultusministerium* endorsed a plan for a unified art school that stressed the handicrafts; it faltered once more on the opposition of the academy professors.[129] What can be said is that the government and the institutional art world perhaps did not participate as enthusiastically as elsewhere in the process of constructing a new broad-based democratic culture that included expressionism and vice versa. The *Kultusministerium,* although it promoted the interests of the New Secession, rejected from a Glass Palace exhibition the work of the former Brücke artists Ernst Ludwig Kirchner and Karl Schmidt-Rottluff, along with that of Otto Dix, as "bolshevist."[130] On the other side, with the exception of Theodor Pilartz (who organized the jury-free sculpture section),[131] not a single member of the Action Committee, the New Secession, or the Group of 100 participated in the Glass Palace exhibition that year.

Many of the artists in the Action Committee now left Munich for good. Those expressionist artists who remained in the city no longer expected official recognition, nor did they anticipate any longer a "spiritual community" with the proletariat. It became evident that in Munich, at least, they could expect little support from the organized left. Led by party political stalwarts, the USPD had achieved an amazing electoral resurgence in response to the brutal suppression of council rule; in local June elections they received 32 percent of the vote, more than any other party. But the party showed no inclination to promote expressionist art. Nor did the communists, who had certainly offered no encouragement during the second council republic. Expressionism's most enthusiastic support had come primarily from those with anarchist leanings; after the suppression of the revolution, though, the anarchist movement ceased to be a significant factor in Munich politics. Faced with this reality, expressionist artists retreated from political activism and reconciled themselves to the economics and political ideology of a capitalist art market, which, by fall of 1919, seemed more and more to promise financial security. As *Der Weg* reported in its next-to-last issue, the September exhibition at Hans Goltz's gallery, a virtual who's who of expressionism, was a huge financial success.[132]

The Munich experience was the most dramatic of the expressionist artists' forays into revolutionary politics in Germany. Buoyed by the quixotic success of anarchism in Munich and the protective patronage of Gustav Landauer, the small Action Committee of Revolutionary Artists for the briefest period of time actually gained control over the institutional art world. While they had little time to enact a program, they made headlines in the art world when the professors at the city's two art schools were summarily dismissed. They undoubtedly shocked the entire city when readers of Munich's two largest newspapers awoke on the first day of the council republic to find Aloys Wach's woodcuts emblazoned across the front pages. For the next several days the public was bombarded by excursuses on the new art and by passionate pleas for the revolutionary legitimacy and timely relevance of expressionism. Although most of the members of the Action Committee were young, and all but a few relatively unknown, they had confidence that they could usurp the authority of the larger Council of Artists and wrest the mantle of revolutionary expressionism from the more conservative (both politically and artistically) New Secession.

Their efforts remained speculative; they found no support from the communists and little immediate comprehension from the working class. With the suppression of the second council republic, the association by guilt of modern art with the radical left facilitated their persecution. Several members of the Action Committee were arrested, and others fled the city as the government and the public came to accept at face value the political claims made for expressionism. Nor could they escape these political associations, no matter how resolutely they now tried to divorce their art from politics. Fritz Schaefler and Aloys Wach, the two artists most closely associated with the Action Committee from the beginning, soon witnessed the rapid eclipse of their reputations. They had come from relative obscurity to produce the most highly visible graphics for Munich's newspapers and art journals. Wach is perhaps the more extreme case: he directed almost all his artistic efforts toward promoting in quasi-religious terms the redemption of mankind with the revolution. Combining Gustav Landauer with the anthroposophist Rudolf Steiner, anarcho-socialism and theosophy,[133] Wach conceived of revolution as class reconciliation, not class struggle. With the suppression of the revolution, his pathetic worker types, and the earnestness of his religious metaphors, became a liability in a Munich art world that sought to expunge the revolutionary associations of expressionist art. Hans Goltz, who gave Wach his first break, distanced himself from this revolutionary artist as loudly and as publicly as possible. With his departure from Munich, Wach lost both a sense of artistic community and a public for his art. He continued his expressionist woodcuts for a time in exile, with at least enough success in German exhibitions to facilitate his move to Braunau-am-Inn.[134] Late in 1919 he published a pamphlet (probably self-financed) that sought to explain, on his own terms, his art to a new public in Austria. *Aloys Wach: Holzschnitte 1918* resembled nothing so much as a religious tract.

Quotes from Steiner and Goethe, which testified in mystical terms to the spiritual transformation of material reality in "true" art, accompanied poor-quality reproductions of his religious woodcuts. But as Wach later wrote: "In the rural environs [of Braunau-am-Inn] expressionism did not thrive."[135] He soon abandoned expressionism and, in search of patrons, became a painter of traditional religious art.

Fritz Schaefler, too, had developed a public persona based on his involvement with the revolution, first with his own quasi-religious woodcuts for the *Süddeutsche Freiheit* and then with his woodcut portraits of Kurt Eisner. He also produced numerous woodcut portraits of left-leaning artists and writers (including Georg Kaiser, Aloys Wach, and Felix Stiemer) that appeared regularly in *Der Weg* and *Die Bücherkiste*. Probably as a result of his high visibility in Munich, he was offered a joint exhibition with Paul Klee and Theodor Pilartz to open the new Zingler gallery in Frankfurt. In his catalog essay, the Action Committee member Eduard Trautner lamely tried to describe Schaefler as more than just a "hostile, destructive, overpowering, formidable" artist; nevertheless, such adjectives appeared over and over in the text. Schaefler's identity as an artist rested almost exclusively on his association with contemporary political events, as confirmed by Trautner in his text. "Schaefler's world is that of today, of the present moment," he wrote, "that of machines, of the world war, of socialization, of force and of revolt."[136]

The period of the revolution was the high point of Schaefler's career; in the months from November 1918 until December 1919 he had some six exhibitions throughout Germany. In the following year he had only one exhibition at a relatively obscure gallery. Although it might be tempting to speculate that after the suppression of the revolution Schaefler rejected an exhibition strategy as part of some radical ideology, the evidence points elsewhere, probably that he was still too closely identified—in the minds of the gallery directors and the public—with the failed revolution. Schaefler did not abandon the friendships made in the Action Committee, and for a while they helped guarantee him a modest livelihood. Although he fled Munich first to Passau and then to Prien at Chiemsee, in June 1919 he completed lithographs for a printing of Georg Kaiser's *Fire in the Opera House* and was contracted by the Munich National Theater to provide set decorations and costumes for Shakespeare's *Much Ado About Nothing* and Kaiser's *Sorina*. Soon he joined Eugen Felder's New Theater in Munich, a cooperative workers' theater which performed Kaiser's *From Morning Till Midnight* with professional and lay actors under the direction of Oskar Maria Graf, another Action Committee member.[137] Despite Schaefler's gradual withdrawal from an explicitly political—or even contemporary—subject matter in his painting, he suffered relative obscurity and economic hardship until he abandoned expressionism and moved to Cologne in 1927, where he established himself as a successful religious artist. The former member of the Action Committee of Revolutionary Artists later joined the National Socialist Party, receiving commissions to decorate National Socialist youth buildings even while his early work was being purged from museums in Hannover, Mannheim, Munich, and Halle.[138]

This last legacy of the Action Committee was an ominous one: as the National Socialists under Adolf Hitler gained increasing support in Bavaria, they made sure that the association between expressionism and bolshevism outlasted the revolutionary period. No matter how few had taken seriously the revolutionary ambitions of expressionism in 1919, no matter how many had sought to distance the new art from the revolution after its suppression, the political rhetoric that surrounded the movement came back to haunt it once more.

THE END OF EXPRESSIONISM 5

In November 1918 the art world appeared to expressionist artists as a *tabula rasa,* an opportunity for them to inscribe their own ambitions and desires for art on a new social order. They imagined a new relevance for their work, an end to their outsider status and to the privileged exclusivity of their art. They would no longer be dependent on a philistine bourgeoisie whose values they scorned, but would find acclaim from a revolutionary proletariat and protection from its government. All this, it seemed, could be accomplished in one decisive stroke. The war years, and the success of their art with a bourgeois clientele, were a brief interlude to be erased from memory, part of a new paradigm of forgetting in a post-war German society eager to put the hardships of the past four years behind it. Instead they focused on the freedoms promised by an end to imperial art tutelage: the freedom to reorganize the entire profession, from the way they learned to the way they reached the public; the freedom to create what they wanted with no outside pressures or interference; the freedom to gain direct access to the "people" without the intrusion of hostile state functionaries and reactionary art administrators. The sacrifices they had to make were minimal—a new emphasis on the handicrafts, a downplaying of individual genius. But these minor concessions promised compensatory rewards and even conferred a new moral dimension to their profession: they could now ethically equate their labors to that of the worker. However naïve, their attempts to radically rethink the role of art and artists in society, and to reconsider how art functioned under both capitalism and socialism, were both serious and passionate.

It is easy to imagine the euphoria these artists felt, congregating with their colleagues, writing manifestos, following the latest political developments, arguing late into the night. As they looked about them, they sensed profound support from diverse groups: sympathetic art critics nationwide, members of the socialist press, some political leaders, and even segments of the establishment art community. As word slowly filtered in from Russia—particularly from the acknowledged leader of the expressionist movement, Wassily Kandinsky—their expectations must have soared. Almost every artists' council in Germany, no matter how large or how small, quickly sent greetings to their colleagues in Russia and dreamed for a similar victory at home.

But from the start the revolution was ambiguous, simultaneously a revolution from above and from below, and revolution was a word manipulated to represent the interests of those both in and out of power. The new code words trotted out with the revolution—words like "community" (*Gemeinschaft*) and "people" (*Volk*)—soon became mere narrative clichés for resolving conflict. Expressionist artists, too, had to work their way through this political and rhetorical minefield, carefully considering which course might best further their goals. In this they fared no better than most, equally unable to fathom a political situation that was confusing at best, hopeless at worst. How much credence was to be given to the Social Democrats' claim that order was the paramount political concern given the threat of Allied intervention and mass starvation? And how much to their claim that significant change would come about, but only gradually? How much help could be expected from the Independent Social Democrats—initially sympathetic to their efforts—when the party was hopelessly split, with one wing supporting the government and the other working for its downfall? And what about the Communist Party, which had shown the least interest in their work? The party organ, *Die Rote Fahne*, did not comment on the arts at all in 1919, being more concerned at the time with the political struggle. While many artists sympathized with its martyred leaders, the putschism of the KPD (despite no mass support) and its unwillingness to participate in electoral politics alienated even more. Under this political constellation, what often emerged from the artists' groups were impromptu responses, dizzying reversals, and displays of confusion. Only gradually did they come to understand that the art world was not a blank slate on which they could inscribe their desires, but rather an entrenched bureaucracy that proved exceedingly difficult to dislodge. Many now feared that, despite cosmetic changes, the institutional art world would survive the revolution intact. As Adolf Behne wrote in late January: "What has happened in the ten weeks of the revolutionary period? The spirit of the old regime has returned to our people after a few short days of initial enthusiasm. Ideally, they want to set the old machine in motion again, only slightly repainted."

With political and economic stabilization, expressionist artists were confronted with a new set of problems. Was inclusion in a broad-based democratic arts program enough to satisfy their demands for radical change? Could they accommodate themselves to the new republic, or were they to be forced into political opposition? Was it still possible to believe in the revolutionary nature of their art as a challenge to contemporary society, or would their art have to change? Still unanswered was whether expressionism as a style was marked by its destructive or constructive relationship to reality. Did it fragment reality in order to destroy it, reassemble it, or both? In the early days of the revolution sympathetic critics generally emphasized the constructive aspect of expressionism; the new art was called upon, like any other productive work, to reconstruct a new society on the ashes of the one destroyed by the war. In an effort to discredit it, though, conservative critics kept alive its destructive side, equating its shattering of forms with the violence of the bolshevists in Russia—and by implication with the communists at home. Finally, critics on the left, disappointed in the failure of the revolution, once more resurrected a destructive (or at least dialectical) version of expressionism, promoting it for its subversive resistance to bourgeois authority.

Even with the apparent failure of the revolution, artists and critics struggled to keep alive their politically progressive notions of expressionism. Their attitude was reinforced by persistent attacks from the right, which equated their art with political radicalism, even bolshevism, and conversely by occasional support from the political left. But their arguments were vague and lacked specifics. The discussions of expressionism and revolution that filled the pages of the art press had surprisingly little to say about individual artists or individual works of art. Questions as to what revolutionary art should look like, or what its subject matter should be, were almost nowhere in evidence. Although most art critics assumed significant changes in the art world as the result of the revolution, much of their criticism conformed to certain unwritten rules in which the language of culture did not partake of the language of politics. Critics referred obliquely to the "events of November," but rarely to specific episodes, political personalities, or even parties. Whereas journals as diverse as *Die Aktion* and *Die neue Rundschau* wrote weekly about political events, the same vocabulary was often withheld from their art criticism.

The lofty, generalized tone of German art-political writing may have been a legacy of press censorship during the war, a force of habit rather than a necessity. For some authors, it may have been a protective measure against political persecution. The possibility also suggests itself, however, that the nature of the argument advanced by the critics necessitated its tone. Because most of these writers were concerned with upholding the viability of expressionist art, they set about explaining away what could not be explained away: the indissoluable link between expressionism and capitalism that had emerged in Germany.

In the long run, many of the aims of the expressionist artists promoted under the slogan "art and revolution" were in fact realized: they were now represented in state museums, their opinions were now sought by the state bureaucracy, and they gradually began to infiltrate the state art schools. By the early 1920s many expressionists had been appointed to academies throughout Germany, including Heinrich Campendonk at the Essen School of Decorative Arts, Oskar Kokoschka at the Dresden Academy, Otto Mueller at the Breslau Academy, Cesar Klein at the Berlin Museum of Decorative Arts, and Georg Tappert at the State Academy for Art Education in Berlin. The Bauhaus, in which Walter Gropius hoped to enact the program of the Working Council for Art, opened in Weimar under the auspices of a local Social Democratic government. Lyonel Feininger and Gerhard Marcks were among the first appointed, followed by Paul Klee and Wassily Kandinsky. There is no question that these artists profited from the new art-politics of the Weimar government. But although some reforms had indeed occurred, it was essentially only new people in the old positions. Like so many other institutions in Weimar Germany, the art establishment survived essentially unchanged: cosmetically altered, but structurally intact.

The responses of expressionist artists to the simultaneous success and failure of their cause remained, not surprisingly, inconclusive. Many struggled for a time to keep alive the politically progressive notions of their art. Among those was Hans Richter, the leader of the Action Committee of Revolutionary Artists during the second council republic in Munich. After his arrest and expulsion from Munich, he briefly returned to Zurich, where he futilely attempted to revive the League of Radical Artists on its original premises, despite his experiences in Munich. The effort failed on the objections of several members, at least one of whom now questioned the original political assumptions of the group. The sculptor P. R. Henning, a member of the original group, wrote in a letter to Walter Gropius:

> I have benefitted here from the insight of how strongly the emotional state of the revolutionary element only polishes the surface anew . . . Hans Richter, who has now gone to Berlin, may please some there with his sensationalism . . . Revolution, though, only for its own sake, is the same superstition as was bureaucracy or organization.[1]

Richter now eliminated all figurative elements in his art, resulting in completely abstract geometric compositions, the precursors of his abstract films. He pursued experiments to discover an objective abstract visual language based on such diverse—and increasingly extreme—models as forms in nature and the visual appearance of Chinese letters.

Many other artists, too, struggled to keep their ideals alive, but in the end put their trust in the reformed institutions of the new parliamentary democracy. Among the more dramatic examples was Paul Klee, the "silent" member of the Action Committee of Revolutionary Artists, who was "coopted" into the group only days before it disbanded. Initially, Klee had stood cautiously to the right of the Action Committee, fearful about the outcome of the revolution. If anything, he became closely identified with the Council of Artists and with the anti-bolshevik line of the *Münchner Blätter,* on whose editorial board he sat. At some point, however, Klee's sympathies shifted to the more radical of Munich's artists' groups. The depth of his emotional commitment to the goals of the Action Committee can be gauged from a letter he began on 12 May—that is, after the suppression of the second council republic—to his close friend Alfred Kubin:

> Of however little permanence this communist republic appeared from the very beginning, it nevertheless presented an opportunity for an assessment of the subjective possibilities of existence in such a community. It was not without a positive result. Naturally a pointedly individualistic art is not suitable for appreciation by all, it is a capitalist luxury. However, we ought to be more than curiosities for rich snobs. And that part of us which somehow strives beyond this to eternal values would be better able to experience support in a communist community . . . We should be able to conduct the results of our activity as discoverers directly to the people's body. This new art could then penetrate into the crafts and make them flourish. Then academies would not exist any more, only art schools for craftsmen. . . .
>
> Thus the Council Republic also brought for us many an insight. A practical realization is now less than ever to be thought of. . . . Perhaps this does not interest you so much, but it has preoccupied me very much for a time.[2]

Klee's letter amounted to a summary of the radical artistic manifestos circulating throughout Germany (questioning art as a luxury commodity, calling for an art for the "people," advocating the effective utilization of art through the crafts, opposing academies), with a special nod to Hans Richter and the League of Radical Artists in his borrowing of the term "people's body" from their manifesto. At the same time, however, it was an admission of failure and a painful recognition that his individualistic art might after all be only a capitalist luxury. These reflections gained urgency as he completed and mailed the letter on the eve of his hasty departure from Munich for Switzerland, when the fear of reprisal finally caught up with the least visible member of the Action Committee.

While Klee was in Switzerland, he was in touch with Marcel Janco and Viking Eggeling, whom Richter had proposed as professors at a reformed Munich academy.[3] He also planned to meet with Richter, who had escaped prosecution but had been expelled from Munich.[4] While in Switzerland, Klee missed the opening of the summer exhibition of the Munich New Secession, where beside his usual fairy-tale paintings and watercolors was one dramatic departure, a small oil on cardboard titled *Young Proletarian* (fig. 5.1). The round, roughly painted face of a young proletarian boy fixes his stare on the viewer. The symmetrical composition, contrasting red and green colors, and the slightly elevated viewpoint combine to form an unsettling, even aggressive portrait. It stood in a curious relationship with Aloys Wach's worker portraits: although it shared the downcast heavy eyelids, the absence of a cubist breakup of space gave a more solid presence to the figure. Klee's proletarian was simultaneously oppressed and defiant, a figure of the period after the suppression of the revolution. The topical subject matter and the new, relatively crude realistic style, were a marked departure for Klee. It may have been Klee's fleeting, almost wistful, attempt at a popular art, one which escaped the individualism of the capitalist luxury problematized in his letter to Kubin.

Curiously, reviewers of the show never mentioned the painting. For critics such as Ernst Grünthal, writing in *Der Weg*, this was symptomatic of an attempt to avoid any further political persecution of expressionist art. Hermann Esswein of the SPD *Münchner Post*, however, used his generally negative review of the exhibition to attack Klee and, for the first time, link his name in print with the extreme left:

> Among the fantasy artists Paul Klee carries special weight as a totally special phenomenon. I find only that he actually has no fantasy, but indulges in foolishness like a child . . . For the sake of curiosity it may be mentioned that Paul Klee was considered by the art dictators of the council republic as a graphic instructor at the Munich School of Arts and Crafts. . . . However in the final analysis all of this total salon-bolshevism, also in art, is only a specialty for educated rabble.[5]

The sales results of the exhibition unequivocally showed Klee how the art-buying public responded to *Young Proletarian*. Of the top priced pictures, all were sold except *Young Proletarian*. Klee quickly aban-

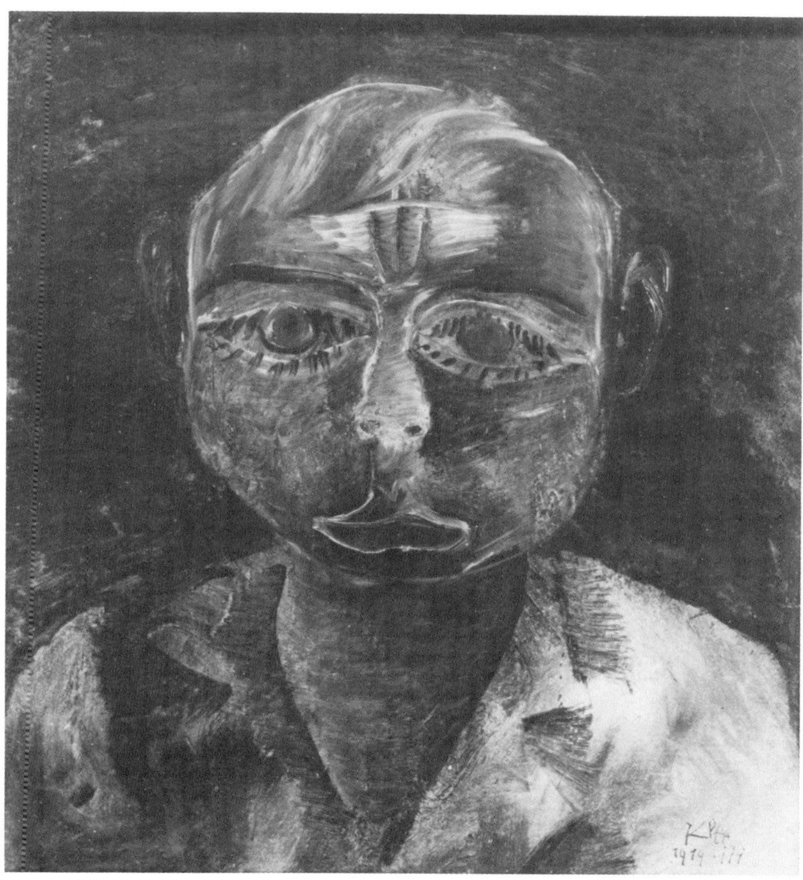

5.1 Paul Klee, *Junger Proletarier (Young Proletariat)*, 1919. Oil on board, 25 x 23.5 cm. © 1988, copyright by Cosmopress, Geneva.

doned the new style; its confrontational physiognomy was the antithesis of the image Klee now projected, which was apparent in his own self-portrait, *Absorption* (fig. 5.2). Here Klee conspicuously emphasized the tightly closed eyes and the missing ears of the artist mystically withdrawn from the world, a reversal of his short-lived stance of political engagement. On 1 October 1919 Klee signed a sales contract with Hans Goltz, whose *Der Ararat* had described revolutionaries as "psychopaths" and the Freikorps as "rescue troops." In the imaginary polarity Klee had laid out in his letter to Kubin—art for the people or art as a capitalist luxury—it was the latter which prevailed.

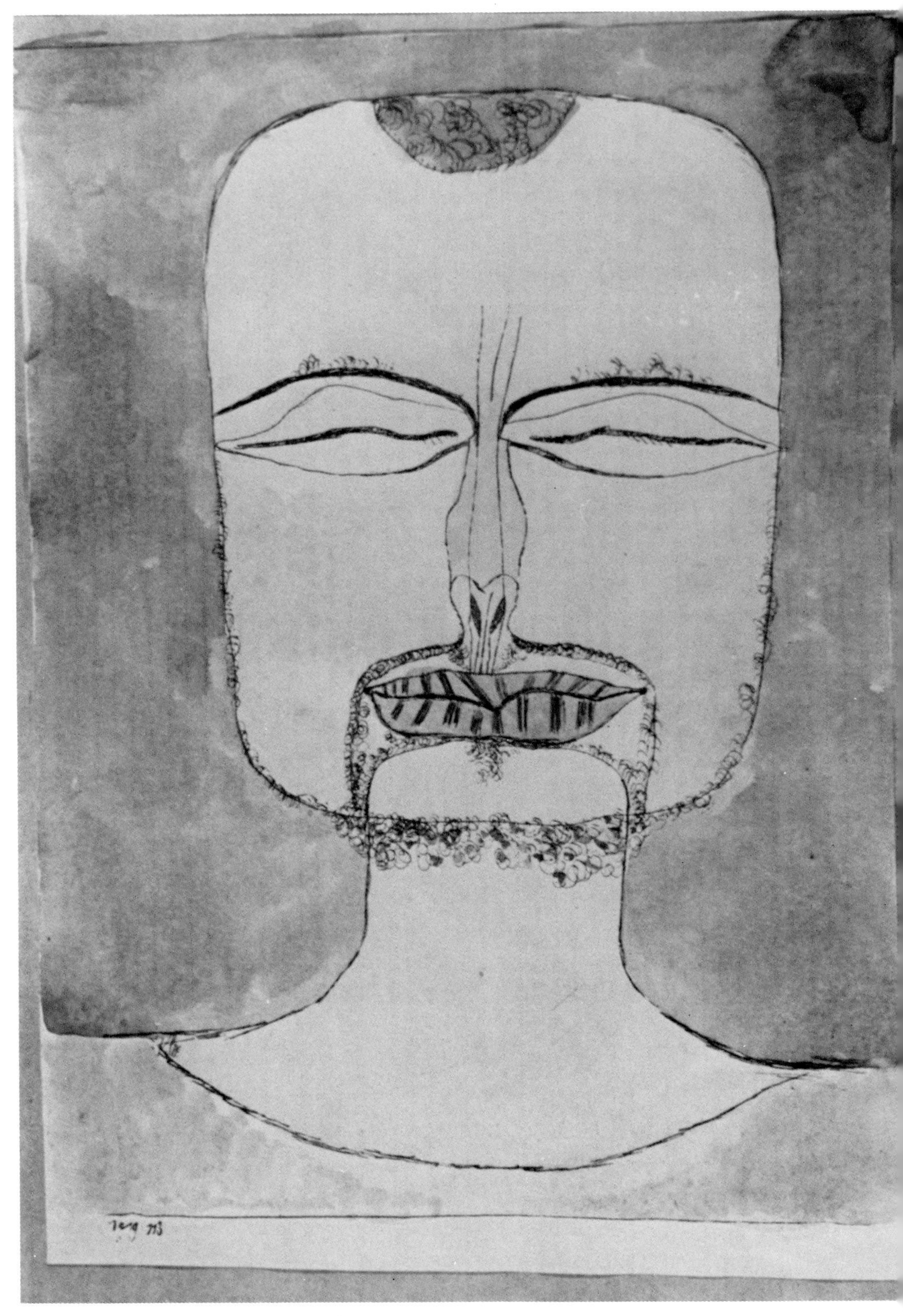

5.2 Paul Klee, *Versunkenheit (Selbstporträt)* [*Absorption (Self-portrait)*], 1919. Colored lithograph, 25.6 x 18 cm. © 1988, copyright by Cosmopress, Geneva.

If artists such as Klee made their peace with the new republic, others were less sanguine about the compromise. Highly disillusioned, their revolutionary hopes defeated, they began to reassess both their art and their politics. Bruno Taut was one of them. He grew increasingly skeptical about his earlier faith in art to renew society and in his own utopian architectural schemes. As early as February 1920 he wrote to his patron Karl Ernst Osthaus that he was finishing his book *The Dissolution of the Cities* (a romantic view of decentralization heavily reliant on the ideas Kropotkin and Landauer) and that he would then leave utopia behind and hopefully work in the "realm of the practical."[6] Taut even began to distance himself from the Working Council for Art and from the modishness of its more utopian manifestations. His differences became apparent when in May 1920 he withdrew his work from the final exhibition of the Working Council for Art after its run in Berlin. He was apparently distressed when critics concerned themselves almost exclusively with the formal characeristics of his utopian drawings, paying little attention to their social concerns. He may also have been alarmed at the way in which the crystalline towers and spiky mountain peaks of his own utopian drawings had found their most practical expression as decorations in places such as the Skala dance casino (fig. 5.3), a Berlin restaurant and nightclub.

Taut expressed his disillusionment in a poignant letter[7] that came to terms with almost two years of passionate involvement in groups such as the Working Council for Art and the Cooperative Society of Socialist Artists. He wrote: "Our age has one great strength: it wishes for better things. The great and the humble, faith and tragedy simultaneously. To wish for better but be unable to do anything, to achieve nothing—that is the meaning of the age." For Taut, expressionism had become discredited: "Out of step with the age: death of Expressionism. Absorbed into literariness and vaudeville." He was equally disenchanted with politics; neither capitalism nor communism seemed to offer any viable alternative:

Strangle the "beautiful soul" of politics. Collaboration with politics pointless. Politics is in its essence mundane, materialistic. The devil's work of mechanization: bourgeois, capitalism. . . .

Socialization: political consequences, inexorable death of the industrial state (from the standpoint of industry uneconomic, senseless).

Enforced death of too many. Safety valve against overpopulation: hunger, plague, civil war.

Chaos. Decline of the West.

Consequence of the East, Bolshevism: quicker, more conscious disintegration than in the West. Also Chaos.[8]

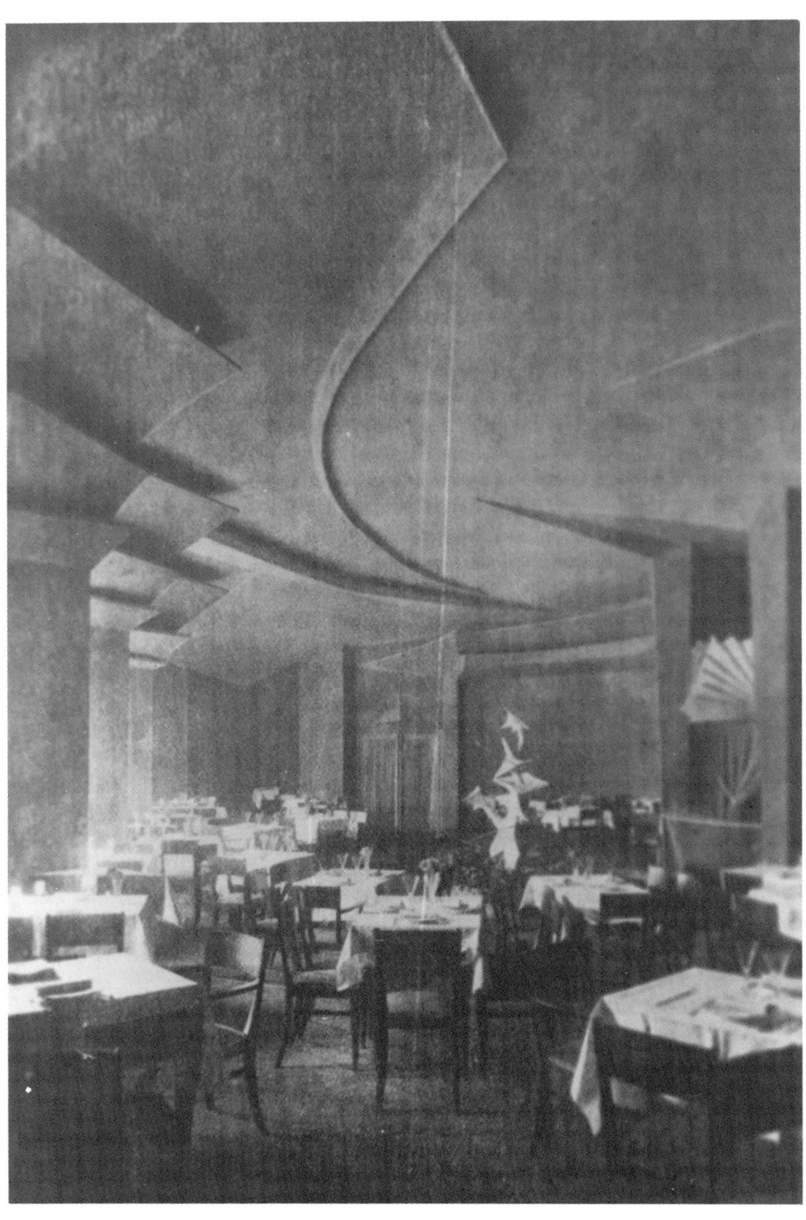

5.3 Walter Wurzbach and Rudolf Belling, interior of Skala Dance-Club, Berlin, 1920.

By the following year, Taut left utopia behind. He took up a position as City Architect in Magdeburg, where he reorganized the planning office, worked with the building cooperatives, and developed future projects for the city. He, too, made a kind of peace with the republic, but on a different basis. He now devoted most of his efforts to providing working-class housing, usually in collaboration with socialist building guilds, but dependent, nonetheless, on local social democratic governments.

In his disillusionment Taut had spoken of the death of expressionism, "absorbed into literariness and vaudeville." He was not the only one to announce the demise of the movement. The institutionalization of expressionism, its celebration as an official style, soon had about it a funereal aspect. As the right attacked expressionist art for its leftist political associations, as some critics defensively sought to extricate it from its revolutionary connections, and as others insistently upheld their politically progressive notions of it, many eventually abandoned it. Many of the most influential critics in Germany now proclaimed with apodictic certainty the end of expressionism. This did not mean that they expected it to disappear overnight, with its practitioners suddenly abandoning it or its patrons abruptly deserting it. Rather, it was the first sign that the fateful history of expressionism during the revolution had destroyed confidence in its ability to serve the avant-garde notion of the relationship between art and politics.

Among the first to suggest an end to expressionism was the critic Willi Wolfradt, writing in the June 1919 issue of the liberal journal *Die Neue Rundschau*. Central to Wolfradt's argument was this: expressionism was inextricably tied to the revolution, meaning not revolution in general, but the November Revolution in particular. Among other things, Wolfradt based his observations on the formal aspects of expressionism: "The fever of revolution hammers in every curve, color, prosody, dissonance."[9] To show the thoroughgoing nature of this phenomenon, he described—in violent metaphor—the dismemberment of form in expressionist art. He summed up his case as follows: "Art did not lend itself to the revolution; it was it [revolution] itself."[10]

But if expressionism had tied itself to the November Revolution, it was a union that, in Wolfradt's estimation, had failed:

> The revolutionary forms itself in art. If art is submerged in the actuality of the revolution—that is, politicizes itself in such a way that it remains tied to an actual goal to be realized—then, as soon as this goal begins to emerge from the utopian phase, art dies. One used to think that in a perfect world there would be no art. This is correct and only expresses the deep relationship between art

and dissatisfaction, the revolutionary character not only of today's, but of all and every art.[11]

In this passage Wolfradt summoned up the notion of the end of art as conceived by Hegel. If art prefigured an ideal state of being, then as soon as it was imagined that this state might actually be reached, it also became conceivable that art would lose its purpose.

For Wolfradt, the political concerns of expressionism no longer made sense, for politics was no longer the realm where revolution could succeed. He concluded: "All politics are irrevolutionary." He reasserted instead an idealist conception of the inherently revolutionary nature of art and postulated an alternative to the "baroque of expressionism," which was "inwardly exhausted." This he described as a "new classical period," characterized by a "new strengthened lawfulness, melody, quiet, substantiality;" that is, an antithesis of expressionism as he defined it, the reverse of Wölfflin's transition from classical to baroque.

Other, more supportive critics, also wrote the obituary of expressionism—even if they foresaw its demise further in the future. The author Kasimir Edschmid had stated his fears about the institutionalization of expressionism already in 1917.[12] In a 1920 lecture he admitted that public recognition had brought to a close the oppositional phase of expressionism ("the forward thrust of yesterday became . . . the yawn of today"), but still upheld the viability of the first generation of expressionists, while dismissing the legions of newcomers. In the end, though, he suggested a possible shift toward realism—but in a still distant future.[13] Edschmid's summary judgment came at the opening of an expressionist exhibition in Darmstadt that already had about it the feel of a retrospective.

Among the most influential critics to repudiate expressionism was Wilhelm Hausenstein, one of its earliest champions on the left. It was Hausenstein who as early as 1913 had described expressionism as the art of a future socialist society. Within the space of a year, though, Hausenstein gave up not only his leftist political convictions but his enthusiasm for expressionist art.[14] Already in his essay "Art and Revolution," published in the *Neue Merkur* and in a catalog for the Alfred Flechtheim gallery, Hausenstein had rejected any precipitous link between art and the politics of the new state—in order, as he saw it, to safeguard the revolutionary nature of art. Although clearly disillusioned with the course of the revolution, he still held out in his concluding words the faint hope that the new state might produce a "new collectivity" rather than "revolutionary gestures." Late in 1919 he cautiously reconfirmed his earlier assessment that expressionism was a sign of a coming collectivist, socialist society. This confirmation of his earlier views came in an expanded version of his 1913 book *Bild und Gemeinschaft: Entwurf einer Soziologie der Kunst,* which he republished "despite the reservations of today, despite the skepticism of hindsight."[15]

In a *volte-face* in Munich in April 1920, however, Hausenstein publicly renounced his support for expressionism, questioning its viability, its problematic relationship to reality, and its institutionalization. In his 1920 book *Die Kunst im diesem Augenblick* he expanded the theme of this lecture and made it clear that the failure of expressionism was also a failure of politics. In a bitter political reckoning he wrote: "Socialism, which once promised rescue, entered into bankruptcy with the revolution." The "metaphysical stupidity of the nationalist sphere and the dilettantism of the left," he lamented, had become "only the hopeless pendants around the hopeless stupidity of the democratic middle."[16] As for expressionism, he reversed his earlier characterization of the new art as a sign of a coming collective society and relegated it instead to a mere sign of its time: "horribly misformed . . . hacked to pieces, sick, displaced."[17] With its institutionalization had come its demise: "Expressionism today has its Glass Palace. It has its salon. No cigarette poster, no nightclub manages without expressionism. It is loathsome."[18] Hausenstein delivered the final death knell: expressionism had "come to an end," he wrote. "Expressionism is dead."[19]

In *Die Kunst in diesem Augenblick,* Hausenstein, like Wolfradt, introduced cautiously, if unspecifically, a realist alternative to expressionism in a "return to nature."[20] His renunciation of expressionism was at the same time a renunciation of political involvement. Now, he turned for consolation to the world of art, where he looked for the "rescue of a miserable world" from "a totally different, only spiritual region."[21]

Such pronouncements of the end of expressionism did not go unchallenged. But even the most ardent supporters had to admit that expressionism had become derivative, even mere fashion. Responding to Hausenstein's speech, Paul Westheim wrote in *Das Kunstblatt:* "The expressionist Academy, expressionist fashion, expressionist fellow-travelers, that catchphrase expressionism with which the smart art dealers and clever art critics practice their propaganda; would that it was already at an end!"[22] What Westheim wanted an end to was not expressionism, but its pale imitators. Like Edschmid, he tried to distinguish between an authentic, first-generation expressionism, and its new acolytes—and thus rescue the movement from its own demise.

Hausenstein, Wolfradt, and others, disappointed in the outcome of the revolution, fled the world of politics for that of art, announcing the end to their political hopes with the end of expressionism. From another quarter, though, came a more trenchant critique of expressionism, one waged still in the name of revolutionary politics. This was the assault of Berlin Dada, which seemed to call not just for an end to expressionism, but an end to art.

Dada first came to Berlin from Zurich in 1917 in the person of the poet/physician Richard Huelsenbeck, whose anti-war stance was quickly taken up by a number of artists and writers who became known as the Berlin Dada group. The core group included George Grosz, a bohemian artist of working-class origins who had recently been discovered and promoted by the critic Theodor Däubler and the art dealer Hans Goltz; the brothers Wieland Herzfelde and John Heartfield, sons of the socialist poet Franz Held and the working-class activist Alice Stolzenberg; and Raoul Hausmann, a member of the Expressonist Working Group in Dresden and co-editor of the anarchist journal *Die Freie Strasse*. Their scorn for the war and for German society soon manifested itself in a series of outrageous performances modeled on the programs of the Cabaret Voltaire. In one of the most famous, Grosz performed an obscene tap dance in which he relieved himself in pantomime before a Lovis Corinth painting with the words "Art is shit."[23] They restyled their lives and their appearances as an insult to German militarism and patriotism. Grosz and Heartfield anglicized their names to protest anti-British propaganda, and they all assumed provocative dress: Huelsenbeck, for instance, wore the uniform of an army doctor, a monocle, and carried a riding crop; Grosz often wore a military uniform, complete with a monocle, a huge cardboard Iron Cross hung around his neck, and a gigantic papier-mâché death mask. Even in private Grosz acted the role of a Prussian general, ordering people about and slapping their faces with his glove.[24]

This combination of insult and humor was directed at the hypocrisy of German society: its reverence for culture—and its penchant for brutality. The mocking skepticism with which they confronted the world around them soon found an outlet in the Malik Verlag, a clandestine publishing house they founded and which was always just a step ahead of the censors. The pamphlets and portfolios they published redirected their liberal opposition to the war into an aggressive attack on German culture, which they held culpable for the war. The first George Grosz portfolio, published by the Malik Verlag in 1917, included a number of hard-edged drawings of rape, murder, assault, and insanity in the big city—symbols of a society gone absolutely mad. One of their prime targets soon became the expressionists, whose growing success—and "spiritualization"—they saw as part of an escapist bourgeois culture responsible for the war and its carnage. As Grosz later wrote:

> The German Dada movement had its roots in the perception that came to some of my comrades and to me at the same time that it was complete nonsense to believe that spirit or anything spiritual ruled the world. Goethe in bombardments; Nietzsche in knapsacks; Jesus in trenches. But there were still people who thought spirit and art had power . . . Dada was not an ideological movement, but an organic product which arose as a reaction to the cloud-wandering tendencies of the so-called sacred art that found meaning in cubes and Gothic, while the field commanders painted in blood.[25]

The attack on expressionism went public when Huelsenbeck read the first German Dada manifesto (co-written with Hausmann) at a 12 April 1918 Dada evening in Berlin. Here Huelsenbeck challenged the widening appeal of expressionist art as symptomatic of a withdrawal from the brutal realities of war:

> Art in its execution and direction is dependent upon the time in which it lives, and artists are creatures of their epoch. The highest art will be that which in its conscious content presents the thousandfold problems of the day, the art which has been visibly shattered by the explosions of last week, which is forever trying to collect its limbs after yesterday's crash . . . Has expressionism fulfilled our expectations for such an art which is a public vote on our most vital concerns?
>
> No! No! No!
>
> Under the pretense of internalization, the expressionists in literature and in painting have joined together to form a generation which already today longingly awaits its literary and art historical appreciation and is a candidate for an honorable recognition by the bourgeoisie. Under the pretense of propagating the soul, they have, in their struggle against naturalism, found their way back to those abstract-pathetic gestures which presuppose an empty, comfortable and inflexible life.[26]

This assault on expressionism was also taken up by the Dadaists in Zurich; the Rumanian Tristan Tzara charged in a 1918 manifesto: "We have enough cubist and futurist academies: laboratories of formal ideas. Is the aim of art to make money and cajole the nice-nice bourgeois?"[27]

With Germany's military defeat and the November Revolution, the Dadaists' broadside on German society moved more and more out of the realm of art and into that of radical politics. On 31 December 1918, George Grosz, John Heartfield, and Wieland Herzfelde joined the German Communist Party, receiving their membership cards from Rosa Luxemburg herself.[28] With the deaths of Karl Liebknecht and Rosa

Luxemburg, and the suppression of revolutionary activity in Berlin, they devoted themselves to fighting the new republic and the "traitors" of the revolution. Together they published a succession of short-lived journals, including *Jedermann sein eigner Fussball* and *Die Pleite,* which were continually banned by the authorities. Articles on the bankruptcy of the SPD and in praise of the KPD were accompanied by Grosz's satirical drawings, which now acquired a new political directness. The cover of the first issue of *Die Pleite* (fig. 5.4), for example, depicted the new chancellor Friedrich Ebert as a capitalist emperor, ensconced in an armchair with a pillow under his feet and a cigar in his hand. Wearing a monocle and a crown with a tottering Iron Cross, Ebert is served a gigantic snifter of champagne by a military officer. These attacks apparently struck a raw nerve; when street fighting broke out in Berlin in March, Herzfelde was taken into "protective custody" and spent almost two harrowing weeks in the Lehrter prison without even a hearing. Grosz, fearful of being arrested, briefly went into hiding after his studio was searched by the military.[29]

With the revolution the Dadaists kept up their attack on German culture in general and on the expressionists in particular. Their satirical Dada anti-councils, including the Dada Revolutionary Central Council and the Council of Unpaid Workers, mocked the expressionists' councils. The Dada manifesto "What is Dada and What Does It Want in Germany?" written in April or May 1919 by Raoul Hausmann, Richard Huelsenbeck, and Jefim Golyscheff, called for a "brutal battle" against "expressionism and the neoclassical culture as it is represented by *Der Sturm.*"[30] The second issue of the journal *Der Dada,* edited by Hausmann, declared that spirit was dead, expressionism was dead, and art was dead.[31]

Yet for all the attacks, the political distinctions between the Dadaists and the expressionists in 1919 were less clear-cut than they appear retrospectively. At times, they were deceptively fluid. The early Berlin Dada publications featured poems by leading expressionist writers, including Theodor Däubler, Albert Ehrenstein, and Else Lasker-Schuler. Although the manifesto "What Is Dada and What Does It Want in Germany?" explicitly rejected "Sturm art," some of its utopian artistic ideas sounded suspiciously close to those put forward by the artists' councils. For example, the manifesto echoed the Working Council for Art in promoting the building of "light and garden cities which advance mankind in the direction of freedom."[32] Despite the critique of expressionism, at least a few members of the Dada group joined the November Group—including Grosz, who did not resign until 1921.[33] The first Dada exhibition (about which so little is known) was not the famous

1920 Dada Fair, but a March 1919 exhibition that preceded the Exhibition of Unknown Architects at I. B. Neumann's fashionable gallery on the Kurfürstendamm. In fact, both exhibitions at Neumann's gallery featured the work of Jefim Golyscheff, who was enthusiastically championed by both groups. Raoul Hausmann wrote of Golyscheff's

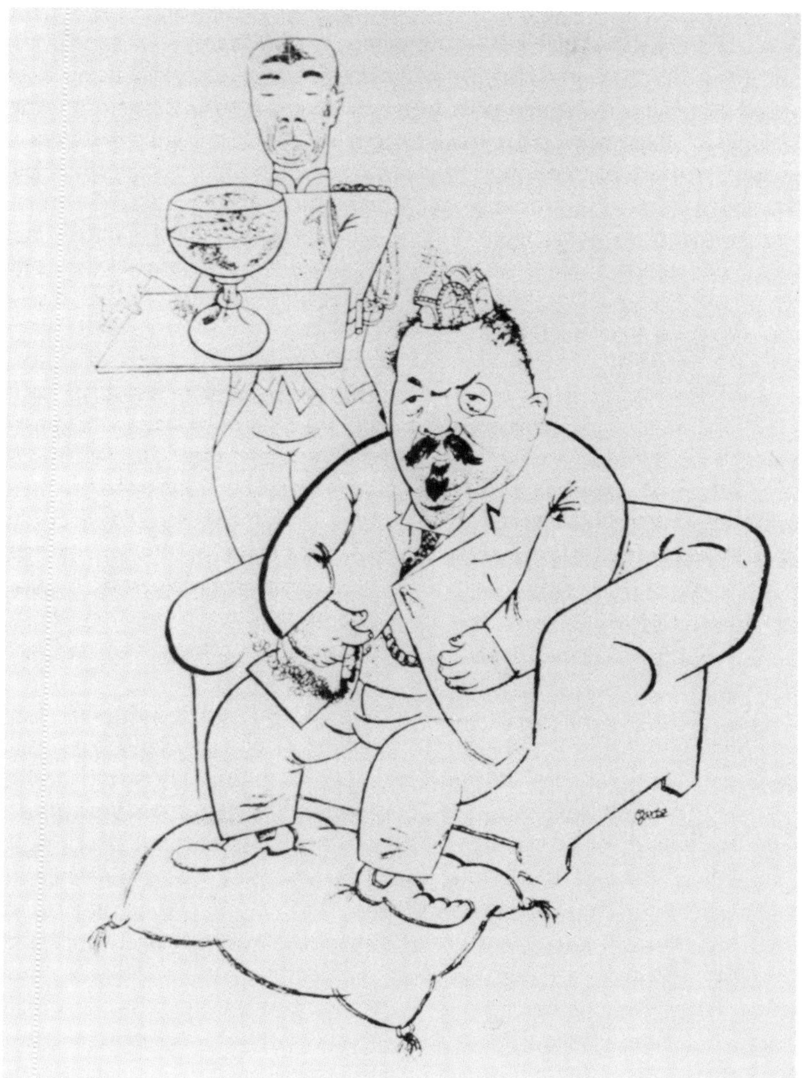

5.4 George Grosz, *By the Grace of Money Bags,* cover illustration for *Die Pleite* 1, no. 1 (1919). Estate of George Grosz, Princeton, New Jersey.

contributions to the first Dada exhibition that he brought "assemblages such as had never been seen before: things grafted together out of cans, small bottles, bits of cardboard, lumps of wood, scraps of plush and tufts of hair. An incredible optical spectacle: before then it had been impossible to show anything like this."[34] Golyscheff's constructions appealed to the nihilism of Dada, with its attention to everyday objects rather than art. Yet his childlike architectural sketches in the Exhibition for Unknown Architects, which followed immediately at I. B. Neumann's gallery, epitomized what Gropius had been looking for: utopia. For a brief moment, at least, the two enterprises did not seem totally incompatible. Golyscheff eventually came to stand for a compromise between the two: when he edged away from the Dada group late in 1919, Adolf Behne promoted him as the heir apparent to expressionism (increasingly abandoned by Behne since it was under assault). His previous Dada connections and his unconventional art assured that he could be disassociated from criticism that expressionism had become the plaything of a moneyed public; his move away from the Dadaists guaranteed that he did not totally reject art.[35]

By early 1920, however, the divisions became more clear-cut, and the choice for artists became one between artistic accommodation and outright political opposition to the new republic. But even for those who chose the latter, the form that opposition would take was still open to debate. Was the only consciously revolutionary art anti-art, either collections of the mundane refuse of contemporary life or satirical cartoons attacking the ruling class? Or was a more positive, even heroic, art of the working class possible? And how was one to create revolutionary art but survive financially in a capitalist economy? And even more importantly, how was one to avoid cooptation?

Among those who now sought to discredit the new republic in their art were the Dresden artists Conrad Felixmüller and Otto Dix. Although Felixmüller left the Dresden Secession Group while Dix remained a member, both gained reputations as politically committed artists. Their approaches to political art, though, diverged considerably. Still, both were forced through it all to reckon with the realities of artistic production in a capitalist state.

By late 1919 Felixmüller had become an adherent of Otto Rühle, the renegade Dresden communist whom he sketched and painted repeatedly in the following year. Rühle, who opposed Russian domination of the German Communist Party, was expelled from the party in October 1919 for his views, whereupon he helped establish the syndicalist Communist Worker's Party of Germany (KAPD). Whether Felixmüller followed Rühle into the KAPD is unknown, but his contributions to *Die*

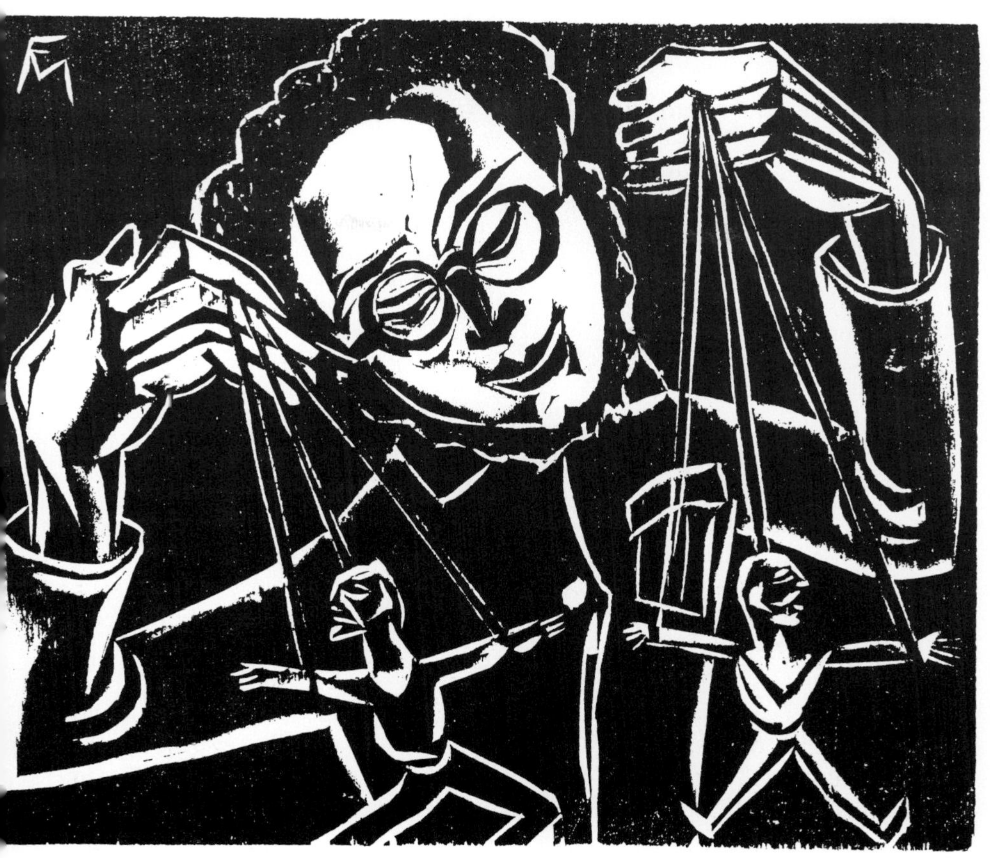

5.5 Conrad Felixmüller, *Karl Radeks Traum (Karl Radek's Dream)*, 1920. Woodcut, 13.5 x 17 cm. Photo courtesy of Titus Felixmüller.

Aktion in 1920 made clear his sympathies with Rühle's political position. In *Karl Radek's Dream* (fig. 5.5), for example, he showed the Russian emissary to Germany manipulating the "puppet" leaders of the KPD.[36]

With Felixmüller's intensified political commitment in 1920 came a change in his art, described by the artist in his thinly veiled autobiographical statement for *Die Aktion*. After the suppression of the revolution, he wrote there, his task was to create a proletarian art:

As is generally known, the revolution was betrayed and bloodily suppressed . . . Crimes against brave revolutionaries depressed Pönnecke [Felixmüller] so much that he ceased to work. It was clear to him: there is no other task than to be a revolutionary . . . If the proletariat has the political power, the power that it needs to develop itself, it will create from this tradition of struggle and of final victory its culture and its art: the art of simple men, devoid of luxury; the art of love, of human relation.

With the 8,000 marks he received from the Rome prize awarded his painting *Pregnant Woman in the Forest,* Felixmüller traveled not to Italy but to the Ruhr in 1920.[37] He now painted a number of partisan leftist paintings inspired by the workers' militancy in that area. In the wake of the March 1920 Kapp Putsch, a right-wing attempt to oust the government which failed when workers went out on strike, a red army of over fifty thousand formed in the Ruhr. Felixmüller's *Ruhr District II* (fig. 5.6) depicts members of this red army—armed workers with red arm bands who patrol the entrance to a factory. His new art was one response to the perceived failure of his expressionism to live up to its revolutionary claims: from the "destructive synthetic cubism" of his work in the war years, and the affirmative spiritualization of expressionism in 1918–19, Felixmüller developed a partisan leftist art, which now promoted the beliefs of the KPD and the KAPD that workers' resistance to the Kapp Putsch signaled the opportunity for the left to seize power. He retained the expressive colors and even the exaggerated features of his earlier art, but now tied them to a new, politically conscious subject matter.

Felixmüller explained his new position in a letter to one of his patrons, Heinrich Kirchhoff:

There [the Ruhr] I felt again Schiller's words: All men become (are!) brothers—and understood still more strongly that work is holy . . . I am still more convinced after this trip through the places of serious essential work that it is bad and repugnant to be a "Dadaist"; that is, to make fun of everything, to cause an upheaval. For man certainly becomes noble through serious work.[38]

Felixmüller's belief in a positive expressive partisan art, and his rejection of the satirical anarchic Dada art, brought him into conflict with his protégé Dix. Their relationship had always been difficult, even competitive. After one of the Dresden Secession Group exhibitions Dix had complained bitterly about a speech Felixmüller had given; the recounting of one of their private conversations, he believed, had served to discredit his art and thereby potentially hurt him financially. Dix wrote in anger to Felixmüller:

I am dependent neither on the recognition of the philistine [*Spiesser*] or the non-philistine, but, to be sure, on the money of the first—you brought yourself forward afterwards and told bombastic trash about your pictures. I do not doubt the effect of this contrast [between our work]—in any case I must draw my conclusions from all this.[39]

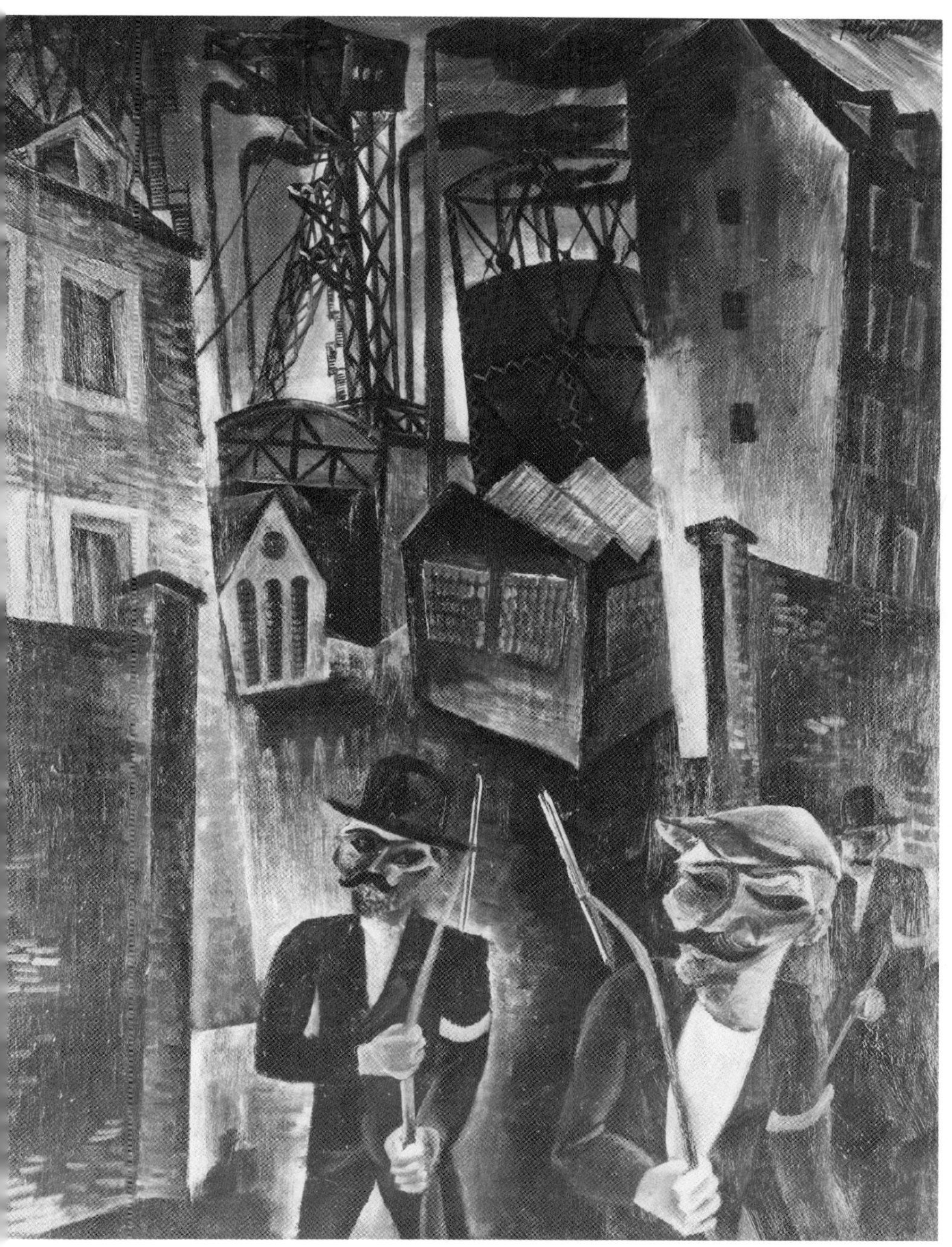

Conrad Felixmüller, *Ruhrrevier II (Ruhr District II)*, 1920. Oil on canvas, 95 x 75
Private Collection.

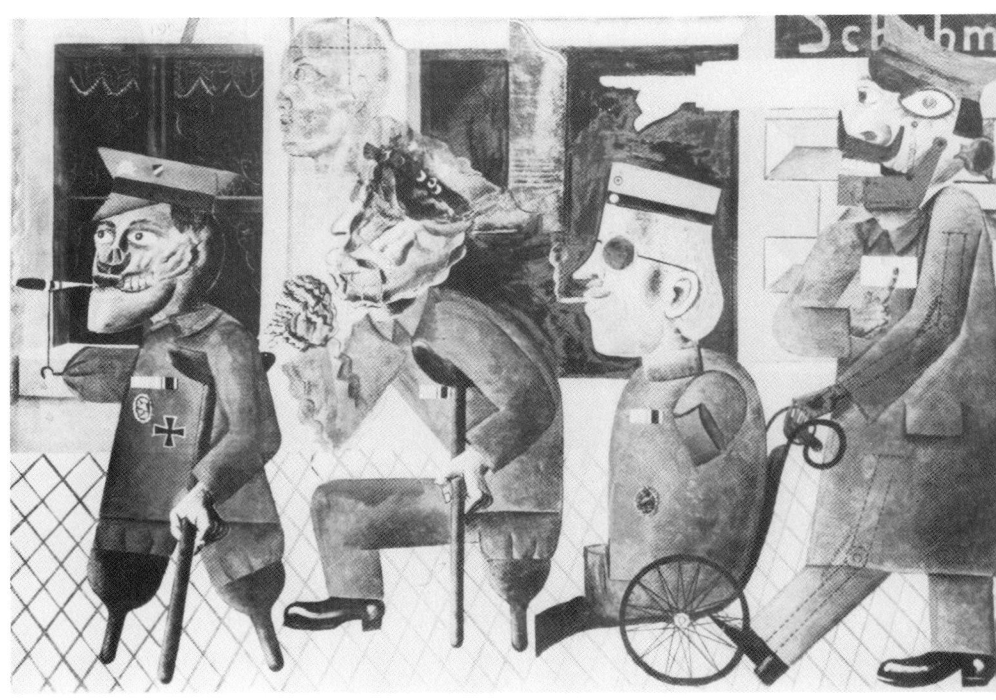

5.7 Otto Dix, *Kriegskrüppel (War Cripples)*, 1920. Oil on canvas, 150 x 200 cm. Formerly Stadtmuseum Dresden, now lost.

Dix, too, soon developed a politically committed art, but one quite different from Felixmüller's. He was influenced by the Dada movement in Dresden, which attracted a small group of students at the academy, and soon came into contact with the Dada artists in Berlin. Dix's new socially conscious paintings and collages of 1920, works such as *War Cripples* (fig. 5.7), used caricature to attack the persistence of militarism in the Weimar Republic. There was little trace any longer of expressionism in his new Dada anti-art. His rejection of expressionism was even more explicit in his *Match Seller I* (fig. 5.8). Dix showed a crippled war veteran selling matches to oblivious, well-dressed passersby. The work, however, was not only an attack on Weimar society, but on a co-member of the Dresden Secession Group, Oskar Kokoschka. In the days following the Kapp Putsch a battle had taken place on the Postplatz in Dresden between federal troops and demonstrating workers in which fifty-nine people were killed. After a stray bullet damaged a Rubens painting in the Zwinger museum, Kokoschka

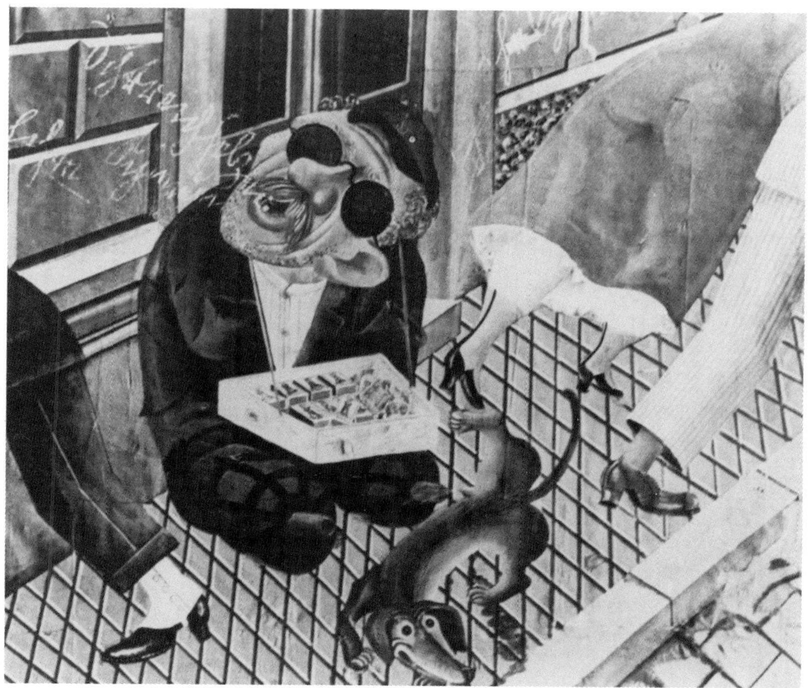

5.8 Otto Dix, *Streichholzhändler I (Match Seller I)*, 1920. Oil on canvas, 141 x 166 cm.

issued a public appeal inviting the contestants to transfer their fighting to a parade ground outside the city where they would not endanger works of art. The preservation of masterpieces, Kokoschka wrote, took precendence over political struggle. Dix provided his own response by placing Kokoschka's appeal in the gutter in his painting.

Felixmüller rejected what he perceived as a prevailing negativity in Dix's art. In the same letter to Heinrich Kirchhoff in which he praised the nobility of the workers he was painting, Felixmüller wrote of Dix: "Unfortunately the man is again completely Dadaist and 'paints' pornographic pictures of the worst kind; I consider him lost . . ."[40] Felixmüller and Dix already in 1920 posed two alternative strategies toward producing politically progressive art, one which eventually led to internecine conflict within the communist party in the 1920s: positive, heroic, didactic depictions of the working class vs. anti-art caricatures of the capitalist exploiter.

Felixmüller and Dix, though, also posed another unresolved dilemma of the revolution. Felixmüller's depictions of the proletariat found their way not to the "finest understanding and the most respectful-loving protection in the worker's living room," as the leftist critic Carl Emil Uphoff had put it in *Der Cicerone,* but to the private collections of his wealthy though politically enlightened patrons. And although Dix produced art-critical attacks on the political bankruptcy of expressionism, and even explicit critiques of the Weimar government, he was simultaneously mindful of seeking if not the "recognition" of the "philistine," then certainly his "money," as he had put it in his letter to Felixmüller. While distancing himself from expressionism, he continued to exhibit in expressionist shows, whether with the Dresden Secession Group, the November Group, or in the annual state-run salon in Berlin. This was equally true of other Dada artists. Subversion of the establishment could be tolerated, it seems, as long as it was accompanied by a simultaneous compromise with it. Even the communist artist George Grosz gained acclaim exhibiting with the reactionary Munich dealer Hans Goltz, with whom he had a contract.

With its fateful involvement in the revolution, expressionism had, in a sense, proven itself both too political and not political enough. Under these circumstances, the new social democratic art policies could be used to buttress the party's revolutionary rhetoric, but also by its critics to prove its anti-revolutionary stance. Expressionism therefore seemed perfectly suited to represent the greatest cultural achievement of the revolution, the illusion of successful revolution. Nowhere was this illusion more dazzling than in the much anticipated opening of a new theater for the masses in Berlin. With the construction of the Grosses Schauspielhaus, expressionism, now well into its deathwatch, enjoyed its final triumph.

Sensing the revolutionary enthusiasm around him, the director Max Reinhardt seized upon the idea of breaking down the barriers between art and the "people." He wanted to create a colossal new theatrical space—a theater for five thousand spectators. To the flamboyant theater impresario, theater was "food for the hungry."[41] In collaboration with the architect Hans Poelzig, a member of the Working Council for Art, he set about transforming the dilapidated former Schumann Circus in Berlin, one of the few existing structures large enough to accommodate so many people. The exterior of the building was only slightly modified, and they had it painted a bright burgundy red. This was enough to convince the conservative critic Karl Scheffler that it was nothing less than "a threatening image of red revolution."[42] It was the interior of the building that underwent a more dramatic change. Poelzig designed an enormous panoramic stage in an amphitheater vaulted by a huge dome. In the foyer, the walls and ceiling seemed to merge together in one continuous form painted a submarine green. The auditorium, painted a pale yellow, featured an even more fantastic vision: stalactites seemed to grow downward from the ceiling into slender sup-

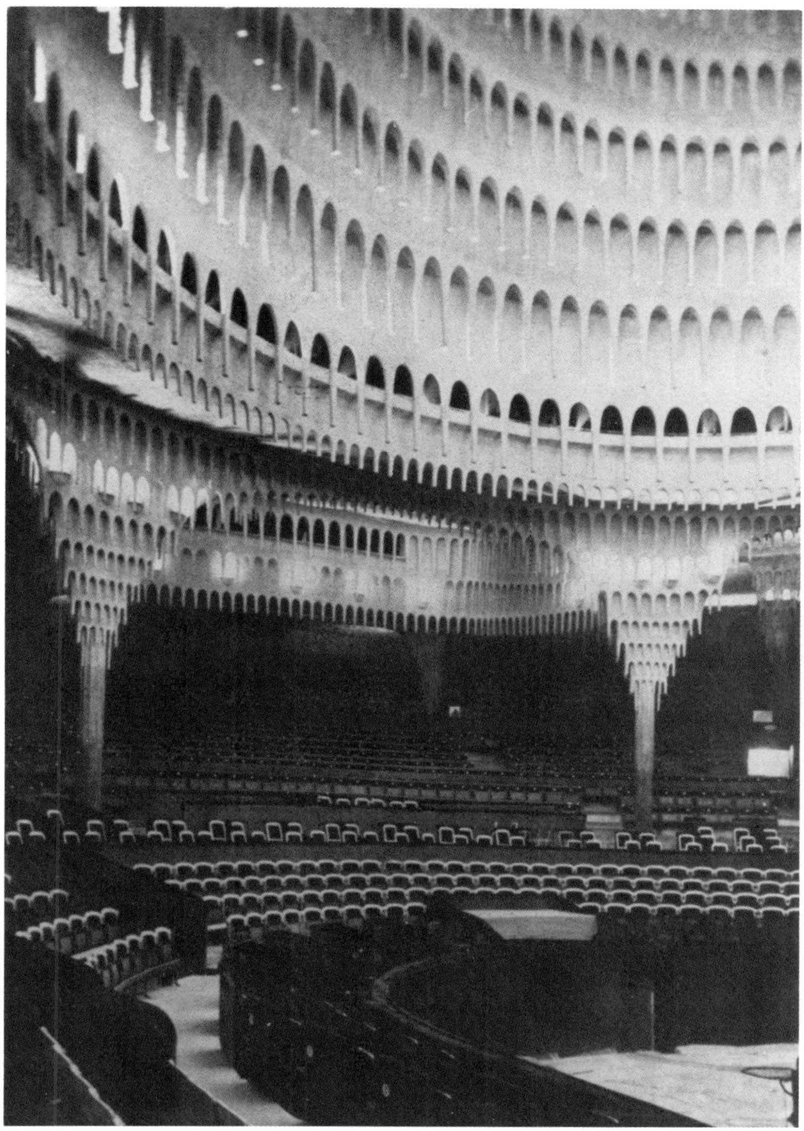

5.9 Hans Poelzig, *Grosses Schauspielhaus*, (Orchestra), Berlin, 1919.

ports (fig. 5.9). These stalactites were studded with colored bulbs, which appeared from below as constellations in the night sky. The effect was clearly meant to dazzle the masses. Despite interruptions by strikes and severe shortages of materials, the impressive dome took only four months to complete. The theater opened on 28 November 1919 with a performance of Aeschylus' *Oresteia,*[43] and vast numbers of spectators flocked to the enormous theater with its dramatically reduced ticket prices.

Here was the one utopian architectural project actually realized in the new republic. Here was culture for the masses and expressionist architecture as the ultimate work of art. But what did it amount to in the final analysis? In Poelzig and Reinhardt's building, the theatrical experience was not designed to educate or uplift, but to dazzle and stupefy. Even the construction of the Theater of the Five Thousand underscored its illusory nature; the plaster stalactites and the other gimmicky effects were fitted over the existing fabric of the old building, merely hiding its architectural seams. As with many of the institutions in the new republic, it was the by-now familiar case of putting a new face on the old.

Expressionism fell short of its expressed ideals in the Grosses Schauspielhaus because it was not really revolutionary, but merely revolutionary spectacle. In the absence of real change, its illusion was artfully sustained. This truth was captured by the social critic Kurt Tucholsky, who in February 1920 attended—along with thousands of others—Reinhardt's staging of Romain Rolland's play *Danton.* The critics were enthusiastic, but Tucholsky left the theater and wrote a poem called "Danton's Death." It read in part:

'Revolution!' the People howls and cries
'Freedom, that's what we're needing!'
We've needed it for centuries—
our arteries are bleeding.
   The stage is shaking. The audience rock.
   The whole thing is over by nine o'clock.

The day looks grey as I come to.
Where is that People—remember?—
that stormed the peaks from down below?
What happened to November?
   Silence. All gone. Just that, in fact.
   An act. An act.[44]

Notes

Chapter 1. Introduction

1. Quoted in Peter Paret, *The Berlin Secession* (Cambridge, 1980), 26–27.

2. Art historians, until recently, have largely ignored the issue of art and revolution in Germany. Beginning with the revival of vanguard German art after its suppression by the National Socialists, writers such as Werner Haftmann and Will Grohmann avoided any mention of the revolution in which so many expressionist artists had been so passionately involved. They subscribed to the theory of modern art as an inevitable, integrative international phenomenon, with German art taking its place in this development. At the same time, art historians in the German Democratic Republic, while noting the issue, avoided any close examination of the subject, limiting their discussion only to issues central to orthodox communist definitions of revolutionary art (realism, the partisan function of art, and art at the service of the state). Beginning in 1969, a few art historians in the German Federal Republic and the United States began to reconsider the issue, perhaps under the influence of the student revolts of the late 1960s. Such accounts, however, still presented the history of the artists' groups as static, ignoring the realities of rapidly changing, chaotic political and economic struggles that forced artists to redefine their positions almost day by day. For a reference to the most recent literature that constitutes the bibliographical foundation for this study, see the acknowledgments section.

3. Georg Meyer's 1977 *Bibliographie der deutschen Revolution 1918/19* alone contains over 2,500 titles. Interpretations of the revolution have been fraught with ideological biases. After World War II, historians tended to interpret the revolution in view of the Cold War. Historians in the German Federal Republic generally stressed the liberal achievements of social democracy in 1918, while historians in the German Democratic Republic attempted to trace the origins of their country to the suppressed revolution. More recently, the perceived failures of communism and the shift of revolutionary conflict to the Third World have caused many leftist historians to reassess the November Revolution and the failure of revolution in the country with the largest organized working class before World War I. Several of these historians have focused almost exclu-

sively on political institutions as the primary target of study: either concentrating on how the SPD alienated its own constituency, or arguing that had the revolution not taken place, not even evolutionary socialism would have occurred. Other historians have recently undertaken a reassessment of the council movement, often focusing on "missed opportunities" in an attempt, it seems, to prove that the revolution might have succeeded were it not for SPD duplicity. Alternatively, still others have aimed at a more comprehensive social history of the revolution, which does not study the revolution in order to assess blame or to validate a contemporary political strategy. I do not want to enter into this complex historical debate here; however, I have found it useful to draw on the work of Gerald Feldman, Eberhard Kolb and Reinhard Rürup, particularly their joint effort in "Die Massenbewegung der Arbeiterschaft in Deutschland am Ende des Ersten Weltkrieges (1917–1920)," *Politische Vierteljahresschrift* 13, no. 2 (August 1972): 84–105.

4. The council movement did not instantaneously materialize in November 1918. It underpinned a spontaneous mass movement that developed in the final years of the war separate from, and even in opposition to, the traditional socialist organizations of party and trade union. The aims of the councils were for the most part radical democratic. Although many historians emphasize the basic reformist character of the councils, it should not be overlooked that the Congress of Councils in December 1918 still demanded socialization for "ripe" industries and the formation of a Red Guard. Still, the role of the councils was ambiguous, being technically only a consulting body to the Council of People's Representatives, a political entity negotiated by the leadership of the socialist parties. See Eberhard Kolb, *Die Arbeiterräte in der deutschen Innenpolitik 1918–1919* (Düsseldorf, 1962), 405.

5. The SPD was reformist before the war, and in 1914 it voted for war credits and collaborated with industry in support of the war effort.

6. Wilhelm Groener, chief of staff of the Supreme Command, and Friedrich Ebert, head of the SPD and member of the Council of People's Representatives, reciprocally agreed in a telephone conservation on 10 November 1918 that the army would support the new government and that the new government would oppose the Spartacists and guarantee public security and order.

7. This stabilization had already, in a sense, been anticipated and prepared for before the revolution. Anxiety over chaotic demobilization and insufficient food supplies drove leading industrialists and trade union leaders together as early as October 1918 to manage the economy. On 15 November the Stinnes-Legien agreement was signed, in which industrialists conceded the eight-hour day, pledged to improve working conditions, and agreed to adopt a policy of social insurance. In return the trade unions agreed to increase productivity and tacitly to oppose nationalization. The industrialists reneged on the agreement once order was restored.

8. Inflation led to the virtual extinction of the national and corporate debt. It conferred on export industries a distinct advantage as the external value of the mark dropped faster than its internal value. See Stephen A. Schucker, "Fi-

nance and Foreign Policy in the Era of the German Inflation," in Otto Büsch and Gerald Feldman, *Historische Prozesse der deutschen Inflation* (Berlin, 1978), 350; see aso Gerald Feldman, *Iron and Steel in the German Inflation 1916–23* (Princeton, 1977).

9. Arbeitsrat für Kunst, "Ein neues künstlerisches Programm," reprinted in *Arbeitsrat für Kunst 1918–1921* (Berlin, 1980), 87.

10. "Diese alte feiste pervertierte Rentnerin . . . Mumienreich des Anton von Werner, Franz von Stuck . . . den Siegesallee-Handwerkern . . . dieser Schundanhäufung." Hermann von Wedderkop, "Revolution in der Kunst," *Ostern 1919* (Potsdam, 1919), 48.

11. In the decade before the war these attacks on modern art were nowhere more evident than in the controversies that erupted in the press. Among the most vehement were the debates over the art critic and historian Julius Meier-Graefe's acclaim for French impressionist and neoimpressionist art in his book *The Case of Böcklin* and the nationalist attack on the influence of French on German art in the 1911 *A Protest of German Artists*. For a detailed discussion of these debates, see Paret, *The Berlin Secession*, 170–99.

12. Rudolf Kurtz, "Programmatisches," *Der Sturm* 1, no. 1 (1910):2.

13. Although numerous studies exist on other facets of working-class culture, there is not even a general study of SPD policies toward the visual arts in imperial Germany—let alone avant-garde art. Cultural matters were rarely the center of debate at party meetings and were seriously discussed for the first time only at the 1906 meeting in Mannheim. At this meeting, Klara Zetkin asserted the class character of culture and warned against the assimilation of bourgeois culture without first reevaluating it for potential use in the political struggle. To what extent others adhered to this view is not certain. The most explicit public debate about reformist tendencies in social democratic cultural practice came with the debate about naturalism. While such party organs as *Sozialistische Monatshefte* promoted naturalism for its "socialist traces," Franz Mehring, among others, attacked it as reformist, claiming that under capitalism there was no chance for productive artistic activity on the part of the proletariat and that all attention instead must be directed to economic and political issues. See Georg Fülberth, "Sozialdemokratische Literaturkritik," *alternative* 14, no. 76 (1971): 6–7. At least two of the most influential critics supporting expressionism, though—the Social Democratic Party members Wilhelm Hausenstein and Adolf Behne—promoted expressionism in the party press and taught in socialist workers' night schools.

14. See advertisement in *Die Aktion* 3, no. 3 (15 January 1913): col. 90.

15. Franz Luft, "Revolutionsball der Aktion," *Die Aktion* 3, no. 8 (19 February 1913): cols. 233–35.

16. Karl Scheffler, "Kunstausstellungen," *Kunst und Künstler* 12, no. 2 (November 1, 1913): 120; also cited in Paret, *The Berlin Secession*, 208.

17. Gustav Pauli, "Reiseberichte," Hamburg Kunsthalle, Archiv 119a, 9 July 1917; quoted in Theda Shapiro, *Painters and Politics* (New York, 1976), 165.

18. Wilhelm Hausenstein, *Der nackte Mensch in der Kunst aller Zeiten und Völker* (Munich, 1913), 192.

19. In the nineteenth century, Bavarian monarchs, for the most part, tried to challenge the authority of the Catholic church and to align themselves with the middle classes by fostering a certain liberalism and secularism, particularly in education, science, and the arts. See Peter Jelavich, *Munich and Theatrical Modernism: Politics, Playwriting, and Performance 1890–1914* (Cambridge, 1985).

20. See the manifesto of the Munich Secession in Ekkehard Mai, "Problemgeschichte der Münchner Kunstakademie bis in die zwanziger Jahre," in Thomas Zacharias, ed., *Tradition und Widerspruch. 175 Jahre Kunstakademie München* (Munich, 1985), 125.

21. The attacks on naturalist art came primarily from the Catholic press, which called the naturalists "socialists in tailcoats" and identified them with the goals of social democracy. As Peter Jelavich has shown, though, after an initial attempt to forge an alliance with the SPD, the Munich naturalist writers, at least, succeeded in alienating not only the church, but the working-class movement as well. See Jelavich, *Munich and Theatrical Modernism,* 41–42.

22. The debate was begun by Hans Rosenhagen in the Berlin newspaper *Der Tag* and was quickly joined by the Munich press. See Winfried Nerdinger, "Die 'Kunststadt' München," in Christoph Stoelzl, ed., *Die Zwanziger Jahre in München,* Catalog Münchner Stadtmuseum (Munich, 1979), 94.

23. The Gruppe Tat was never really successful and may even have attracted some to meetings only for the free beer. It dissolved in 1912 due to a dearth of followers and continued police harassment of Mühsam. See Jelavich, *Munich and Theatrical Modernism,* 275–78.

24. "Revolution ist die Bewegung zwischen zwei Zuständlichkeiten. Hierbei stelle man sich nicht das Bild einer sich langsam drehenden Rolle vor, sondern eines ausbrechenden Vulkans, einer explodierenden Bombe oder auch einer sich entkleidenden Nonne.

"Alle Revolution ist aktiv, singulär, plötzlich und ihre Ursachen entwurzelnd. . . .

"Zerstörung und Aufrichtung sind in der Revolution identisch. Alle zerstörende Lust ist eine schöpferische Lust (Bakunin). Einige Formen der Revolution: Tyrannenmord, Absetzung einer Herrschaftsgewalt, Etablierung einer Religion, Zerbrechen alter Tafeln (in Konvention und Kunst), Schaffen eines Kunstwerks, der Geschlechtsakt." Erich Mühsam, "Revolution," *Revolution* 1, no. 1 (15 October 1913): 2.

25. Mühsam elsewhere rejected the SPD for trying to turn the worker into a bourgeois. See Jelavich, *Munich and Theatrical Modernism,* 275.

26. Johannes R. Becher, "Freiheitslied," *Revolution* 1, no. 1 (15 October 1913): 2; quoted in Jelavich, *Munich and Theatrical Modernism,* 279.

27. "Ich finde das Blatt night 'revolutionär' genug. Zuviel Lyreskes (*sic*); zu wenig Dolche, Schwerter, Fahnen." "Ein Brief an die Revolution," *Revolution* 1, no.2 (1 November 1913): 2.

28. "Wo 'stürmt' etwan (*sic*) der 'Sturm'? Bestenfalls im Herbstsalon." "Adam: Gegen Zuständliches," *Revolution* 1, no. 2 (1 November 1913): 2.

29. *Dresden. Geschichte der Stadt in Wort und Bild* (Dresden, 1985), 114, 130.

30. The Arnold gallery, which also featured older art, became very successful after 1900. In the 1890s it averaged yearly sales of 60,000–80,000 RM; in 1912, 500,000 RM. It is unclear what percentage of sales resulted from their sponsorship of modern art. *Leben und Wirken eines Dresdner Kunsthändlers: Ludwig Gutbier* (Dresden, 1934), 5.

31. Fritz Löffler, "Die Dresdner Sezession, Gruppe 1919. 1919 bis 1925," in *Kunst im Aufbruch: Dresden 1918–1933,* Gemälde Galerie Neue Meister (Dresden, 1980), 39.

32. Actually, the debate seems to have ceased as early as 1913. The signposts of this change were the rejection of the academy director Anton von Werner's paintings from the 1913 salon, the efforts by the *Kultusministerium* to include the Secession in the 25th anniversary salon exhibition (the Secession rejected the idea), and the rallying of most factions of the German art world around the war effort the following year. (The rejection of Anton von Werner's paintings in 1913 had to do with the political tensions before World War I, with Germany avoiding a diplomatic affront to France.)

33. See Adolf Behne, "National-antinational," *Zeit-Echo* 1, no. 18 (1915–16): 273; and Adolf Behne, "Organisation, Deutschtum und Kunst" *Zeit-Echo* 1, nos. 23–24 (1915–16): 361–64.

34. Quoted in Shapiro, *Painters and Politics,* 154.

35. The Worpswede artist Heinrich Vogeler in an open letter to the Kaiser protested the Brest-Litovsk treaty, leading to his confinement in an insane asylum for the remainder of the war. See Shapiro, *Painters and Politics,* 164.

36. *Conrad Felixmüller: Werke und Dokumente* (Nürnberg, 1981), 60–61.

37. "'Auf dem Felde der Ehre' / Diese Schädelstätte von Mord / Gepflügt und gepflegt von geldstinkenden Händen und Lügenwort!" Richard Fischer, "Feld der Ehre," *Menschen* 1, no. 3 (15 May 1918): 1.

38. Paul Cassirer and Leo Kestenberg, "Zur Einführung," *Der Bildermann* 1, no. 1 (5 April 1916); quoted in Paret, *The Berlin Secession,* 240.

39. See O. K. Werckmeister, "Klee im Ersten Weltkrieg," in *Versuche über Paul Klee* (Frankfurt am Main, 1981), 86–87.

40. See, for instance, Wilhelm Worringer, *Abstraktion und Einfühlung* (Munich, 1908).

41. *Das Kunstblatt* was first put out with financial help from the art dealer I. B. Neumann, who owned the Graphisches Kabinett on the Kurfürstendamm. The October 1917 issue on Oskar Kokoschka was so popular that a second run was printed. See Paul Westheim, "Wie *Das Kunstblatt* entsteht," in *Expressionismus: Aufzeichnungen und Erinnerungen der Zeitgenossen* (Otten, 1965), 67.

42. Werckmeister, "Klee im Ersten Weltkrieg," 85.

43. Other patrons included Anne Friedländer-Fuld, wife of the coal magnate and founder of the Chemische Fabriken AG; the eye specialist Dr. Max

Linde; heirs of great fortunes, such as Karl Ernst Osthaus and Count Harry Kessler; and the Elberfeld banker August Freiherr von der Heydt. The Stuttgart industrialist Bosch opposed heavy industry's wartime boom, criticized strict adherence to unreasonable war aims, and advocated internal political reform. Rathenau, head of the War Raw Materials Department, in his 1917 book *Of Things to Come,* predicted that the state would play an ever increasing role in economic life after the war and would be organized on a more collective and egalitarian basis than before. On Bosch see Gerald Feldman, "German Business Between War and Revolution," *Entstehung und Wandel der modernen Gesellschaft: Festschrift für Hans Rosenberg* (Berlin, 1970), 318.

44. See the statement ridiculing "flight into another land which cultivates fantastic-poetic mirages" and the "Sturm von Aktionen" in *Menschen* 1, no. 1 (15 January 1918): 4. The editors rejected as well the intransigent personal politics followed by Pfemfert in *Die Aktion,* which tended to deter unified action. Pfemfert rejected almost anyone from *Die Aktion* who had ever supported the war, even if they had recanted their position.

45. Ludwig Rubiner, "Dem Zeichner Frans Masereel," *Zeit-Echo* 3 (August-September, 1917): 49.

46. "Unter dem Vorwand der Verinnerlichung haben sich die Expressionisten in der Literatur und in der Malerei zu einer Generation zusammengeschlossen, die heute schon sehnsüchtig ihre literatur- und kunsthistorische Würdigung erwartet und für eine ehrenvolle Bürger-Anerkennung kandidiert. Unter dem Vorwand, die Seele zu propagieren, haben sie sich . . . zu den abstrakt-pathetischen Gesten zurückgefunden, die ein inhaltloses, bequemes und unbewegtes Leben zur Voraussetzung haben." See Richard Huelsenbeck, "First German Dada Manifesto," in Raoul Hausmann, *Am Anfang war Dada,* first edition, (Steinbach/Giessen, 1972), 23–24.

47. *Kunst und Künstler* reported in December on the possibility of raising the luxury tax to 20 percent, further threatening the art market. See *Kunst und Künstler* 17, no. 3 (1 December 1918): 116–17.

48. "Stehen wir viel besser und gesicherter in der Gesellschaft als der Proletarier?! Sind wir nicht wie Bettler abhängig von den Launen der kunstsammelnden Bourgeoisie!" Ludwig Meidner, "An alle Künstler, Dichter, Musiker," *An alle Künstler!* (Berlin, 1919), 8.

49. Letter by Oskar Schlemmer to Otto Meyer, 25 January 1919, reprinted in Tut Schlemmer, *The Letters and Diaries of Oskar Schlemmer* (Middletown, 1972), 65.

Chapter 2. Berlin

1. "A New Artistic Program" was published in *Vorwärts* on 11 December 1918 and one day later in *Die Freiheit.* The first public notice mentioning the WCA was actually a small announcement in the conservative *Kunstchronik und Kunstmarkt,* reporting on the formation of a relief fund, with private means,

for needy artists returning from the war. The announcement was signed by Hans Purrmann for the *Freie Sezession* and by Theo von Brockhusen for the WCA. Contributions were to be sent to Dr. Wilhelm Valentiner. See "Notizen," *Kunstchronik und Kunstmarkt* 30, no. 7 (29 November 1918): 143.

2. "Kunst und Volk müssen eine Einheit bilden. Die Kunst soll nicht mehr Genuss weniger, sondern Glück und Leben der Masse sein. Zusammenschluss der Künste unter den Flügeln einer grossen Baukunst ist das Ziel. Fortan ist der Künstler allein als Gestalter des Volksempfindens verantwortlich für das sichtbare Gewand des neuen Staates. Er muss die Formgebung bestimmen vom Stadtbild bis herunter zur Münze und Briefmarke." "Ein neues künstlerisches Programm," reprinted in *Arbeitsrat für Kunst 1918–1921*, 87.

3. "Beseitigung der künsterlisch wertlosen Denkmäler sowie aller Bauten, deren Kunstwert im Missverhältnis zu dem Wert ihres anders brauchbaren Materials steht. Verhinderung voreilig geplanter Kriegsdenkmale und unverzügliche Einstellung der Arbeiten für die in Berlin und im Reich vorgesehenen Kriegsmuseen." Ibid.

4. Demand no. 3: "Umwandlung des künstlerischen und handwerklichen Unterrichts von Grund auf. Bereitstellung staatlicher Mittel dafür und für Meistererziehung in Lehrwerkstätten." Ibid.

5. The party-political affiliations of only a few of the members are known: John Schikowski and Käthe Kollwitz were members of the SPD, Adolf Behne joined the USPD, and Hugo Simon was the USPD finance minister in November.

6. Iain Boyd Whyte, *Bruno Taut and the Architecture of Activism* (Cambridge, 1982), 44. He worked in a munitions firm in Brandenburg and later in the war worked in the office of the Stellawerk stove factory in Bergisch-Gladbach.

7. Bruno Taut, "Eine Notwendigkeit," *Der Sturm* 4, no. 196/197 (February 1914): 174–75.

8. "I joined the party [SPD] . . . I stood it only for two months, as I thought the slogans of the party of too primitive a kind and dealing too much with too low a level of intelligence and education." Valentiner Papers, *Archives of American Art,* Roll #2140, 625. In his unpublished "Reminiscences," Valentiner reports that he was mistakenly listed in the *Vossische Zeitung* as a co-founder of Rathenau's DDP. His letter to that paper claiming that his name had been used by the party without his knowledge or permission led to a break with Rathenau.

9. Margaret Sterne, *The Passionate Eye* (Detroit, 1980), 117–24.

10. Valentiner Papers, *Archives of American Art,* Roll #2140, 633.

11. Sterne, *The Passionate Eye,* 117–24.

12. Whyte details these intellectual sources, particularly the influence of Peter Kropotkin's and Gustav Landauer's anarcho-syndicalist ideas on mutual aid and decentralization. Whyte, *Bruno Taut and the Architecture of Activism,* 101–2.

13. Heinrich Richter-Berlin, "Mein Leben," *Kunstblätter der Galerie Nierendorf* (Berlin, 1974), no. 32, 9.

14. Protocol of meeting of 3 December 1918, reprinted in Helga Kliemann, *Die Novembergruppe* (Berlin, 1969), 55 n. 11.

15. The leadership had already solicited statements of support from artists in other cities. Listed in the protocol were Otto Hettner and Hans Purrmann (Berlin); Heinrich Campendonk, Schlicht, Heinrich Bachmaier, Fritz Schaefler, H. Mauermayer, A. Wachlmayer and J. Nitsche (Munich); Rüdiger Berlit, M. Schwimmer and Fredwaak (Leipzig); E. Timm (Hamburg); and Curt Stoermer (Worpswede).

16. Although four of the five NG leaders were members of the WCA (Pechstein, Tappert, Klein, and Richter-Berlin), the majority of painters assembled on 3 December had not signed the WCA manifesto. Attending the meeting were: Rudolf Belling, Georg Leschnitzer, Otto Mueller, Oskar Moll, M. Frey, R. Steiner, Karl Jacob Hirsch, Miss I. Stern, Bruno Krauskopf, Rudolf Bauer, W. Schmid, Berhard Hasler, Erich Mendelsohn, Richard Janthur and Otto Freundlich. Only Krauskopf and Bauer signed the WCA's "A New Artistic Program."

17. "Die Zukunft der Kunst und der Ernst der jetzigen Stunde zwingt uns Revolutionäre des Geistes (Expressionisten, Kubisten, Futuristen) zur Einigung und engem Zusammenschluss. Wir richten daher an alle Künstler, welche die alten Formen in der Kunst zerbrochen, die dringende Aufforderung, ihren Beitritt zur Novembergruppe zu erklären." Circular letter of 13 December 1918, reprinted in Kliemann, *Die Novembergruppe,* 55 n. 11.

18. "Aufstellung und Verwirklichung eines weitgefassten Programms, welches mit Vertrauensleuten in den verschiedenen Kunstzentren durchzusetzen ist, soll uns engste Vermischung von Volk und Kunst bringen." Ibid.

19. Ibid., 56. The draft is undated and does not seem to have been published in the art press.

20. "Wir stehen auf dem fruchtbarsten Boden der Revolution. Unser Wahlspruch heisst: Freiheit, Gleichheit, Brüderlichkeit. . . . Wir . . . wollen mutig und ohne Scheu mit allen uns zur Verfügung stehenden Kräften Rückstand und Reaktion bekämpfen." Ibid.

21. Ibid., 57.

22. Ibid.

23. The broadsheet was issued in the name of the Central Work-Committee, made up of the painters Rudolf Bauer, Bernhard Hasler, Cesar Klein, Moriz Melzer, Heinrich Richter-Berlin, Max Pechstein, and Georg Tappert; the sculptor Belling; and the architect Erich Mendelsohn. Missing from the Work-Committee announced in the circular letter of 13 December were Bruno Krauskopf, Hans Steiner, and Wilhelm Schmid; they were replaced by Hasler and Mendelsohn.

24. "Ihre Anwesenheit wäre mir auch insofern erwünscht gewesen, als die Gesamtstimmung der Versammlung Ihnen gezeigt hätte, wie recht meine Meinungsäusserungen in dieser Richtung bisher gewesen sind. Ob Spartakus oder U.S.,—die Leute wollen von Ihnen, von uns nichts wissen, auch der proletarische Halskragen hilft uns nicht dazu, Vertrauen und Verständnis zu erhoffen.

Was wir treiben ist ihnen fremd. Sie haben auch nicht den Wunsch es zu verstehen, es ist ihnen gleichgültig und wird es noch in 10 bis 15 Jahren sein! Die proletarische Jugend von 1900 wäre ein viel geeigneteres Objekt für die Aktion und ihre Bestrebungen gewesen. In derselben war eine Gier nach Literatur, nach Kunst, nach Bildung! Diese Jugend stand noch 2 Stunden vor Einlass vor den Theatern, um auf dem Olymp seelische und geistige Empfängnis zu erhalten. Der heutige, junge Proletarier tut dies nicht mehr. Das Klassenbewusstsein, die politische Aufklärung hindert ihn daran, da er nicht im Parkett sitzen kann, verzichtet er vollends. . . .

"Sie werden mir nicht Recht geben wollen, werden meinen, ich beurteile die Verhältnisse als Künstler, als Besitzer geistiger Werte. Dem möchte ich entgegenstellen, dass ich als Sohn eines überzeugten Sozialisten in den Lehren des Sozialismus aufgewachsen bin, das Parteileben in all' seinen Formen kennengelernt habe, wie das Proletariat in all' seinen Höhen und Tiefen. Von dem Moment an, als ich mich entschloss, Maler zu werden, wurde ich als Abtrünniger, als Bourgeois, angesehen. . . .

"Ihre politische Arbeit in der Aktion wird nicht vom Genossen, dem Handarbeiter anerkannt. Sie reden nicht dessen Sprache . . . Sie werden im besten Falle geduldet, aber nicht verstanden. Mit der Spartakus-Gruppe wird es Ihnen ebenso gehen, heut sind Sie,—wir, als Mitläufer willkommen, in der kommenden Revolution schlagen sie Ihnen den Laden ein, und sofern sie zur Macht gelangen, dekretieren sie, was Sie herausgeben dürfen. Geben Sie 10.000 Arbeitern das letzte rote Hahnheft: Rottluff-Brust in die Hand, sie werden damit nichts anzufangen wissen, heut' nicht, in 5 Jahren nicht, denn sie stehen auf dem Boden des Naturalismus, dem Boden der realen Anschauung. Der Proletarier ist der irrigen Anschauung, dass die gesamte neue Kunst, ein Produkt der bürgerlichen Gesellschaft ist, und verlangt nun, dass er als Diktatur den Künstlern vorschreibt, in welchen Bahnen die neue (jetzt natürlich sozialistische) Kunst sich bewegen soll." Letter Georg Tappert to Franz Pfemfert, 20 November 1918, reprinted in Gerhard Wietek, *Georg Tappert* (Munich, 1980), 48–49.

25. Ibid.

26. "Das Kunstblatt . . . braucht jetzt nicht mit neuem Programm und neuen Versicherungen vor seine Leser hinzutreten. . . . In der Kunst hat schon lange eine Revolution eingesetzt." Paul Westheim, "Jenseits der Gräber weiter!" *Das Kunstblatt* 3, no. 1 (January 1919): 1.

27. "Bezüglich des Verständnisses ist diese Krise zeitlich, da ja die sozialisierte Menschheit die Lebenshaltung aller Mitglieder der menschlichen Gestaltung auf den Stand der Lebenshaltung des heutigen Bürgertums und darüber hinaus schliesslich auf den des heutigen Hofes heben wird." Peter Bender, "Der Künstler und die Revolution," *Die Aktion* 8, no. 49/50 (14 December 1918), col. 655.

28. Lu Märten, "Sozialismus und Künstler," *Die Freiheit* 1, no. 21 (26 November 1918).

29. Hellmuth Falkenfeld, "Der geistige Arbeiter im sozialistischen Staat

II," *Die Freiheit* 1, no. 53 (13 December 1918) and "Der geistige Arbeiter im sozialistischen Staat III," *Die Freiheit* 2, no. 5 (3 January 1919).

30. "Ist es ein blosser glücklicher Zufall, dass gleichzeitig mit der sozialen und politischen Revolution eine Umwälzung auf künstlerischem Gebiete sich vollzieht? Ein neuer Geist geht durch die Kunst, ein Drang nach Verinnerlichung und Vertiefung, der die Seelen erheben, hinreissen und erbauen und den Freigewordenen das bedeuten will, was den Geknechteten einst die Religion bedeutete." John Schikowski, "Die Revolution und die Kunst," *Vorwärts* 35, no. 314a (14 November 1918).

31. Henry Pachter, "Expressionism and Cafe Culture," in Stephen Eric Bronner and Douglas Kellner, *Passion and Rebellion: The Expressionist Heritage* (U.S.A., 1983), 50.

32. "Expressionisten, lasst euch nicht führen von Leuten, die als 'geistige' versuchen, die Pseudokulturgüter des Kapitalismus in die neue Freiheit hinüberzuretten." Letter by Curt Stoermer to the November Group, 28 November 1919, reprinted in Will Grohmann, "Zehn Jahre Novembergruppe," *Kunst der Zeit* 3, nos. 1–3, special number (1928): 30.

33. ZStP *Informationsstelle der Reichsregierung,* 07.05. According to this summary, Zech served from 1 December 1918 until 30 September 1919, when the Publicity Office was merged with the *Reichszentrale für Heimatdienst.* The *Reichszentrale* was established on 21 October 1918 and was previously known as the *Zentralstelle für Heimataufklärung im Geschäftsbereich des Pressechefs beim Reichskanzler.* On 15 November 1918, Dr. Landsberg was named head of the *Reichszentrale,* which on 16 August 1919 was subsumed by the *Vereinigten Presseabteilung der Reichsregierung.* Rigby, quoting Heinrich Inheim, "Das Berliner Plakatjahr 1918," *Das Plakat* 10, no. 1 (January 1919), states that the Publicity Office was under the direction of Reckendorf, who had overseen wartime poster production. (See Ida Katherine Rigby, *An alle Künstler! War-Revolution-Weimar* [San Diego, 1983], 34.) Reckendorf continued to play a significant role in the Publicity Office. On Zech's politics, see Paul Zech, *Deutschland, dein Tänzer ist der Tod* (Rudolstadt, 1980), n.p.

Although an expressionist writer was in charge of commissioning posters, only a handful were given to expressionist artists. It was precisely these posters, though, which generated the most public discussion. Several artists who had produced war-bond posters were also commissioned by the Publicity Office to produce posters during the revolution. For example, A. M. Cay, who produced one of the first posters for the Publicity Office (*Der Trommler*) in 1918 was also responsible for the wartime propaganda poster *Alter Fritz.*

34. Although I have found no records of the Publicity Office, an October 1919 report by the organization that took over the Publicity Office indicates that the posters were directed against the "bolshevist danger." ZStP, 90Ha4, Nachlass Hänisch, no. 457.

35. See, for example, posters for the seventh and eighth war bonds drives reproduced in *Ein Krieg wird ausgestellt* (Frankfurt, 1976), 128 and 129.

36. Posters that relied on more realistic figures or on simplified, uncluttered

advertising techniques were typical. See, for instance, the rather cloying *Mother! Think of me!* with its detailed drawing of a young waif by Kirchbach, or the more effective *Social Democrats to the Red Ballot-Box* with masses of tiny figures streaming toward the red urn.

37. Hänisch and Hoffmann disagreed about almost every policy matter, with their conflict eventually demanding the attention of the Central Council. Their most vehement disagreement concerned the extent and timing of the separation of church and state in matters of education. Their disputes often carried over to other members of the ministry, who often took sides along party lines. See Eberhard Kolb and Reinhard Rürup, eds., *Der Zentralrat der deutschen sozialistischen Republik* (Leiden, 1968), 138–39.

38. See, for example, *Münchner Neueste Nachrichten* (25 November 1918).

39. The account of the meeting appears in Hermann Schmitz, *Revolution der Gesinnung!: Preussische Kulturpolitik und Volksgemeinschaft seit dem 9. November 1918* (Neubabelsberg, 1931), 50–51. Whyte uses this same source, but mistakenly identifies Hoffmann as the SPD member of the ministry.

40. Letter by Bruno Taut to Konrad Hänisch, 3 December 1918, ZStP, 90Ha4, Nachlass Hänisch, Nr.453, Bl.17.

41. "Wir wollen nicht etwa eine Diktatur des Expressionismus aufstellen, wir wollen aber für unsere künstlerischen Bestrebungen die gleichen Rechte, auch die staatliche Unterstützung und Hilfe erhalten wie alle übrigen Richtungen in der Kunst." Letter by Herwarth Walden to Konrad Hänisch, 12 November 1918, ZStP, 90Ha4, Nachlass Hänisch, no. 452.

42. Letter by Konrad Hänisch to Herwarth Walden, 13 November 1918, ZStP, 90Ha4, Nachlass Hänisch, no. 452.

43. "Auch Ihnen möchte ich sagen, dass die künstlerischen Fragen, so sehr gerade ich ihre Bedeutung anerkenne, jedenfalls in diesen ersten Wochen noch vor *Dringenderem* zurückstehen müssen." Letter by Konrad Hänisch to Rudolf Bauer, 13 November 1918, ZStP, 90Ha4, Nachlass Hänisch, no. 452.

44. "Nationalgalerie," *Das Kunstblatt* 3, no. 7 (July 1919): 213–21; also *Ostern*, catalog of the Flechtheim gallery (Düsseldorf, 1919), 15–17. See also Andreas Hünecke, "Expressionistische Kunst in deutschen Museen bis 1919," in *Das Schicksal einer Sammlung. Die neue Abteilung der Nationalgalerie im ehemaligen Kronprinzen-Palais*, Staatliche Museen zu Berlin (Berlin, 1986).

45. Justi described the Kaiser's attitude toward modern art as follows: "So beschränkte er sich nicht darauf, die neue Kunst nicht zu fördern, sondern hielt es für seine Pflicht, ihre Anerkennung durch den Staat zu verhindern." Ludwig Justi, *Die Nationalgalerie und die moderne Kunst* (Leipzig, 1918), 6. He also wrote that because of frustration with the Kaiser's policies he had wanted to quit his post in 1917. The *Kultusminister* Schmidt-Ott asked him urgently to stay, promising to loosen the grip of the Provincial Art Commission on the museum. According to Justi, Hugo von Tschudi convinced him he was morally bound to stay to bring about this needed reform. See also Annegret Janda, "Die Gemälde und Bildwerke der Expressionistischen im ehemaligen Kronprinzen-Palais. Ein Ausschnitt aus der Geschichte der Neuen Abteilung der

National-Galerie von 1918 bis 1945," in *Das Schicksal einer Sammlung. Die Neue Abteilung der Nationalgalerie im ehemaligen Kronprinzen-Palais,* Staatliche Museen zu Berlin (Berlin,1986).

46. This was the Cornelius-Saal, given over to contemporary art in January 1918. Justi, *Die Nationalgalerie und die moderne Kunst,* 18.

47. The "small commission" was made up of two artists, two patrons, the minister, and the director. Ibid., 30–31.

48. ". . . sollte sich die staatliche Kunstpflege nicht darauf beschränken, Werke zu kaufen und auszustellen, die eigentlich ins Bürgerhaus gehören, sondern es müssten Aufträge zum grosszügigen Schmuck öffentlicher Gebäude gegeben werden." Ibid., 41.

49. Paul Westheim, "Die Nationalgalerie," *Frankfurter Zeitung* (12 December 1918).

50. Paul Westheim, "Die Nationalgalerie und die moderne Kunst," *Frankfurter Zeitung* (31 January 1919).

51. Valentiner had already published his basic program in an article entitled "Die Museen als Bildungsstätten für das Volk," *Vorwärts* 35, no. 339 (10 December 1918).

52. Monika Flake-Knoch, "Wilhelm R. Valentiners Museumskonzeption von 1918 und die zeitgenössischen Bestrebungen zur Reform der Museen," *Kritische Berichte* 8, no. 4/5 (1980): 55.

53. "Sie hält das ganze Konzept weder für freiheitlich noch für demokratisch." G. Ring, "Falsche Propheten," *Die Hilfe* 25, no. 24 (12 June 1919): 300.

54. "Er vergisst dabei, dass die besten Künstler für ihre Werke die bescheidenste Wand einer Arbeiterwohnung der Totenkammer vorziehen." Carl G. Heise, "Das Museum," *Genius* 2, no. 1 (1920): 2.

55. Ludwig Justi, "Valentiners Vorschläge zur Umgestaltung der Museen," *Zeitschrift für bildende Kunst* 54, Neue Folge no. 30 (May 1919): 200.

56. "Und die Kunst wird neu und schön. Sonst konnte Justi kein Bild kaufen für die Nationalgalerie, wenn der Kaiser nicht mochte. Nun möchte er kaufen, aber nun sagt ihm Westheim, dass er dann keinen Charakter hat. Er muss gekreuzigt werden. Rosa Luxemburg weiss dann sicher einen guten Nachfolger." Friedrich Paulsen, "Das neue Leben," *Wachtfeuer* 5, no. 3 (1919): 18.

57. Sitzung des Senats beider Sektionen der Akademie, Berlin, 3 December 1918, no. 2074, Akademie der Künste, Berlin, Registratur 3, no. 693a, "Reform." The other members of the commission were President Manzel; Professors Engel, Geyger, Koch, Schumann and Seiffert; Privy Councillor Hoffmann; and the two permanent secretaries.

58. Sitzung der Kommission für Reformvorschläge der Akademie, Berlin, 7 December 1918, Akademie der Künste, Berlin, Registratur 3, no. 693a, "Reform."

59. His 1904 publication *Kunst und Staat* had accused the Berlin Secession of working against the national interest. Paret, *The Berlin Secession,* 90 n. 67.

60. ZStP 90 Ha 4, Nachlass Hänisch, no. 452.

61. Sitzung des Senats beider Sektionen der Akademie, Berlin, 3 December 1918, no. 2074, Akademie der Künste, Berlin, Registratur 3, no. 693a, "Reform."

62. Paul Westheim, "Die Ausstellung," *Frankfurter Zeitung* (28 December 1918). Westheim's argument was not as radical as it may seem. He also argued that an all-inclusive exhibition was not necessary since nonacademic artists had ample opportunities to exhibit, thanks to the success of the secession movement. If the state still felt compelled to sponsor exhibitions, Westheim advocated as an alternative that the state should make exhibition space in many cities available to all artists' groups on a rotating basis, thereby allowing them access to a public.

63. Almost every Berlin daily newspaper carried notices assuring the reader that the cultural heritage of the German nation was being safeguarded during the revolution. See, for example, "Schutz der Kunstsammlungen," *Berliner Tageblatt*, no. 591 (11 November 1919).

64. "Der Krieg hat am Wesen der Kunst nichts geändert; die Revolution wird es auch nicht thun." Karl Scheffler, "Die Kunst und die Revolution," *Kunst und Künstler* 17, no. 30 (February 1919): 165.

65. Scheffler did not refer to the WCA by name, but referred to their manifesto: "Was helfen solche Programmworte (Die Kunst und das Volk müssen eine Einheit bilden), wenn die Kunst nicht kann und das Volk unfähig ist und gar nicht will. Kunst und Volk haben nie eine Einheit gebildet." Ibid., 165–66.

66. Scheffler's battle with the radical proposals of the modern artists was carried out beyond the pages of *Kunst und Künstler* in the ensuing months. The forces he opposed were temporarily victorious when, in July 1919, members of the WCA blocked him from addressing the first annual meeting of the Werkbund after the war. See Joan Campbell, *The German Werkbund* (Princeton, 1978), 131.

67. Artur Degner, "Die Kunst der neuen Zeit," *Die Freiheit* 2, no. 40 (23 January 1919).

68. "Früher gab es wohl keinen Sozialdemokraten, der nicht schon im Namen des guten Geschmacks gegen die wilhelminische Kunstverschandelung protestierte, aber heute wagt eine sich sozialistische nennende Regierung, die so hurtig Maschinengewehre und schwere Artillerie gegen Arbeiter auffahren lässt, die Denkmäler einer befleckten Vergangenheitsepoche nicht anzutasten! Wie viel unblutiger wäre das doch. Wir haben einen in der Revolution geschaffenen 'Arbeitsrat für Kunst,' aber über seine Vorschläge und Proteste geht man nichtachtend hinweg." E. B., "Revolutionäre Kunstpolitik," *Die Freiheit* 2, no. 125 (15 March 1919).

69. "Freigabe der Geistesfreiheit," *Die Freiheit* 2 (23 February 1919).

70. See, for example, the *Berliner Lokal Anzeiger* (18 March 1919).

71. The *Landeskunstkommission* had previously decided on acquisitions by

the National Gallery until Ludwig Justi had insisted on a smaller commission for those decisions. Even that smaller committee was no longer active as several members had resigned over the acquisition of a painting by Oskar Kokoschka.

72. Sitzung der Kommission für Reformvorschläge der Akademie, Berlin, 3 February 1919, Registratur 3, no. 693a, "Reform."

73. Sitzung der Kommission für Reformvorschläge der Akademie, Berlin, 22 March 1919, Registratur 3, no. 693a, "Reform." Nentwig, an assistant to Hänisch, eventually proposed a system of "associates" to the academy, in effect junior members, modeled on the London academy. This was also rejected. Sitzung der Kommission für Reformvorschläge der Akademie, Berlin, 16 April 1919, Registratur 3, no. 693a, "Reform."

74. " . . . Herr Nentwig erwidert, dass von einem Misstrauen gegen die Akademie beim Ministerium keine Rede sei. Man stürme eben jetzt gegen alles Bestehende an, und man muss demgegenüber bestrebt sein, den jungen Leuten, die sich unterdrückt hinstellen, den Wind aus den Segeln zu nehmen." Sitzung der Kommission für Reformvorschläge der Akademie, Berlin, 26 March 1919, Registratur 3, no. 693a, "Reform."

75. Sitzung der Kommission für Reformvorschläge der Akademie, Berlin, 2 April 1919, Registratur 3, no. 693a, "Reform."

76. The essays in *The Spirit of the New National Community* included, among others, Wichard von Moellendorff writing on Walter Rathenau's economic proposals, Gustav Radbruch on the justice system, Kasimir Edschmid on literature, Peter Behrens on art education, and Arnold Zweig on the theater.

77. See note 33 above.

78. "Die revolutionäre Bewegung der Gesellschaft . . . gibt das Recht zu sagen: dass das Leben der Menschen in eine neue Ordnung hineinführt, dass alle zukünftigen Dinge, gleichgültig ob sie religiöser, kultureller oder wirtschaftlicher Art sind, in die Tiefe einer neuen europäischen Gesinnung hineingestellt sein werden. Nichts ist wesentlicher, als uns von dem Irrtum zu erlösen, dass es sich bei der Revolution um die nackte Gebärde eines von katastrophalem Unglück heimgesuchten, vom Hunger entnervten Geschlechtes handle, das den Zusammenbruch und nur diesen wollte." "An das deutsche Volk," *Der Geist der neuen Volksgemeinschaft* (Berlin, 1919), 1.

79. The *Zentrale Bildungsausschuss* of the SPD also advocated the extension of bourgeois art and artistic norms to the proletariat, promoting the publication of masterworks and "artistically worthwhile" literature. Such proposals also preceded the First World War, when the arts were also part of the general political reconciliation. A signpost was the integration of the *Freie Volksbühne* and the *Neue Freie Volksbühne* to form the *Verband der Freien Volksbühnen* in February 1914. See Christoph Rülcker, "Arbeiterkultur und Kulturpolitik im Blickwinkel des 'Vorwärts' 1918–28," *Archiv für Sozialgeschichte* 14 (1974): 118–19 and Herbert Scherer, *Bürgerlich-oppositionelle Literaten und sozialdemokratische Arbeiterbewegung nach 1870* (Stuttgart, 1974), 213.

80. It is difficult to reconstruct with any precision the economic realities of art production in 1919; no sales records are extant for any of the major galleries

supporting expressionist art, and the evidence of individual artists is at best fragmentary. Secondary sources, however, particularly the art press, allow these cautious observations.

81. "Auf keinem anderen Gebiet . . . haben sich die Folgeerscheinungen des Umsturzes so stark und einschneidend bemerkbar gemacht, wie auf dem der Kunst. Während in den Wochen vor Ausbruch der Revolution schon die alten Kriegshochkonjunkturpreise nicht mehr zu halten gewesen waren, setzt seit dem 9. November überhaupt jedwedes Interesse für alle Arten von Kunstwerken von seiten des kaufkräftigen Publikums völlig aus. Genau wie in den Antiquitätengeschäften zeigen sich auch in den Verkaufsläden moderner Kunstwerke keine Käufer mehr." *Der Kunsthandel* 11, no. 1 (January 1919).

82. "Aber wovon soll er leben, wenn niemand geneigt ist, ihm in dieser unsicheren, alles in Frage stellenden Zeit einen Auftrag zu erteilen?" Dr. Georg Jahn, "Die Künstler und die Revolution," *Der deutsche Künstler* 5, no. 9 (15 December 1918): 165.

83. Letter by Lyonel Feininger to Alfred Kubin; quoted in June Ness, *Lyonel Feininger* (New York, 1974), 54–55.

84. Felix Szkolny, "Die Besteuerung der Kunst," *Kunst und Künstler* 17, no. 3 (1 December 1918): 116–17; and Felix Szkolny, "Die Besteuerurg der Kunst," *Kunst und Künstler* 17, no. 8 (1 May 1919): 334–39.

85. Such demands were not limited to expressionist artists. The conservative *Der deutsche Künstler,* associated with the Economic Associations of German Artists, outlined a plan in its 15 January 1919 issue for a government office for artists that would make exhibition rooms available, provide for traveling exhibitions, reform art education, provide financial assistance for impoverished artists, and guarantee old-age pensions. See Eduard Deventer, "Ein Staatsamt für bildende Kunst," *Der deutsche Künstler* 5, no. 10 (15 January 1919): 173–74.

86. Carl Emil Uphoff, "Künstler, Kunst, Sozialismus," *Der Cicerone* 11, no. 5 (1919): 121–25.

87. Letter by Max Ernst to John Schikowski, 7 January 1919; quoted in Shapiro, *Painters and Politics,* 292 n. 25.

88. "Wirtschaftliche Forderungen haben nur die Armen zu stellen, nicht die Künstler." Herwarth Walden, "Kunst und Leben," *Der Sturm* 10, no. 1 (April 1919): 2. See also Herwarth Walden, "Künstler, Volk und Kunst," *Der Sturm* 10, no. 1 (April 1919): 12. Referring to Taut and the WCA he wrote: "Sie machen etwa die Entdeckung, dass nur in Glas gebaut werden kann . . . Anderes Material ist noch keine Kunst. Und Material ist nie schöpferisch, auch wenn manche Menschen unter Glas besser träumen können als unter Eisen. Träumen ist nämlich noch keine Kunt." Ibid., 10–12.

89. Werckmeister, "Klee im Ersten Weltkrieg," 88.

90. "Im neuen Bunde aller Künste mit einer . . . freien sozialistischen Gesellschaft müssen die Vorbedingungen einer neuen Menschheitskultur geschaffen werden. Der Expressionismus, der kein Begriff mehr ist, sondern eine herrliche Wirklichkeit, findet in der beginnenden Weltrevolution seine

Bestätigung." I. B. Neumann, *Im neuen Bunde* (Berlin, 6 March 1919), I. B. Neumann papers, Archives of American Art, Roll no. N69–96, 4.

91. "Die Künstler 'gehören' weder mir noch anderen Kunsthändlern . . . sondern der Menschheit." Ibid.

92. "Die 'Novembergruppe' ist kein wirtschaftlicher Schutzverband, kein (blosser) Ausstellungsverein." Richtlinien der Novembergruppe, reprinted in Kliemann, *Die Novembergruppe*, 57, illustration d.

93. "Sommerausstellung der 'Novembergruppe,'" *Berliner Zeitung am Mittag* 42, no. 86 (19 April 1919).

94. Evidence that *An alle Künstler!* was sponsored by the Publicity Office includes not only the office's insignia on Pechstein's cover illustration, but a letter from Dr. Paul Landau of the Publicity Office to Konrad Hänisch on 18 January 1919 soliciting his contribution to a brochure in which German artists would state their views on art in the socialist state (ZStP 90 Ha 4, Nachlass Hänisch, no. 454) and the inclusion of three essays from an earlier Publicity Office brochure. The undated brochure was apparently published in April.

95. In the January 1919 Publicity Office brochure the author is identified as the expressionist author Kurt Erich Meurer.

96. "Bürgerlicher missleiteter Ehrgeiz kokettiert mit dem patriotischen Mord nun immer noch." (Kurt Erich Meurer) "Aufruf zum Sozialismus," *An alle Künstler!* (Berlin, 1919), 4.

97. "Es war zu wenig Flamme in den Gassen, wie soll sich der Phönix herausgebären? Was wir seit November erleben, ist höchstens Klischee einer Revolution." Ibid.

98. "Warum floss nicht Wein statt Blut?" Ibid., 5.

99. Günter Krüger, "Die Rolle von Brücke und Blauem Reiter beim Durchbruch zur Moderne in Deutschland," in *Der Blaue Reiter* (Bern, 1987), 259. Marc also writes of Pechstein in 1913: "Mir ist höllisch Angst vor einer Popularität wie der seinen." Ibid., 260.

100. Schulz's name never appeared in the journal; he is listed in the *Deutsches Bücherverzeichnis* for 1919–20 as the publisher. From the editorial line it seems likely it was the same Max Schulz of the Berlin businessman's association. He had already written on social and political issues for various periodicals and had been commissioned by the Council of People's Representatives to write "Tariff Agreements, Arbitration of Work Disputes, and the Factory Council Laws," indicating he may have been sympathetic to the SPD.

101. "Wenn Liebknecht siegen würde . . . Gebrüll—Mord—Wahnsinn—Pest—Verwesung—Chaos." "Revolutionsschlamm," *An die Laterne* 1, no. 1 (n.d.): 5. On 4 January 1919, the Prussian government (whose USPD members had just resigned) attempted to dismiss Eichhorn from his post as police president of Berlin. The leadership of the 5 January mass demonstration decided to resist his dismissal, which contributed to the occupying of the Berlin press offices. After the ensuing Freikorps suppression of the mass protests, Eichhorn went into hiding.

102. See the advertisement in *An die Laterne* 1, no. 2 (n.d.).

103. "Die Revolution hat uns die Freiheit gebracht, jahrelange Wünsche zu äussern und zu verwirklichen. . . . Die soziale Republik gebe uns Vertrauen, Freiheit haben wir, und bald blühen aus trockener Scholle Blumen zu ihrer Ehre." Max Pechstein, "Was Wir Wollen," *An alle Künstler!*, 20–22.

104. "Auf der Basis des . . . Handwerks soll uns die Morgenröte der Einheit 'Volk und Kunst' erglänzen. . . . muss den Söhnen des Volks die Möglichkeit geboten werden, durch das Handwerk weiter zu schreiten zur Kunst. Kunst ist keine Spielerei, sondern Pflicht dem Volk gegenüber. Sie ist eine öffentliche Angelegenheit. Die auf der Strecke Liegengebliebenen sind dann auch nicht nutzlose Drohnen, sondern immer noch tüchtige handwerkliche Qualitätsarbeiter, welche dem Staate als solche nützen." Ibid, 19.

105. Victor Miesel, *Ludwig Meidner: An Expressionist Master*, Exibition catalog (Ann Arbor, 1978), 11.

106. Meidner also altered the titles of pre-war apocalyptic scenes following his turn to religious art. For example, in 1918 he exhibited the 1912 painting *Battlefield (The Trench)* as *Waiting for Judgment*. Ibid., 20, n. 28.

107. "Es darf keine Ausbeuter und Ausgebeuteten mehr geben! Es darf nicht länger sein, dass eine gewaltige Mehrheit in den kümmerlichsten, unwürdigsten und entehrendsten Verhältnissen leben muss, während eine winzige Minderheit am übervollen Tisch vertiert. Wir müssen uns zum Sozialismus entscheiden: zu einer allgemeinen und unaufhaltsamen Vergesellschaftung der Produktionsmittel, die jedem Menschen Arbeit, Musse, Brot, ein Heim und die Ahnung eines höheren Zieles gibt." Ludwig Meidner, "An alle Künstler, Dichter, Musiker," *An alle Künstler!*, 7.

108. "Uns Maler und Dichter verbinde mit dem Armen eine heilige Solidarität! Haben nicht auch viele unter uns das Elend kennengelernt und das Beschämende des Hungers und materieller Abhängigkeit? Stehen wir viel besser und gesicherter in der Gesellschaft als der Proletarier?! Sind wir nicht wie Bettler abhängig von den Launen der kunstsammelnden Bourgeoisie!" Ibid., 7–8.

109. "Wir müssen uns der Arbeiterpartei anschliessen, der entschiedenen, unzweideutigen Partei." Ibid., 10.

110. "Ich bin organisierter Sozialdemokrat gewesen seit fünfzehn Jahren, aber ich habe die Jahre nutzlos vertan, die Zeit vertrödelt, verträumt." Ludwig Meidner, "An alle Künstler, Dichter, Musiker," *Der Anbruch* 2, no. 1 (January 1919): n.p.

111. "Wir müssen wahrhaft sozialistische Kämpfer werden . . . und wenn die Stunde kommt—mitangetreten, in Reih und Glieder gestellt—mit der Flinte gegen den Feind . . ." Ibid.

112. "Werdet Kommunisten wie ich!" Ludwig Meidner, "Brüder, zünd' die Fackel an," *Die Erde* 1, no. 4 (15 February 1919): 115–18.

113. "Die Kunst kann nur gedeihen in vollkommener Freiheit . . . Der Künstler muss als Künstler Anarchist sein und als soziales Mitglied, als ein auf die Befriedigung der Lebensnotdurft angewiesener Bürger Sozialist." Kurt Eisner, "Der sozialistische Staat und der Künstler," *An alle Künstler!*, 25.

114. ". . . der bildende Künstler sollte nur in den Feierstunden seiner Inspiration schaffen, er sollte nicht die Kunst zur Ware machen unter dem Zwang wirtschaftlicher Existenznotwendigkeit . . . Deshalb habe ich den Gedanken aufgegriffen, ob gerade der bildende Künstler nicht von seinem eigenen Handwerk ausgehen soll, ob er seine wirtschaftliche Existenz auf sein Handwerk gründen soll, der Bildhauer, z.B. als Steinmetz arbeiten und nur in den Feierstunden seiner Inspiration am Kunstwerk schaffen soll . . ." Ibid.

115. Deleted in *An alle Künstler!* are the introductory paragraph explaining that Eisner is speaking to the Provisional Revolutionary National Assembly in Bavaria and a reference to Eisner's attendance at a meeting of Munich artists. Also deleted is a brief criticism of ministers in the imperial government; Hänisch was among those appointed before the revolution.

116. Hubertus Hendrikus Verstegen, *Het Phoenix-Motief: Bijdrage tot die studie van de humanistische visie op de vorst* (Nijmegen, 1950).

117. "Hier ist man ganz von kniegebeugten Bürgern umgeben, unter denen aufrecht zu bleiben fast über die Kraft geht. Es bleibt uns jetzt nur übrig, die reale Welt zu ignorieren und sich seine eigene innere Welt abgesondert zu erbauen . . . Denn auch der Sozialismus ist durch diese gemeine Zeit so beschmutzt und bis auf die Knochen blamiert, dass er lange brauchen wird, ehe er sein Schild wieder reinwäscht." Letter by Walter Gropius to Karl Ernst Osthaus, 2 February 1919, reprinted in *Arbeitsrat für Kunst,* 117.

118. Adolf Behne, "Unsere moralische Krisis," *Sozialistische Monatshefte* 25, no. 1 (1919): 38; quoted in Whyte, *Bruno Taut and the Architecture of Activism,* 115.

119. Reginald Isaacs, *Walter Gropius: Der Mensch und sein Werk* (Berlin, 1983), 127–35.

120. Letter by Walter Gropius to Karl Ernst Osthaus, 24 April 1917, Ibid., 176.

121. Letter by Walter Gropius to his mother, 22 June 1918, Ibid., 179.

122. Letter by Walter Gropius to Karl Ernst Osthaus, 23 December 1918, reprinted in Herta Hesse-Frielinghaus, *Karl Ernst Osthaus: Leben und Werk* (Recklinghaus, 1971), 471.

123. "Der Mord an Liebknecht und Rosa ist gemein, schlimmer als alles, was die Spartakisten taten." Letter by Walter Gropius to his mother, undated, in Isaacs, *Walter Gropius: Der Mensch und sein Werk,* 194. Also: "Dies waren reine Idealisten, die für ihre Idee wie wenige lebten und starben. Leider nur machten sie denselben Fehler wie die Antipoden und griffen auch zur Gewalt." Letter by Walter Gropius to his mother, undated, Ibid. Gropius chastised his mother for condemning the two slain KPD leaders.

124. Walter Gropius, no title, in Annalise Schmidt, ed., *Der Bolschewismus und die deutschen Intellektuellen: Äusserungen auf eine Umfrage des Bundes deutscher Gelehrter und Künstler* (Berlin, 1919), 14. (The responses to this inquiry by the *Bund deutscher Gelehrter und Künstler* on "Bolshevism and German Intellectuals" were written in January 1919).

125. Whyte, *Bruno Taut and the Architecture of Activism,* 7.

126. "Er (Der Sturm) will die Isolation, die Beziehungslosigkeit der Kunst, rennt an gegen die Verbindung von Kunst und Leben . . . und tut doch alles nur Menschenmögliche diese Kunst innig mit dem besseren Bürgertum zu verschweissen." Adolf Behne, "Kunstwende?" *Sozialistische Monatshefte* 24, no. 23–24 (October 1918): 946.

127. "Der Kubist will mehr als reine Malerei und reine Plastik. Über aller Methode und Systematik baut er mit an der Welt." Ibid.

128. Letter by Walter Gropius to Adolf Behne, 6 March 1919, reprinted in *Arbeitsrat für Kunst,* 119.

129. "Am Sonnabend (1.3) Nachmittag 4 Uhr findet in der Deutschen Gesellschaft, Wilhelmstr. 67 eine entscheidende Sitzung des Arbeitsrats für Kunst statt, zu der wir Sie hiermit dringend einladen. Nach anfänglichen Unklarheiten hat sich der A.f.K. endlich zu der Ansicht durchgerungen, dass er die Idee seiner Gründung nur dann erspriesslich verfolgen kann, wenn die Grenzen zwischen den einzelnen Kunstgruppen Architektur, Malerei, Plastik fallen und ein gemeinsamer, *durchaus radikal gerichteter Arbeitsausschuss* gewählt wird und zunächst in aller Stille vorbereitende Arbeit leistet, bis bei einer vielleicht nicht allzu fernen zweiten Revolution der Augenblick gegeben erscheint, mit den Forderungen der radikalen Künstler an die Öffentlichkeit zu treten. In der Sitzung am Sonnabend soll dieser Arbeitsausschuss gewählt werden, von dessen Zusammensetzung natürlich alles Weitere abhängt. Wir bitten Sie eindringlich, an dieser Sitzung teilzunehmen, damit der äusserste linke Flügel kompromisslos . . . zum Ausdruck kommt." Letter by Walter Gropius to Ludwig Meidner, 26 February 1919, reprinted in Ibid., 117–18.

130. A letter written by the art historian Friedrich Perzynski to Gropius gives some indication of this. As early as 5 February Perzynski responded to Gropius's intention to rid the group of "fellow-travelers," endorsing his plan "to form a narrower circle of those radically inclined." Perzynski named Theodor von Brockhusen as one of those fellow-travelers because he had not followed through on his initial commitment to push for dissolution of the academy. See the letter by Perzynski to Gropius, Berchtesgarden, 5 February 1919, Bauhaus Archiv, Briefe AfK 1919/21, GN 10/16/367–392.

131. Gropius had worked hard to put the group together. Schmidt-Rottluff initially refused, both on the grounds of temperament and because he saw no immediate goal which could bring the arts together. (Letter by Karl Schmidt-Rottluff to Walter Gropius, 5 March 1919, reprinted in *Arbeitsrat für Kunst,* 119.) Gropius prevailed upon him to attend the next meeting and apparently changed his mind.

132. Marcks doubted the wisdom of an alliance with the working class—at least one which ignored the peasantry. Yet he was still concerned with asserting his own revolutionary credentials: "In my defense I recall that ten years ago I was the only one in our circle who perceived the capitalist art economy as inhumane." Letter by Gerhard Marcks to Walter Gropius, 9 March 1919, reprinted in Ibid., 118–19.

133. In addition to the business committee there was now a nineteen-

member "artistic works committee," also with several well-known names including the curator Walter Kaesbach and the painters Emil Nolde, Lyonel Feininger, Georg Tappert, and Moriz Melzer. Also on this committee were many of the younger Berlin artists who tended toward abstraction in their work: Rudolf Belling, Jefim Golyscheff, P. R. Henning, Fritz Stuckenberg, and Arnold Topp. The other committee members were Artur Degner, Otto Freundlich, August Grisebach, Erwin Hass, Karl Jacob Hirsch, Otto Mueller, Franz Mutzenbecher, Friedrich Perzynski, and Richard Scheibe. The WCA also had a third committee of "friends of the WCA" with sixty members. Ibid., 89.

134. "Ich bin mir vollkommen klar darüber, dass von der jetzigen Regierung für unsere Bestrebungen kaum nennenswerte Unterstützung zu erwarten ist." Letter by Walter Gropius to Friedrich Perzynski, 13 March 1919, Bauhaus Archiv, Briefe AfK 1919/21, GN 10/16/367–392.

135. Gropius's speech to the membership, 22 March 1919, Bauhaus Archiv, Vorgeschichte des Bauhauses, 2/3.

136. "Es bleibt uns also nichts anderes übrig als uns an die Proletarier zu wenden, dass heisst an jene Menschen, die Besitz verschmähen, in denen das Gefühl tiefster Zusammengehörigkeit über alle Grenzen hin lebt, die Voraussetzungslosen, die Vorurteilslosen, deren vollkommenstes Beispiel Dostojewski ist, der sich ja selbst als Proletarier bezeichnet hat." Behne, "Unsere moralische Krisis," 38.

137. The exchanges between German and Russian avant-garde artists before the war were in large part orchestrated by Kandinsky. Both Kulbin and Burliuk had contributed to the *Blaue Reiter Almanac;* in 1910 Kandinsky had invited the Burliuks to contribute to the second exhibition of the *Neue Künstlervereinigung* in Munich; that same year Kandinsky took part in the Jack of Diamonds exhibition in Moscow; and in 1912 Kandinsky invited the Burliuks, Goncharova, and Larinov to the second Blaue Reiter exhibition.

138. Letter by Oskar Schlemmer to Otto Meyer, 25 January 1919, in Schlemmer, *The Letters and Diaries of Oskar Schlemmer,* 65.

139. The Executive Council relented on its decision the following day, but it was too late for the emissaries to influence the outcome of the congress. Karl Radek, who managed nonetheless to slip into the country, was arrested during the suppression of the so-called Spartacist uprising in January.

140. Peter Nisbet, "Some Facts on the Organizational History of the Van Diemen Exhibition," in *The First Russian Show,* catalogue of the Annely Juda Fine Gallery (London, 1983), 67.

141. Cesar Klein was also at the meeting but did not sign the telegram. See the letter by Gropius to Perzynski, 13 March 1919, Bauhaus Archiv, Briefe AfK 1919/21, GN 10/16/367–392.

142. Telegram to Moscow, Bauhaus Archiv, GN 10/3/93. It is not clear to which organiztion the "Assembly of Plastic Artists" refers.

143. Harry Graf Kessler, *Tagebücher, 1918–1937* (Frankfurt am Main, 1962), 91.

144. "Wir wollten schon seit Monaten zu Euch sprechen, doch die 'Land-

grenzen' versperrten den Weg. Wir fühlen uns eins mit Euch in dem festen Willen, für unser Teil alles zu tun, dass die Kluft, die die Machtpolitik zwischen den Völkern aufgerissen hat, sich wieder schliesse." Aufruf an die revolutionären Künstler Russlands, 25 March 1919, Bauhaus Archiv, GN 10/3/62–96.

145. " . . . die Solidarität der Mitschaffenden an einem und demselben Werke, das Bewusstsein der erhabenen, allgemein menschlichen Bedeutung dieses Werkes, das ideale Schaffen, das ethische Schaffen—all das . . . erfüllt seine Werke mit geistigem Inhalt." A. Lunatscharski (*sic*) "Proletkult," *Die Aktion* 9, no. 10–11 (15 March 1919), col. 151. Lunacharsky's full text was soon published in Franz Pfemfert's *Rote Hahn* series.

146. "Das Kunstprogramm des Kommissariats für Volksaufklärung in Russland," *Das Kunstblatt* 3, no. 3 (March 1919), 91.

147. "Die Arbeiterschaft, sagte er, will eine vollkommen freie Kunst haben, die aussschliesslich der Schönheit dient. . . . Und ich als einer der Arbeiter, der Arbeiter war und bleibt, bedanke mich von Herzen bei den Künstlern, die mir das Leben bereichern." Wassily Kandinsky, "Kunstfrühling in Russland," *Die Freiheit* 2, no. 171 (9 April 1919).

148. Kandinsky's views on art, particularly his conception of art as a mediator of subjective and metaphysical vibrations of feeling, were already under attack in Russia and were officially rejected in early 1920 by most of the members of INCHUK, who were more interested in objective, exact empirical methods in art. See Hubertus Gassner and Eckhart Gillen, *Zwischen Revolutionskunst und Sozialistischem Realismus: Dokumente und Kommentare. Kunstdebatten in der Sowjetunion von 1917 bis 1934* (Cologne, 1979), 20.

149. "Machen Sie doch einige Skizzen ganz ohne Architektur. Eine ganze Reihe anderer Maler haben auch Ideenskizzen geliefert, meist allerdings ganz utopischer Art, und die sind uns ja auch für den vorliegenden Zweck am liebsten." Letter by Gropius to Pechstein, Bauhaus Archiv, Briefe AfK 1919/21, GN10/16/367–392. Pechstein was apparently not represented in the exhibition.

150. Bruno Taut, "Idealisten," *Die Freiheit* (28 March 1919), reprinted in *Arbeitsrat für Kunst,* 91.

151. See Wassily Kandinsky, "On the Question of Form" in *The Blue Rider Almanac* (London, 1974), 174–75.

152. Adolf Behne, "Zur Einführung in die Ausstellung 'Für unbekannte Architekten,'" *Sozialistische Monatshefte* 25, no. 4 (March 1919), reprinted in: *Arbeitsrat für Kunst,* p. 92. Behne still promoted cubist-influenced art as being the most "architectonic" and, therefore, preferred the works of Johannes Molzahn, Oswald Herzog, and Arnold Topp.

153. "(Er) will mit seinen Zeichnungen, die er Proletariern zudenkt, die Lust anregen, selbst zu produzieren, selbst so etwas Einfaches und Hübsches zu machen," Adolf Behne, "Werkstattbesuche: Jefim Golyscheff," *Der Cicerone* 11, no. 2 (1919): 722.

154. Letter by Walter Gropius to Jefim Golyscheff, 22 March 1919, quoted in Whyte, *Bruno Taut and the Architecture of Activism,* 137.

155. A(lfred) W(iener), "Ausstellung für unbekannte Architekten," *Die Kunst* 40, no. 22 (9 June 1919): 272.

156. " . . . endlich etwas Neues, endlich etwas Originelles . . . Mir gefällt am besten die Freiheit, mit der jeder zu Worte kommt . . . Bei meinem nächsten Lotteriegewinn soll uns der Architekt Finsterlin ein Schloss in seiner Art bauen—das Grundstück befindet sich auf dem Monde." Bruno Taut, "Eine Volksabstimmung," *Die Freiheit* 2, no. 194 (23 April 1919).

157. "Es lebe die Revolution von Ewigkeit zu Ewigkeit! Amen." Ibid.

158. "Dass der Snob architektonische Entwürfe kauft, erwarten wir ja nicht! . . . Dass das interessierte Publikum und dass die Käufer unserer Ausstellung ganz andere sind, als bisher in den Salons als Käufer auftraten, ist wohl sicher." Adolf Behne, Flugblatt zur Ausstellung "Für unbekannte Architekten", reprinted in *Arbeitsrat für Kunst,* 91.

159. "Produktionsgenossenschaft sozialistischer Künstler," *Berliner Zeitung am Mittag* 42, no. 78 (9 April 1919).

160. "Die Genossenschaft sozialistischer Künstler," *Die Freiheit* 2, no. 141 (24 March 1919).

161. "Die Genossenschaft sozialistischer Künstler," *Berliner Tageblatt* 48, no. 373 (12 August 1919).

162. Friedrich Natteroth, "Richtlinien der Genossenschaft sozialistischer Künstler," *Die Freiheit* 2, no. 186 (17 April 1919).

163. "Eine sozialistische bildende Kunst, als Ausdruck sozialistischen Fühlens, besteht erst in den ersten Anfängen—darüber sind wir uns einig. Wie sollte es auch anders sein, da bis gestern kapitalistischer Staat und Gesellschaft die Kunst beherrschten. Es wäre auch verfehlt, die neuesten radikalen Kunstströmungen als sozialistisch oder kommunistisch zu deklarieren, obwohl sie in Russland Kraft der Diktatur—und nicht aus dem Volkswillen heraus—zur offiziellen Kunst der Räteregierung gestempelt wurden." K.H.D., "Eine Ausstellung sozialistischer Künstler," *Vorwärts* 36, no. 317 (24 June 1919).

164. "Zum Glück ist von politischen Absichten in den ausgestellten Arbeiten nichts zu spüren." Fritz Stahl, "Sozialistische Künstler," *Berliner Tageblatt* 48, no. 293 (30 June 1919).

165. *Berliner Tageblatt* 48, no. 322 (16 July 1919).

166. "Die Arbeiterkunstausstellung der Genossenschaft sozialistischer Künstler," *Berliner Tageblatt* 48, no. 354 (2 August 1919).

167. *Vorwärts* 36, no. 485 (22 September 1919).

168. *Vorwärts* 36, no. 399 (7 August 1919); no. 403 (9 August 1919); and no. 410 (13 August 1919).

169. Baluschek's illustrations were republished in 1920 in the *Gartenlaube* accompanying an inflammatory right-wing article decrying the horrors of the revolution.

170. Kollwitz's *Memorial to Karl Liebknecht* is often mistakenly cited as evidence of her allegiance to the KPD during the revolution.

171. " . . . wenn Wahl zwischen Diktatur Ebert und Diktatur Liebknecht, ich bestimmt Ebert wählen würde. Auf einmal aber fällt mir ein, was die

eigentlichen Revolutionäre doch geleistet haben. Ohne diesen steten Druck von links hätten wir auch keine Revolution gehabt, hätten wir den ganzen Militarismus nicht erlöscht. Sie wollte immer nur evolutionieren. Und die Konsequenten, die Unabhängigen, die Spartakusleute, sind auch jetzt wieder die Pioniere, sie drängen immer *vorwärts,* wie es auch liegt. Auch wenn es Blödsinn ist, auch wenn Deutschland darüber kaputt geht. Man wird sie jetzt knebeln müssen, um aus dem Chaos herauszukommen, und es besteht ein gewisses Recht dazu . . . Faktisch muss man mit den Mehrheitssozialisten gehen." Diary entry 8 December 1918, in Hans Kollwitz, ed., *Ich sah die Welt mit liebevollen Blicken: Käthe Kollwitz, Ein Leben in Selbstzeugnissen* (Hannover, 1968), 191.

172. See letter from Käthe Kollwitz to Hanna Mendel, 29 July 1919, in Käthe Kollwitz, *Briefe der Freundschaft* (Munich, 1966), 31.

173. Privately Kollwitz claimed she had not wanted to accept the appointment, but once it had been made public was loathe to create a scandal by refusing it. See a letter by Käthe Kollwitz to Beate Bonus-Jeep, 1919, in Kollwitz, *Ich sah die Welt mit liebevollen Blicken,* 195.

174. Letter by Käthe Kollwitz to Max Barthel, quoted in Whyte, *Bruno Taut and the Architecture of Activism,* 154.

175. The League for Proletarian Culture, however, soon turned its attention toward the development of a proletarian theater and abandoned any efforts in the pictorial arts.

176. Also considered were the Ordenspalais and the Schloss Bellevue. The finance minister finally suggested the Kronprinz Palais because it would probably be ceded to the state in negotiations with the former crown. See Paul Ortwin Rave, *Die Geschichte der Nationalgalerie Berlin* (Berlin, 1968), 83.

177. Ibid.

178. Ibid., 87.

179. The primary supporters of expressionism were the Brücke painter Erich Heckel and Hugo Simon, the USPD finance minister in the provisional socialist government. Besides Heckel and Simon, the commission included the artists Slevogt, Dettmann, Lederer, Gaul, and Kolbe; the art critics/historians Goldschmidt, Glaser, and Grisebach; and the collectors Arnhold and Brugger.

180. See a letter by Julia to Lyonel Feininger, 20 June 1919, Feininger Papers, Houghton Library, Harvard University, bMs Ger 146.1 (609).

181. "Gemacht hat natürlich Kaesbach die ganze Geschichte, und als Justis Heldentat steht sie dann verbucht in der Geschichte. Es ist schon eine Schweinerei." Ibid.

182. See *Dresdner Nachrichten* 63, no. 263 (23 September 1919); see also a letter by Heckel to Kaesbach, 28 June 1919, Germanisches Nationalmuseum, Kaesbach correspondence, I.C. ZR ABK 478. South Seas watercolors by Emil Nolde were finally lent to the museum by the Reichskolonialamt.

183. "Hastig wurden die öffentlichen Sammlungen . . . so umgeordnet und ergänzt, dass der radikale Flügel keinen Anlass zur Opposition findet." Otto Grautoff, *Die neue Kunst* (Berlin, 1921), 133.

184. Wilhelm von Bode, "Die 'Not der Geistigen Arbeiter,'" *Kunst und Künstler* 18, no. 7 (1 April 1920): 297.

185. Letter by Walter Gropius to Georg Tappert, 28 August 1919, Kunstarchiv Arntz. Taut feared that the current plans for reform were nothing more than an attempt to maintain the status quo under the guise of radical change. See Bruno Taut "Zuviel Gerede vom Architektur-Unterricht," *Die Bauwelt* 10, no. 32 (7 August 1919): 9.

186. The government had chosen a design by Prof. Emil Döpler. In late October the Werkbund commissioned Prof. Otto Hupp to design an alternative. (Its objections to the Döpler design were purely technical.) Behne seized on this as typical of the lingering conservatism of the Werkbund: "If only the Werkbund had suggested a new symbol instead of the disgraced bird of prey!" The government sought to dampen the furor by declaring that the eagle would be gold and black, rather than the imperial red and black. At some point the Werkbund responded to this crititicism and asked Schmidt-Rottluff to try his hand at a design. On this affair see, *Vorwärts* 36, no. 506 (3 October 1919); Karl Ernst Osthaus Archiv, Hagen, DWB 1/283; *Sozialistische Monatshefte* 54, no. 26 (26 January 1920).

187. Also suggested were Wätzoldt and Oldenbourg. See the minutes of the meeting of the Werkbund on 5 November 1919, DWB 1/285, Karl Ernst Osthaus Archiv, Hagen.

188. Karl Ernst Osthaus Archiv, Hagen, DWB 1/293, Besprechung mit dem Vorsitzenden, 12 January 1920; see also, John Schikowski, "Der Reichskunstwart," *Vorwärts* 37, no. 23 (13 January 1920).

189. "Berliner Auktionen," *Kunstchronik und Kunstmarkt* 30, no. 47 (19 September 1919).

190. Lothar Brieger, "Jahresbilanz," *Der Kunsthandel* 11, no. 12 (December 1919): 186.

191. "Auf dem Kunstmarkt herrscht fieberhafte Bewegung. Unbesehen fast wird gekauft und überall fehlt es an Ware. Wohin mit dem Papiergeld? . . . Da erinnert man sich, dass Bilder, Graphik, Bücher und Antiquitäten Wertobjekte sind. Von schwankendem Kurswert zwar, aber vor der Hand doch von steigendem Kunstwert . . . In den Ausstellungen prangt an jedem dritten Bild ein Zettel 'verkauft.' Und da es eine reaktionäre Kunst nicht mehr gibt, da jederman modern malt und zeichnet, so wird der gestern noch verlachte Expressionist über Nacht zum Publikumskünstler und zum Kapitalisten. Er knurrt nun seinerseits über das Papiergeld, fürchtet Vermögensabgaben, sucht Häuser oder Bauernhöfe zu kaufen und wird zurückhaltend mit seinen Werken." "Ausverkauf," *Kunst und Künstler* 18, no. 5 (1 February 1920): 191.

192. Stephen Schuker, "Finance and Foreign Policy in the Era of the German Inflation: British, French and German Strategies for Economic Reconstruction after the First World War," in Otto Büsch and Gerald D. Feldman, eds., *Historische Prozesse der deutschen Inflation 1914 bis 1924* (Berlin, 1978), 350.

193. "Wie Pilze schiessen die Kunsthandlungen aus dem Boden, die 'neuen' Kunstfreunde sind zahlreicher denn die alten. Begreiflich: Sie ziehen es vor, ihre Lebensversicherung, ihre Valutapapiere, ihre Kriegs- und Revolutionsgewinne in der Form von Kunstwerken an die Wand zu hängen, bevor sie durch die Papiergeldkatastrophe völlig entwertet werden. . . . Neueste Kunst, etwa ein Kirchner, noch vor zwei Jahren mit 300 Mark bewertet, bringt es heute auf 10,000 Mark." Dr. Bruno Rauecker, *Die Proletarisierung der geistigen Arbeiter* (Munich, 1920), 8.

194. Karl Ernst Osthaus Archiv, Hagen, F2/83/11/1, F2/83/11/2, F2/83/15, R/F.DM.P. 44.

195. Lyonel Feininger Papers, Harvard University, bMs Ger 146.1(609).

196. Feininger's expenses, however, were also substantial, with his wife Julia spending 2,500 marks for the Berlin household in April and his own room and board in Weimar costing some 900 marks per month. Feininger's letters from Weimar to his wife Julia in Berlin read like accounting books, with discussions of sales, prices, and exhibition strategy dominating to the exclusion of almost all other subjects. See a letter by Julia to Lyonel Feininger, 27 May 1919 and a letter by Lyonel to Julia Feininger, 28 May 1919, Lyonel Feininger Papers, Harvard University, bMs Ger 146.1(590, 1787).

197. Feldmann, Kolb, and Rürup, "Die Massenbewegung der Arbeiterschaft am Ende des Ersten Weltkrieges (1917–1920)," 89.

198. Fritz Hellwag, "Die derzeitige wirtschaftliche Lage der bildenden Künstler," in Ernst Francke and Walther Lotz, eds., *Die geistigen Arbeiter,* vol. 2 (Munich, 1922), 162–65. Hellwag's text was apparently written in 1920, but not published until 1922. He referred specifically to the events of 1919.

199. Ibid., 151.

200. Konrad Hänisch, *Die Not der geistigen Arbeiter* (Leipzig, 1920), 42.

201. On the November Group commission were Georg Tappert, Heinrich Richter-Berlin, Rudolf Belling, Bernhard Hasler, Oswald Herzog, Cesar Klein, Ludwig Meidner, Moriz Melzer, and Max Pechstein. The Free Secession commission included Walter Bondy, Arthur Degner, Georg Kolbe, Käthe Kollwitz, Georg Mosson, Otto Mueller, Wolf Röhricht, Richard Scheibe, and Karl Schmidt-Rottluff. (See the catalog *Kunstausstellung Berlin 1919,* Glaspalast am Lehrter Bahnhof, 24 July–30 September 1919, Introduction, n.p.) Degner, Kolbe, Mueller, Scheibe, and Schmidt-Rottluff were all members of the WCA. The entire exhibition was headed by a twelve-man organizing committee composed of representatives from each group. Representing the November Group were Heinrich Richter-Berlin and Georg Tappert; from the Free Secession were Walter Bondy and Arthur Degner. The other members were Georg Hacker (Düsseldorf), Willi Jaeckel, Arthur Lewin-Funcke, Hans Looschen, Ernst Oppler, Walther Peterson (Düsseldorf), Leonhard Sandrock and Max Schlichting. The members of the committee were first publicly announced in the *Berliner Tageblatt* 48, no. 272 (19 June 1919).

202. "Nach der billigen Psychologie der ungebildeten Periode, in der wir

leben, muss die Kunst in einer politisch wilden Zeit auch ihrerseits wild sein." Fritz Stahl, "Kunstausstellung Berlin 1919," *Berliner Tageblatt* 48 (24 July 1919).

203. "Dann kommt die tröstliche Erkenntnis, dass doch wohl die grosse Mehrheit der jungen Herren bloss Simulanten sind, die mit kalter Methode Züge von fremder Tollheit reproduzieren." Ibid.

204. A. von Montbe, "Berliner Bilder," *Dresdner Nachrichten* 63, no. 254 (14 September 1919).

205. "Mit Interesse erwartete man das erste öffentliche Auftreten der Novembergruppe. Der Zusammenschluss aller frischen und lebendigen künstlerischen Kräfte war ja für Berlin schon längst zu einer Dringlichkeit geworden. Die Novembergruppe ist dieser Zusammenschluss nicht. Sie hat nicht die Geister aufzubringen vermocht, die als die eigentlichen Träger der Entwicklung erscheinen, statt dessen überwuchert auch bei ihr ein verantwortungsloses Mitläufertum, dem noch breitere Propagandamöglichkeiten zu beschaffen keine Notwendigkeit bestand." Walter Ley, *Das Kunstblatt* 3 (1919): 320.

206. Paul Westheim, *Frankfurter Zeitung,* as reported in *Der Kunsthandel* 11, no. 8 (August 1919): 116.

207. See, for example, John Schikowski, "Die Expressionisten im Landesausstellungsgebäude," *Vorwärts* 36, no. 465 (11 September 1919) and the *Sozialistische Monatshefte* 25, no. 56 (29 September 1919).

208. "Man steht wie vor einem Verhängnis, und man fragt sich, ob es so hat kommen müssen, ob unsere Zeit dazu verurteilt ist, die Formen der alten Kunst zu zerschlagen, wie die Bolschewisten in Russland die Formen des Gesellschaftslebens zertrümmern und behaupten, nur darauf komme es heut' an, der Wiederaufbau sei die Frage einer künftigen Zeit." Curt Glaser, "Kunstausstellung Berlin 1919," *Kunstchronik und Kunstmarkt* 30, no. 45 (5 September 1919): 962.

209. "Das sei die 'Kunst,' die unser Vaterland herabringe und entehre . . . Der Nihilismus, der alles stürze, was bisher in der Kunst feststand, habe auch im öffentlichen Leben den Umsturz herbeigeführt." "Bilderstürmer im Glaspalast," *Berliner Zeitung am Mittag* (5 September 1919).

210. "Kunstdebatten-Kunstskandale," *Vorwärts* 36, no. 457 (7 September 1919).

211. Schikowski, "Die Expressionisten im Landesausstellungsgebäude."

212. Ludwig Reve, "Bilderstürmer im Glaspalast," *Berliner Zeitung am Mittag* (5 September 1919); "Bildstürmer im Berliner Glaspalast," *Dresdner Nachrichten* (9 September 1919); and "Notizen," *Kunstchronik und Kunstmarkt* 30, no. 47 (19 September 1919): 1002.

213. "Den Anlass zu diesen Vorgängen versucht die eine Partei der anderen zuzuschreiben, und die ganze Angelegenheit wird wieder auf das politische Gebiet hinübergespielt. Man spricht von Agenten gegenrevolutionärer Gruppen, die das Publikum durch geschickte Agitation aufstacheln. Es zeigt sich auch hierin, dass der Versuch gemacht wird, einerseits die Kunst zum Mittel des politischen Kampfes zu benutzen, andrerseits die Revolutionskonjunktur

auszubeuten, um die jüngsten Erscheinungen auf künstlerischem Gebiet tendenziös mit den am weitesten links stehenden Parteigruppen in Beziehung zu bringen, wie es in Russland bereits mit Erfolg versucht worden ist. Aber was in Russland auf dem Wege der Diktatur erreicht wurde, muss bei uns auf dem des Mehrheitswillens kläglich misslingen, wie nun auch die Stellungnahme des Glaspalastpublikums schlagend erweist." "Notizen," *Kunstchronik und Kunstmarkt* 30, no. 47 (19 September 1919): 1002.

214. *Sitzungsberichte der verfassungsgebenden Preussischen Landesversammlung*, Tagung 1919/21, vol. 6 (Berlin, 1921), 90. Sitzung, 4 December 1919, col. 7314.

215. ". . . sicher ist die Demokratisierung in der Kunst nicht angebracht; hier gilt nun einmal das aristokratische Prinzip ganz unleugbar." Ibid., col. 7319.

216. ". . . wir müssen hierbei der Befürchtung Ausdruck geben, dass leider auch jetzt wieder eine Art von offizieller Kunst aufzukommen scheint, nur nach der andern Richtung hin . . . Heute machen sich zu unserm Bedauern Anzeichen bemerkbar, dass ein Kunstwerk allein danach bewertet wird, welcher politischen Richtung sein Schöpfer angehört . . . Es gibt nur Kunst als solche, das heisst gute oder schlechte Kunst, . . . aber es gibt keine proletarische Kunst und auch keine kapitalistische Kunst . . ." Ibid., col. 7343–44.

217. "Solche Bilder brauchen ja auch nicht im Übermass beschafft zu werden . . ." Ibid.

218. ". . . wir können gleich konstatieren, dass die Revolution an der Tatsache nichts geändert hat, dass es kunstarme, kulturell besitzlose Schichten, die Masse des Volkes unten gibt . . . Da wir kein einheitliches Volksganzes haben, haben wir selbstverständlich auch kein einheitliches Kunstleben. . . . weil wir in einer gärenden, sozial gärenden Zeit leben, ist bei der Kunst dasselbe der Fall. . . . Das finden wir z.B. in den beiden Kunstrichtungen in der Malerei verkörpert, die wir . . . einerseits als die Verteidigerin des Bestehenden bezeichnen können, und diejenige, die wir als die expressionistische ansprechen, die das Neue formen, die durch die Kunst eine Willensbildung der Gesellschaft zum Ausdruck bringen . . . , die die Kunst in den Dienst der neuen sozialen Formen stellen will. Die künstlerische und intellektuelle Jugend ist bei uns, bei der Arbeiterklasse . . ." Ibid., col. 7333–44.

219. ". . . die Revolution (hat) die harte Muschelschale der militaristisch-imperialistischen Zensur . . . vernichtet, so dass heute die Kunst freiere und bessere Bahnen gehen kann." Ibid., col. 7261.

220. ". . . der Künstler ist auch heute noch immer von der Bourgeoisie, d.h. der kapitalkräftigen Bürgerschaft abhängig. Meine Parteifreunde aber sind der Ansicht, . . . dass die Kunst nicht etwa nur eine Kunst für das seichte und perverse Kurfürstendammpublikum sein soll, sondern vielmehr eine Kunst für die breite Volksmasse, eine gesunde Volkskunst." Ibid.

221. "Es verlangt niemand, dass Sie diese Leute lieben; aber man bemüht sich nicht, diese Künstler zu verstehen, nur weil sie etwas Neuartiges sind, weil sie Revolutionäre der Kunst sind. Das ist grundfalsch. Geben Sie diesen

Künstlern soviel soziales Mitempfinden, soviel Liebe, dass sie wenigstens leben können, dann werden Sie sehen, was geleistet wird. In jeder Revolution wird nach links oder rechts manchmal ein etwas kühner Bocksprung gemacht; das ist eben die logische Folgerung jeder Revolution; ob das in der Kunst oder in der Politik geschieht, das ist gleichgültig." Ibid., col. 7268.

222. "Es gibt immer noch kunstliebende Bürger, denen ein Inbeziehungsetzen der beiden Dinge—kurz gesagt: Expressionismus und Weltrevolution—unsympathisch ist. Sie finden es unsachlich, die Dinge in einem Atem zu nennen. . . . Mit den Befreiungsenergien der neuen Kunst haben sie sich abgefunden, aber sie wünschen auf keinen Fall, dass die hier als interessant empfundenen Energien über den Bildrahmen hinaus weiter wirken. Die Wirkung soll also eine ästhetische auf den Kreis der Kenner beschränkt bleiben. . . . Kunst hat nichts mit Politik zu tun. . . .

"Wenn jetzt dieselben kunstliebenden Bürger angefangen haben, expressionistische Kunst zu kaufen und zu sammeln, so schliessen sie selbstredend wieder einen Kompromiss. Sie empfinden nicht das Geistige der neuen Kunst, das ja ihrem Geiste feindlich ist, sondern sehen ausschliesslich die ihren Augen ungewohnte Oberfläche, die sie als Überraschungsreiz geniessen. Der Kompromiss besteht darin, dass sie eine Kulturbewegung vor sich selbst zu einer Mode degradieren,—um sie mitmachen zu können." Adolf Behne, "Graphik und Plastik von Mitgliedern der Novembergruppe Berlin," *Menschen* 2, no. 14 (81/86) (December 1919): n.p.

223. ". . . solange ein Mitglied einer Künstlergruppe vor Fritz Ebert, dem Bestätiger von Todesurteilen . . . (und) Personifizierung bourgeoiser Indolenz katzbuckelt, solange hat die Künstlervereinigung verdammt wenig Recht, sich radikal oder gar revolutionär zu nennen." Franz Schulz, "Kunst, Bürger, Staat," *Das Forum* 4, no. 9 (June 1920): 656.

224. ". . . (sie) führt ihn mit ehrerbietigem Lächeln und freundlichen Bücklingen vor die Parade junger, radikaler, revolutionärer Kunst. Doch der Vielgeprüfte verliert die Fassung nicht und dieweil im Ruhrgebiet irgendwo das Kommando 'Feuer' ertönt, sucht er auch der radikalen revolutionären Kunst gerecht zu werden. Immerhin: verhaltenes Lachen erschüttert die elegante Weste des Landesvaters und das Gerechtwerden wird ihm offenbar nicht leicht. Der führende Expressionistenführer expliziert devot, als hätte er es mit einem mäzenatischen Bierbrauer zu tun, die Schar der kleinen Expressionisten horcht gespannt . . ." Ibid., 655–56.

225. "Open Letter to the November Group," *Der Gegner* 2, no. 8/9 (1920/21); 297; reprinted in Kliemann, *Die Novembergruppe,* 62. Signing the letter were Otto Dix, Max Dungert, George Grosz, Raoul Hausmann, Hannah Höch, Ernst Krantz, Franz Mutzenbecher, Thomas Ring, Rudolf Schlichter, Georg Scholz, and Willy Zierath.

226. It was referred to as the Weimarer-Belvedere-Berg. See protocol of 18 November 1919, meeting of WCA, partially reprinted in *Arbeitsrat für Kunst,* 108.

227. See a letter by Walter Gropius to Adolf Behne, 15 May 1920, reprinted in Ibid., 124.

228. Ich meine damit, der A.f.K. muss Mittel und Wege finden, dem Arbeiter beizubringen, dass er sich durch seine unsinnigen Lohnforderungen selbst schädigt, kulturhindernd wirkt und uns Künstler, die ja dort seine Interessen vertreten, grossen Schaden [anrichtet]." Letter by Rudolf Belling to Walter Gropius, n.d., Bauhaus Archiv, Briefe AfK 1919/21, GN 10/9/192–210. The clipping was from the *8 Uhr Abendblatt* (18 March 1919).

229. See *Deutsche Bauzeitung* 53, no. 71 (3 September 1919). The German government never came up with a plan that satisfied the French. In July 1921 Walter Rathenau and Louis Loucheur were still trying to work out an agreement by which Germany would meet its reparation payments in German goods and workmanship. Twenty-five thousand prefabricated houses made in Germany were to be erected in France. Many French critics were opposed to the idea for fear that German goods and workmen would result in "colonization" of an area just devastated by the Germans. See Mary McLeod, "Architecture or Revolution," *Art Journal* 43, no. 2 (Summer 1983): 147 n. 110.

230. Protocol of 18 November 1919 meeting of WCA, Bauhaus Archiv, Briefe AfK 1919/21, GN 10/2/35–61.

231. As late as January 1920, WCA members were still searching for an appropriate building project. Georg Tappert wrote to Behne in January 1920 concerning an announcement in the *Verlag der Neuen Buddhistischen Zeitschrift Zehlendorf,* which discussed future plans for a "Buddhist house" and possible Buddhist settlement. Tappert thought this might be the "ideal project" the WCA was still looking for. Behne was interested enough to note in the margin of the letter: "order this issue." Letter by Georg Tappert to Adolf Behne, 26 January 1920, Staatsbibliothek Preussischer Kulturbesitz Berlin, N1. Behne, no. 36.

232. The history of the founding of the Bauhaus in Weimar is outside of the parameters of this discussion. For two excellent accounts see, Marcel Franciscono, *Walter Gropius and the Creation of the Bauhaus in Weimar* (Urbana, 1971) and Reginald R. Isaacs, *Walter Gropius: Der Mensch und sein Werk* (Berlin, 1983).

233. Isaacs, *Walter Gropius: Der Mensch und sein Werk,* 206–7.

234. There were thirteen questions in all, addressing: (1) educational reform; (2) state support; (3) housing policy; (4) artists retraining in the handicrafts; (5) the artist in the socialist state; (6) art exhibitions; (7) unification of the arts; (8) color in the city; (9) decoration of public buildings; (10) the relationship of art to the people; (11) methods for presenting work to the public; (12) contacts with foreign artists' groups; (13) anonymity of art works. *Ja! Stimmen des Arbeitsrates für Kunst* is reprinted in full in *Arbeitsrat für Kunst,* 10–76.

235. The respondents were Adolf Allwohn, Adolf Behne, Rudolf Belling, Heinrich Campendonk, Hermann Finsterlin, Walter Gropius, Bernhard Has-

ler, Erwin Hass, P. R. Henning, Oswald Herzog, Cesar Klein, Eva Lau, Gerhard Marcks, Moriz Melzer, Franz Mutzenbecher, Hermann Obrist, Karl Ernst Osthaus, Friedrich Perzynski, Richard Scheibe, Werner Scheibe, John Schikowski, Karl Schmidt-Rottluff, Milly Steger, Georg Tappert, Bruno Taut, Max Taut, Arnold Topp, and Wilhelm Valentiner.

236. "Dem Reglement haben wir kein besseres Reglement entgegenzusetzen, sondern unsere und des Volkes künstlerische Spontanität. . . . Hier lautet unsere Aufgabe: Zerstörung der Bildung." *Arbeitsrat für Kunst,* 20.

237. "Abschaffung und Reorganisation des bisherigen Zeichenunterrichtes. Vollständiges Gewährenlassen der kindlichen Phantasie im Kinderheim und der Schule bis etwa zum 10. Lebensjahre. . . . Förderung des kindlichen Ausdruckszeichens durch Lehrer, deren Aufgabe es nicht sein soll, die Zeichnungen auf Richtigkeit, technische Sauberkeit und dergleichen Dinge zu korrigieren. Aufgabe des Lehrers muss es sein, die Phantasie des Kindes anzuregen . . ." Ibid., 66.

238. "Die gründlichste Reform würde durch eine (wenigstens zeitweise) Abschaffung aller Schulen erreicht. Vielleicht wird die Kunst besser, wenn sie einmal wieder wild wächst, wie es im Anfang aller Dinge war, als sich eine naive Kunst bildete." Ibid., 75.

239. "Der Staat ist seinem Wesen nach kunstfeindlich." Ibid., 20.

240. "Kunst und Staat sind unvereinbare Begriffe." Ibid., 31.

241. "Der Staat muss ganz ignoriert werden." Ibid., 68.

242. "Sozialisierung. Die Kunst muss sozialisiert werden." Ibid., 39.

243. "Anregung, Belehrung und Beeinflussung der Jugend ist notwendig, damit diese die Bestrebungen der modernen Künstler in den Kreis der Familie und in die Arbeitsstuben und Werkstätten trägt." Ibid., 67.

244. Brochure announcing sale of the volume, Bauhaus Archiv, AfK.

245. Ulrich Linse, *Die anarchistische und anarcho-syndikalistische Jugendbewegung 1919–1933* (Frankfurt am Main, 1976), 58.

246. See Ernst Friedrich, "Etwas über Expressionismus," *Freie Jugend* 1, no. 5 (1919) 2.

247. "Der Arbeitsrat wollte den Kunstsalons nicht ihre Ausstellungen nachmachen. Er wollte auch nicht eine Perlenkette expressionistischer Meisterwerke aneinanderreihen." Adolf Behne, "Kunstausstellung für Arbeiter," *Die Freiheit* 3, no. 8 (5 January 1920).

248. Walter Passarge, "Eine Ausstellung Arbeiter-Kunst in Berlin," *Der Cicerone* 12, no. 4 (1920): 167.

249. Linse, *Die anarchistische und anarcho-syndikalistische Jugendbewegung 1919–1933,* 58.

250. "Die Ausstellung im Osten Berlins," Bauhaus Archiv, AfK, no number.

251. Ibid.

252. "Berichte der Geschäftsführung," 31 March 1920, Bauhaus Archiv, Briefe AfK 1919/21, GN 10/111–34.

253. I have not been able to locate any issue of the *Agrar-Korrespondenz* other than the April 1920 issue, which is in a press clipping file in the Staatsarchiv,

Potsdam. The content of previous articles on the exhibition can only be inferred from this issue.

254. "Ein Wort noch über Ihre zwar nicht bewiesene aber apodiktisch aufgestellte Behauptung, dass Sozialismus und Expressionismus zusammengehören. . . . Er ist also letzten Endes ganz exklusiv, aristokratisch, einsam, ungenossenschaftlich. Wo steckt da die Verwandtschaft mit dem Sozialismus? Wird hier nicht etwa Sozialismus und Revolution miteinander verwechselt? . . . Denn wo hat er seine Hauptanhänger? In Berlin WW, Kurfürstendamm, wo die Novembersozialisten und Salonspartakisten sitzen!" Ph. Leuthold, "Arbeiterkunstausstellung: Entgegnung," *Beilage der freien wissenschaftlichen sozialistischen Agrar-Korrespondenz* (April 1920).

255. Protocol of the meeting of the business committee 30 May 1921 (22 June 1921), Bauhaus Archiv, AfK, no number.

256. "Den expressionistischen Künstler aber wird die Revolution zur Erde zwingen und seinem Stil etwas von dem schweren Tritt der proletarischen revolutionären Massen verleihen. Sie wird ihm die gefährliche Sucht nach treibhausgezüchteter Geistigkeit nehmen und sie wird ihm durch das Bewusstsein, Mitkämpfer zu sein in den Reihen des revolutionären Proletariats, die Gefühlsechtheit erringen lassen, nach deren Ausdruck er strebt." Heinrich Stern, "Bildende Kunst und Revolution," *Die Aktion* 9, no. 47/48 (29 November 1919): col. 780.

Chapter 3. Dresden

1. David W. Morgan, *The Socialist Left and the German Revolution* (Ithaca, 1975), 170.

2. Horst, Dörrer, *Die Herausbildung einer revolutionären Massenpartei in Ostsachsen bei besonderer Berücksichtigung der Vereinigung des linken Flügels der Unabhängigen Sozialdemokratischen Partei Deutschlands mit der Kommunistischen Partei Deutschlands (1914 bis 1920)*, Habilitationsschrift, Karl Marx University (Leipzig, 1968), 124.

3. The two leaders of the unified council were Albert Schwarz (SPD) and Otto Rühle (Spartacists). Ibid., 124–25.

4. Morgan, *The Socialist Left and the German Revolution*, 170.

5. Horst Beutel, "Die Novemberrevolution von 1918 in Lepizig und die Politik der Leipziger USPD-Führung bis zum Einmarsch der konterrevolutionären Truppen des Generals Maercker am 12. Mai 1919," *Wissenschaftliche Zeitschrift der Universität Leipzig* 7 (1957/58): 390.

6. *Dresdner Anzeiger* 189, no. 318 (16 November 1918).

7. *Dresdner Anzeiger* 189, no. 319 (17 November 1918).

8. Gasch applied for and received assistance from the Saxony "Künstlerhilfsbund" and became active in a group seeking financial assistance for artists returning from the front. Staatsarchiv Dresden, MdInnern, 17448 (no. 16) and 17460 (no. 17). Gasch's revolutionary stance during 1918–19 is never com-

mented on in GDR literature, possibly because he later became a Nazi sympathizer.

9. "Herunter von den Thrönchen mit den alten selbstherrlichen Kunstpäpsten! Nieder mit allem Akademismus! . . . Weg mit allen Ordenspflästerchen und geheimen Titeln!" "Ein Arbeiterrat bildender Künstler," *Dresdner Volkszeitung* 29, no. 269 (18 November 1918).

10. "Es sei kein Ruhm für die Künstler, dass sie es den Arbeitern und Soldaten überlassen haben, die Verhältnisse umzustürzen. Die Künstler würden es ihnen nicht vergessen, was sie für sie geleistet haben!" Ibid.

11. "[Wir] begrüssen den neuen sozialistischen Freistaat und die sich bildende vereinigte deutsche Republik . . . [Wir] hoffen, dass die Neugestaltung und Befreiung von brutalen Mächten die Welt zugleich von dem Materialismus der letzten Epochen reinigen und dadurch auch die Kunst verinnerlichen und erhöhen wird. Die Versammlung . . . betrachtet sich als Sprecher und wesentlichen Vetreter der Dresdener Künstlerschaft, um so mehr, als die Anregung zu ihr von den jüngeren Künstlern ausgegangen ist und als sie keine Persönlichkeit in sich enthält, die nicht mit der künstlerischen Jugend und mit allen Anforderungen der Zeit Schritt zu halten gewillt ist. Die hier versammelte Künstlerschaft wird niemals Schlupfwinkel einer künstlerischen oder andern Reaktion sein." "Der Künstlerrat," *Dresdner Neueste Nachrichten* 26, no. 316 (19 November 1918).

12. "Die Künstler nach der Revolution," *Dresdner Volkszeitung* 29, no. 280 (2 December 1918).

13. *Dresdner Neueste Nachrichten* 26, no. 344 (18 December 1918).

14. "Die Vereinigung umfasst *nicht* vorzugsweise die extremen Elemente, vielmehr haben ihre Bestrebungen von Anfang an ein Gegengewicht schaffen wollen gegen die in den ersten Revolutionstagen auftauchenden radikalen Absichten und Kundgebungen der Gruppe des Malers Gasch . . . Diese radikal gerichtete Gruppe ist, wie es scheint, durch einen geschickten Gegenzug der Gründer des Künstlerrats in diesen aufgenommen worden . . ." Report by Dr. Grohmann(?) to Dresden mayor, 17 April 1919, Stadtarchiv Dresden, Hauptkanzlei, 741/19 (no. 18).

15. "Entwurf der Geschäftsführung," December 1918, Staatsarchiv Dresden, MdInnern, 17271, no. 60.

16. Ibid. Other members included Dreher, Wrba, Duelfer, Poelzig, Mendelsohn, Meier-Graefe and Zehder.

17. Richard Stiller, "Die Dresdner Kunst in den Kriegsjahren," in *Dresdner Kalender 1919* (Dresden, 1919), 93.

18. *Sächsische Volkszeitung* 17, no. 276 (2 December 1918).

19. "Sie sind zum Teil ökonomisch und gehen auf eine Sicherung der wirtschaftlichen Existenz der Künstler hinaus; insoweit wird für den Staat nur die Frage entstehen, ob und in welcher Weise eine *Selbsthülfe* der Künstler, wie sie etwa im Künstlerhülfsbund sich entwickelt, gefördert und vielleicht . . . unterstützt werden kann." Letter by Richard Lipinski to the Academic Council, 4 January 1919, Staatsarchiv Dresden, Md.Innern, 17271, no. 3.

20. ". . . die lebensfähigsten zeitgenössischen Kunstbestrebungen . . ." Ibid.

21. Rühle, a member of the USPD since its founding, in November formed the International Communists with ties to the Bremen anarcho-syndicalist movement. He apparently joined the KPD soon after its founding, but constantly fought with the party leadership. See Dörrer, *Die Herausbildung einer revolutionären Massenpartei in Ostsachsen bei besonderer Berücksichtigung der Vereinigung des linken Flügels der Unabhängigen Sozialdemokratischen Partei Deutschlands mit der Kommunistischen Partei Deutschlands (1914 bis 1920)*, 132.

22. Ibid., 149. Beutel reports that twelve were killed and fifty-two wounded. See Beutel, "Die Novemberrevolution von 1918 in Leipzig und die Politik der Leipziger USPD-Führung bis zum Einmarsch der konterrevolutionären Truppen des Generals Maercker am 1. Mai 1919," 396 and 401.

23. Letter by Conrad Felixmüller to Dieter Gleisberg, 18 January 1971, reprinted in *Conrad Felixmüller: Werke und Dokumente* (Nürnberg, 1981), 75. See also the letter to Horst Michel, 15 November 1975, reprinted in *Kunst im Aufbruch: Dresden 1918–1933*, exhibition catalog, Gemäldegalerie Neue Meister (Dresden, 1980), 44.

24. See the two drafts of Felixmüller's unpublished autobiography (called "recollections"), n.d., Archiv für bildende Kunst, Germanisches Nationalmuseum, Nürnberg, Felixmüller Papers, Teil 10, Karton no. 16.

25. "1. Die Sezession 'Gruppe 1919' wird von einer Anzahl Künstler gebildet, die im Sinne ihrer Kunst ideelle Unternehmungen vorhaben, welche sie, wie auch ihre Kunst, notwendigerweise von den bisherigen Künstlern trennen. Hauptgrundsätze sind: Wahrheit—Brüderlichkeit—Kunst. Der Elan der Zeit hat die Gruppe hervorgebracht, und der kommende kann sie vernichten: Wir werden dazu beitragen, indem wir den kommenden den Weg bereiten, der wir eben schon sind. 2. Neue Mitglieder können nur einstimmig von sämtlichen Mitgliedern der Gruppe aufgenommen werden; entscheidend ist jedesmal der Mut und die innere notwendige Überzeugung, die aus den Werken des Aufzunehmenden sprechen; Dresdner Künstlervereinigung anzugehören, ist nicht erlaubt, auswärtigen nur nach gemeinsamen Beschluss. . . . 4. Ausstellungen werden in Dresden nur als Gruppe veranstaltet, in besonderen Fällen können nach Beschluss Ausnahmen gemacht werden. Juriert wird von allen Mitglieder der Gruppe gemeinsam." Fritz Löffler and Emilio Bertonati, eds., *Dresdner Sezession 1919–1925* (Munich, 1977), n.p.

26. "Der Proletensohn wurde gefördert, protegiert und gelangte in die 'Obere Gesellschaftsklasse,' die ihn aufnahm und ihn, den Begabten, zu ihrem Künstler machte . . . der bisher ungekannte Luxus . . . , die Gespräche über 'das neue Gedicht,' 'abstrakte Kunst,' 'Expressionismus,'—wankten den hochgehenden Sohn der ärmsten schuftenden Menschen . . . , sodass er inmitten der 'Bourgeois' in Kunst versank . . . Damit verriet der Proletensohn seinen Ursprung und wurde Künstler . . . In dieser Zeit ekstatischer Begeisterung brach der Krieg aus . . . Visionär sah er die gebückten Proleten der ganzen Welt im Kampf um ihre Existenz, sah er sie nun auch im Krieg, als Masse, als

Kanonenfutter: Da fühlte er sich wieder als ihresgleichen, als Kampfgenosse . . . Fühlt sich selbst als Verräter und rebellierte . . . Jeder Tag und jede Stunde entfernten ihn von den 'Oberen,' die er als Verbrecher sah und hasste; ebenso hasste wie das artistische Bluffen in der heutigen Kunst, das ihn nun quälte und als seine Mitschande erschien . . . Sein Wille war gegen den Krieg; glühend verweigerte er den Militärdienst . . . Er widersetzte sich dem Moloch Krieg und Militarismus, den Bezirkskommandeuren und Irrenärtzen . . . und ertrug mit fester Ruhe und starkem, zielbewusstem Willen Verhaftung und Irrenhausinternierung . . . Zu dieser Zeit existierte ein geheimer Bund, hauptsächlich bestehend aus Literaten. Man diskutierte nächtelang. Man machte anarchistische Pläne, revolutionäre Gedichte, reichte verbotene Schriften herum, wollte Militärdienstverweigerung unterstützen und Streiks vorbereiten helfen. Schliesslich endete die Sache literarisch, wurde zu schöner Geste, die leer blieb, wurde Snob. Das war der Bruch . . . Wie allgemein bekannt, wurde die Revolution verraten und blutig niedergehalten . . . Verbrechen gegen tapfere Revolutionäre deprimierten Pönnecke so sehr, dass er aufhörte zu arbeiten. Es war ihm klar: es gibt keine andere Aufgabe als Revolutionär zu sein . . . Wenn das Proletariat die politische Macht hat, die Macht, die es braucht, um sich zu entfalten, wird es aus seiner Tradition des Kampfes und des endlichen Sieges seine Kultur und seine Kunst schaffen: die Kunst des einfachen luxuslosen Menschen; die Kunst der Liebe, der menschlichen Beziehung." Conrad Felixmüller, "Der Prolet (Pönnecke)," *Die Aktion* 10, no. 23/24 (12 June 1920), reprinted in *Conrad Felixmüller: Werke und Dokumente*, 79–81.

27. A letter from Maria Müller to his aunt Julie, dated 11 May 1917, reports that he had been called up for military service. In *Conrad Felixmüller: Werke und Dokumente*, 62.

28. In a letter to Peter August Böckstiegel, probably dating from January 1918, Felixmüller wrote: "You know of my stay in the mental asylum from Hanna [his sister]." It is not clear whether this refers to his service as a hospital orderly or to actual confinement in an asylum for his refusal to perform military duty. Letter reprinted in Ibid., 66.

29. "Fern aller Verliebtheit in ekstatischer Verzückung wird der Kampf gegen Selbstbeharrung aufgenommen; keine Flucht mehr in ein anderes Land, das phantastisch-poetische Spiegelungen kultiviert, kein Sturm von Aktionen, die in giftiger Ressentimentspolemik versanden, sondern gemeinsamer Angriff, Forderung und Verheissung." *Menschen* 1, no. 1 (15 January 1918), 4. In the 15 June 1918 issue of *Menschen,* the editors attacked Pfemfert for refusing permission to publish several poems, despite the fact that *Menschen* provided him with free advertising for *Die Aktion.*

30. Pfemfert rejected almost anyone from *Die Aktion* who had ever supported the war effort, even if they had changed their position. Such was the case with Ludwig Meidner, whom Pfemfert suspected of creating a drawing which could be construed as supportive of the war.

31. "Alle würden sofort gesund und glücklich sein, wenn man ihnen sagte: 'Krieg ist vorbei' . . ." Conrad Felixmüller, "Militär-Krankenwärter Felixmül-

ler XI Arnsdorf," *Menschen* 1, no. 3 (15 May 1918), reprinted in Gerhart Söhn, ed., *Conrad Felixmüller: von ihm—über ihn* (Düsseldorf, 1977), 19–20.

32. Still, at times early in the year he worried about finances, even considering applying for a job as artistic director of the New Hamburg Kammerspiel. See a letter by Conrad Felixmüller to Peter August Böckstiegel, n.d. (before 4 April 1918), reprinted in Ibid., 82.

33. Letter by Conrad Felixmüller to Peter August Böckstiegel, 1918, reprinted in Ibid., 68. Felixmüller even moved to Wiesbaden with his new wife to be closer to his most important patron, returning to Dresden only when French troops advanced on the city.

34. " . . . es herrscht schlimmere Militär-Diktatur als vor dem 9. Nov. Die Helden der Revolution sitzen wieder in Festungen; die Arbeiter haben in Berlin und andren Städten bewaffnete Aufstände versucht, sind aber nach anfangs herrlichen Siegen (alle Zeitungen, Arsenals, Polizeibüros, Markthallen, Bahnhöfe) von Fronttruppen! niedergeknüppelt worden. Russische Genossen haben den Arbeitern Geld und Waffen geliefert, haben mitgekämpft—jetzt sind sie verhaftet, erschossen; auch Liebknecht und Rosa Luxemburg sind tot! Hier in Dresden gab es auch Maschinengewehrfeuer, auf Proletarier und Soldaten, die eine Demonstration machten; unsre Genossen sind verhaftet worden; 14 Tote, 60 Verwundete—ich kam mit dem Leben davon. Der Proletarier blutet wie nie zuvor—der Bürger freut sich." Letter by Conrad Felixmüller to Peter August Böckstiegel, 23 January 1919, reprinted in *Conrad Felixmüller: Werke und Dokumente,* 72.

35. *Neue Blätter* steered clear of politics in its pages during the war. Curiously, though, the *Dresdner Neueste Nachrichten* reported that four 1918 issues of the *Neue Blätter* were confiscated; *Menschen,* on the other hand, with its outright anti-war stance seems to have escaped trouble with the censors. See *Dresdner Neueste Nachrichten* 26, no. 335 (2. Ausgabe) (8 December 1918).

36. "Gründung einer sozialistischen Gruppe der geistigen Arbeiter," *Dresdner Neueste Nachrichten* 26, no. 319 (23 November 1918).

37. "Was ist der Sozialismus nicht? . . . Sozialismus ist nicht Aufhebung des Individualismus . . . Der Sozialismus ist nicht die Herrschaft einer Klasse. Der Sieg der Arbeiterklasse ist das Mittel (dessen Notwendigkeit wir gesehen haben), nicht aber das Ziel des Sozialismus. Der siegreiche Sozialismus bringt . . . die Auflösung allen Klassenbewusstseins in Gemeingefühl und zugleich Freiheitsgefühl . . . Der Sozialismus ist seinem Wesen nach nicht irreligiös, denn er fordert die Freiheit und Selbständigkeit der Religion." *Zweites Flugblatt der sozialistischen Gruppe der Geistesarbeiter,* Archiv für Bildende Kunst, Germanisches Nationalmuseum, Nürnberg, Felixmüller Papers, Teil 10, Karton 10.

38. Paul Adler, "Vom Sozialismus zur Utopie," *Neue Blätter für Kunst und Dichtung* 1, no. 8 (December 1918): 170–71.

39. "Die sozialistische Gruppe der Geistesarbeiter," *Menschen,* Montagsblatt, 1, no. 4 (20 January 1919): 3.

40. "Aus tiefer Versöhnung, dem Kampf folgend, steigt eine neue Schön-

heit empor." Hugo Zehder, "1919 Neue Blätter für Kunst und Dichtung," reprinted in Löffler and Bertonati, *Dresdner Sezession 1919–1925*, n.p.

41. Will Grohmann, "Dresdner Sezession 'Gruppe 1919,'" *Neue Blätter für Kunst und Dichtung* 1, no. 11 (March 1919): 257–60.

42. See *Dresdner Neueste Nachrichten* 27, no. 9 (11 January 1919) and no. 18 (19 January 1919). Richter may have purchased some of these works himself as an investment. The situation of the art market in Dresden remains unclear for lack of evidence.

43. "Ein Aufruf der russischen Künstler," *Neue Blätter für Kunst und Dichtung* 1, no. 10 (February 1919): 213–14.

44. "Während deutsche Künstlerräte ziemlich hilflos herumtappen, haben Russlands junge Künstler ihn [einen neuen Weg] entschlossen beschritten." Ibid.

45. Letter by Conrad Felixmüller to Otto Gussmann, 24 February 1919, reprinted in *Conrad Felixmüller: Werke und Dokumente*, 76.

46. Draft proposal, Archiv für bildende Kunst, Germanisches Nationalmuseum, Nürnberg, Felixmüller Papers, Teil 10, Karton no. 10.

47. "Der Künstlerrat ist gegründet worden, um die Ursachen der Missstände im Kunstleben des Landes aufzudecken, die Möglichkeiten für eine Besserung zu untersuchen, und die daraus folgenden Reformen den Behörden zur Einführung vorzuschlagen. Er setzt sich aus Künstlern aller Richtungen zusammen und kann schon heute als die Vertretung der gesamten Künstlerschaft gelten." "Dresdner Künstlerrat," n.d. (March 1919), Staatsarchiv Dresden, MdInnern, 17271, nos. 49–59.

48. "Der Sozialismus verlangt eine Begrenzung des Privateigentums an Kunstwerken. Das Interesse des Künstlers strebt zu einer Beteiligung an dem Wertzuwachs des verkauften Werkes, der sich im Laufe der Zeit im Kunsthandel ausdrückt." Ibid.

49. On the executive committee were: Böckstiegel, Dreher, Dülser, Felixmüller, Fischer, Godenschweg, Gross, Gussmann, Hettner, Jahn, Arthur Lange, Otto Lange, v. Ledebur, Mendelsohn, Poelzig, Schmitz, Schubert, Wrba, Zehder, and Werner. *Dresdner Neueste Nachrichten* 27, no. 70 (19 March 1919).

50. "Der Akademische Rat kann sich nicht verhehlen, dass die Neugestaltung der politischen Verhältnisse auch auf die Zuständigkeit und Zusammensetzung des Akademischen Rates selbst zurückwirken muss." Letter from the Academic Council to the Interior Ministry, 13 February 1919, Staatsarchiv Dresden, M.d.Innern, 17271, no. 19.

51. Ibid. See also Dr. Carl Pützfeld, "Wandel an der Kunstakademie," *Dresdner Neueste Nachrichten* 27, no. 78 (22 March 1919).

52. Ibid. The two academy professors would serve for six years, the others for three.

53. Letter by Conrad Felixmüller to Peter August Böckstiegel, 2 August 1917. Sonje Böckstiegel kindly provided me with a copy of this unpublished letter.

54. Letter by Otto Dix to Alfred Günther, n.d., reprinted in *Kunst im Aufbruch: Dresden 1918–1933*, 41.

55. See the minutes of the Lehrerversammlung, 25 February 1919 and 12 March 1919, Sitzungsprotokolle der Kunstakademie, Archiv der Hochschule für bildende Kunst, Dresden.

56. Letter from the Academic Council to the Interior Ministry, 23 April 1919, Staatsarchiv Dresden, M.d.Innern, 17271, no. 64.

57. On 22 March, for instance, the *Dresdner Neueste Nachrichten* warned: "Für die Kunst selbst ist noch nichts gewonnen, wenn man ihre akademische Verwaltung im Sinne der Zeitforderungen demokratisiert . . . Das Kunstschaffen ist . . . eine Angelegenheit nur der Besten und eine 'Demokratisierung' nach jener Richtung durchaus widersinnig." Dr. Carl Pützfeld, "Wandel an der Kunstakademie," *Dresdner Neueste Nachrichten* 27, no. 78 (22 March 1919).

58. Minutes of Lehrerversammlung, 26 March 1919, Sitzungsprotokolle der Kunstakademie, Archiv der Hochschule für bildende Kunst, Dresden.

59. Archiv für bildende Kunst, Germanisches Nationalmuseum, Nürnberg Felixmüller Papers, Teil 10, Karton no. 10. The first page of the draft contract in the Felixmüller papers is missing.

60. Announced in *Dresdner Neueste Nachrichten* 27, no. 85 (29 March 1919). In May part of the first exhibition of the Dresden Secession Group 1919 traveled to Berlin where it was shown in the Free Secession exhibition.

61. The following comments are based on the works illustrated in the catalog and works mentioned in the criticism. Unfortunately, the catalog does not list all the works shown at the exhibition.

62. One hundred copies of Hartmann's book were offered to the public for 10 marks, with ten luxury editions priced at 500 marks each.

63. "Alles in allem zeigt die Ausstellung, dass nicht der Sturm unserer Tage diese Gebilde als etwas . . . Neues ans Licht gebracht hat, sondern die Keime und Anfänge schon Jahre vor dem Kriege sich zu entfalten begannen." R. S., "Die Dresdner Sezession 'Gruppe 1919,'" *Dresdner Anzeiger* 189, no. 100 (6 April 1919).

64. "Sächsischer Kunstverein," *Dresdner Volkszeitung* 30, no. 33 (10 February 1919).

65. "Bildende Kunst," *Dresdner Volkszeitung* 30, no. 92 (23 April 1919): 6.

66. For the complicated chronology of *Menschen* and the confusing numbering of its issues, see Paul Raabe, *Die Zeitschriften und Sammlungen des literarischen Expressionismus* (Stuttgart, 1964), 70–73.

67. "O, welcher Freund der Menschen wäre nicht Sozialist?" *Menschen,* Montagsblatt, Werbeblatt, no. 11 (December 1918).

68. Schilling occasionally printed dissenting opinions. In an essay titled "The Spiritual Proletarian," Raoul Hausmann warned outright that "the spirit is misused as a new means for the stabilization of the . . . bourgeoisie" and called on artists to subordinate their interests to those of the proletariat. Raoul Hausmann, "Der geistige Proletarier," *Menschen,* Montagsblatt, 1, no. 8 (17 February 1919): 3.

69. Late in January Schilling resigned the editorship, claiming that the "sense of the revolution"—"spirit against un-spirit—was being betrayed by "tactics, parties, methods." Heinar Schilling, "Innere Notwendigkeit," *Menschen,* Montagsblatt, 1, no. 6 (3 February 1919). The Socialist Group may have experienced internal dissension in the wake of the government calling out troops against the demonstrators in January. After March the "Monday Paper" changed its name to the *Dresden Monday Newspaper* and was published by the Socialist Group until it ceased publication in June.

70. "In der Politik heisst dieser Idealismus *anationaler Sozialismus,* der *unbedingt* und *radikal* gefordert wird, *nicht nur im Geiste, sondern in der Tat!*" (Walter Rheiner), *Menschen* 2, no. 1 (12) (January 1919): 1.

71. On the founding of the A-National Socialist Party, see Kolinsky, *Engagierter Expressionismus,* 85–90. The precise relationship between the A-National Socialist Party, the International Communists, and the KPD remains unclear.

72. Felixmüller had done the woodcut in 1916 for *Die Aktion* from a photograph, but it was not published at the time.

73. "Karl Liebknecht und Rosa Luxemburg hielten als Einzige dieser vier Jahre die Fahne der Revolution hoch. Sie wurden heute durch die Massnahmen der 'revolutionären' Regierung ermordet. Die Bestie triumphiert über den Geist des Sozialismus! Die feile Journaille jubelt über 480 Leichen und 1000 Verwundete überzeugungstreuer Ideenkämpfer. MENSCHEN! Die Regierung ist des vielfachen Mordes schuldig! Die Menschenschlächter des Militarismus sind ihre gedungenen Schergen. Ehre und Ruhm ihren toten Gegnern! Wir neigen uns vor ihnen zur Erde. Klärt auf! Sprecht! Redet! Schreit!" *Menschen* 2, no. 2 (15) (15 January 1919): 1.

74. "Menschen, Proletarier, Arbeiter! Und ihr, die 'Geistes-Arbeiter-Räte'! Wie lange noch wollet ihr solches dulden?" Walter Rheiner, "Die Schande der Revolution," *Menschen* 2, no. 4 (22 (15 February 1919).

75. Walter Rheiner, "Erklärung der Schriftleitung," *Menschen* 2, no. 5 (25) (1 March 1919).

76. The other graphic contributions were from artists outside of Dresden, including George Kind, Walter O. Grimm, Eugen Gattermann, and Oskar Nerlinger.

77. Dörrer, *Die Herausbildung einer revolutionären Massenpartei in Ostsachsen bei besonderer Berücksichtigung der Vereinigung des linken Flügels der Unabhängigen Sozialdemokratischen Partei Deutschlands mit der Kommunistischen Partei Deutschlands (1914–1920),* 157.

78. Beutel, "Die Novemberrevolution von 1918 in Leipzig und die Politik der Leipziger USPD-Führung bis zum Einmarsch der konterrevolutionären Truppen des Generals Maercker am 12. Mai 1919," 397.

79. Dörrer, *Die Herausbildung einer revolutionären Massenpartei in Ostsachsen bei besonderer Berücksichtigung der Vereinigung des linken Flügels der Unabhängigen Sozialdemokratischen Partei Deutschlands mit der Kommunistischen Partei Deutschlands (1914 bis 1920),* 161.

80. Morgan, *The Socialist Left and the German Revolution,* 240.

81. Ibid.

82. Beutel, "Die Novemberrevolution von 1918 in Leipzig und die Politik der Leipziger USPD-Führung bis zum Einmarsch der konterrevolutionären Truppen des Generals Maercker am 12. Mai 1919," 409.

83. Letter from the Academic Council to the Interior Ministry, Staatsarchiv Dresden, MdInnern, 17271, no. 64.

84. "Niemand wird es bezweifeln, dass auf keinem Gebiete eine Überspannung des demokratischen Prinzipes weniger am Platz ist als auf dem der Kunst . . ." Letter from the Interior Ministry to the Council of Artists, 30 April 1919, Staatsarchiv Dresden, MdInnern, 17271, no. 66.

85. " . . . von einseitiger Herrschaft einzelner Richtungen . . ." Ibid.

86. Boris Kuschner, "Die Kunst der Gemeinschaft," *Neue Blätter für Kunst und Dichtung* 2, no. 1 (May 1919): 35.

87. "Durch den Willen der Mehrheit des Volkes und seiner parlamentarischen Vertreter sind Sie berufen worden, den Neubau der Republik Sachsen zu leiten. . . . Es ist anzunehmen, dass Sie die junge, fortschrittliche Kunst als einen Eckstein zum grossen Bau betrachten, den Sie zu errichten gedenken, denn Sie haben nicht die Absicht, altes und schon verbrauchtes Material hierfür zu verwenden. Der Widerwille aller . . . unter den Trägern der Neuen Kunst . . . gegen das bisher geübte System bürokratischer Bevormundung, ausgeübt von zum Urteilen Unberufenen, und gegen die durch keine sachlichen Gründe zu rechtfertigende Bevorzugung einer Kunst, welche nicht mehr vom Rhythmus der Gegenwart getragen wird, ist stark." Hugo Zehder, "Offenes Schreiben an das Ministerkollegium der Republik Sachsen," *Neue Blätter für Kunst und Dichtung* 2, no. 2 (June 1919): 56.

88. Zehder wrote in the August 1919 *Neue Blätter* that he had left the group for "principle and personal reasons." "Anmerkungen," *Neue Blätter für Kunst und Dichtung* 2, no. 5 (August 1919): 101.

89. "Die überreichen Vorschläge der anderenorts entstandenen Kunsträte . . . (auch die organisatorische Tätigkeit des Kommissariats für Kunst in Russland) sollten zugleich als Unterlage dienen." Zehder, "Offenes Schreiben an das Ministerkollegium der Republik Sachsen," *Neue Blätter für Kunst und Dichtung* 2, no. 2 (June 1919): 56.

90. Minutes of Lehrerversammlung, 2 July 1919, Sitzungsprotokolle der Kunstakademie, Archiv der Hochschule für bildende Kunst, Dresden. It is not clear why Pechstein declined the position. The position for which Kokoschka was proposed was not the same one; he was to replace Carl Bantzer. At the same time, the vote to appoint Dreher as professor was nine in favor, one abstention. Kokoschka's salary was 4,800 marks, with a 1,824-mark cost-of-living bonus, and a housing subsidy of 540 marks. He received the largest and best studio space.

91. Kokoschka had tried through influential friends since at least 1917 to be appointed to the Dresden academy and had asked Kurt Wolff during the war to intercede on his behalf with the royal family to secure a position for him in

Darmstadt. See a letter from Oskar Kokoschka to Kurt Wolff, 27 November 1917, Kurt Wolff Papers, Beinecke Library, Yale University.

92. "Seine Kunst und Persönlichkeit wurzeln in dem, was man . . . 'modern' nennt, im problematischen. Aufs äusserste sensitiv und spontan in der Technik, exklusiv in der Geschmacksrichtung, ist seine Kunst freilich nicht jedermann zugänglich. Sie enthält aber in ihrer merkwürdigen zusammengesetzten Art, in ihrem geistreichen und glänzenden Kolorismus, ihrer seltsamen mystischen Versonnenheit Werte, welche den Lehrlingen in dieser Form fehlen, und welche eine notwendige und wertvolle Ergänzung der übrigen Lehrkräfte bilden." Letter Lehrerversammlung to the Minister of the Interior, Professor Richard Dreher, Personalakte, 1919, Archiv der Hochschule für bildende Kunst, Dresden.

93. "Auf diesen Bilder sah man eine Reihe Menschen, mit aufreizender Zähigkeit immer wieder von neuem gemalt, deren Ausdruck irgendeine geheimnisvolle Beziehung mit denen zu verbinden schien, die auf der Strasse riefen; es war als ob eine Bewegung von den Köpfen und Händen der Leinwand zu den grossen Plätzen ausging, wo sich das Schauspiel der Welt erfüllte . . . Denn die Gesichter, die in der Schreckenskammer eingesperrt waren, rennen heute auf den Strassen herum!" Walter Hasenclever "Oskar Kokoschka," *Menschen*. Montagsblatt 1, no. 3 (19 January 1919): 2.

94. For instance, when the expressionist journal *Die Sichel* attacked the conservative *Fränkische Kurier* for calling a Kokoschka drawing "the height of idiocy," a court proceeding was initiated by the Nürnberg newspaper. See *Vorwärts* 37, no. 63 (4 February 1920).

95. Dr. Carl Pützfeld, "Wandel an der Kunstakademie," *Dresdner Neueste Nachrichten* 27, no. 78 (22 March 1919).

96. A poster in the collection of the Museum of Modern Art in New York titled "Nieder mit dem Bolschewismus" was probably done by Kokoschka.

97. See Dr. Carl Pützfeld "Neue Kunst in deutschen Museen," *Dresdner Neueste Nachrichten* 27, no. 203 (31 July 1919). The museum also owned a quasi-expressionist work by Erbsloh.

98. See undated statement written by Segall for the Dresdner Arbeiter-Kunst-Gemeinschaft in Löffler and Bertonati, *Dresdner Sezession 1919–1925*, n.p.

99. "Einige Museumsdirektoren, die bis jetzt der neuen Kunst sehr wenig oder gar kein Interesse entgegengebracht haben, kaufen zur Zeit moderne Bilder. Kommt das Verständnis für die neue Kunst so plötzlich? Wir glauben, es wird nur äusserlich die Mode mitgemacht und irgendwelches persönliche Gefühl kommt als Wertung nicht in Frage." Conrad Felixmüller and Otto Lange, "Zur Umgestaltung der Dresdner Galerie," *Dresdner Neueste Nachrichten* 27 (26 July 1919), reprinted in *Conrad Felixmüller: Werke und Dokumente*, 78.

100. " . . . dass das Volk . . . die abfälligsten . . . Urteile über gewisse pathologische Auswüchse und kindliche Rückfallserscheinungen der modernsten und revolutionärsten Kunst fällt." Dr. Wilhelm Junius, "Zur Umgestal-

tung der modernen Galerie Dresdens," *Dresdner Nachrichten* 63, no. 205 (27 July 1919).

101. *Sachsen: Kultur und Arbeit des sächsischen Landes* (Berlin, 1928), 143.

102. "Neuerwerbungen für die Dresdner Gemäldegalerie," *Dresdner Anzeiger* 189 (8 August 1919).

103. See *Dresdner Nachrichten* 63, no. 207 (29 July 1919) and *Dresdner Anzeiger* 189 (30 July 1919).

104. *Sachsen: Kultur und Arbeit des sächsischen Landes*, 70.

105. Heinar Schilling, "Sozialisierungsgesetze," *Menschen* 2, no. 10 (September 1919), quoted in Wolfram Göbel, "Sozialisierungstendenzen expressionistischer Verlage nach dem ersten Weltkrieg," *Internationales Archiv für Sozialgeschichte der deutschen Literatur* 1 (1976): 198. The socialization was announced only in the September issue.

106. "Die Kunst ist vorhanden nicht für, sondern gegen die Gesellschaft." Paul Nicolaus Steiner, "Über Genie und Gesellschaft," *Menschen* 2, no. 5 (46/49) (6 and 13 July 1919): 6.

107. "Die Mehrheit hat niemals das Recht auf ihrer Seite." Will Erich Peuckert, "Mehrheit und Spartakus," *Menschen* 2, no. 5 (46/49) (6 and 13 July 1919): 7.

108. " . . . die Schuld müsse zum grössten Teil dem pp. Autor zugemessen werden, der mit solchen Bohemelehren die Gesellschaft unterwühle und alle Grundfesten des Staates ins Wanken bringe." Ibid.

109. "Solange noch Menschen in Taylorsysteme gespannt sind, die Verhältnisse also nicht geändert, kann von einer Änderung des Menschen nicht gesprochen werden . . . Denn solange Interessen nicht befriedigt sind, bleibt jedes Ideal Geschwätz . . . Wo wirtschaftliche Voraussetzungen nicht erfüllt sind, bleibt jede andere Möglichkeit abgeschnitten." Felix Stiemer, "Grenzbestimmung," *Menschen* 2, no. 5 (46/49) (6 and 13 July 1919): 9. The same article was published in the Munich art journal *Der Weg* 1, no. 6 (July 1919): 6, which, by that time, was being published in Berlin.

110. Other writers loosely associated with *Menschen* and the Secession Group 1919 also questioned the fundamental premises of a "spiritual" revolution in July. For instance, the Dresden playwright Friedrich Wolf, a contributor to *Menschen* and a friend of Felixmüller's, in the July 1919 issue of *Die rote Erde* complained that all that had occurred since the revolution was endless talk and that belief in the brotherhood of all men, which stood as the basis of so many of the presuppositions of the artists' and intellectuals' councils, had in no way proved itself valid. See Friedrich Wolf, "Präludium zu den nächstkommenden Tagen," *Die rote Erde* 1, no. 2 (July 1919): 59.

111. "Jahrzehntelang habt ihr geschaffen, mitgeholfen an der sehr späten Empörung, gegrollt, gerufen, zusammengeschlagen und nun?" Walther Georg Hartmann, "Revolution, ihr Künstler und Kameraden!!" *Menschen* 2, no. 5 (46/49) (6 and 13 July 1919): 10.

112. "Auf den Thronen . . . in unserem Lande sitzen immer noch die ge-

schwollenen Prinzen und betrügen das gehorsame Volk mit ihren Geist-Atrappen, ihrem Kunst-Schwindel, ihren Patronaten-Gesten. Jetzt ist es Zeit, mit allem treuherzigen Betrug aufzuräumen, allen verbindlichen Lügnern den Garaus zu geben . . . Nieder die Fälscher, die in der Pose des Geistes den Geist verraten!" Ibid., 10–11.

113. "Sollen die, die Gold für unsre Arbeit erhalten, uns Pfennige vorwerfen?" Ibid., 11.

114. "Seine Sprache ist gegen, seine Form ist über unserer Zeit . . . Zwei seiner nackten Menschen treten den elenden lächerlichen Ballast unserer jahrhundertealten 'Kultur': die Ästhetik = tot. Bei ihm gibt es nichts 'ästhetisch-schönes' . . . Rücksichtslos hat Schmidt-Rottluff alle Systeme, die uns umgeben, auf uns sitzen, zerreiben, aussagen, niederdrücken, blind, tot machen—niedergetreten . . ." Conrad Felixmüller, "Schmidt-Rottluff," *Menschen* 2, no. 5 (46/49) (6 and 13 July 1919): 11.

115. "Schmidt-Rottluff ist die Manifestation unseres Wollens und Zieles: Befreiung vom Sklavenlos, den lebendigen Menschen—das göttliche Wesen der Weltschöpfung—für die Intensität seines Leibes und Geistes in Freiheit." Ibid.

116. Two 1919 lithographic portraits of Pfemfert and his wife by Felixmüller date from this stay in Dresden. See Gerhard Söhn, ed., *Conrad Felixmüller: Das Graphische Werk 1912–1974* (Düsseldorf, 1975), nos. 195 and 196, p. 88. Felixmüller did not earn anything from the graphics for Pfemfert; Pfemfert did not pay artists for their contributions and kept the originals. See Peter Günther, "Bemerkungen zum 'jungen Felixmüller,'" in *Conrad Felixmüller: Werke und Dokumente*, 12.

117. These are the words of von der Heydt's biographer, who described the Baron's enlightened art patronage in a 1919 book. Karl Georg Heise, *Die Sammlung des Freiherrn August von der Heydt* (Munich, 1919), xiv.

118. Letter by Dr. Hans Koch to Conrad Felixmüller, 10 July 1919, reprinted in *Conrad Felixmüller: Werke und Dokumente,* 79–80.

119. " . . . bestimmt von der Geist-Ära unserer Zeit . . . : Schnelligkeit, Mechanik; Politik, Religiosität; Luxus, Krieg; unser Krieg; unsere Schnellbahnen, Aeroplans, Autos, Lazarette, Strassenkämpfe—die Revolution des Menschen . . . Nicht das Individuum—sondern sein nächstes, die Masse. Die Kunst der Masse, für sie, als Produkt der Masse vom Mensch-Künstler, dem Massenträger, der Aller Lust und Qual spürt als seine Lust und Qual . . ." Conrad Felixmüller, "Künstlerische Gestaltung," *Das Kestnerbuch* (Hannover, 1919), reprinted in Söhn, *Conrad Felixmüller—von ihm—über ihn,* 32–33.

120. See *Münchner Neueste Nachrichten* 72 (27 March 1919).

121. Feininger was solicited in May by Lasar Segall to participate in the exhibition. When he responded that he had no new work ready to show, Segall convinced him to send one of his older works. It arrived only after the opening of the exhibition. See a letter by Lasar Segall to Lyonel Feininger on the stationery of the Richter gallery, 21 May 1919, Harvard University, Feininger Papers, bMs Ger 146 (1373); see also *Dresdner Neueste Nachrichten* 27, no. 174

(29 June 1919). Other "guests" participating in the show were Achmann (Regensburg), Bechstein (Munich), Burchartz (Hannover), Fabry (Wiesbaden), Gleichmann (Erfurt), Grosz (Berlin), Lohse (Dresden), Bierbach (Dresden), Delavilla (Frankfurt), Spiess (Dresden), Schwitters (Hannover), Glatter (Dresden) and Godenschweg (Dresden). See *Ausstellung Gruppe 1919 mit Gästen*, catalog of the second exhibition of the Dresden Secession Group 1919 (Dresden, 1919), n.p.

122. "Lasst ihr euch nicht mehr irre machen durch das köstliche Spiel der schönen Form." Rudolf Probst, *Ausstellung Gruppe 1919 mit Gasten*, catalog of the second exhibition of the Dresden Secession Group 1919 (Dresden, 1919), n.p.

123. "Jetzt . . . scheint alles Gewesene radikal auseinander gesprengt—dazwischen klafft der entsetzliche Abgrund, in dem alle vorige Geltung rettungslos versunken ist. Das Dasein selbst ist aufgerissen wie in Pubertät. Spürt ihr das Werden einer neuen Zeit nicht alle im eigenen Blut? Ein neues Menschheitsbewusstsein kämpft sich hervor." Ibid.

124. "Dresdner Sezession Gruppe 1919," *Dresdner Anzeiger* 189, no. 266 (8 July 1919).

125. Dr. Carl Pützfeld, "Ausstellung der Gruppe 1919," *Dresdner Neueste Nachrichten* 27, no. 186 (12 July 1919).

126. Ibid.

127. "Das ist zumeist noch alles so ungeklärt in der Auffassung und so gesucht und gequält in der Darstellung . . . , dass ein tieferes Versenken ganz unmöglich wird." "mm" (Menzer), "Bildende Kunst," *Dresdner Volkszeitung* 30, no. 152a (6 July 1919).

128. "Dresdner Sezession Gruppe 1919," *Dresdner Anzeiger* 189, no. 266 (8 July 1919).

129. Dr. Carl Pützfeld, "Ausstellung der Gruppe 1919," *Dresdner Neueste Nachrichten* 27, no. 186 (12 July 1919).

130. " . . . Otto Dix (verfällt) plötzlich darauf, statt bunter Splitter zur Abwechselung wirklich Blasen zu malen, sphärische Gallerte gedunsener Leiber, die rot oder blau glühen und von Sternen umtanzt werden. Das ist ein ganz willkürlicher, im einzelnen kindisch spielend durchgeführter Malerscherz, der niemanden von seiner inneren Notwendigkeit überzeugen kann. Solche Atelierwitze schädigen den Ruf der neuen Kunst." F. Z., "Dresdner Sezession," *Dresdner Nachrichten* 63, no. 204 (26 July 1919).

131. Dr. Carl Pützfeld, "Ausstellung der Gruppe 1919," *Dresdner Neueste Nachrichten* 27, no. 186 (12 July 1919).

132. Claus Baumann, *Kurt Günther* (Berlin, 1977), 7. Other Dresden artists in the Dada circle were Kurt Günther, Otto Griebel, and Sergius Winckelmann.

133. Dr. Carl Pützfeld, "Ausstellung der Gruppe 1919," *Dresdner Neueste Nachrichten* 27, no. 186 (12 July 1919).

134. Letter by Lyonel Feininger to Julia Feininger, 25 September 1919, reprinted in Ness, *Lyonel Feininger*, 111.

135. Rudolf Herbert Kämmerer, "Dresdner Sommerausstellungen," *Die junge Kunst* 1, no. 6 (August 1919): 11–12.

136. Posse, Introduction, *Künstler-Vereinigung, Dresden,* catalog of the summer exhibition of the Künstler-Vereinigung, Dresden (Dresden, 1919), n.p.

137. Dr. Carl Pützfeld, "Künstler-Vereinigung Dresden," *Dresdner Neueste Nachrichten* 27, no. 182 (6 July 1919).

138. See "Künstlervereinigung Dresden," *Dresdner Neueste Nachrichten* 27, no. 215 (10 August 1919).

139. Morgan, *The Socialist Left and the German Revolution,* 270.

140. "'Wie male ich expressionistisch?' Diese Frage der Unzulänglichen und Zuspätkommenden, welchen heute das zweifelhafte Glück zuteil wird, aus der Verbürgerlichung einer radikalen Kunstbewegung Kapital zu schlagen, hat sich Otto Dix niemals gestellt. . . . Natürlich fiel es Dix nicht ein, den Ruf zur Freiheit als einen neuen Befehl zum Marsch in Reih' und Glied aufzufassen, als Erlaubnis, mit dem grossen Tross der Umlerner die Revolution ordnungsgemäss zu vollziehen. Sein prachtvolles Temperament lässt sich nicht zu einem Spaziergängerschritt einladen, der allerlei Familienfreunde, Stammtischbedenken und die berühmten 'ewigen Ideale' und 'heiligsten Güter' als guten Ballast im Rucksack mit sich führt. Er ist ein Indianer, ein Sioux-Häuptling. Immer auf dem Kriegspfad. Wie eine Axt schwingt er den Pinsel und jeder Hieb ist ein Farbenschrei." H(ugo) Z(ehder), "Otto Dix," *Neue Blätter für Kunst und Dichtung* 2, no. 6 (September 1919): 119.

141. ". . . [werden auch] Predigten [gehalten] über neues Weltbewusstsein, expressionistische Religiosität und den kosmischen Revolutionär, nicht ohne schmeichelhafte Beziehungen zu einer Vergangenheit, die sich von der Gegenwart am vorteilhaftsten dadurch unterschied, dass sie zu ihrer Selbstbehauptung keiner erdachten Beziehungen bedurften." Ibid., 120.

142. Carl Emil Uphoff, "Kunst, Künstler, Sozialismus," *Der Cicerone* 11, no. 5 (1919): 125.

143. "Und zwar deshalb nicht, weil der Staat nichts mehr und nichts weniger ist als eine Entgleisung des Menschen vom Wege zur vollendeten, weltumfassenden Persönlichkeit auf dem Weg zum unpersönlichen Herdenwesen." Carl Emil Uphoff, "Kunst, Künstler und Staat," *Der Cicerone* 11, no. 9 (1919): 364.

144. The precise date of the *Menschen* issue on the Secession Group 1919 is unclear, since the special issues were often undated. The special issue which preceded it by two (no. 6) was dated 20 and 27 July, that which followed it (no. 9) was dated 14 September; therefore, it was most likely published either in late August or early September.

145. "Expressionismus—für viele nur Stilzwang der Zeit, Erlebnis aus dritter Hand und darum Ästhetik. Selten war ein Wort so rasch diskrediert. Nun fragt der Chor: wo ist die Ekstase, die Vision, die Geistigkeit, wo bleibt das heimliche Wunder? . . . Was geht mich der Geist an? Dann lieber Brot. Gewiss, dann lieber Brot. Denken wir nicht an die Macher, nicht an das Wort. Schaut und prüft. Um weniger Gerechter willen durften die andern weiterle-

ben." Will Grohmann, "Sonderheft von Graphik der Gruppe 1919 Dresden," *Menschen* 2, no. 8 (62/65), n.d.

146. See, for example, the summary of his speech to the Sächsischer Künstlerhilfsbund in *Dresdner Nachrichten* 63, no. 179 (1 July 1919).

147. Göbel, "Sozialisierungstendenzen expressionistischer Verlage nach dem ersten Weltkrieg," 198. See also Kolinsky, *Engagierter Expressionismus,* 114f.

148. *Menschen* 3, no. 1 (87/91) (January 1920): 64 and 70. Schilling later became a National Socialist sympathizer.

149. ". . . lehnte Otto Lange ab: er sei gewerkschaftlich organisiert und Gegner der KPD. Otto Schubert desgleichen—er habe fünf Jahre an der Front gelegen—nun wolle er Ruhe haben. Heckrott erklärte, er sei Offizier gewesen und die KPD käme nicht für ihn in Frage. Segall, er sei Jude und Pole, also Ausländer—deshalb könne er keiner deutschen Partei angehören. Dix—lassen Sie mich mit Ihrer dämlichen Politik in Ruhe—ich gehe lieber in den Puff. Nur Konstantin von Mitschke-Collande trat der KPD bei." Letter by Conrad Felixmüller to Dieter Gleisberg, Director of the Lindenau Museum, Altenburg, 18 January 1971, reprinted in *Conrad Felixmüller: Werke und Dokumente,* 75.

150. "Die Ausstellung wird kaum wesentlich werden . . . ich bin eben mit dieser Sezession als solcher nicht emphatisch verkoppelt. Mit Felixmüller ist sozusagen der Rahm abgeschöpft." Letter by Dr. Hans Koch to Conrad Felixmüller, 12 August 1919, reprinted in Ibid., 79.

151. P. F. Schmidt, review of the third exhibition of the Dresden Secession Group, reprinted in Löffler and Bertonati, eds., *Dresdner Sezession 1919–1925,* n.p. Loffler and Bertonati give no indication where the review was published.

152. The academy awarded prizes to Lange, Schubert, Böckstiegel, Voll, and Heckrott in 1920. Minutes of the Lehrerversammlung, 12–13 March 1920, Sitzungsprotokolle der Kunstakademie, Archiv der Hochschule für bildende Kunst, Dresden.

Chapter 4. Munich

1. Karl-Ludwig Ay, ed., *Appelle einer Revolution: Dokumente aus Bayern zum Jahr 1918/1919* (Munich, 1968), 16.

2. Willy Albrecht, "Das Ende des monarchisch-konstitutionellen Regierungssystems in Bayern," in *Bayern im Umbruch* (Munich, 1969), 287.

3. Heinrich Hillmayr, "München und die Revolution von 1918/19," in *Bayern im Umbruch,* 460.

4. The provincial Diet and the King tried to preempt the revolution with a 2 November 1918 agreement introducing the long-demanded parliamentary system and proportional voting in Bavaria. The Social Democrats supported this effort before 7 November.

5. Albrecht, "Das Ende des monarchisch-konstitutionellen Regierungssystems in Bayern," 285.

6. Hillmayr, "München und die Revolution von 1918/19," 478.

7. *Münchner Neueste Nachrichten* 71 (20 November 1918). The groups included the Wirtschaftsverband bildender Künstler, Bund zeichnender Künstler, Die Juryfreien, Illustratorenverband, Künstlergenossenschaft, Künstlerinnenverein, Luitpoldgruppe, Radierverein, Sezession, and the Münchner Bund.

8. The leaders of the Group of 100 were Joseph Eberz, Edwin Scharff, Max Unold, and Richard Seewald, all members of the New Secession. It claimed to represent the "young, energetic art of the future." See *Münchner Neueste Nachrichten* 72 (13 February 1919).

9. "Die Kunstpflege des Volksstaats, dem mit dem Zusammenbruch des alten Systems . . . eine Reihe wichtiger Aufgaben zufallen, behält als ihr Ziel im Auge, dass die Kunst nicht Luxus- und Ausnahmezustand sein darf, dass sie vielmehr das ganze Volk und das tägliche Leben durchdringen, nicht einzelnen, sondern allen erreichbar sein soll, und dass ihre höchsten Leistungen . . . der Allgemeinheit gehören." *Münchner Neueste Nachrichten* 72 (22 November 1919).

10. "Unser klassisches Zeitalter flüchtete aus dem Reich der unmöglichen Politik in das Reich des Schönen. Dass Freiheit nur im Reich des Schönen gedeihen könnte und nicht in der Welt, war ein Dogma verzweifelter Resignation. In der heutigen Zeit und in der Zukunft scheint es mir, als ob diese Flucht in das Reich des Schönen nicht mehr notwendig sein sollte, dass die Kunst nicht mehr ein Asyl für Verzweifelte am Leben sein soll, sondern dass das Leben selbst ein Kunstwerk sein müsste und der Staat das höchste Kunstwerk." Kurt Eisner, "Die Stellung der revolutionären Regierung zur Kunst und zu den Künstlern," in Kurt Eisner, *Sozialismus als Aktion. Ausgewählte Aufsätze und Reden* (Frankfurt am Main, 1975), 114.

11. Ibid., 118.

12. "Die Künstlerschaft muss aus ihrer unpolitischen Haltung herauskommen. Wenn Forderungen der Kunst und der Künstlerschaft volkstümlich werden und im Volkswillen Ausdruck finden sollen, muss die Künstlerschaft an der gesamten politischen Arbeit aktiven Anteil nehmen. Manche von uns, vielleicht die meisten, werden sich sträuben, ein so wenig anreizendes Gebiet zu betreten, allein es geht nicht anders. . . . Es müssen Künstler ins Parlament, aber nicht nur, um bei den seltenen Kunstdebatten sachverständig Stellung zu nehmen, sondern um sich an der ganzen politischen Arbeit mitzubeteiligen . . ." *Satzungen des Rates der bildenden Künstler Münchens*, BHStA MA 92225.

13. Dr. Hans von Kunstrat, "Kunst und Revolution," *Bayerischer Kurier* 62, no. 365 (31 December 1918); also 63, nos. 1–2 (1–2 January 1919) and no. 10 (10 January 1919).

14. Stölzl, *Die Zwanziger Jahre in München*, 141.

15. William Bischoff, "Artists, Intellectuals and Revolution: Munich 1918–1919," Unpublished Doctoral Dissertation (Harvard University, 1970), 155.

16. See *Münchner Neueste Nachrichten* 72 (24 March 1919).

17. Winfried Nerdinger, "Fatale Kontinuität: Akademiegeschichte von den

zwanziger bis zu den fünfziger Jahren," in Zacharias, *Tradition und Widerspruch: 175 Jahre Kunstakademie München*, 179.

18. *Münchner Neueste Nachrichten* 72 (1 April 1919).

19. "Ich komme nun zu . . . [den] intensivsten Gegnern der Akademie . . . , ich meine die Vertreter der allerjüngsten Richtung, die ich hier der Bequemlichkeit halber als *Expressionisten* oder *Futuristen* bezeichnen will. . . . Logischerweise müssten sie jegliche Art von Lehranstalt des Lernenden zum Adepten ablehnen, die für sie hauptsächlich mit der Befruchtung seiner Phantasie und mit einer allgemein ästhetischen Würdigung seiner Arbeiten oder mit kunstphilosphischem Gedankenaustausch erledigt ist, kann diese Art von Erziehung mit viel geringeren Kosten auf einem Spaziergang oder in einer traulichen Plauderstunde erledigt werden. . . .

"[So gut ich es verstehe,] . . . so würde man sich doch eine schwere Verantwortung aufbürden, . . . wenn man . . . in künstlerischen Dingen äussere Umstände wie z.B.—die momentane Verteilung der politischen Machtfaktoren—als 'Zwangsmittel' für Erreichung künstlerischen Zwecke heranziehen würde . . ." Archiv für Bildende Kunst, Germanisches Nationalmuseum, Nürnberg, ZR ABK 816, Riemerschmid Papers, B197.

20. "Uns bleibt nur eines: auf der Wacht sein und an den Geist glauben. Denn das ist unser Schicksal." Renatus Kuno, "Saturnalien des Krieges," *Münchner Blätter für Dichtung und Graphik* 1, no. 1 (January 1919): 6.

21. "Zuerst verlas der jüdisch-polnische Expressionist Stückgold ein doktrinär-fanatisches Glaubensbekenntnis voll schwerer, dunkler, mythologischer Worte . . . [Die Ausführung von einem Maler], der dem Futurismus sehr nahesteht [sagte]: . . . Der Künstlerrat entspreche nicht der neuen Zeit . . . Die Betitelten und Beamteten dürften nichts mehr mitzureden haben . . . Ein drittes Referat von Bildhauer Pilartz, reichlich durchtränkt von politisch-revolutionären Grundanschauungen . . . machte den 'Hofkünstlern' heftige Vorwürfe, die sich nicht in die neue Regierung vordrängen dürften." *Bayerischer Kurier* 62, nos. 357–58 (24–25 December 1918).

22. After the January elections Stückgold and Pilartz, along with Josef Eberz and Fritz Schaefler, unsuccessfully attempted to orgnize a group called the Independents. It is unclear whether the name was chosen to indicate support for the USPD. Among those invited to join the group were: Davringhausen, Campendonk, Seehaus, Bloch, Lass, Laubscher, Laurent, Mauermayer, Kars, Kisling, Ruttmann, Wach, and Bechstein. Schaefler's address was given as the return address. Archiv für Bildende Kunst, Germanisches Nationalmuseum, Nürnberg, Felixmüller Papers, Teil 10, Karton no. 10.

23. The papers of Fritz Schaefler, art editor of *Der Weg*, were unavailable at the time of publication. They will be published in a forthcoming study on art and revolution in Munich by Justin Hoffmann. It is my hope that this study will clarify the operation of the journal, including the process of editorial decision making. At this point it is still difficult to judge whether seeming inconsistencies are a result of conflict in editorial policies or simply the rush to get issues to press.

24. "Unser Weg wird gegangen von jedem, der an den Menschen glaubt. Vielleicht ist dies allein revolutionäre Gesinnung: an den Menschen zu glauben. Unwesentlich ist es, Bürgern, Akademikern, Reaktionären, aber auch den Radikalen aus Klugheit, den antikapitalistischen Ökonomisten die Kappe abzureissen. . . . Es gibt einen Weg, und wir alle gingen ihn: den Weg vom einfachen Ich zum liebenden Ich." Otto Zareck, "Unser Weg," *Der Weg* 1, no. 1 (January 1919): 4.

25. "Würde man heute alle Mitglieder einer Klasse ausrotten, in einiger Zeit wäre die Lücke durch Zuwachs aus anderen Klassen ausgefüllt und wieder hergestellt. Bestehende Klassen sind aus der Art bestehender Menschen hervorgewachsen und begreiflich. Klassenvernichtung würde eine Wunde reissen, für die Heilung nur in annähernder Wiederherstellung vorherigen Zustands zu erwarten wäre.

"Ehe man die andere Gesellschaft errichtet, muss man den anderen Menschen haben, der sie zusammensetzt. Hier ist die Voraussetzung allen Gelingens, und Erfüllung muss umso heisser und fanatischer angestrebt werden, je menschlicher und tiefer Verständnis und Nachsicht gegenüber gegenwärtigem Siechtum sind." Eduard Trautner, "Glosse," *Der Weg* 1, no. 1 (January 1919): 6.

26. For details on Schaefler's early career, see *Fritz Schaefler: Ein unbekannter Expressionist*, exhibition catalog, Suermondt-Ludwig-Museum (Cologne, 1983), 52–62.

27. *Süddeutsche Freiheit* first appeared in November 1918 edited by Hans Wagenseil, a Schwabing writer. Klingelhöfer became editor on 23 December 1918. Klingelhöfer joined the SPD in November 1918 and switched to the USPD three months later. Bischoff, *Artists, Intellectuals and Revolution: Munich 1918–1919*, 202–7.

28. "Unser Ziel: Die nationale grossdeutsche Bundesrepublik. Der nationale sozialistische Volksstaat. Überwindung des imperialistischen Kapitalismus. Die nationale und internationale Werkgenossenschaft der Völker.

"Unser Weg: Die Überwindung des preussischen Machtzentralismus. Bekämpfung jedes Herrentums der Person und der Klassen. Erziehung aller zur politischen und sozialen Verantwortlichkeit. Pflege der internationalen Solidarität des Geistes." *Süddeutsche Freiheit* 1, no. 9 (13 January 1919).

29. "Sie fragen mich, ob es unbedingt notwendig sei, dass das Titelblatt der Süddeutschen Freiheit ein expressionistisches Bild, 'das keiner versteht,' zeigt. Ja, das ist notwendig. Denn aus demselben revolutionären Geist aus dem der Inhalt unserer Zeitung geboren wird, gehen diese Bilder hervor. Das Proletariat hatte bisher zu wenig Zeit sich um Dinge zu kümmern, die nicht unmittelbar mit seiner Existenzfrage zusammenhingen. Die Revolution hat hierfür Abhilfe geschaffen und nun ist das Proletariat verpflichtet, sich etwas mehr um Fragen zu kümmern, die ihn (*sic*) früher nicht interessierten. Das Proletariat soll sich mit der neuen Kunst befassen, denn auch sie ist Revolution.

"Die Künstler, die unsere Titelblätter entwerfen, entstammen meist dem Proletariat oder stehen ihm jedenfalls in ihrer Gesinnung nahe. . . . Und das

Proletariat ist verpflichtet, sich wenigstens zu bemühen, die neue Kunst zu verstehen. Ebenso wie es von der Bourgeoisie verlangt, dass sie die Revolution versteht." Staatsarchiv München, Stanw. Mue. I 2077, Gustav Klingelhöfer, 16 January 1919; quoted in Justin Hoffmann, "Der Aktionsausschuss revolutionärer Künstler Münchens," *München 1919. Bildende Kunst/Fotografie der Revolutions- und Rätezeit* (Munich, 1979), 57–58. Klingelhöfer erred when he assumed that artists such as Schaefler came from proletarian backgrounds: Schaefler's father, for example, was a tax collector.

30. "Neuerwachtes Interesse entdeckt das Proletariat . . . Oft nennen Angst (Sklavenhalterangst) und Misstrauen sich Menschenliebe . . . Tüchtigkeit wittert Geschäft (Proletariat = Betätigungsmöglichkeit, wenn Übersee verschlossen ist)." E. Trautner, "Glossen," *Der Weg* 1, no. 2 (February 1919): 4.

31. "Es ist an der Zeit, dass die Revolution eine Revolution, eine Reformation schaffe. Die Stunde schreit nach der Politik der Sache. Ein misslich Tun ist es, an die selbsttätige Kraft des Geistes zu glauben und vertrauen, dass Ausruf, Programm und Idee evolutionär siegen müssen. . . . Politiker des Geistes sind ein fruchtloser Begriff; die Diktatur . . . allein erzwingt wahre Politik. . . . Mag Einer stehen, in welchem Lager er will, unter dem stürmischen Zwang der Notwendigkeit entgeht er dem Sozialismus nicht." Kurt Bock, "Voran!" *Der Weg* 1, no. 2 (February 1919): 10.

32. See, for instance, Heinrich Mann's speech to the PRGA in *Münchner Neueste Nachrichten* 71 (1 December 1918).

33. BHStA, MA 92225.

34. Waggi Herz, "Heinrich Hoffmann und die Revolution—zur Genese faschistischer Fotografie," in *München 1919*, 148.

35. Ernst Toller, *Eine Jugend in Deutschland* (Reinbeck bei Hamburg, 1963), 94; Oskar Maria Graf, *Wir sind Gefangene* (Munich, 1927), 386.

36. Ulrich Linse, *Organisierter Anarchismus im Deutschen Kaiserreich von 1871* (Berlin, 1969), 300–301.

37. See the letter by Gustav Landauer to Leo Kestenberg, 13 December 1917, in Gustav Landauer, *Sein Lebensgang in Briefen*, vol. 2 (Frankfurt am Main, 1929), 201 and 326. Beside the edition of 250, it was also published in a cheaper edition for a working-class audience.

38. See the letter by Gustav Landauer to Hugo Warnstedt, 1 July 1916, Ibid., 153.

39. Charles B. Maurer, *Call to Revolution: The Mystical Anarchism of Gustav Landauer* (Detroit, 1971), 164.

40. "Die Unwandlung der Gesellschaft kann nur in Liebe, in Arbeit, in Stille kommen." Gustav Landauer, *Aufruf zum Sozialismus* (Frankfurt am Main, 1967), 50.

41. Linse, *Organisierter Anarchismus im Deutschen Kaiserreich von 1871*, 327.

42. Ibid., 366.

43. *Münchner Neueste Nachrichten* 72 (10 April 1919).

44. Letter by Bruno Taut to Karl Ernst Osthaus, 16 May 1919, Karl Ernst Osthaus Archive, Hagen, Kue 351/4.

45. "Das ist keine Pressefreiheit, was wir haben. Dagegen erkläre ich, wir sind in der Revolution, wir sind in der Gefahr, die Republik ist in Gefahr durch diese Stimmungsmache . . . mit Hilfe sogenannter öffentlicher Meinung bereiten sich immer wieder gegenrevolutionäre Putsche vor." Gustav Landauer, speech to the Provisional National Assembly, 30 December 1918, reprinted in Wolf Kalz, *Gustav Landauer: Kultursozialist und Anarchist* (Meisenheim am Glan, 1967), 75.

46. When the editors of the *Münchner Neueste Nachrichten* and the *Bayerischer Kurier* refused to submit to the censorship of the Central Council, the Central Council took over publication and named Titus Tautz, a member of the Action Committee, editor. See *Münchner Neueste Nachrichten* 72 (9 April 1919).

47. See the letter by Gustav Landauer to Hans Franck, 27 September 1918, in Landauer, *Sein Lebensgang in Briefen*, 262.

48. He had hoped Kollwitz would provide a portrait illustration of Shakespeare for a book he was planning in 1917. See the letter by Gustav Landauer to Adolf Neumann, 13 June 1917, Ibid., 183.

49. Letter by Gustav Landauer to August Hauschner, 26 December 1918, Ibid., 342.

50. Letter by Gustav Landauer to his daughters, 30 December 1918, Ibid., 344.

51. Only one letter survived confiscation during the suppression of the second council republic. See Ibid., 44.

52. Landauer was not the only member of the council government to promote expressionist art. Edgar Jaffe, for example, the minister of finance under Eisner, had become a patron of modern art before the war. See Martin Green, *The von Richthofen Sisters* (New York, 1974), 28 and 89.

53. Wach diary, written in the late 1920s and early 1930s, in the possession of Margarete Döppler, Braunau-am-Inn, Austria, n.p.

54. Letter by Titus Tautz to Justin Hoffmann, 12 October 1978, reported in Hoffmann, "Der Aktionsausschuss revolutionärer Künstler Münchens," 47.

55. "Ehe die politische Revolution war, war die Revolution der Kunst. Lange bevor das Ende des Weltkrieges dem Geist der neuen Zeit politisch die Bahn frei gemacht hat, war dieser Geist in der neuen Kunst lebendig geworden. Das ist es, was heute das werktätige Volk wissen muss, dass die jungen Künstler und die junge Kunst seine Bundesgenossen sind. Es ist der Geist der brüderlichen, der alles umfassenden Gemeinsamkeit, es ist der Geist der lebendigen Massenbewegung, der diese Kunst erzeugt hat, der ihre Formen gebiert und sie durchstrahlt. . . .

"Gerade weil die neue Kunst sich ihrem Geiste nach völlig der herrschenden Überlieferung entgegenstellte, ist auch ihre Form ein völlig Neues, ein Fremdes, das die Menschen noch seltsam anmutet, das die Vielen des Volkes, welche diese Kunst nicht haben wachsen sehen, noch nicht erkennen als das zu ihnen Gehörige. . . .

"Sie will dem werktätigen Volke zeigen, dass sie für es arbeitet und mit ihm eines Sinnes ist. Bald wird die Zeit da sein, wo jeder Volksgenosse fühlt: das ist meine Kunst, das ist die Kunst des Volkes. Habt ein wenig Geduld und ihr werdet diese Formen, die euch befremden, lieben . . . Die neue Kunst jubelt der Weltrevolution zu. Sie weiss, dass nun auch der Tag ihres eigenen Sieges gekommen ist." Ludwig Coellen, "Die neue Kunst," *Münchner Neueste Nachrichten* 72 (9 April 1919).

56. "Sie [die Kunst] hat keinen Zweck in sich, sie hat dem neuen Leben, das wahre Gemeinschaft sein soll, zu dienen, zu ihm auszurufen und anzufeuern. Sie hat die Menschen reif zu machen und ihnen das Gewissen und die reine Schönheit zu geben, die alle menschlichen Beziehungen von nun an lebendig bestimmen sollen.

"Endlich ist der Künstler an die Stelle gerückt, die ihm gebührt, in die Mitte und in den fruchtbaren Anschluss an . . . den sinnvollen Plan der allgemeinen Arbeit. . . . Nur der hat ein Recht, sich Künstler zu nennen, dessen Arbeit . . . notwendig und gut für den Menschen ist, um sich als Mensch zu fühlen, um seine menschliche Aufgabe zu begreifen und stärker und selbstgewisser zur Vollkommenheit aufzustreben.

"Kunst ist weder Luxus noch Vergnügen.

"Kunst ist Brot; der unterdrückte, leidende, endlich sich befreiende Mensch ist hungrig nach Wahrheit und Schönheit. Nur was diesen Hunger stillt, ist Kunst. Die Kunst ist allen Menschen zugänglich zu machen. Sie ist rein zu halten von den leeren, überflüssigen . . . und verseuchenden Erzeugnissen der alten Gesellschaft." Titus Tautz, "Die Kunst und das Proletariat," *Münchner Neueste Nachrichten* 72 (9 April 1919).

57. "Aber, dass künstlerische Erziehung etwas ist, was so notwendig ist wie Brot, muss jeder einsehen, der weiss, wie abhängig die endliche und wahrhafte Durchführung des sozialistischen Gedankens von einer grundlegenden Veränderung der menschlichen Psyche ist." Justus Bier, "Revolutionierung der künstlerischen Erziehung," *Münchner Neueste Nachrichten* 72 (11 April 1919).

58. ". . . Suchen nach eigenem Ausdruck kraftvoller Persönlichkeit, Kampf des Geistes gegen äussere Fessel nur scheinbarer Welt. . . . Dieser Kunst ethisches Ziel aber ist Erziehung zur Menschlichkeit." Hans Theodor Joel, "Zur neuen Kunst," *Münchner Neueste Nachrichten* 72 (12/13 April 1919).

59. ". . . es [ist] natürlich, dass diese Künstlergeneration, im Gegensatz zur vorhergehenden, die die Aussenwelt wie auf einem Instrument auf sich spielen liess, politisch werden musste—und zwar sozialistisch-revolutionär, dass das einzige expressionistisch-politische Programm ist mit dem Ziel, die Aussenwelt nach einem menschlich Innern zu gestalten, den Menschen zum Beherrscher und Ordner der Materie zu machen. . . . Ihrer [expressionistische Politik] grössten Künder [sind] Plato und Christus, die radikalen Förderer nicht des Zuständlich-Zufälligen, sondern des Geistig-Ewigen." Richard Fischer, "Expressionismus und Politik," *Münchner Neueste Nachrichten* 72 (12/13 April 1919).

60. "Aufklärende Vorträge über Neue Kunst," *Münchner Neueste Nachrichten* 72 (12 April 1919).

61. "Denn nur das neue Schaffen, das kurz vor der Welterschütterung entstanden ist, kann mit dem Rhythmus des neu sich bildenden Lebens im Einklang stehen." D. P. Sterenberg, "Aufruf der russischen fortschrittlichen bildenden Künstler an die deutschen Kollegen," *Münchner Neueste Nachrichten* 72 (9 April 1919).

62. "Mit der Ausrufung der baierischen Räterepublik wollen wir uns die Möglichkeit schaffen, unsere Pläne, die sich völlig mit den Euren decken, zu verwirklichen." Ibid. A list of signatories followed, the first public listing of the members of the Action Committee. Listed were: Heinrich Bachmaier, Max Bethke, Friedrich Burschell, W. Ludwig Coellen, Georg Kaiser, Otto Lerchenfeld, Wilhelm Petersen, Felix Stiemer, Titus Tautz, Alfred Wolfenstein, Walt Laurent, T. C. Pilartz, Hans Richter, Fritz Schaefler, Georg Schrimpf, Stanislaus Stückgold, and Aloys Wach.

63. Wilhelm Hausenstein, "Über Expressionismus in der Malerei," *Tribüne der Kunst und Zeit,* no. 2 (1919): 71–72. This text, published in 1919, was a reworked version of speeches to the *Deutsche Gesellschaft 1914* in March 1918 and the *Bund Deutscher Gelehrter und Künstler* in Berlin in September 1918.

64. Letter by Wilhelm Hausenstein to Herbert Schweitzer, 14 August 1946, quoted in O. K. Werckmeister, "Kairuan: Wilhelm Hausensteins Buch über Paul Klee," in Ernst-Gerhard Güse, ed., *Die Tunisreise: Klee, Macke, Moilliet* (Stuttgart, 1982): 80.

65. Staatsarchiv München, Staatsanwaltschaft München, no. 2242/II, Blatt 120, Exhibit in Toller's trial. I thank O. K. Werckmeister for providing me with a copy of this memorandum.

66. Wilhelm Hausenstein, "Kunst und Revolution," *Der Vorläufer: Sonderheft des Neuen Merkur* 3 (1919): 77–86; and *Ostern 1919* (Potsdam, 1919), 25–40. The essay was also published unchanged in Hausenstein's collected essays *Zeiten und Bilder* (Munich,1920), 25ff., and there dated "Ende 1918."

67. "Die Kunst kann entscheidende Bedeutung letzten Endes nur aus ihrer eigenen künstlerischen Tatsächlichkeit gewinnen. Der Weg der politischen Insinuation gibt der Kunst selbst keine Bürgschaft, und es ist gänzlich gleichgültig, ob dieser Weg von der Reaktion, vom Krieg oder von der Revolution ausgeht. Kunst beruht in sich, nicht in Verbindungen der Macht." Hausenstein, "Kunst und Revolution," in *Ostern 1919,* 28.

68. Zillibiller diary, quoted in Bischoff, *Artists, Intellectuals and Revolution: Munich 1918–1919,* 260.

69. Letter by Max Unold to Paul Klee, 11 April 1919 (Unold called on Klee to join the executive committee). I thank O. K. Werckmeister for sharing the contents of this letter with me.

70. The four were Urban, Mühlbauer, Püttner, and Scharff.

71. "Neuaufgabe der Münchner Kunstgewerbeschule," *Münchner Neueste Nachrichten* 72 (11 April 1919).

72. BHStA, MK 14344.

73. Hansen was listed in a 22 April 1919 protocol as a member of the Action

Committee and his essay in *Der Weg* suggests he was familiar with the Munich art scene.

74. "Euch ist Revolution und Kunst wie jeder Atemzug Eures dürftigen Lebens Konjunktur." Hans Hansen, "Revolutionäre Künstler," *Der Weg* 1, no. 4 (April 1919): 4.

75."Ihr möchtet Euch an ihm [the spirit of the revolution] hinaufschwingen, um womöglich aus königlichen Lakaien revolutionäre Minister zu werden." Ibid.

76. "Der Expressionismus—die revolutionäre Kunst, wie sie der bürgerliche Revolutionär begreift, ist die Revolutin auf der Palette und im Tintenfass. Das Herrliche und Beste an ihm ist, dass er zu nichts verpflichtet. Der Künstler kann als Künstler getrost Anarchist sein. Die anarchistische Kunst wird bezahlt. Es lässt sich leben mit ihr; sie dient dem Kapital und der Bourgeoisie wie zuvor." Ibid.

77. "Der Sozialismus, der sich verwirklicht, macht sofort alle schöpferischen Kräfte lebendig; in Ihrem Werke aber sehe ich, dass Sie auf wirtschaftlichem und geistigem Gebiet . . . sich nicht darauf verstehen. Diese Mitteilung bleibt von mir streng privat; es liegt mir fern, das schwere Werk der Verteidigung, das Sie führen, im geringsten zu stören. Aber ich beklage aufs schmerzlichste, dass es nur noch zum geringsten Teil mein Werk, ein Werk der Wärme und des Aufschwungs, der Kultur und der Wiedergeburt, ist, das jetzt verteidigt wird." Letter by Gustav Landauer to Aktionsausschuss, 16 April 1919, reprinted in Hansjörg Viesel, ed., *Literaten an der Wand: Die Münchner Räterepublik und die Schrifsteller* (Frankfurt am Main, 1980), 268.

78. "Der Aktionsausschuss revolutionärer Künstler erklärt hiermit, dass er allein als Vertreter der Künstlerschaft der Stadt München und ganz Baierns zu betrachten ist. Er stellt sich auf den Boden kommunistischer Prinzipien und erkennt die Diktatur des Proletariats als den wahren und einzigen Weg zur Verwirklichung der proletarischen Räterepublik und des Kommunismus an." 'Revolutionäre Künstler," *Mitteilungen des Vollzugsrats der Betriebs- und Soldatenräte* (15 April 1919), reprinted in Max Gerstl, *Die Münchner Räterepublik* (Munich, 1919), 63.

79. "Wir erklären: Wir sind nicht die 'Vertreter' der Münchner, der Bayerischen oder sonst irgendwelcher Künstler, die zu dem kapitalistischen Zeitalter gehören, wir sind die Vertreter und Bevollmächtigten einer Idee, und unser Ziel ist, an dem Aufbau der neuen Gemeinschaft und deren ideellen Entwicklung praktisch mitzuarbeiten." "Revolutionäre Künstler," *Mitteilungen des Vollzugsrat der Betriebs- und Soldatenräte* (16 April 1919), reprinted in Ibid., 64.

80. Hans Richter, "Vorwort," *XXIX- Kollektiv-Ausstellung Richter/Heckel,* Neue Galerie Hans Goltz (Munich, 1916). Around 1913 Richter had abandoned a realist style for cubist and expressionist influenced form and subject matter; it was these later works which dominated the Goltz gallery exhibition.

81. Hans Richter, "Ein Maler spricht zu den Malern," *Zeit-Echo* 3 (May 1917): 3–5.

82. Richard Sheppard, "Dada and Politics," *Journal of European Studies* 9, pt. 1/2, no. 33/34 (March/June 1979): 50.

83. Reported in a letter from Ferdinand Hardekopf to Olly Jacques, 19 April 1919, reprinted in Richard Sheppard, "Ferdinand Hardekopf and Dada," *Jahrbuch der deutschen Schiller-Gesellschaft*, no. 20 (1976): 144–45.

84. "Wir Künstler als Vertreter eines wesentlichen Teils der Gesamtkultur wollen uns 'mitten in die Dinge' hineinstellen und die Verantwortung für die kommende, ideelle Entwicklung im Staate mit übernehmen. . . . Wir verkünden, dass das künstlerische Bewegungsgesetz unserer Epoche in umfassender Formulierung bereits vorliegt. Die Geistigkeit einer abstrakten Kunst (siehe Ausführungsprogramm) bedeutet die ungeheure Erweiterung des freiheitlichen Gefühls des Menschen. Unser Glaubensziel ist die brüderliche Kunst: neue Sendung des Menschen in der Gemeinschaft. Die Kunst im Staat muss den Geist des gesamten Volkskörpers widerspiegeln. Kunst zwingt zur Eindeutigkeit, soll Fundament des neuen Mensch bilden, jedem einzelnen und keiner Klasse gehören." "Manifesto of the League of Radical Artists, Zurich," reprinted in Justin Hoffmann, "Hans Richter und die Münchner Räterepublik," *Hans Richter 1888–1976*, Akademie der Künste (Berlin, 1982), 22. Also published in the *Neue Züricher Zeitung* (Sechstes Blatt), no. 655 (4 May 1919).

85. *Hans Richter 1888–1976*, Akademie der Künste (Berlin, 1982), 56–57.

86. Minutes of the Action Committee meeting in Landtag building, 22 April 1919; a copy is in the Library of Congress, Washington, D.C., Rehse Collection, container no. 439.

87. Ibid.

88. It is not known whether Campendonk accepted. I have not been able to identify Holzer or Janes.

89. "Der Aktionsausschuss revolutionärer Künstler möge ganz über meine künstlerische Kraft verfügen. Dass ich mich dahin zugehörig betrachte ist ja selbstverständlich, da ich doch mehrere Jahre vor dem Krieg schon in der Art produzierte, die jetzt auf eine breitere öffentliche Basis gestellt werden soll. Mein Werk und meine sonstige künstlerische Kraft und Erkenntnis stehen zur Verfügung!" Letter by Paul Klee to Fritz Schaefler, 12 April 1919, reprinted in *Fritz Schaefler: Ein unbekannter Expressionist*, 19.

90. Paul Klee, *The Diaries of Paul Klee* (Berkeley, 1964), 406.

91. Hoffmann, "Hans Richter und die Münchner Räterepublik," 24.

92. Kehr, "Kunsterzieher an der Akademie," in Zacharias, *Tradition und Widerspruch: 175 Jahre Kunstakademie München*, 294.

93. *Münchner Post* 33, no. 158 (10 July 1919).

94. Hermann Esswein, art critic of the SPD *Münchner Post*, attended the meeting at which the action was supposedly taken and was later surprised by the outcome; he claimed the proposal, made by Richter and Pilartz, was never formally adopted and therefore invalid. Hermann Esswein, "Das Schicksal der Kunstgewerbeschule: Erklärung," *Münchner Post* 33, no. 106 (5 May 1919). (The article was written on 30 April but not published until 5 May.)

95. "Der weite Ruck nach links, die Kommunisten-Herrschaft, brachte nun

auch den radikalsten Richtungsflügel der zur Zeit in München debattierenden Künstlerschaft zum Zug und ich muss offen gestehen, der Wortführer der kommunistischen Künstlerkommission, wie ich verstand ein Herr Richter aus Zürich, hat mir besser gefallen als die oben beleuchtete Gruppe. Ein klarer Standpunkt, ein vernehmbares Ja oder Nein ist Goldes wert, und liegt auch noch kein Anlass vor, bestimmte Forderungen und Pläne des Herrn Richter, seines Gesinnungsfreundes H.C. Pillarz [*sic*] und ihrer Auftaggeber vor der Öffentlichkeit zu besprechen, so verdient doch die Hauptsache, in deren Namen die Herren gekommen sind, ein Wort der Aufklärung. Die Herren sprachen im Namen des Expressionismus, meldeten die Ansprüche der Neuen Kunst an und der von ihr ergriffenen jungen geistig-revolutionären Generation." Hermann Esswein, "Das Schicksal der Kunstgewerbeschule," *Münchner Post* 33, no. 99 (29 April 1919).

96. *Die Geistesarbeiter,* no. 7 (11 May 1919), quoted in William Bischoff, "The Action Committee of Revolutionary Artists in the Munich Revolution of 1918–1919," *Studies in Modern European History and Culture* 3 (1977): 25.

97. "Fidelis," "Gustav Landauers Kulturprogramm," *Das Forum* 4, no. 8 (May 1920): 579. "Fidelis" published what he claimed was Landauer's outline for the reorganization of education and the arts, along with his own commentary. The original manuscript by Landauer is in the Jewish National and University Library, Jerusalem, Arc. 432/113.

"Fidelis" may have been Alexander Strasser, a KPD member and the nephew of Franz Pfemfert, or Hans Bloch, who worked for a brief time in Landauer's office. Viesel, *Literaten an der Wand: Die Münchner Räterepublik und die Schriftsteller,* 808. He undoubtedly used a pseudonym to escape political persecution.

98. "Die neue Ära der Menschheitsgeschichte hat in den Monumenten und öffentlichen Gebäuden, die von jetzt ab errichtet werden, ihren Ausdruck zu finden. Bei Staatsaufträgen sind überall auch die jungen Künstler heranzuziehen; dies gilt für alle Künste. Malerei und Plastik sind von vornherein in die Architektur einzugliedern." "Gustav Landauers Entwurf zu seinem Kulturprogramm," Gustav Landauer Papers, Jewish National and University Library, Jerusalem, Arc. 432/113.

99. "Malerei und Plastik: Förderung der lebenden Künstler und modernen Richtungen durch Staatsankäufe. Errichtung eines Museums für moderne Kunst. Der Staat stellt Staatsgebäude für Ausstellungen zur Verfügung und sorgt für Wanderausstellungen." "Gustav Landauers Entwurf zu seinem Kulturprogramm," Jewish National and University Library, Jerusalem, Arc. 432/113.

100. "Fidelis'" text read: "Malerei und Plastik. Neugründung von Museen. Staatsankäufe. Staatsgebäude für Ausstellungen. Wanderausstellungen." "Fidelis," "Gustav Landauers Kulturprogramm," 582.

101. ". . . das prachtvolle Pferd des Colleoni oder eine Tierfigur eines 'impressionistischen' Bildhauers wie Gaul. Sie haften beide am Äusserlichen. Man möchte das Pferd des Colleoni besteigen, man möchte die Tierfigur von Gaul

streicheln. Ganz anders die eines Expressionisten, etwa eine solche von Marc. In seinen Pferden ist das 'Ur'-Pferd enthalten. Das ist nicht mehr ein beliebiges Pferd, sondern es ist schlechtweg *das* Pferd.

"Diese Beispiele mögen genügen. Sie genügen auch, um das Wesentliche zu erkennen. Jene haften am Figürlichen, diese kommen zum 'Kommunen,' zum 'Allgemeingültigen.' In jedem Punkt, in jeder Linie, in jeder Fläche und ebenso in jeder Farbe drückt sich das Ringen des neuen Künstlers aus. Das Figürliche kann dabei, wie bei Kandinsky, ganz schwinden. Nach geistig-religiöser Verinnerlichung strebt die Künstlerschaft und mit ihr die Masse, die nicht-satte, nicht bourgeoismässige Masse. . . . Die neue Kunst wird eine Proletarierkunst sein." Ibid., 586–87.

102. "Leviné lehnte das Programm ab, da es ihm zu sehr im hergebrachten, bürgerlichen zu haften schien . . ." Ibid. Despite this report, "Fidelis" blamed the rejection on the personality clash between Landauer and Leviné rather than any disagreement over principles.

103. Hoffmann, "Hans Richter und die Münchner Räterepublik," 22. Artists and writers outside the Action Committee were also arrested. The actress Tilla Durieux, for example, wife of Paul Cassirer, may have been briefly arrested for "bolshevik intrigue." (See telegram from Berlin requesting her release, Library of Congress, Washington, D.C., Rehse Collection, Eisner Police File, container no. 420, no. 294.) Even Rainer Maria Rilke was kept under surveillance because of his friendship with Toller and other literary figures involved in the first council republic. Richard Grunberger, *Red Rising in Bavaria* (London, 1973), 147.

104. On the arrest and release of Schrimpf, Achenbach, and Graf, see Viesel, ed., *Literaten an der Wand: Die Münchner Räterepublik und die Schriftsteller,* 116. On the arrest and release of Pilartz, see *Münchner Post* 33, no. 107 (8 May 1919).

105. Viesel, ed., *Literaten an der Wand: Die Münchner Räterepublik und die Schriftsteller,* 725–26.

106. StMue, SAM, I, 1915.

107. *Fritz Schaefler: Ein unbekannter Expressionist,* 9–10.

108. Statement by Fritz Schaefler, 12 July 1919, StAMue, SAM 1915, no. 37.

109. Wach diary, n.p.

110. Letter by Paul Klee to Lily Klee, 28 June 1919, in Paul Klee, *Briefe an die Familie,* II (Cologne, 1979), 957.

111. "Von einem Deutschen! Wehe Euch jüdischen Schweinehunden! Euch Spartakisten! Nichtskönner! Spekulanten! Hunde! Gesindel! Wehe Euch, die ihr das deutsche Vaterland und die deutsche Kunst ruiniert! . . . Dasselbe Gesindel wie Mühsam, Levien etc. und Konsorten. Kokoschka! Heckel! Kirchner! Eberz! Unold! Seewald! Dawringhausen! [*sic*]" *Der Weg* 1, no. 5 (May/June, 1919), 14.

112. "Dem Künstlerrat war bekannt, dass ein Aktionsausschuss revolutionärer Künstler sich gebildet hatte, der auf die Ausrufung der Räterepublik

wartete, um sofort mit radikalsten Massnahmen vorzugehen. Die Tendenz dieses Aktionsausschusses war orientiert nach dem Moskauer künstlerischen Programm, die Sozialisierung der Kunst sofort in die Wege zu leiten unter diktatorischer Führung der Kunstrichtung, die man unter dem Namen Expressionismus zusammenfasst." Hermann Urban, *Münchner Neueste Nachrichten* 72 (15 May 1919).

113. See *Münchner Neueste Nachrichten* 72 (17 May 1919).

114. "Ich gehöre überhaupt keiner politischen Partei an und verfolgte als Mitglied des revolutionären Künstlerrats rein künstlerische Ziele." T. C. Pilartz, "Erklärung," *Münchner Post* 33, no. 107 (8 May 1919). The purpose of the statement was clear when Esswein followed it with the words: "Nach der vorstehenden Erklärung dürfte also ein Anlass zur weiteren Verhaftung des Herrn Pilartz nicht vorliegen."

115. Mayer's essay may have been written before the military suppression of the council republic, in the wake of the suspension of the academy professors, and in response to Hansen's charges in *Der Weg*.

116. "Dabei ist es bemerkenswert, dass die meisten dieser Künstler als Menschen ganz auf dem Boden der jeweiligen Gesellschaftsordnung standen, korrekte, ja beinahe spiessige Bürger waren." August L. Mayer, "Revolution und Kunst," *Münchner Blätter für Dichtung und Graphik* 1, no. 4 (April 1919): 64. The issue was delayed because of the general strike.

117. Karl Konstantin Löwenstein, "Mord der Moderne," *Münchner Blätter für Dichtung und Graphik* 1, no. 10 (October 1919): 160.

118. "Ist der 16–30 jährige Metallarbeiter, welcher bis 1000 Mark im Monat verdient hat und in den Jahren 1917 und 1918 den Sekt aus Masskrügen trank . . . ein Proletarier? Ist ein Oberlandesgerichtsrat, der mit Frau und 4 Kindern von 1915–1919 sein kleines Vermögen verzehren musste, um seine Lieben nicht hungern zu lassen, ein Bourgeois?" Anonymous, "Heraus aus dem Gefängnis des Schlagworts und der Phrase," *Der Ararat* 1, no. 3 (19 May 1919).

119. "Aufruf der Unbeteiligten," *Münchner Neueste Nachrichten* 72 (9 May 1919).

120. "Der Weg zu diesem Tempel ist aber steil und steinig. Für Prozessionen und Völkerwanderungen ist er zu schmal. Offen aber für jeden, ob im Arbeiterkleid oder im Bratenrock. . . . Die Kunst [steht offen] zwar nicht für das Volk, aber für jeden aus dem Volke, der nicht aus Neugier, sondern aus dem heissen Bedürfnis seines Herzens heraus sie aufsuchen will." Hans Goltz, "Ehrfurcht," *Der Ararat* 1, no. 3 (19 May 1919).

121. ". . . man bringt einen um und 'beweist' nachher, dass er ein Mörder war." Eduard Trautner, "Terror," *Der Weg* 1, no. 5/6 (May/June 1919): 4.

122. "Man könnte fragen: Ist es nötig, dass der Staat so verfährt?—Ja! Es ist nötig! Es ist nicht nur nötig, sondern selbstverständlich, solange Staat identisch mit Herrschaft ist und nicht mit Gemeinschaft." Ibid., 6.

123. Felix Stiemer, "Grenzbestimmung," *Der Weg* 1, no. 7 (July 1919): 8.

124. Ernst Grünthal, "Neue Sezession München," *Der Weg* 1, no. 7 (July 1919): 2.

125. "Der Künstler, der in den alten Traditionen seines Berufes weiter schafft, kann ebenso wohl politisch radikal gesinnt sein wie derjenige der künstlerisch neue Bahnen sucht, im Banne des schroffsten Kapitalismus stehen kann. Es war ein verfehlter Versuch, in den ersten Tagen der Räterepublik eine bestimmte Kunstrichtung zu Kunst der Revolution stempeln zu wollen. . . . Denn es handelt sich hier gewiss nicht um Volkskunst, sondern um eine Kunstrichtung, welche bis heute in Kreisen gepflegt wird, die dem Volksempfinden meist herzlich wenig Verständnis entgegenbringen." Anonymous, "Kunst und Politik II," *Neue Zeitung* 1, no. 139 (26 June 1919).

126. "Wenn er sagen durfte, dass Sozialismus keine Wissenschaft, sondern Kunst sei, muss von seinen Jüngern gefordert werden, dass sie den Begriff Kunst ebenso umwerten, wie Marx den Begriff Wissenschaft erneuert hat. Wir müssen fordern, dass vor den kommunistischen Geist die kommunistische Wirtschaft gesetzt wird: vorher haben wir kein Recht zu geistigen Forderungen an das Proletariat." Felix Stiemer, "Gustav Landauer," *Die Bücherkiste* 1, no. 8/9/10 (December 1919): 100.

127. Bayerisches Kriegsarchiv, Munich, Gruppenkommando 4, Bund 53, Akt. 12, Tk.Z. No. 1370.

128. Letter from the Bayerisches Staatsministerium für Unterricht und Kultus to the Arbeitsausschuss bildender Künstler, Munich, BHStA, MA 92225.

129. Nerdinger, "Fatale Kontinuität: Akademiegeschichte von den zwanziger bis zu den fünfziger Jahren," 185.

130. Winfried Nerdinger, "Die 'Kunststadt' München," in Stölzl, *Die Zwanziger Jahre in München*, 101.

131. *Münchner Post* 33, no. 151 (2 July 1919).

132. "Ankündigung," *Der Weg* 1, no. 10/11 (October/November 1919): 17.

133. Wach had been briefly associated with Rudolf Steiner's anthroposophy group in Munich in 1914 and was one of the signatories to Steiner's proposal to restructure the parliamentary system that was published in the 17 March 1919 *Süddeutsche Freiheit*. See the Wach diary, n.p.

134. Letter by Aloys Wach to his mother, 21 September 1919. In the possession of Margarete Döppler, Braunau-am-Inn, Austria.

135. Wach diary, n.p.

136. "Schaeflers Welt ist die heutige, augenblickliche: die der Maschinen, des Weltkriegs, der Sozialisierung, der Gewalt und des Aufruhres . . ." Eduard Trautner, "Fritz Schaefler," in *Zinglers Kunstkabinett* (Frankfurt am Main, 1919), 16.

137. *Fritz Schaefler: Ein unbekannter Expressionist*, 10.

138. Ibid., 12–14.

Chapter 5. The End of Expressionism

1. "Ich habe hier viel Einblick geniessen müssen, wie stark das Affektvolle des revolutionären Elementes im Menschen die Oberfläche neu poliert . . .

Hans Richter, der nun nach Berlin gegangen ist, mag Sensationslustigen dort einen Gefallen tun . . . Revolution, nur um ihrer selbst willen, ist derselbe Aberglaube als es die Bureaukratie oder die Organisation war." Letter by P. R. Henning to Walter Gropius, Davos, 28 June 1919, Bauhaus Archiv, Briefe AfK 1919/21, GN 10/13/289–319.

2. "So wenig dauerhaft diese kommunistische Republik von Anfang an schien, so gab sie doch Gelegenheit zur Überprüfung der subjektiven Existenz-Möglichkeiten in einem solchen Gemeinwesen. Ohne positives Ergebnis war sie nicht. Natürlich eine zugespitzte, individualistische Kunst ist zum Genuss durch die Gesamtheit nicht geeignet, sie ist kapitalistischer Luxus. Aber wir sind doch wohl mehr als Kuriositäten für reiche Snobs. Und das was uns irgendwie darüber hinaus Ewigkeitswerten zustrebt, das würde im kommunistischen Gemeinwesen eher Förderung erfahren können. . . . wir würden die Ergebnisse unserer Erfindertätigkeit dem Volkskörper zuleiten können. Denn Akademien gäbe es nicht mehr, sondern nur Kunstschulen für Handwerker.

Also hat die Räte-Republik auch für uns manche Erkenntnis gebracht. An eine praktische Durchführung ist nun erst recht nicht mehr zu denken. . . . vielleicht interessiert Sie das nicht so sehr, aber es hat mich zeitweise sehr beschäftigt." Letter by Paul Klee to Alfred Kubin, 12 May 1919, reprinted in *Paul Klee: Das Frühwerk 1883–1922,* exhibition catalog Städtische Galerie im Lenbachhaus (Munich, 1979), 93. For a more comprehensive account of Klee and the Munich revolution, see O. K. Werckmeister, *The Making of Paul Klee's Career, 1914–1920* (Chicago, 1989).

3. Letters by Paul Klee to Lili Klee, 22 June 1919 and 25 June 1919, reprinted in Paul Klee, *Briefe an die Familie 1893–1940* (Cologne, 1979), 954 and 956.

4. See the letter by Paul Klee to Lili Klee, 19 June 1919, Ibid., 954.

5. "Unter den Phantasiekünstlern gilt Paul Klee als ein ganz besonderes Phänomen, ich finde nur, dass er eigentlich keine Phantasie hat, sondern Torheiten treibt wie ein Kind . . . Der Kuriosität halber mag erwähnt werden, dass Paul Klee von den Kunstdiktatoren der Rätezeit als Graphik-Lehrer an der Münchner Kunstgewerbeschule in Aussicht genommen war. . . . aber schliesslich ist dieser ganze Salon-Bolschewismus auch in der Kunst nur eine Spezialität für gebildetes Lumpengesindel . . ." Hermann Esswein, "Die Sommerausstellung der Neuen Sezession III," *Münchner Post* 33, no. 158 (10 July 1919).

6. Whyte, *Bruno Taut and the Architecture of Activism,* 206.

7. The letter, dated Christmas 1920, is unsigned. Whyte suggests it was written by either Taut or Hans Scharoun, but argues convincingly that the style seems closer to Taut's. Ibid., 208.

8. Letter by Taut(?) to Gläserne Kette, Christmas 1920, Hans Scharoun-Nachlass, Akademie der Künste, Berlin; quoted in Ibid.

9. "Das Fieber der Revolution hämmert in jeder Kurve, Farbe, Metrik, Dissonanz." Willi Wolfradt, "Kunst und Revolution," *Die neue Rundschau* 30, part 1 (1919): 750.

10. "Die Kunst lieh sich nicht der Revolution, sie war sie selbst." Ibid.

11. "In der Kunst gestaltet sich das Revolutionäre. Geht die Kunst in der Tatsächlichkeit der Revolution auf, das heisst politisiert sich derart, dass sie ans faktische Verwirklichungsziel gehaftet bleibt, sobald dieses aus der utopischen Phase herauszutreten beginnt, so stirbt die Kunst. Man hat gemeint, in einer vollkommenen Welt werde es keine Kunst geben. Das ist richtig und druckt nur den tiefen Zusammenhang zwischen Kunst und Unzufriedenheit, den revolutionären Charakter nicht nur heutiger, sondern aller und jeder Kunst aus." Ibid., 753.

12. Edschmid's speech, "Über den dichterischen Expressionismus," was reprinted in *Tribüne der Kunst und Zeit,* no. 1 (Berlin, 1921), 39–78.

13. Kasimir Edschmid, "Stand des Expressionismus," in *Deutscher Expressionismus Darmstadt,* exhibition catalog (Darmstadt, 1920). Edschmid tried to defend a first generation of expressionists from the legions of followers and imitators. For a fuller discussion of the Darmstadt exhibition and Edschmid's lecture, see the forthcoming Ph.D. dissertation on New Objectivity painting by Sanda Agalidi, University of California, Los Angeles.

14. For a fuller account of Hausenstein's position, see O. K. Werckmeister, "Kairuan: Wilhelm Hausensteins Buch über Paul Klee," 79–96.

15. Wilhelm Hausenstein, *Bild und Gemeinschaft: Entwurf einer Soziologie der Kunst* (Munich, 1920), 9.

16. "Der Sozialmus, der einmal eine Rettung versprach, ist mit der Revolution in einen Bankerott eingetreten. . . . als ob nicht die allerdings metaphysische Dummheit der nationalistischen Sphäre und der Dilettantismus der Linken nur die hoffnungslosen Pendants um die hoffnungslose Dummheit der demokratischen Mitte wären." Wilhelm Hausenstein, *Die Kunst in diesem Augenblick* (Munich, 1920), 43–44.

17. Ibid., 40.

18. "Expressionismus hat heute seinen Glaspalast. Er hat seinen Salon. Kein Zigarettenplakat, keine Bar kommt heute ohne Expressionismus aus. Es ist ekelhaft." Ibid., 17.

19. Ibid., 11, 35.

20. Ibid., 39.

21. Ibid., 45.

22. "Die expressionistische Akademie, die expressionistische Mode, das expressionistische Mitläufertum, jener Schlagwort-Expressionismus, mit dem smarte Kunsthändler und gewandte Kunstliteraten ihre Propaganda betrieben, wäre es schon am Ende!" Paul Westheim, "Das 'Ende des Expressionismus,' " *Das Kunstblatt* 4, no. 6 (June 1920): 188.

23. Beth Irwin Lewis, *George Grosz: Art and Politics in the Weimar Republic* (Madison, 1971), 57.

24. Ibid.

25. George Grosz, "Abwicklung," *Das Kunstblatt* 8, no. 2 (Feburary 1924), 37, quoted in Ibid., 53.

26. "Die Kunst ist in ihrer Ausführung und Richtung von der Zeit abhän-

gig, in der sie lebt, und die Künstler sind Kreaturen ihrer Epoche. Die höchste Kunst wird diejenige sein, die in ihren Bewusstseinsinhalten die tausendfachen Probleme der letzten Woche werfen liess, die ihre Glieder immer wieder unter dem Stoss des letzten Tages zusammensucht . . . Hat der Expressionismus unsere Erwartungen auf eine solche Kunst erfüllt, die eine Ballotage unserer vitalsten Angelegenheiten ist?

"NEIN! NEIN! NEIN! . . .

"Unter dem Vorwand der Verinnerlichung haben sich die Expressionisten in der Literatur und in der Malerei zu einer Generation zusammengeschlossen, die heute schon sehnsüchtig ihre literatur- und kunsthistorische Würdigung erwartet und für eine ehrenvolle Bürger-Anerkennung kandidiert. Unter dem Vorwand, die Seele zu propagieren, haben sie sich im Kampf gegen den Naturalismus zu den abstrakt-pathetischen Gesten zurückgefunden, die ein inhaltlos, bequemes und unbewegtes Leben zur Voraussetzung haben." Richard Huelsenbeck, "First German Dada Manifesto," reprinted in Raoul Hausmann, *Am Anfang war Dada* (Steinbach/Giessen, first edition, 1972), 23–24.

27. *Dada: Eine literarische Dokumentation* (Hamburg, 1964), 47.

28. Lewis, *George Grosz: Art and Politics in the Weimar Republic,* 67.

29. Ibid., 74–75.

30. Raoul Hausmann, Richard Huelsenbeck, and Jefim Golyscheff, "Was ist der Dada und was will er in Deutschland," *Der Dada* 1, no. 1 (June 1919).

31. Lewis, *George Grosz: Art and Politics in the Weimar Republic,* 59.

32. Whyte, *Bruno Taut and the Architecture of Activism,* 140.

33. The date Grosz joined the November Group is still unknown; he did not formally resign until 1921.

34. Raoul Hausmann, *Phases* II, first edition (Paris, 1967), quoted in Whyte, *Bruno Taut and the Architecture of Activism,* 138.

35. See Adolf Behne, "Werkstattbesuche: Jefim Golyscheff," 722.

36. For another example of an attack on the KPD by Felixmüller, see *Die Aktion* 10, no. 31/32 (7 August 1920). Pfemfert, who held antiparliamentary views, was expelled from the KPD in October 1919. In 1920 he was one of the founders of the KAPD, along with Rühle. See Kolinsky, *Engagierter Expressionismus,* 87–88.

37. Post-war relations may have prevented the usual Rome-prize trip to Italy. Felixmüller wrote to his brother in 1971 that he did not go to Rome because of the rampant inflation there. See the letter by Conrad Felixmüller to Helmut Müller, 16 May 1971, *Conrad Felixmüller: Werke und Dokumente,* 87.

38. "Dort unten fühlte ich wieder Schillers Wort: Alle Menschen werden (sind!) Brüder—und begriff immer noch stärker, dass die Arbeit heilig ist . . . Ich bin noch überzeugter nach dieser Reise durch die Stätten der ernsten sachlichen Arbeit, dass es schlecht und widerlich ist 'Dadaist' zu sein, d.h. alles zu verulken, Klamauk zu machen; denn der Mensch wird durch ernste Arbeit bestimmt edel." Letter by Conrad Felixmüller to Heinrich Kirchhoff, 27 July 1920, reprinted in *1920–1980: Sechzig Jahre Galerie Nierendorf* (Berlin, 1980), 18.

39. "Ich bin weder auf die Anerkennung durch die Spiesser oder Nichtspiesser angewiesen wohl aber auf das Geld der ersteren—du hast Dich nachher hingestellt und bombastisches Zeug über Deine Bilder erzählt. An der Wirkung dieses Gegensatzes zweifele ich nicht—ich muss jedenfalls meine Konsequenzen aus all dem ziehen." Letter by Otto Dix to Conrad Felixmüller, n.d. (1919), reprinted in *Conrad Felixmüller: Werke und Dokumente,* 76.

40. "Leider ist der Mann wieder vollkommen Dadaist und 'malt' pornographische Bilder übelster Art; ich halte ihn für verloren . . ." *1920–1980. Sechzig Jahre Galerie Nierendorf,* 18.

41. Pehnt, *Expressionist Architecture,* 16.

42. Quoted in Ibid., 13.

43. Ibid.

44. John Willett, *Art and Politics in the Weimar Period: The New Sobriety 1917–1933* (New York, 1978), 57.

Select Bibliography

Primary Sources

Archives

Akademie der Künste, Berlin
- Sitzungsprotokolle des Senats beider Sektionen der Akademie
- Sitzungsprotokolle der Kommission für Reformvorschläge

Archiv der Hochschule für bildende Kunst, Dresden
- Sitzungsprotokolle der Kunstakademie
- Personalakte

Archiv für bildende Kunst, Germanisches Nationalmuseum, Nürnberg
- Conrad Felixmüller Papers
- Walter Kaesbach Correspondence
- Richard Riemerschmid Papers

Archives of American Art
- I. B. Neumann Papers
- Wilhelm Valentiner Papers

Bauhaus Archiv, Berlin

Bayerisches Geheimes Staatsarchiv, Munich

Bayerisches Hauptstaatsarchiv (BHStA), Munich

Beinecke Library, Yale University, New Haven
- Kurt Wolff Papers

Houghton Library, Harvard University, Boston
- Lyonel Feininger Papers

Jewish National and University Library, Jerusalem
- Gustav Landauer Papers

Karl Ernst Osthaus Archiv, Hagen

Library of Congress, Washington, D.C.
- Rehse Collection

Staatsarchiv Dresden
- Ministerium des Innerns (MdInnern)

Staatsarchiv Oberbayern, Munich (StMue)
- Staatsanwaltschaft München (SAM)

Staatsbibliothek Preussischer Kulturbesitz, Berlin
Stadtarchiv Dresden (Hauptkanzlei)
Aloys Wach Papers, in possession of Margarete Döppler, Braunau-am-Inn
Zentrales Staatsarchiv Potsdam (ZStP)

Newspapers (November 1918 to January 1920)

Bayerischer Kurier (Munich)
Berliner Lokal Anzeiger (Berlin)
Berliner Tageblatt (Berlin)
Berliner Zeitung am Mittag (Berlin)
Dresdner Anzeiger (Dresden)
Dresdner Nachrichten (Dresden)
Dresdner Neueste Nachrichten (Dresden)
Dresdner Volkszeitung (Dresden)
Frankfurter Zeitung (Frankfurt)
Die Freiheit (Berlin)
Münchner Neueste Nachrichten (Munich)
Münchner Post (Munich)
Neue Zeitung (Munich)
Die Rote Fahne (Berlin)
Sächsische Volkszeitung (Leipzig)
Süddeutsche Freiheit (Munich)
Vorwärts (Berlin)

Journals

Die Aktion (1914–20)
An die Laterne (1919)
Der Ararat (1919)
Der Anbruch (1919)
Der Bildermann (1916)
Die Bücherkiste (1919)
Der Cicerone (1917–19)
Der Deutsche Künstler (1918–19)
Die Erde (1919)
Das Forum (1919–20)
Freie Jugend (1918–19)
Die Hilfe (1919)
Die Junge Kunst (1918–19)
Kriegszeit (1914–16)
Die Kunst (1914–19)
Kunst und Künstler (1914–20)
Das Kunstblatt (1917–19)
Kunstchronik und Kunstmarkt (1918–19)
Der Kunsthandel (1918–19)
Menschen (1917–19)

Münchner Blätter für Dichtung und Graphik (1918–19)
Neue Blätter für Kunst und Dichtung (1918–19)
Die Neue Rundschau (1919–?)
Das Plakat (1919)
Die Rote Erde (1919)
Sozialistische Monatshefte (1917–19)
Der Sturm (1915–19)
Die Tat (1919)
Wachtfeuer (1918–19)
Der Weg (1919)
Zeit-Echo (1914–17)

Books, Articles, Pamphlets

Adler, Paul. "Vom Sozialismus zur Utopie." *1918. Neue Blätter für Kunst und Dichtung* 1, no. 8 (December 1918): 170–71.

Anonymous. "Adam: Gegen Zuständliches." *Revolution* 1, no. 2 (1 November 1913): 2.

———. "Ein Aufruf der russischen Künstler." *Neue Blätter für Kunst und Dichtung* 1, no. 10 (February 1919): 213–14.

———. "Ausstellungsbericht Gruppe 1919." *Der Cicerone* 11, no. 11 (June 1919): 340.

———. "Ausverkauf." *Kunst und Künstler* 18 (February 1920): 191–95.

———. "Berliner Auktionen." *Kunstchronik und Kunstmarkt* 30, no. 47 (19 September 1919).

———. "Ein Brief an die Revolution." *Revolution* 1, no. 2 (1 November 1913): 2.

———. "Das Ergebnis des Briefmarken-Wettbewerbs." *Mitteilungen des Reichskunstwarts*, no. 1 (Berlin, 1920).

———. "Heraus aus dem Gefängnis des Schlagworts und der Phrase." *Der Ararat* 1, no. 3 (19 May 1919): n.p.

———. "Die künstlerische Gestaltung des Reichsadlers." *Mitteilungen des Reichskunstwarts*, no. 2 (Berlin, 1920).

———. "Das Kunstprogramm des Kommissariats für Volksaufklärung in Russland." *Das Kunstblatt* 3, no. 3 (March 1919): 91–93.

———. "Nationalgalerie." *Das Kunstblatt* 3, no. 7 (July 1919): 213–21.

———. "Notizen." *Kunstchronik und Kunstmarkt* 30, no. 47 (19 September 1919): 1002.

———. "Revolutionsschlamm." *An die Laterne* 1, no. 1 (n.d.): 5.

———. "Die sozialistische Gruppe der Geistesarbeiter." *Menschen* (Montagsblatt) 1, no. 4 (20 January 1919): 3.

Ausstellung Gruppe 1919 mit Gästen. Catalog of the Second Dresden Secession Group 1919 Exhibition (Dresden, 1919).

Behne, Adolf. "Alte und neue Plakate." In *Das politische Plakat* (Berlin, 1919).

———. "Graphik und Plastik von Mitgliedern der Novembergruppe Berlin." *Menschen* 2, no. 14 (81/86) (December 1919): n.p.

______. "Der Hass der Neutralen." *Die Tat* 7, no. 4 (July 1915): 340–41.
______. "Ist das Schwäche?" *Sozialistische Monatshefte* 23, no. 25/26 (1917): 1286.
______. "Kritik des Werkbundes." *Die Tat* 9, no. 1 (August 1917): 430–38.
______. "Kunstwende?" *Sozialistische Monatshefte* 24, no. 23/24 (1918): 946–52.
______. "Unsere Moralische Krisis." *Sozialistische Monatshefte* 25, no. 1 (1919): 34–38.
______. "National-antinational." *Zeit-Echo* 1, no. 18 (1915–16): 273.
______. "Organisation, Deutschtum und Kunst." *Zeit-Echo* 1, no. 23–24 (1915–16): 361–64.
______. "Werkstattbesuche: Jefim Golyscheff." *Der Cicerone* 11, no. 2 (1919): 722–26.
______. *Die Wiederkehr der Kunst* (Leipzig, 1919).
Bender, Peter. "Der Künstler und die Revolution." *Die Aktion* 8, no. 49/50 (14 December 1918): col.654–56.
Bock, Kurt. "Voran!" *Der Weg* 1, no. 2 (February 1919): 10.
Bode, Wilhelm von. "Die 'Not der Geistigen Arbeiter.'" *Kunst und Künstler* 18, no. 7 (1 April 1920): 297–300.
Brieger, Lothar. "Deutscher Kunst-Katzenjammer." *Der Kunsthandel* 11, no. 2 (February 1919): 17–18.
______. "Jahresbilanz." *Der Kunsthandel* 11, no. 12 (December 1919): 186–87.
Burchard, Dr. Ludwig. "Von den Gründen der Rekordpreise für Kunstwerke." *Der Kunsthandel* 10, no. 2 (February 1918): 17–20.
Däubler, Theodor. "Künstlerische Neuerscheinungen Hans Richter." *Die Aktion* 6, no. 13 (25 March 1916): col.181–82.
Deventer, Eduard. "Ein Staatsamt für bildende Kunst." *Der deutsche Künstler* 5, no. 10 (15 January 1919): 173–74.
Edschmid, Kasimir. "Stand des Expressionismus." In *Deutscher Expressionismus Darmstadt,* exhibition catalog (Darmstadt, 1920).
______. "Über den dichterischen Expressionismus." *Tribüne der Kunst und Zeit* 1 (1921): 39–78.
Ehmcke, F. H. *Zur Krisis der Kunst: Ein Beitrag zu Münchener Kunstschulfragen in ihrer symptomatischen Bedeutung für die deutsche Kunsterziehung* (Jena, 1920).
Eisner, Kurt. "Der sozialistische Staat und der Künstler." In *An alle Künstler!* (Berlin, 1919): 25–36.
Estee, O. *München auf dem Kopf: Die Geschichte einer Räterepublik in 40 Bildern* (Munich, 1919).
Fechter, Paul. *Der Expressionismus* (Munich, 1914).
Felixmüller, Conrad. "Militär-Krankenwärter Felixmüller XI Arnsdorf." *Menschen* 1, no. 3 (15 May 1918): n.p.
______. "Der Prolet (Pönnecke)." *Die Aktion* 10, no. 23/24 (12 June 1920): col.333–36.

———. "Schmidt-Rottluff." *Menschen* 2, no. 5 (46/49) (6 and 13 July 1919): 10–11.

———. "Zur Kunst." *Die schöne Rarität* 2 (April 1918): 40.

"Fidelis." "Gustav Landauers Kulturprogramm." *Das Forum* 4, no. 8 (May 1920): 577–99.

Fischer, Richard. "Feld der Ehre." *Menschen* 1, no. 3 (15 May 1918): 1.

Friedeberger, Hans. "Das Künstlerplakat der Revolutionszeit." *Das Plakat* 10, no. 4 (July 1919): 260–77.

Friedrich, Ernst. "Etwas über Expressionismus." *Freie Jugend* 1, no. 5 (1919): 2.

Gehrig, Oscar. *Plakatkunst und Revolution* (Berlin, 1919).

Der Geist der neuen Volksgemeinschaft; eine Denkschrift für das deutsche Volk (Berlin, 1919).

Gerstl, Max. *Die Münchner Räterepublik* (Munich, 1919).

Glaser, Curt. "Kunstausstellung Berlin 1919." *Kunstchronik und Kunstmarkt* 30, no. 45 (5 September 1919): 962.

Goltz, Hans. "Ehrfurcht." *Der Ararat* 1, no. 3 (19 May 1919): n.p.

Graf, Oskar Maria. *Wir sind Gefangene* (Munich, 1927).

Grautoff, Otto. *Die neue Kunst* (Berlin, 1921).

Grohmann, Will. "Dresdner Sezession 'Gruppe 1919.'" *Neue Blätter für Kunst und Dichtung* 1, no. 11 (March 1919): 257–60.

———. "Sonderheft von Graphik der Gruppe 1919 Dresden." *Menschen* 2, no. 8 (62/65) (n.d.).

———. "Zehn Jahre Novembergruppe." *Kunst der Zeit*, special issue no. 3, no. 1–3 (1928): 30.

Grünthal, Ernst. "Neue Sezession München." *Der Weg* 1, no. 7 (July 1919): 2–4.

Hänisch, Konrad. *Kulturpolitische Aufgaben: Aus dem Vortrag des Kultusministers gehalten Montag, den 3. Februar in der Handelshochschule zu Berlin* (Berlin, 1919).

———. *Die Not der geistigen Arbeiter, ein Alarmruf. Nach einem im Leipziger Buchhändlerhause gehaltenen Vortrag* (Leipzig, 1920).

Hansen, Fritz. "Der Kunsthandel als Objekt der Luxussteuer." *Der Kunsthandel* 11, no. 10 (October 1919): 152–53.

Hansen, Hans. "Revolutionäre Künstler." *Der Weg* 1, no. 4 (April 1919): 2–6.

Hartmann, Walther Georg. "Revolution, ihr Künstler und Kameraden!!" *Menschen* 2, no. 5 (46/49) (6 and 13 July 1919): 10.

Hasenclever, Walter. "Oskar Kokoschka." *Menschen* (Montagsblatt) 1, no. 3 (19 January 1919): 2.

Hausenstein, Wilhelm. *Bild und Gemeinschaft. Entwurf einer Soziologie der Kunst* (Munich, 1920).

———. *Die bildende Kunst der Gegenwart* (Stuttgart, 1914).

———. *Die Kunst in diesem Augenblick* (Munich, 1920).

———. *Der nackte Mensch in der Kunst aller Zeiten und Völker* (Munich, 1913).

———. "Kunst und Revolution," *Der Vorläufer: Sonderheft des Neuen Merkur* 3 (1919): 77–86. Also in *Ostern 1919,* Galerie Flechtheim, Düsseldorf, 25–40 (Potsdam, 1919).
———. "Musae inter arma." *Zeit-Echo* 1, no. 14 (1915–16): 212–15.
———. "Über Expressionismus in der Malerei." *Tribüne der Kunst und Zeit* 2 (1919): 71–72.
Hausmann, Raoul, Richard Huelsenbeck, and Jefim Golyscheff. "Was ist der Dada und was will er in Deutschland?" *Der Dada* 1, no. 1 (June 1919): n.p.
Heise, Carl Georg. "Das Museum." *Genius* 2, no. 1 (1920): 1–4.
———. *Die Sammlung des Freiherrn August von der Heydt* (Munich, 1919).
Hellwag, Fritz. "Die derzeitige wirtschaftliche Lage der bildenden Künstler." In *Die geistigen Arbeiter,* edited by Ernst Franke and Walther Lotz, vol. 2 (Munich, 1922).
Inheim, Heinrich. "Das Berliner Plakatjahr 1918." *Das Plakat* 10, no. 1 (January 1919): 75.
Jahn, Dr. Georg. "Die Künstler und die Revolution." *Der deutsche Künstler* 5, no. 9 (15 December 1918): 165.
Justi, Ludwig. *Die Nationalgalerie und die moderne Kunst* (Leipzig, 1918).
———. "Valentiners Vorschläge zur Umgestaltung der Museen. *Zeitschrift für bildende Kunst* Neue Folge 54, no. 30 (May 1919): 190–200.
Kämmerer, Rudolf. "Brief aus Dresden." *Die junge Kunst* 1, no. 3 (July 1919): 13–15.
———. "Dresdner Sommerausstellungen." *Die junge Kunst* 1, no. 6 (August 1919): 11–12.
Kandinsky, Wassily. "On the Question of Form." In *The Blue Rider Almanac,* edited by Wassily Kandinsky (London, 1974).
Kühn, Herbert. "Expressionismus und Sozialismus." *Neue Blätter für Kunst und Dichtung* 2 (May 1919): 28–30.
Kuno, Renatus. "Saturnalien des Krieges." *Münchner Blätter für Dichtung und Graphik* 1, no. 1 (January 1919): 6.
Künstler-Vereinigung, Dresden. Catalogue of the Summer Exhibition of the Künstler-Vereinigung Dresden (Dresden, 1919).
Kunstausstellung Berlin 1919. Glaspalast am Lehrter Bahnhof, 24 July–30 September 1919.
Kurtz, Rudolf. "Programmatisches." *Der Sturm* 1, no. 1 (1910): 2.
Kuschner, Boris. "Die Kunst der Gemeinschaft." *Neue Blätter für Kunst und Dichtung* 2 (May 1919): 35.
Landau, Dr. Paul. "Flugblatt und Flugschrift." In *Das Politische Plakat* (Berlin, 1919).
Leuthold, Ph. "Arbeiterkunstausstellung." *Beilage der Freien wissenschaftlichen sozialistischen Agrar-Korrespondenz* (April 1920): n.p.
Löwenstein, Karl Konstantin. "Mord der Moderne." *Münchner Blätter für Dichtung und Graphik* 1, no. 10 (October 1919): 160.
Löwing, Herbert. "Warum sozialistische Propaganda?" In *Das Politische Plakat* (Berlin, 1919).

Luft, Franz. "Revolutionsball der Aktion." *Die Aktion* 3, no. 8 (19 February 1913): col.233–35.

Lunatscharski (*sic*) A. "Proletkult." *Die Aktion* 9, no. 10/11 (15 March 1919): col.145–53.

Mayer, August. "Revolution und Kunst." *Münchner Blätter für Dichtung und Graphik* 1, no. 4 (April 1919): 6.

Meidner, Ludwig. "An alle Künstler, Dichter, Musiker." In *An alle Künstler!* (Berlin, 1919).

———. "An alle Künstler, Dichter, Musiker." *Der Anbruch* 2, no. 1 (January 1919): n.p.

———. "Brüder, zünd' die Fackel an. Zum Gedächtnis Carl (*sic*) Liebknecht und Rosa Luxemburg." *Die Erde* 1, no. 4 (15 February 1919): 115–18.

Mühsam, Erich. "Revolution." *Revolution* 1, no. 1 (15 October 1913): 2–3.

XXIX Kollektiv-Ausstellung: Richter/Heckel. Neue Galerie Hans Goltz (Munich, 1916).

Ostern 1919. Galerie Flechtheim, Düsseldorf (Potsdam, 1919).

Passarge, Walter. "Eine Ausstellung Arbeiter-Kunst in Berlin." *Der Cicerone* 12, no. 4 (1920): 167.

Paulsen, Friedrich. "Das neue Leben." *Wachtfeuer* 5, no. 3 (1919): 18.

Pechstein, Max. "Was wir wollen." In *An alle Künstler!* (Berlin, 1919).

Peuckert, Will Erich. "Mehrheit und Spartakus." *Menschen* 2, no. 5 (46/49) (6 and 13 July 1919): 7.

Das politische Plakat (Berlin, 1919).

Rauecker, Bruno. *Die Proletarisierung der geistigen Arbeiter* (Munich, 1920).

Rheiner, Walter. "Die Schande der Revolution." *Menschen* 2, no. 4 (22) (15 February 1919): 1.

Richter, Hans. "Ein Maler spricht zu den Malern." *Zeit-Echo* 3 (June 1917): 49.

Riemerschmid, Richard. *Künstlerische Erziehungsfragen II* (Munich, 1919).

Ring, G. "Falsche Propheten." *Die Hilfe* 25, no. 24 (12 June 1919): 300.

Rubiner, Ludwig. "Mitmensch." *Zeit-Echo* 3 (May 1917): 10–13.

———. "Neuer Inhalt." *Zeit-Echo* 3 (May 1917): 2–5.

———. "Dem Zeichner Frans Masereel." *Zeit-Echo* 3 (August–September 1917): 49.

Rührt Euch! Pamphlet of the Werbedienst (Berlin, 1919).

Schapire, Rosa. "Schmidt-Rottluffs religiöse Holzschnitte." *Die rote Erde* 1, no. 6 (November 1919).

Scheffler, Karl. "Die Kunst und die Revolution." *Kunst und Künstler* 17 (February 1919): 165–67.

———. "Kunstausstellungen." *Kunst und Künstler* 12 (November 1913): 120.

———. "Die Zukunft der deutschen Kunst." *Kunst und Künstler* 17 (May 1919): 309–28.

Schilling, Heinar. "Innere Notwendigkeit," *Menschen* (Montagsblatt) 1, no. 6 (3 February 1919).

Schmidt, Annalise, ed. *Der Bolschewismus und die deutschen Intellektuellen. Äus-*

serungen auf eine Umfrage des Bundes deutscher Gelehrter und Künstler (Leipzig, 1920).

Schmidt-Rottluff, Karl. "Notizen." *Kunstchronik und Kunstmarkt* 30, no. 8 (6 December 1918).

Schmitz, Hermann. *Revolution der Gesinnung! Preussische Kulturpolitik und Volksgemeinschaft seit dem 9. November 1918* (Neubabelsberg, 1931).

Schulz, Franz. "Kunst, Bürger, Staat." *Das Forum* 4, no. 9 (June 1920): 655–60.

Steiner, Paul Nicolaus. "Über Genie und Gesellschaft." *Menschen* 2, no. 5 (46/49) (6 and 13 July 1919): 6.

Stern, Heinrich. "Bildende Kunst und Revolution." *Die Aktion* 9 no. 47/48 (29 November 1919): col.775–80.

Stiemer, Felix. "Grenzbestimmung." *Der Weg* 1, no. 6 (July 1919): 6. Also in *Menschen* 2, no. 5 (46/49) (6 and 13 July 1919): 9.

______. "Gustav Landauer." *Die Bücherkiste* 1, no. 8/9/10 (December 1919): 100.

Stiller, Richard. "Die Dresdner Kunst in den Kriegsjahren." In *Dresdner Kalender 1919*, 93ff. (Dresden, 1919).

Styx, Eugen. "Worte zur Revolution." *Menschen* 2, no. 5 (46/49) (6 and 13 July 1919): 6.

Szkolny, Dr. Felix. "Die Besteuerung der Kunst." *Kunst und Künstler* 17 (December 1918): 116–17.

______. "Die Besteuerung der Kunst." *Kunst und Künstler* 17 (May 1919): 334–39.

______. "Kunstauktion und Luxussteuer." *Der Kunsthandel* 11, no. 9 (September 1919): 129–30.

Taut, Bruno. "An die sozialistische Regierung." *Sozialistische Monatshefte* 24, no. 51 (26 November 1918): 1050–52.

______. "Eine Notwendigkeit." *Der Sturm* 4, no. 196/197 (February 1914): 174–75.

______. "Der Sozialismus des Künstlers." *Sozialistische Monatshefte* 25 (1919): 259–62.

______. "Zuviel Gerede vom Architektur-Unterricht." *Die Bauwelt* 10, no. 32 (7 August 1919): 9–10.

Trautner, Eduard. "Glosse." *Der Weg* 1, no. 1 (January 1919): 6.

______. "Glossen." *Der Weg* 1, no. 2 (February 1919): 4.

______. "Terror." *Der Weg* 1, no. 5/6 (May/June 1919): 4–6.

Uphoff, Carl Emil. "Künstler, Kunst, Sozialismus." *Der Cicerone* 11, no. 5 (1919): 121–25.

______. "Kunst, Künstler und Staat." *Der Cicerone* 11, no. 9 (1919).

______. "Die Sozialisierung der Kunst." *Der Cicerone* 11, no. 7 (1919).

Valentiner, Wilhelm. *Umgestaltung der Museen im Sinne der neuen Zeit* (Berlin, 1919).

Walden, Herwarth. *Expressionismus: die Kunstwende* (Berlin, 1918).

______. "Künstler Volk und Kunst" *Der Sturm* 10, no. 1 (April 1919): 10–13.

———. "Kunst und Leben." *Der Sturm* 10, no. 1 (April 1919): 2–3.
Wedderkop, Hermann von. "Revolution in der Kunst." In *Ostern 1919*. Galerie Flechtheim Düsseldorf (Potsdam, 1919).
Westheim, Paul. "Das 'Ende des Expressionismus.'" *Das Kunstblatt* 4, no. 6 (June 1920): 187–88.
———. "Jenseits der Gräber weiter!" *Das Kunstblatt* 3, no. 1 (January 1919): 1.
Wichert, Fritz. "Die bildende Kunst und der soziale Staat." In *Der Geist der neuen Volksgemeinschaft; eine Denkschrift für das deutsche Volk*, 111–15. (Berlin, 1919).
W(iener), A(lfred). "Ausstellung für unbekannte Architekten." *Die Kunst* 40, no. 22 (9 June 1919): 272.
Wolf, Friedrich. "Präludium zu den nächstkommenden Tagen." *Die rote Erde* 1, no. 2 (July 1919): 59.
Wolf, Georg Jacob. "Kunst und Revolution." *Die Kunst* 39 (1918–19): 217–20.
Wolfradt, Willi. "Kunst und Revolution." *Die neue Rundschau* 30, part 1 (1919) 745–55.
Worringer, Wilhelm. *Abstraktion und Einfühlung* (Munich, 1908).
Zareck, Otto. "Unser Weg." *Der Weg* 1, no. 1 (January 1919): 4.
(Zehder, Hugo). "Anmerkungen." *Neue Blätter für Kunst und Dichtung* 2, no. 5 (August 1919): 101.
———. "Offenes Schreiben an das Ministerkollegium der Republik Sachsen." *Neue Blätter für Kunst und Dichtung* 2, no. 2 (June 1919): 56–57.
———. "Otto Dix." *Neue Blätter für Kunst und Dichtung* 2, no. 6 (September 1919): 119–20.
Zinglers Kunstkabinett. Catalogue of the Opening Exhibition at the Zingler Gallery (Frankfurt am Main, 1919).

Secondary Sources

History

Albrecht, Willy. "Das Ende des monarchisch-konstitutionellen Regierungssystems in Bayern." In *Bayern im Umbruch*, edited by Karl Bosl, 263–99 (Munich, 1969).
Ay, Karl-Ludwig. *Die Entstehung einer Revolution* (Berlin, 1968).
———, ed. *Appelle einer Revolution: Dokumente aus Bayern zum Jahr 1918/1919* (Munich, 1968).
Beutel, Horst. "Die Novemberrevolution von 1918 in Leipzig und die Politik der Leipziger USPD-Führung bis zum Einmarsch der konterrevolutionären Truppen des Generals Maercker am 12. Mai 1919." *Wissenschaftliche Zeitschrift der Universität Leipzig* 7 (1957/58): 385–411.
Bosl, Karl, ed. *Bayern im Umbruch* (Munich, 1969).
Bronner, Stephen Eric, ed. *The Letters of Rosa Luxemburg* (Boulder, 1978).
Büsch, Otto, and Gerald Feldman, eds., *Historische Prozesse der deutschen Inflation 1914 bis 1924* (Berlin, 1978).

Dörrer, Horst. *Die Herausbildung einer revolutionären Massenpartei in Ostsachsen bei besonderer Berücksichtigung der Vereinigung des linken Flügels der Unabhängigen Sozialdemokratischen Partei Deutschlands mit der Kommunistischen Partei Deutschlands (1914 bis 1920)*. Habilitationsschrift, Karl Marx University (Leipzig, 1968).

Dorst, Tankred, ed. *Die Münchner Räterepublik* (Frankfurt am Main, 1966).

Dresden. Geschichte der Stadt in Wort und Bild (Dresden, 1985).

Eckhardt, Günther. *Industrie und Politik in Bayern* (Berlin, 1976).

Eisner, Kurt. *Sozialismus als Aktion. Ausgewählte Aufsätze und Reden* (Frankfurt am Main, 1975).

Evans, Richard J., ed. *The German Working Class 1888–1933: The Politics of Everyday Life* (London, 1982).

Feldman, Gerald. "German Business between War and Revolution." In *Entstehung und Wandel der modernen Gesellschaft: Festschrift für Hans Rosenberg*, 312–41 (Berlin, 1970).

______. *Iron and Steel in the German Inflation 1916–23* (Princeton, 1977).

Feldman, Gerald, Eberhard Kolb, and Reinhard Rürup. "Die Massenbewegung der Arbeiterschaft in Deutschland am Ende des Ersten Weltkrieges (1917–1920)." *Politische Vierteljahresschrift* 13, no. 2 (August 1972): 84–105.

Grunberger, Richard. *Red Rising in Bavaria* (London, 1973).

Hillmayr, Heinrich. "München und die Revolution von 1918/19." In *Bayern im Umbruch,* edited by Karl Bosl, 453–504 (Munich, 1969).

______. *Roter und Weisser Terror in Bayern nach 1918* (Munich, 1974).

Hunt, Richard. *The Creation of the Weimar Republic* (Lexington, 1969).

Kalz, Wolf. *Gustav Landauer: Kultursozialist und Anarchist* (Meisenheim am Glan, 1967).

Kluge, Ulrich. "Quellen zur Geschichte der Rätebewegung 1918/1919 in Archiven des Bundesgebietes." *Internationale Wissenschaftliche Korrespondenz zur Geschichte der Deutschen Arbeiterbewegung* 11/12 (April 1971): 39–46.

Kolb, Eberhard. *Die Arbeiterräte in der deutschen Innenpolitik* (Düsseldorf, 1962).

Kolb, Eberhard, and Reinhard Rürup, eds. *Der Zentralrat der deutschen sozialistischen Republik 19.12.1918–8.4.1919. Vom Ersten zum Zweiten Rätekongress* (Leiden, 1968).

Landauer, Gustav. *Sein Lebensgang in Briefen* 2 vols. (Frankfurt am Main, 1929).

Linse, Ulrich. "Die anarchistische und anarcho-syndikalistische Jugendbewegung 1919–1933." In *Quellen und Beiträge zur Geschichte der Jugendbewegung* 18 (Frankfurt am Main, 1976).

______. *Die Anarchistische und anarcho-syndikalistische Jugendbewegung 1918–1933: Zur Geschichte und Ideologie der anarchistischen, syndikalistischen und unionistischen Kinder- und Jugendorganisationen 1918–1933* (Frankfurt am Main, 1976).

______. "Die Anarchisten und die Münchener Novemberrevolution." In *Bayern im Umbruch,* edited by Karl Bosl, 37–73 (Munich, 1969).

———. *Gustav Landauer und die Revolutionszeit* (Berlin, 1974).

———. *Organisierter Anarchismus im Deutschen Kaiserreich von 1871* (Berlin, 1969).

Lunn, Eugene. *Prophet of Community: The Romantic Socialism of Gustav Landauer* (Berkeley, 1973).

Maurer, Charles B. *Call to Revolution: The Mystical Anarchism of Gustav Landauer* (Detroit, 1971).

Meyer, Georg. *Bibliographie der deutschen Revolution 1918/19* (Göttingen, 1977).

Morgan, David. *The Socialist Left and the German Revolution* (Ithaca, 1975).

Sachsen: Kultur und Arbeit des sächsischen Landes (Berlin, 1928).

Schuker, Stephen A. "Finance and Foreign Policy in the Era of the German Inflation." In *Historische Prozesse der deutschen Inflation 1914–1924*, edited by Otto Büsch and Gerald D. Feldman, 343–61 (Berlin, 1978).

Sitzungsberichte der verfassungsgebenden preussischen Landesversammlung, Tagung 1919/21 (Berlin, 1921).

Ryder, A. J. *The German Revolution of 1918* (Cambridge, 1967).

General

Bardi, Pietro Maria. *Lasar Segall* (Milan, 1959).

Baumann, Claus. *Kurt Günther* (Berlin, 1977).

Benson, Timothy. *Raoul Hausmann and Berlin Dada* (Ann Arbor, 1987).

Bischoff, William. "The Action Committee of Revolutionary Artists in the Munich Revolution of 1918–19." *Studies in Modern European History and Culture* 3 (1977): 7–36.

———. "Artists, Intellectuals and Revolution: Munich 1918–19." Ph.D. Dissertation, Harvard University (Cambridge, 1970).

Bronner, Stephen Eric, and Douglas Kellner, eds. *Passion and Rebellion: The Expressionist Heritage* (1983).

Burschell, Friedrich. "'Revolution' und 'Neue Erde.' München 1918/19. Aus meinen Erinnerungen." *Imprimatur* Neue Folge 3 (1961/62): 244–48.

Campbell, Joan. *The German Werkbund* (Princeton, 1978).

Conrad Felixmüller: Werke und Dokumente. Archiv für Bildende Kunst am Germanischen Nationalmuseum (Nürnberg, 1982).

Conzelmann, Otto. *Der andere Dix. Sein Bild vom Menschen und vom Krieg* (Stuttgart, 1983).

Conzelmann, Otto, ed. *Otto Dix: Handzeichnungen* (Hannover, 1968).

Dada: Eine literarische Dokumentation (Hamburg, 1964).

Dokumente zu Leben und Werk des Malers Otto Dix. Germanisches Nationalmuseum Nürnberg (Nürnberg, 1977).

Fischer, Lothar. *Otto Dix: Ein Malerleben in Deutschland* (Berlin, 1981).

Flake-Knoch, Monika. "Wilhelm R. Valentiners Museumskonzeption von 1918 und die zeitgenössischen Bestrebungen zur Reform der Museen." *Kritische Berichte* 8, no. 4/5 (1980): 49–58.

Franciscono, Marcel. *Walter Gropius and the Creation of the Bauhaus in Weimar* (Urbana, 1971).

Frecot, Janos. "Bibliographische Berichte: Adolf Behne." *Werkbundarchiv* 1 (1972): 81–116.

Frommhold, Erhard. *Lasar Segall and Dresden Expressionism* (Milan, 1972).

Fülberth, Georg. "Sozialdemokratische Literaturkritik vor 1914." *alternative* 14, no. 76 (February 1971): 2–24.

Gabler, Karlheinz, ed. *Erich Heckel und sein Kreis: Dokumente- Fotos- Briefe- Schriften* (Berlin, 1983).

Gassner, Hubertus, and Eckhart Gillen. *Zwischen Revolutionskunst und Sozialistischem Realismus. Dokumente und Kommentare. Kunstdebatten in der Sowjetunion von 1917 bis 1934* (Cologne, 1979).

Gerstenberg, Kurt. "Die Radierungen von Fritz Schaefler." In *Das Kunstwerk*, 51 (Baden-Baden, September 1955).

Gleisberg, Dieter. "Conrad Felixmüller und die Gründung der 'Sezession Gruppe 1919.'" In *Dezennium 2. Zwanzig Jahre VEB Verlag der Kunst Dresden* (Dresden, 1972).

______. *Conrad Felixmüller: Leben und Werk* (Dresden, 1982).

Göbel, Wolfram. *Der Kurt Wolff Verlag 1913–1930* (Frankfurt am Main, 1977).

______. "Sozialisierungstendenzen expressionistischer Verlage nach dem Ersten Weltkrieg." *Internationales Archiv für Sozialgeschichte der deutschen Literatur* 1 (1976): 178–200.

Gray, Cleve, ed. *Hans Richter* (New York, 1971).

Green, Martin Burgess. *The von Richthofen Sisters* (New York, 1974).

Grochowiak, Thomas. *Ludwig Meidner* (Recklinghausen, 1966).

Günther, Peter. "Bemerkungen zum 'jungen Felixmüller.'" In *Conrad Felixmüller: Werke und Dokumente*. Archiv für Bildende Kunst am Germanischen Nationalmuseum, 11–14 (Nürnberg, 1981).

Halfbrodt, Dirk, and Wolfgang Kehr, eds. *München 1919: Bildende Kunst/ Fotografie der Revolutions- und Rätezeit* (Munich, 1979).

Hausmann, Raoul. *Am Anfang war Dada* (Steinbach/Giessen, 1st edition, 1972).

Heinrich Richter-Berlin. Kunstblätter der Galerie Nierendorf, no. 32 (Berlin, September 1974).

Herz, Waggi. "Heinrich Hoffmann und die Revolution—zur Genese faschistischer Fotografie." In *München 1919: Bildende Kunst/ Fotografie der Revolutions- und Rätezeit*, edited by Dirk Halfbrodt and Wolfgang Kehr, 123–96 (Munich, 1979).

Herzog, G. H., ed. *Conrad Felixmüller: Legenden 1912–76* (Tübingen, 1977).

Hesse-Frielinghaus, Herta. *Karl Ernst Osthaus: Leben und Werk* (Recklinghausen, 1971).

Hodin, Joseph Paul. *Ludwig Meidner: seine Kunst, seine Persönlichkeit, seine Zeit* (Darmstadt, 1973).

Hoffmann, Justin. "Der Aktionsausschuss revolutionärer Künstler Münchens." In *München 1919: Bildende Kunst/ Fotografie der Revolutions- und*

Rätezeit, edited by Dirk Halfbrodt and Wolfgang Kehr, 21–75 (Munich, 1979).

———. "Hans Richter und die Münchner Räterepublik." In *Hans Richter 1888–1976*. Akademie der Künste, Berlin, 21–25 (Berlin,1982).

Hünecke, Andreas. "Expressionistische Kunst in deutschen Museen bis 1919." In *Das Schicksal einer Sammlung: Die neue Abteilung der Nationalgalerie im ehemaligen Kronprinzen-Palais*. Staatliche Museen zu Berlin (Berlin, 1986).

Hüser, Fritz, ed. *Paul Zech. 19. February 1881–7. September 1946* (Dortmund, 1961).

Hütt, Wolfgang, "Materialien zur Darstellung der Novemberrevolution in der bildenden Kunst in Deutschland." *Wissenschaftliche Zeitschrift der Martin-Luther Universität Halle-Wittenberg*. Gesellschaft- und Sprachwissenschaftliche Reihe 8 (November 1958): 161–70.

Isaacs, Reginald R. *Walter Gropius: Der Mensch und sein Werk* (Berlin, 1983).

Janda, Annegret. "Die Gemälde und Bildwerke der Expressionistischen im ehemaligen Kronprinzen-Palais: Ein Ausschnitt aus der Geschichte der Neuen Abteilung der National-Galerie von 1918 bis 1945." In *Das Schicksal einer Sammlung: Die neue Abteilung der Nationalgalerie im ehemaligen Kronprinzen-Palais*. Staatliche Museen zu Berlin (Berlin, 1986).

Jelavich, Peter. *Munich and Theatrical Modernism: Politics, Playwriting, and Performance 1890–1914* (Cambridge, 1985).

Kehr, Wolfgang. "Kunsterzieher an der Akademie." In *Tradition und Widerspruch. 175 Jahre Kunstakademie München*, edited by Thomas Zacharias, 287–314 (Munich, 1985).

Kessler, Harry Graf. *Tagebücher, 1918–1937* (Frankfurt am Main, 1962).

Klee, Paul. *Briefe an die Familie 1893–1940* 2 vols. (Cologne, 1979).

———. *The Diaries of Paul Klee* (Berkeley, 1964).

Kliemann, Helga. *Die Novembergruppe*. Bildende Kunst in Berlin 3, Deutsche Gesellschaft für Bildende Kunst (Berlin, 1969).

Knilli, Friedrich, and Ursula Münchow, eds. *Frühes Deutsches Arbeitertheater 1847–1918* (Munich, 1970).

König, Wieland. *Peter August Böckstiegel* (Ettlingen, 1978).

Kolinsky, Eva. *Engagierter Expressionismus* (Stuttgart, 1970).

Kollwitz, Hans, ed. *Ich sah die Welt mit liebevollen Blicken* (Hannover, 1968).

Kollwitz, Käthe. *Briefe der Freundschaft* (Munich, 1966).

Kreiler, Kurt. *Die Schriftstellerrepublik—zum Verhältnis von Literatur und Politik in der Münchner Räterepublik* (Berlin, 1978).

Kristl, Wilhelm Lukas. "Wie Pflanze im Treibhaus: Zeitschriften aus Süddeutschland um 1918/19." *Börsenblatt für den Deutschen Buchhandel*. Frankfurter Ausgabe, no. 16 (26 February 1974): n.p.

Krüger, Günter. "Die Rolle von Brücke und Blauem Reiter beim Durchbruch zur Moderne in Deutschland." In *Der Blaue Reiter*. Kunstmuseum Bern, 252–60 (Bern, 1987).

Kunst in Dresden. 18.–20. Jahrhundert. Ausstellung zur Erinnerung an die

Gründung der Dresdner Kunstakademie 1764, Kurpfälzische Museum (Heidelberg, 1964).

Landauer, Gustav. *Aufruf zum Sozialismus*. Reprint. (Frankfurt am Main, 1967).

Lane, Barbara Miller. *Architecture and Politics in Germany 1918–1945* (Boston, 1968).

Leben und Wirken eines Dresdner Kunsthändlers: Ludwig Gutbier. Von Freunden der Galerie Arnold (Dresden, 1934).

Lenman, Robin. "A Community in Transition: Painters in Munich, 1886–1924." *Central European History* 15, no.1 (March 1982): 3–33.

Lewis, Beth Irwin. *George Grosz: Art and Politics in the Weimar Republic* (Madison, 1971).

Lischka, Gerhard Johann. *Oskar Kokoschka: Maler und Dichter* (Frankfurt am Main, 1972).

Löffler, Fritz. *Otto Dix 1891–1969* (Recklinghausen, 1981).

Löffler, Fritz, and Emilio Bertonati, eds. *Dresdner Sezession 1919–1925* (Munich, 1977).

Mai, Ekkehard. "Problemgeschichte der Münchner Kunstakademie bis in die zwanziger Jahre." In *Tradition und Widerspruch. 175 Jahre Kunstakademie München,* edited by Thomas Zacharias, 103–43 (Munich, 1985).

McLeod, Mary. "Architecture or Revolution." *Art Journal* 43, no. 2 (Summer 1983): 132–47.

Meissner, Günter. *Hans Baluschek. Leben und Werk*. Ph.D. diss., Leipzig University (Leipzig 1962).

Middleton, J. C. "Dada versus Expressionism or The Red King's Dream." *German Life and Letters,* series 2, 15, no. 1 (October 1961): 37–52.

Müller, Joachim, ed. *Die Akte Paul Zech*. Aus dem Archiv der Deutschen Schillerstiftung, no. 11 (Weimar, n.d.)

Nagel, Otto. *Käthe Kollwitz* (Greenwich, 1971).

Nerdinger, Winfried. "Fatale Kontinuität: Akademiegeschichte von den zwanziger bis zu den fünfziger Jahren." In *Tradition und Widerspruch: 175 Jahre Kunstakademie München,* edited by Thomas Zacharias, 179–203 (Munich, 1985).

______. "Die 'Kunststadt' München." In *Die Zwanziger Jahre in München,* Münchner Stadtmusem, edited by Christoph Stolzl, 93–119 (Munich, 1979).

______. *Richard Riemerschmid. Vom Jugendstil zum Werkbund. Werke und Dokumente* (Munich, 1982).

Ness, June. *Lyonel Feininger* (New York, 1974).

Nisbet, Peter. "Some Facts on the Organizational History of the van Diemen Exhibition." In *The First Russian Show.* Catalogue of the Annely Juda Fine Art Gallery (London, 1983).

O'Konor, Louise. *Viking Eggling 1880–1925* (Stockholm, 1971).

Pachter, Henry. "Expressionism and Cafe Culture." In *Passion and Rebellion:*

The Expressionist Heritage, edited by Stephen Eric Bronner and Douglas Kellner, 43–54 (1983).

Paret, Peter. *The Berlin Secession* (Cambridge, 1980).

Pehnt, Wolfgang. *Expressionist Architecture* (London, 1973).

———. "Gropius the Romantic." *Art Bulletin* 53 (September 1971): 379–92.

Peter, Lothar. *Literarische Intelligenz und Klassenkampf. 'Die Aktion' 1911–32* Sammlung Junge Wissenschaft (Cologne, 1972).

Petersen, Klaus. *Ludwig Rubiner: Eine Einführung mit Textauswahl und Bibliographie* (Bonn, 1980).

Pörtner, Paul. "The Writers' Revolution: Munich 1918–19." *Journal of Contemporary History* 3, no. 4 (October 1968): 137–51.

Raabe, Paul. *Die Zeitschriften und Sammlungen des literarischen Expressionismus* (Stuttgart, 1964).

Rave, Paul Ortwin. *Die Geschichte der Nationalgalerie Berlin* (Berlin, 1968).

Redlich, Fritz. "German Literary Expressionism and Its Publishers." *Harvard Library Bulletin* 17 (1969): 143–68.

Reed, Orrel P., ed. *German Expressionist Art: The Robert Gore Rifkind Collection* Frederick Wight Gallery, UCLA (Los Angeles, 1st edition, 1977).

Reiss, Wolfgang. *Die Kunsterziehung in der Weimarer Republik* (Weinheim, 1981).

Richter, Hans. *Begegnungen von Dada bis heute. Briefe, Dokumente, Erinnerungen* (Cologne, 1973).

———. *Dada Profile* (Zurich, 1961).

———. *Dada—Kunst und Antikunst* (Cologne, 3rd edition, 1973).

———. *Köpfe und Hinterköpfe* (Zurich, 1967).

Richter-Berlin, Heinrich. "Mein Leben," *Kunstblätter der Galerie Nierendorf*, no. 32 (Berlin, 1974).

Rülcker, Christoph. "Arbeiterkultur und Kulturpolitik im Blickwinkel des 'Vorwärts' 1918–1928." *Archiv für Sozialgeschichte* 14 (1974): 115–56.

Rühmer, Eberhard. "Kunst im Zeichen der Sezession." In *Münchner Schule, 1850–1914*, 89–102 (Munich, 1979).

Sanesi, Roberto. *Hans Richter opera grafica dal 1902 al 1969* (Bologna, 1976).

Scherer, Herbert. *Bürgerlich-oppositionelle Literaten und sozialdemokratische Arbeiterbewegung nach 1890* (Stuttgart, 1974).

Schlemmer, Tut, ed. *The Letters and Diaries of Oskar Schlemmer* (Middletown, 1972).

Schmidt, Diether. *Otto Dix im Selbstbildnis* (Berlin, 1978).

Schneede, Uwe M. *Käthe Kollwitz: Das zeichnerische Werk* (Munich, 1981).

Schubert, Dietrich. *Otto Dix in Selbstzeugnissen und Bilddokumenten* (Reinbek bei Hamburg, 1980).

Shapiro, Theda. *Painters and Politics: The European Avant-Garde and Society 1900–1925* (New York, 1976).

Sheppard, Richard. "Dada and Politics." *Journal of European Studies* 9, parts 1/2, no. 33/34 (March/June 1979): 39–74.

———. "Ferdinand Hardekopf und Dada." *Jahrbuch der deutschen Schillergesellschaft* 20 (Marbach 1976): 132–61.

Sheppard, Richard, ed. "33 Letters, Telegrams and Cards from Hans Richter to Tristan Tzara and Otto Flake (1917–26)." In *New Studies in Dada, Essays and Documents* (Driffield, 1981).

Söhn, Gerhart, ed. *Conrad Felixmüller. Das Graphische Werk 1912–1974* (Düsseldorf, 1975).

Söhn, Gerhart. *Conrad Felixmüller: von ihm—über ihn* (Düsseldorf, 1977).

Sterne, Margaret. *The Passionate Eye: The Life of Wilhelm Valentiner* (Detroit, 1980).

Sulzer, Dieter. *Der Nachlass Wilhelm Hausenstein* (Marbach am Neckar, 1982).

Toller, Ernst. *Ein Jugend in Deutschland* (Reinbek bei Hamburg, 1963).

Verkauf, Willy, Marcel Janco, and Hans Bolliger, eds. *Dada: Monograph of a Movement* (New York, 1975).

Verstegen, Hubertus Hendrikus. *Het Phoenix-Motief- Bijdrage tot die studie van de humanistische visie op de vorst* (Nijmegen, 1950).

Viesel, Hansjörg, ed. *Literaten an der Wand: Die Münchner Räterepublik und die Schriftsteller* (Frankfurt am Main, 1980).

Werckmeister, O. K. "Kairuan: Wilhelm Hausensteins Buch über Paul Klee." In *Die Tunisreise. Klee. Macke. Moilliet,* edited by Ernst-Gerhard Güse, 79–96 (Stuttgart, 1982).

———. "Klee im Ersten Weltkrieg." In *Versuche über Paul Klee,* 86–107 (Frankfurt am Main, 1981).

Westheim, Paul. "Wie *Das Kunstblatt* entsteht." In *Expressionismus: Aufzeichnungen und Erinnerungen der Zeitgenossen* (Otten, 1965).

Whyte, Iain Boyd. *Bruno Taut and the Architecture of Activism* (Cambridge, 1982).

Wietek, Gerhard. *Georg Tappert 1880–1957* (Munich, 1980).

Willett, John. *Art and Politics in the Weimar Period: The New Sobriety 1917–1933* (New York, 1978).

Wingler, Hans Maria, ed. *Oskar Kokoschka: Schriften 1907–1955* (Munich, 1956).

Wolff, Kurt. *Briefwechsel eines Verlegers 1911–1963* (Frankfurt am Main, 1966).

Zacharias, Thomas, ed. *Tradition und Widerspruch: 175 Jahre Kunstakademie München* (Munich, 1985).

Zech, Paul. *Deutschland, dein Tänzer ist der Tod* (Rudolstadt, 1980).

Exhibition Catalogs

Arbeitsrat für Kunst Berlin 1918–1921, Akademie der Künste, Berlin (Berlin, 1980).

Peter August Böckstiegel, Staatliche Kunstsammlungen Dresden (Dresden, 1950).

Ein Krieg wird ausgestellt, Historisches Museum, Frankfurt (Frankfurt am Main, 1976).

Kunst im Aufbruch: Dresden 1918–1933, Gemälde Galerie Neue Meister (Dresden, 1980).

Miesel, Victor. *Ludwig Meidner: An Expressionist Master,* University of Michigan Gallery (Ann Arbor, 1978).

1920–1980: Sechzig Jahre Galerie Nierendorf, Galerie Nierendorf (Berlin, 1980).

Revolution und Realismus: Revolutionäre Kunst in Deutschland 1917 bis 1933, Staatliche Museen zu Berlin (Berlin, 1978).

Hans Richter 1888–1976, Akademie der Künste, Berlin (Berlin, 1982).

Rigby, Ida Katherine. *An alle Künstler! War- Revolution- Weimar,* San Diego State University (San Diego, 1983).

Robbins, Daniel, ed. *The World Between the Ox and the Swine: Dada Drawings by Hans Richter,* Museum of Art, Rhode Island School of Design (Providence, 1971).

Roters, Eberhard, ed. *Georg Tappert: Ein Berliner Expressionist 1880–1957,* Berlinische Galerie (Berlin, 1980).

Fritz Schaefler. Ein unbekannter Expressionist, Suermondt-Ludwig Museum (Cologne, 1983).

Otto Schubert. Druckgraphik und Zeichnungen, Kupferstichkabinett der Staatlichen Museen zu Berlin (Berlin, 1957).

Stölzl, Christoph, ed. *Die Zwanziger Jahre in München,* Münchner Stadtmusem (Munich, 1979).

Suckale-Redlefsen, Gude. *Plakate in München 1840–1940. Eine Dokumentation zu Geschichte und Wesen des Plakats in München aus den Beständen der Plakatsammlung des Münchner Stadtmuseums* (Munich, 1975).

Gedächtnisausstellung Aloys Wach, Ausstellungsgruppe Firesü (Braunau-am-Inn, 1979).

Aloys Wach: An Exhibition of Prints and Drawings from the Ernest Tross Collection, Los Angeles County Museum of Art (Los Angeles, 1956).

Wem gehört die Welt: Kunst und Gesellschaft in der Weimarer Republik, Neue Gesellschaft für Bildende Kunst (Berlin, 1977).

Widerra, Rosemarie. *Hans Baluschek: Leben und Werk,* Märkisches Museum (Berlin, 1974).

Zweite, Armin, ed. *Paul Klee: Das Frühwerk 1883–1922,* Städtische Galerie im Lenbachhaus (Munich, 1979).

Index

Page numbers in boldface indicate illustrations.